Gender, Emotion, and the Family

Gender, Emotion, and the Family

Leslie Brody

HARVARD UNIVERSITY PRESS

Cambridge, Massachusetts

London, England

For my family

Second printing, 2001

First Harvard University Press paperback edition, 2001

Library of Congress Cataloging-in-Publication Data

Brody, Leslie.
    Gender, emotion, and the family / Leslie Brody.
        p.   cm.
    Includes bibliographical references and index.
    ISBN 0-674-34186-4 (alk. paper)
    ISBN 0-674-00551-1 (pbk.)
    1. Emotions—Sex differences.
   2. Family—Sex differences.
   3. Sex differences (Psychology)
   4. Stereotype (Psychology)
   5. Interpersonal communication—Sex differences.
   I. Title
   RC455.4.E46B76   1999
   152.4—dc21   98-32351

Acknowledgments

Many friends, colleagues, and family members helped to inspire this book and to make it a reality, especially in the face of the multiple (and often overwhelming) demands faced by an employed mother. I am immensely grateful to all of them. When I started the book, I had two-year-old twins, Rachel and Matthew, and a six-year-old, Jennie. They are now thriving at the respective ages of six and ten. I especially thank them and my husband, Lance, for sharing me with my work, and for their ability to make this book another member of the family. Special appreciation goes to Lance for taking the time to read drafts of my chapters and to provide me with thoughtful feedback, integrating my work into his own busy schedule.

Over the past twenty years, the Psychology Department at Boston University has encouraged me to explore the research that matters the most to me. Many colleagues at Boston University have enriched my thinking about gender and emotion. I especially thank Anne Copeland for her many years of research collaboration and friendship. Fran Grossman and Abby Stewart (now at the University of Michigan) have both been sources of wisdom and support. Bob Harrison helpfully provided his expertise on research methodology and emotion on innumerable occasions. The late Bill Mackavey, former chair of the department, and Henry Marcucella, the current chair, were particularly supportive of my work.

I am grateful to colleagues, both at Boston University and elsewhere, who read parts of the book and provided helpful feedback, including Lisa Feldman Barrett, Michael Baum, Murray Cohen, Alice Cronin-Golomb, Judith Hall, Jackie Liederman, Gretchen Lovas, Kim Saudino, and Abby Stewart. Elizabeth Aries' review of the book in its entirety was thoughtful and insightful. I also thank the many graduate students who dedicated their time, energy, and creativity to research issues related to gender and emotion, including Carrie Beckstein, Susan Doron, Shari Friedkin,

Thierry Guedj, Markey Guyer, Xiaolu Hsi, Helen Hwang, Jody Leader, Tracey Madden, Michael Monuteaux, Dorothy Richardson, Lisa Sutton, and Deborah Wise. I am also appreciative of two research grants that I received from Boston University Graduate School, GRS-959-PSYC and GRS-661-PSYC.

My sister Bunting Fellows in 1994–1995 provided the inspiration and support I needed to begin as well as to complete this project. Florence Ladd, the former director of the Mary Ingraham Bunting Institute, and Renny Harrigan, the assistant director, created a nurturing and stimulating environment in which I could think creatively and freely.

Melanie Northrop Forman was an invaluable assistant in the final stages of this project, tracking down seemingly nonexistent citations and frequently fitting the demands of this project into the demands of her own busy life. Lynissa Stokes provided invaluable help with medical library research. Kiffany Pfister and Catherine Ahn were my Radcliffe Junior Partners in the initial stages of this project, helping me immeasurably with data coding and exhaustive library research. So too did my Boston University undergraduate assistants, including Kim Chernoff, Kristi Gammon, and Yvonne Quilop. I also thank Jeff Gagne for helping out with innumerable editing and administrative tasks related to the book.

The initial project that grounded this research was funded by a Gender Roles grant from the Rockefeller Foundation; I thank them for their support. Esther Altman, Deborah Hay, Karen Levine, Gretchen Lovas, Janet Malley, Jessie Miller, Eric Nass, and Elizabeth Vandewater all enthusiastically helped out with various phases of that project, and I am grateful to them.

My parents, Sydney and Shirley, and my sister, Marilyn, were always encouraging of my work, and my father patiently read early drafts of chapters and gave me thoughtful feedback about what made sense and what didn't. Irene King, our kind and loving babysitter of the past ten years, created an atmosphere that made it possible for me to write, knowing that my children were well cared for. I cannot thank her enough.

Kate Brick, the book's production editor, spent many hours helping to create a more reader-friendly book and answering my queries with good nature. And Elizabeth Knoll, my editor at Harvard University Press, is the model of what an editor should be. I thank her for her wisdom, patience, good judgment, sense of humor, and encouragement.

Contents

1 Introduction   1

I THE NATURE AND EXTENT OF GENDER DIFFERENCES

2 Understanding Emotional Expression   15
3 Words, Faces, Voices, and Behaviors   26
4 Physiological Arousal and Patterns of
  Emotional Expression   58
5 Sad or Mad? The Quality of Emotions   78

II GENDER, BIOLOGY, AND THE FAMILY

6 The State of the Art: Biological Differences?   101
7 Transactional Relationships within Families   128
8 Gender Identification and De-identification
  in the Family   147
9 Fathers and the Family Climate   177

III CULTURAL ORIGINS AND CONSEQUENCES OF
    GENDER DIFFERENCES

10 Social Motives, Power, and Roles   201
11 Stereotypes and Display Rules   227
12 The Power of Peers   244
13 The Health Consequences of Gender-Stereotypic
   Emotional Expression   260
14 Rethinking Gender and Emotion   281

Notes   289
References   303
Index   355

1

Introduction

When I get upset, I can't express myself at all, but if my wife's upset, you'd think you were hearing poetry. She can express exactly what she's feeling inside.

—James, age 47[1]

When my friends ask me what I'm writing about, I invariably reply, "the development of gender differences in emotional expression." And just as invariably, my answer is met with blank stares. So I try to elaborate: "You know, how when they're upset, women say they feel sad and hurt, while men say they feel mad." My friends' eyes light up and their heads nod. "Oh, yes, now we understand. How interesting," they say. I continue, "Yes, and I'm writing about why that happens, a developmental model." My friends query expectantly, "So, what's the model?" "Well," I reply, "it's complicated. There are all kinds of reasons: biological differences, cultural pressures, family relationships, peer interactions . . ." My voice trails off at this point. "Well, it would take me a long time to tell you about everything." And I usually end lamely with, "Maybe you should read my book."

My attempt to encapsulate this complex and burgeoning field for my friends by linking the expression of sadness with women and the expression of anger with men does capture some ubiquitous stereotypes about emotional expression in the two sexes. It is also rooted in data showing that in some anger-inducing situations, both young girls and women express more hurt, disappointment and sadness than do their male counterparts (Brody 1993). For example, in a study I conducted of American middle-aged married couples, women and men said that they would feel equally angry, but women said that they would feel more hurt, disappointed, and sad than men in response to the following story: "You

1

always do favors for Bill. One day you ask Bill to mail an important package for you, and he forgets" (Brody 1993).

But as with any single example, my response belies the complexity of gender differences in emotional expressiveness. In fact, there are many situations, such as marital conflict, in which women actually express more anger than men express. And men respond to anger-inducing situations with a multiplicity of reactions, including cardiovascular reactivity and voice intonation patterns not seen in women (Gottman and Levenson 1992; Siegman 1993). The quality of women's and men's emotional expressiveness depends on a host of interacting factors, including the nature of the situation they find themselves in, who the participants are, what culture they are from, what ages they are, and what social roles they play. Moreover, whether or not there are gender differences in emotion depends on the aspect of emotional expressiveness considered: words, voice intonation, behaviors, physiological arousal, facial expressiveness, or some combination of these.

The idea that gender differences may vary in different situations and as a function of different individual and cultural characteristics is neither a popular nor an easy idea to convey. Generalized stereotypes about women's and men's emotional expressivity tend to be ubiquitous. Yet, understanding the conditions under which gender differences appear and disappear is a valuable enterprise in its own right, one that allows us to transcend our gender stereotypes, affording both women and men their due measure of respect. Perhaps more important, by trying to understand the complexity of how such gender differences emerge and develop we may gain some freedom over the power these often unconscious processes play in our lives and in our relationships.

This book is both a synthesis and an interpretation of the existing literature on gender and emotion. I explore the nature and extent of gender differences in emotional expression, as well as the fascinating question of how gender differences in emotional expression come about. Although there is an inseparable interaction among biological, social, and cultural processes that contributes to gender differences in emotional expressiveness, the current evidence points more confidently to the contributions made by cultural and social processes than to biological ones. Biological sex differences contribute to gender differences in emotion only insofar as representatives of the culture, in the form of parents, peers, teachers, and the media, respond to these biological differences in dissimilar ways, in accordance with cultural values and stereotypes. In fact, we never can be certain if biological differences are the result, not the cause, of different environmental or social stimulation that the two sexes receive (see Dawson et al. 1992, 1997; Shatz 1992). This may be true even when very young infants are studied, since males and females may receive different types of environmental inputs as soon as they are born.

I take a functionalist approach to the study of emotional expression, arguing that the expression of emotions is useful and adaptive for accomplishing our social roles as well as for communicating our needs and goals to ourselves and to others. For example, expressing anger lets us and the people around us know that something is not going well, that something needs to be changed. It may even provide the energy needed to effect change (Campos et al. 1994; Campos, Campos, and Barnett 1989).

Taking a functionalist approach leads me to ask and answer two critical questions. First, how do the social roles, needs, and goals of the two sexes differ? I include in my conception of social roles how power, status, and intimacy differ for men and women, since these processes are fundamental to human social interaction across cultures (Fiske 1991). The sources of power are many, including: social rules that dictate who has power (known as legitimate power); concrete resources, such as money or physical strength; expertise or knowledge; and feelings of confidence. Women have less access than men to most of these bases of power (Hacker 1951; Johnson 1978). Women also have less power than men because they have lower status and prestige. Status is culturally defined by characteristics such as appearance, the insignia of office or rank, clothing, education, sex, age, religion, or race (Winter 1973; Kemper 1978).

Addressing sex differences in power leads to another question: How do the emotions men and women express help them to adapt to their differing levels of power, to the differing circumstances in their lives? For example, the lower power that most women have may contribute to their minimization of expressions of contempt, since contempt may alienate others, and men, who often have higher power, may respond to contemptuous behaviors by potentially hurting or harming women.

Boys' and girls' emotional expressiveness is ultimately (and probably unconsciously) shaped to prepare them for successful completion of their future gender roles, with roles for women emphasizing affiliation and caretaking and roles for men emphasizing competition, power, control, and protecting others. In accordance with these roles, boys are shaped to minimize emotional expressions with some important exceptions: notably anger, pride, and contempt. Girls are shaped to maximize emotions that promote affiliation and restore social bonding, such as warmth, empathic distress, respect, and shame, as well as those that promote helplessness and lower power, such as fear and sadness. The expression of these emotions enables the two sexes to successfully accomplish their future gender roles as well as to maintain the existing power and status differences between the two sexes.

I emphasize family processes, played out within a particular cultural context and within a particular set of cultural values, as formative for gender differences in emotion. I have been strongly influenced by Sara Ruddick's (1982) ideas that one of the primary goals for parents is to raise children who are socially acceptable and well liked by others in the culture. Very few parents want to raise children who don't "fit in," who are isolated or outcast, identified as "different" by teachers and peers. Evidence suggests that when children express emotions in accordance with cultural norms, they are better liked. Some cultural norms, or display rules, dictate that females may express vulnerability and sadness but males may not, while males may express aggression, but females may not. Parents reward their children (both unconsciously and consciously) in subtle and not so subtle ways to conform to the cultural norms and values surrounding gender and emotional expression. Research, for example, shows that in the same setting, some parents minimize the extent to which they refer to "angry" feelings when talking to their preschool daughters, but not to their sons (Fivush 1989, 1993).

I will further emphasize that cultural values surrounding gender and emotion are transmitted not only by parents, but also by other socialization agents, such as peers, with whom being popular comes from expressing emotions in gender stereotypic ways. For American boys, this means acting invulnerable, tough, and "cool"; for girls, it means almost the direct opposite: expressing vulnerable feelings and behaving unaggressively. Gender images in the media also foster prescriptive stereotypes in powerful ways.

Parents and other socialization agents may be driven to respond differently to male and female infants not only because of cultural values, but also because of differing characteristics of female and male infants themselves. I will analyze considerable evidence that boys and girls differ in subtle ways at birth, which may evoke different reactions from their parents. I focus on gender differences in temperament, a construct that refers to relatively stable biologically based behavioral tendencies that are extant early in life (Bates 1989). Commonly studied indices of temperament include the extent to which infants become physically or emotionally aroused in response to stimulation, and the extent to which they can facilitate, inhibit, or minimize their arousal, using such processes as self-soothing, attending, approaching, withdrawing, or attacking (Rothbart 1989). Gender differences in several aspects of infant temperament, such as activity and arousal levels, may evoke different responses from parents, and both parents' and children's temperaments become transformed over time as a result of their repeated interactions with each other. This transformative process is one that developmental psychologists have called a transactional relationship (Sameroff 1975), and I will argue that it gradually shapes the nature and extent of gender differences in emotional expressiveness.

That parents and children exert mutual influences on each others' development is consistent with family systems theories of development, which hold that there are nonlinear influences among cultural processes, parents, and their children. Moreover, family systems theories maintain that the family unit as a whole needs to be taken into account in order to understand how and why gender differences emerge. What this means, for example, is that the effects of mother-child relationships on children's emotional expressiveness cannot be isolated from, and are influenced by, other coexisting family relationships, such as the quality of sibling relationships, or mother-father relationships.

Differing family socialization experiences may have long-term consequences for the kinds of emotions that daughters and sons express toward people outside of the family. This is a perspective emphasized by object relations theorists, such as Fairbairn (1952). Children's early emotional reactions to their parents' behaviors, such as warmth in response to a parent's acceptance, or anger in response to a parent's rejection, are hypothesized to become internalized as templates or models for future emotional responses. Expressing anger may be a way of signalling to the parent that the parent-child relationship is not satisfying, and in fact may be an adaptive communication, perhaps serving to create distance from the parent. For better or for worse, the expression of anger and distress then become habitual and generalized to subsequent social relationships. In fact, people tend to re-create repeatedly the quality of early parental relationships when they become adults, by continuing to respond to their current partners in ways that were characteristic of their early relationships. In doing so, they evoke familiar responses from their partners. For example, they may make mistakes (perhaps unconsciously) in order to evoke criticism from a partner, because they were raised by a critical parent. By re-creating the quality of previous relationships, people reexperience and rework their previous relationships, avoiding the pain of loss and seeking the comfort of well-known feelings (Sandler and Sandler 1986).

Feminist object relations theorists such as Chodorow (1978), Fast (1984), and Benjamin (1988) have argued that girls and boys internalize and experience different kinds of early family relationships because both sexes are parented primarily by women. As a result, their emotional functioning develops differently. By virtue of being the same sex as their primary caretakers, girls identify with them and are hypothesized to internalize a sense of connection to others and of shared and reciprocal emotional experiences. It is only with the onset of adolescence that girls are pressured to become more autonomous. It is hypothesized that girls may use expressions of hostility and distress at this time to facilitate separation from their mothers (Chodorow 1978).

In contrast, boys de-identify with their mothers from a very early age in order to develop a male gender identity. Boys are hypothesized to internalize a sense of being disconnected from others, of becoming different in emotional expressiveness from their mothers.

Feminist object relations theorists also hypothesize that the unequal power and status that men and women wield, both in the family and in the culture, impact the quality of the emotions that boys and girls experience and internalize. One example—the gendered nature of the traditional family structure, in which mothers do more child care and have less power than do fathers, may set into play differing dynamics for mother-child as opposed to father-child relationships.

I question and elaborate the view that the different roles played by mothers and fathers in the family may set into motion different patterns of emotional expression for daughters versus sons (Benjamin 1988; Chodorow 1978; Fast 1984). I explore current data that focus on whether, in fact, early mother-daughter relationships are qualitatively different from early mother-son relationships. In turn, I also review how these relationships relate to daughters' and sons' emotional expressiveness. In particular, I focus on the counter-intuitive idea that the same maternal behavior, for example empathy, may be responded to differently by daughters and sons because the two sexes are under pressure to identify with different gender roles. Current data relevant to these feminist object relations theories are limited but encouraging, suggesting that these theories warrant further attention by researchers.

My research confirms the critical role that fathers play in the emergence of their children's emotional expressiveness. Among others, Nancy Chodorow (1978) has theorized that if fathers play a major role in child care *and* if mothers have valued roles and higher status and power in the culture, then both sons and daughters should develop positive characteristics typical of both their own and the opposite sex, including becoming emotionally expressive, interpersonally oriented, and also goal directed.

My data show this prediction to be correct: when the traditional structure of the family is changed, and fathers play an active role in child rearing, there are shifts in the degree to which their children's emotional expressiveness is gender-stereotyped. Sons in nontraditional families become more emotionally expressive than do their male counterparts from traditional families; daughters in nontraditional families express more competitive themes and less vulnerability, sadness, and fear relative to daughters from traditional families (Brody 1997). Involved fathers may enable sons to learn that masculinity and emotional expression are not necessarily incompatible. Involved fathers may also help daughters to differentiate their emotional expressiveness from that of their mothers, facilitating their expressions of aggression and competition while minimizing their expressions of dysphoric emotions.

I also suggest that boys' and girls' emotional expressiveness may be affected by their parents' stereotypes about emotional functioning in the same and opposite sex. Compared to noninvolved fathers, involved fathers may be less likely to gender stereotype their children, inducing fewer self-fulfilling prophecies in their children's emotional development. Insights gleaned from social psychology research show that people are less likely to stereotype members of their own sex, who constitute an "in-group," than members of the opposite sex, who constitute and "out-group" (see Fiske 1993; Swim 1994). Mothers' stereotypes about their sons' emotional expressiveness may be more distorted than they are about their daughters', while the reverse patterns may be true for fathers. These stereotypes may insidiously affect the development of emotional expressivity in sons and daughters and may also change the quality of family interactions.

The observation that changing the traditional structure of the family affects gender differences in children's emotional expression indicates that social factors construct these differences. This remains true even after acknowledging that at least some formative social factors originate in response to biological gender differences. Although Freud's oft-quoted expression that "anatomy is destiny" has been interpreted to mean that the anatomical differences between males and females determine their differing social roles and fates, I argue that anatomical processes merely contribute to destiny, along with complex social and cultural processes, including the structure of the family itself. Gender differences in emotional expression clearly vary in different social and cultural contexts.

Throughout the book, I draw on a research study I conducted, funded by a Gender Roles Grant from the Rockefeller Foundation, that involved 95 families, with each family including a mother, a father, and at least one school-aged child, aged 6 through 12. Fifty-one of the families in the study had a participating daughter; 44 had a participating son. All of the parents in the study had been married or living together for at least three years prior to the start of the study. The parents in the study ranged in age from 27 to 62, were predominantly European-American, and ranged from lower to upper class, with the majority of the participants being middle-level administrators or white-collar workers. Their education ranged from sixth grade to completion of graduate school with the average educational level being one year of college.[2]

I was interested in the emotional expressiveness as well as in the gender roles of each family member. To measure their gender roles, each member of these families was asked about their participation in household tasks and child care. For example, both mothers and fathers were asked how many hours they were employed per week, as well as how often they and their spouses got their children ready for school in the morning, or went to parent-teacher conferences, or did the laundry or car repairs.[3] All family members were also asked about their attitudes toward women's roles using the Attitudes toward Women Scale (Spence and Helmreich 1972),[4] which included items such as the extent to which they agreed with the statement, "Women should never ask men out on a date." Further, parents were asked about their child rearing practices, including how nurturing or restrictive they were, using the Block Child Rearing Practices Report (Block 1965).

Patterns of emotional expression in family members were measured in two different ways. The first involved asking family members how they would feel in response to stories such as the following: "You're sitting in your room and suddenly you see someone looking in your window." The second involved asking children and parents to write their own stories in response to three pictures. The pictures are displayed in Figure 1 and depict a same-sexed person looking in the mirror, two same-sexed people facing each other, and two opposite-sexed people facing each other. Parents and children were independently asked the following questions about the pictures:

"What's happening in this picture?"
"What's going to happen?"
"How are the people feeling?"
"What are the people thinking?"

Stories were coded for the frequency with which family members used various emotion words, such as sad or happy; portrayed physical aggression or competition themes, such as "Bill and Harry were arguing over who was the better ball player"; and portrayed interpersonal affiliation themes, such as two people discussing something in a positive way. Not only were emotions coded in these stories, but also the identity of the story characters. Did children choose to include mothers, fathers, or themselves and their peers in their stories? These measures were used to explore the quality of family members' relationships to others.

Along with in-depth interviews that were given to sixteen randomly selected families, the analyses of these measures provided some key findings that inform the conclusions I draw about gender differences in emotional expression. I often quote stories written by the participants, as well as the evocative statements they made, which depict some kernel of truth about gender differences in emotional expression. These data are synthesized with other relevant research throughout the book, in an attempt to evaluate what is currently known about gender differences in emotional expression and to understand how such differences come about.

OVERVIEW.   This book explores the existence and emergence of gender differences in emotional expression from a feminist empiricist perspective. I believe that careful research that attends to the experiences of both men and women, and that particularly highlights the cultural and situ-

Same-sex character looking in a mirror

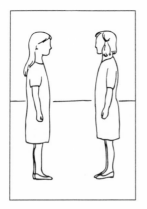 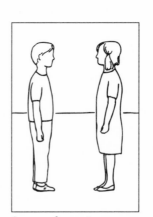 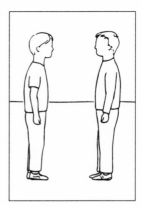

Same- and opposite-sex peers

Fig. 1. Pictures that research participants wrote stories about

ational specificity of gender differences, can make a clear contribution to our understanding of both gender and emotion (Enns 1992). I also believe that empirical evidence concerning gender differences is uninterpretable and often meaningless without an existing theoretical context within which to understand such differences. As discussed above, I draw heavily on two theoretical perspectives for exploring the emergence of gender differences in emotional development: a family systems perspective and a feminist object relations perspective.

My analysis directly contradicts "essentialist" theories by proposing that the differing emotional expressions of women and men are neither inherent in their biological genders nor products of a unitary, shared psychology for either sex (Hare-Mustin and Marecek 1994; see also Assiter 1996). Rather, gender differences in emotional expression are created by complex interactions among biological, social, and cultural factors. The extent to which such differences do or do not exist varies depending on the particular group of women or men under consideration, on their cultural and family backgrounds, and on their historical milieu.

On the other hand, I assume that there are some experiences that most women share: in particular, having lower status and power than males, as well as being stereotypically responded to as "females." I also diverge from some feminist analyses of the family by acknowledging that biological differences between infant boys and infant girls play a role in patterns of interactions between children and their parents.[5] Perhaps my argument can be best categorized as "modernist feminism in a postmodern age," to quote the title of Alison Assiter's (1996) thought-provoking book. In other words, although I acknowledge that there are universal features and experiences that most women share, I also acknowledge the complexities of the social, cultural, and psychological processes that influence these experiences, as well as the particularities of the consequences that ensue as a result. The consequences that ensue for males' and females' emotional expression are neither universal nor essential to the nature of males and females, and have complex biological, developmental, and socio-cultural roots.

I

The Nature and Extent of Gender Differences

2

Understanding Emotional Expression

My expectations of people affect why I get angry—I expect people to be the way I am and they're not, and that's gotten me into a lot of trouble.

—*Lisa, age 43*

What is an emotion? This is a question that has many different answers depending on who is asked, with the answers constituting theoretical points of view rather than precise definitions. The theoretical view I am most comfortable with is that emotions are *motivational systems* with physiological, behavioral, experiential, and cognitive components. Emotions have a positive or negative valence (that is, feel good or bad) and also vary in intensity, or arousal levels, from mild to strong. They are often precipitated by interpersonal situations or by events that warrant our attention because they affect our well-being (Harrison 1986).

Emotions motivate us and guide our actions. We behave in ways that help us to avoid feeling distressed and that increase our feelings of pleasure (Tomkins 1984). We feel pleasure or pride when we achieve our goals or meet our needs, and we feel badly, including guilty, ashamed, or distressed, when we fail at tasks that are important to us. William James (1890/1952) wrote that "the normal provocation of self feeling is one's actual success or failure, and the good or bad actual position one holds in the world (p. 197) . . . the sum total of all that . . . [a person] can call his, not only his body and his psychic powers, but his clothes and his house, his wife and his children, his ancestors and friends, his reputation and works . . . all these things give him the same emotions. If they wax and prosper, he feels triumphant; if they dwindle and die away, he feels cast down" (p. 188). Recent theorists, knowingly or not, have elaborated on James's thinking. For example, Carver and Scheier (1990) have argued that emotions monitor the rate of progress toward attaining important goals. If progress toward a goal is occurring at a rate slower than people expect, they will experience negative emotions, such as disappointment or anxiety. If people are making more rapid progress toward a goal than they expect, they will experience positive emotions, such as feeling elated or joyful.

Emotional Experience versus Expression

Emotional experience and expression are somewhat difficult for researchers to disentangle. Presumably, the expression of an emotion consists of some measurable outward manifestation, like a blood pressure change or a muscle pattern on someone's face. In contrast, the experience of an emotion is a feeling state known only to the individual. This distinction is murky, however, for the only way to really measure experience is to ask people to think about their feeling states. Unfortunately, they must express a feeling using words in order to tell you they've experienced it. The other difficulty with the measurement of emotional experience is that people may not want to admit to painful or socially unacceptable feelings.

Internal experiences of emotions (what people feel inside) signal whether or not their needs and goals are being met and may or may not be communicated to others. Expressing feelings, in contrast, communicates to others the state of people's motives or needs, and potentially modifies the likelihood that people will attain their goals by mobilizing behavioral changes both in themselves and others. This point is highlighted by functionalist theories of emotion, which assert that emotions are in essence and by their very nature useful (Campos et al. 1989; 1994). For instance, expressing anger may help us to convince someone else to do what we would like them to do, and may also help us to feel less conflicted and stressed. Expressing sadness may bring others to our aid. And, as the comedienne Loretta LaRoche says, "The shortest distance between two people is a smile"—the expression of warmth brings others closer to us.

Sometimes, of course, we can express emotions when we are by ourselves. This may either serve a self-communicative function (i.e., we better understand what we have experienced) or it may simply reflect the physiological and behavioral arousal accompanying the emotional experience. It is also possible that such self-expressions serve a cathartic function, in that we may feel better after we express an emotion to ourselves. Most of us have probably experienced the relief of making an angry face or shaking a fist in the absence of the person we are angry at.

Expressing feelings may also help us to identify the nature of an emotional experience. For example, it may be only after we hit someone that we become aware of being angry. The facial feedback hypothesis states that the expression of emotion induces autonomic, hormonal, and behavioral changes that trigger the experience of the emotion. A stronger way of stating this hypothesis is: if you don't express an emotion, you may never experience it (Buck 1980). Studies have shown that asking people to frown increases their feelings of anger; while asking them to smile increases their feelings of happiness, suggesting that facial expressions amplify the experience of the corresponding feeling (Laird 1974). Similarly, asking people to pose various facial expressions such as happiness or disgust for 10 seconds results in larger changes in heart rate and skin temperature than asking them to try to recreate an emotional experience in their imagination for 10 seconds (Ekman, Levenson, and Friesen 1983).

People also use their facial and even vocal expressions as clues as to what they are experiencing or in making judgments about their attitudes. For example, Martin, Harlow, and Strack (1992) asked research participants to hold either a pen between their lips, which generated a smile, or a folded paper towel tightly between their teeth, which activated the muscles associated with anger. The participants then heard a story involving Mike, who had carefully planned a party only to learn that the person who was supposed to bring the music forgot to do so. Participants were asked to say how Mike might feel. The results of the study indicated that participants holding a positive facial expression reported more favorable reactions, including understanding rather than anger, than did those holding angry facial expressions. This effect was significant only after participants had rated their feelings 90 seconds after they had exercised and were physiologically aroused. The study indicated that people make judgments about their feelings based partly on feedback from their facial expressions as well as on their arousal levels.

The facial feedback hypothesis suggests that if women express more feelings using facial expressions than men do, which is indeed the case, then they should experience more feelings as well, a more arguable proposition. Work related to the facial feedback hypothesis also suggests that women, long stereotyped as the "intuitive" sex, should make more judgments based on their emotions than men do, simply because they are more facially expressive than are men. These hypotheses are all speculative at this point.

In this book, I focus on gender differences in the expression or the measurable display of emotion, as distinct from emotional experience or the perception of emotions in others. I hold to the view that the expression and experience of emotion can occur independently of each other. Both everyday experience and clinical neurological evidence support the idea that emotional experience and expression can be independent. There is a curious phenomenon in some patients[1] consisting of involuntary incidents of laughing or crying unaccompanied by the experience of any emotion. The pathological laughing/crying incidents have the same respiratory, secretory, vocal, vascular, and facial muscular sequences as normal emotional laughing/crying, but the patients report no emotional experience and are unable to inhibit the laughing/crying. Thus, the neurological circuits for the facial and motor expression of emotion appear to be separable from the circuits that produce the experience (Rinn 1991).

In infancy, there may well be a one to one correspondence between emotional experience and emotional expression—most infants show directly what they feel inside. (On the other hand, even in infancy, there may be individual differences in the extent to which experience and expression diverge, depending on the infant's temperament). As people age, expression is increasingly affected by cultural values, and emotional experience and expression become more and more disparate.

Often, the separation between experience and expression is due to the conscious use of emotional regulation strategies, in which we monitor and control the quality and intensity of emotions we express, especially those we communicate to others. We don't express every emotion we experience. For example, older children can disguise their disappointment at receiving an unwanted gift better than younger children (Cole 1986; Saarni 1984, 1988). The separation between emotional experience and expression may become so profound that adults can develop "poker" faces.

There is also the complicated question of the role that the unconscious plays in the relationship between the experience and the expression of emotions. The experience of an emotion, such as anger, may actually be an unconscious distortion of some other emotional experience, such as sadness, that was pushed out of consciousness because it was too painful to bear (see Freud 1915). How this influences the nature of emotional expression is an interesting and open question. For example, if someone represses sad feelings and experiences anger instead, do they express their anger differently from someone who simply experiences anger, with no accompanying repression of sadness?

How we regulate our expression of emotions depends on complex interactions among our cultural backgrounds, our current social situations, our social roles, our needs and motives, our temperaments, and our status and power relative to those with whom we are interacting. Some of these processes differ for males and females, contributing to the dissimilar ways in which they express emotions.

I will close this discussion about emotional experience and expression with two somewhat contradictory thoughts. The first is that I believe them to be independent of each other at times, and in some individuals. The second is that they are hard to measure independently. It is often difficult to draw conclusions about whether researchers are studying emotional experience or emotional expression. Some studies blur the two constructs by using verbal self-report measures; for example, asking participants, "How intensely do you feel sad?" Such questions require people both to reflect on their experiences as well as to express their feelings. The evidence I present indicates that although men and women express feelings differently in specific contexts, it is less clear whether or not they actually experience feelings differently.

The Many Dimensions of Emotional Expression

Whether or not there are gender differences in the quality of expressed emotions is a complex question. Emotions may be expressed in "pure" form, such as sadness without other feelings mixed in; or may be expressed in "blended" form, as mixtures of several emotions. Sadness, anger, distress, hurt, and pain may also be expressed as one lump feeling, for example, when people talk about just plain feeling "bad" (Greenberg 1996). Are there gender differences in some, or all of these characteristics of emotional expression? Moreover, are there gender differences in the types of emotions that women and men express, as well as in the frequency, intensity, duration, and lability with which they express them?

Emotional expression turns out to be a multi-dimensional construct. In their recent factor-analytic study of six self-report measures of emotional expression, James Gross and Oliver John (1998) identified five factors, including positive expressivity, negative expressivity, the intensity of emotional expression,[2] expressive confidence (such as enjoying acting and being the center of attention), and masking or emotional regulation (such as suppressing anger, or telling a lie with a straight face). These five factors probably constitute only a limited representation of all possible aspects of emotional expressiveness, since the analysis did not sample the entire range of feelings, nor did it sample all possible ways in which emotions could be expressed—for example, through words versus facial expressions.

A comprehensive look at emotional expression must include all five modalities through which emotions can be expressed, including words, facial and vocal expressions, behaviors, and physiological arousal. You can say what you're feeling in words, show it on your face, change your voice characteristics, behave differently, or manifest a change in your physiology, such as blood pressure or sweating responses. Men and women may differ in some or all of these modalities. To add to the complexity, people may not limit themselves to only one modality to express a feeling, but may use several. So, for example, when two-year-olds feel angry, they may scream, screw up their faces, and hit. Adults have probably learned to simply tell someone how angry they are, although they may experience a rise in blood pressure while doing so. These all constitute patterns in the way individuals express emotions, and the two sexes may differ in some or all of these patterns at various ages.

To answer the question of whether males and females express feelings differently, or even express different feelings, it is also critical to explore contextual questions such as: Which males and females? Which emotions? What setting are they in? What roles are they playing? To whom are they directing the feeling? If there are indeed gender differences, are they constant throughout development, or do they shift at different ages? Do they hold true for all cultures? For all situations? To whom you are expressing emotion makes a tremendous difference in whether and how a particular feeling is expressed. The kinds of feelings people express to a child may differ from those expressed to an adult male. The kinds of feelings people express to and about women may differ from those they express to and about men. For example, one male research participant reported: "If I'm angry at a man, I'd yell and scream at him; then I'd cool down and call him and talk about it and apologize. If it were a woman, though, I'd walk away and keep it all inside so she doesn't get upset and cry. I'd be more angry quicker with a man." My research data, in fact, indicate that women at three different ages: school age, adolescence, and adulthood, are more apt to express fear and anger toward men than toward women (Brody, Lovas, and Hay 1995).

The answers to the questions I have raised about gender differences in emotion turn out to be fascinating and complex. How and when men and women express feelings depends on which emotion they are experiencing, the situational context, and their own particular characteristics, including their age, ethnicity, and cultural background. It also depends on which modality of emotional expression they are using, and whether the frequency or the intensity of emotional expression is measured. Although the face, the voice, words, behavior, and physiological changes can all vividly communicate feelings, each conveys somewhat different information, and men and women use each modality somewhat differently.

Biology, Environment, and Emotional Expression

Arguably, emotional expressions have some "hard-wired" components, with "hard-wired" referring to genetic preprogramming to respond in particular ways. Hard-wiring is suggested by the fact that the particular muscle movements associated with some facial expressions are present at birth and are culturally invariant, including the facial movements associated with anger, disgust, happiness, sadness, fear, and surprise (Ekman and Oster 1979). For example, a brow-raising expression as a form of greeting behavior has been found across diverse cultures in both men and women. Some facial expressions are even found across species (Darwin 1897). Other hard-wired components of emotional functioning may include the capacity to experience pleasure and pain, some voice intonations, and some physiological responses, such as increased heart rate and a higher pitched voice being associated with feelings of panic. The "action tendencies," or characteristic behavioral patterns associated with some emotions, may also be hard-wired, in that they tend to be automatic and involuntary. For instance, blinking may be an action tendency for anxiety, which helps both sexes to avoid potentially harmful incoming stimulation. Similarly, lunging forward may be an involuntary action tendency for anger, which may help to mobilize an individual for action (Campos et al. 1989).

Further, there seem to be universal "dimensions" of emotion that people are able to identify cross-culturally. Researchers have attempted to determine the components of emotion by using multidimensional scaling techniques, in which they ask people to determine which emotion labels are similar by sorting the labels into piles. The number of times that two terms are put into the same pile, or group, is counted as a way of analyzing the similarity of emotion terms (Scherer 1984). For example, anger and fear would be put more often into the same pile than anger and happiness. Using multidimensional scaling techniques across many culturally diverse samples, researchers have found either two or three dimensions of emotions: evaluation or valence (pleasant versus unpleasant, or good versus bad); arousal or intensity (slow versus fast, or mild versus strong) and activity or dominance (dominant versus submissive). The third dimension, activity or dominance, has alternatively been viewed as a social dimension, one that emerges out of an interpersonal context, such as social engagement–disengagement, or the "object" causing the emotion (de Rivera and Grinkis 1986; Markus and Kitayama 1991). Emotions that rank high on social engagement are those that signal or maintain closeness in relationships, such as warmth and guilt. Emotions that rank high on social disengagement are those that signal or maintain distance in relationships, such as hostility. Anger, for example, would have negative valence, high arousal, high dominance, and high social disengagement (see Russell 1991).

The fact that such dimensions are culturally universal implies that there are biological underpinnings to the way in which emotions are experienced and interpreted. Other evidence of hard-wiring is suggested by research showing that particular areas of the brain become activated when processing positive versus negative emotions, which I will discuss at length in Chapter 6. Yet other research indicates that some emotional experiences show modest genetic influences, again indicating biological bases for emotional experiences and expressiveness. For example, levels of contentment, social fearfulness, and anger-proneness are more similar to each other in identical twins than in fraternal twins (Goldsmith, Buss, and Lemery 1997; Lykken and Tellegen 1996).[3] An impressive 44 to 52 percent of the variance in happiness in adults can be accounted for by genetic variation, while family and social factors such as socioeconomic status, educational achievements, family income, marital status, and religious commitment turn out to account for no more than 3 percent of the variance (Lykken and Tellegen 1996).

However, it is important to note that the term hard-wired is somewhat misleading, because in humans, it has been found that neurological development does not occur in the absence of environmental influences. Katz and Shatz (1996) summarize evidence that indicates that in order for fetal and neonatal brain development to occur, the brain must be stimulated in some fashion by the social and physical environment. For example, an altered formation of neurons and axons in the brain characterizes young children who suffer from even one week of sightlessness due to cataracts. In the absence of visual input from the environment, brain development changes. The necessity for environmental inputs to complete the development of the brain is theorized to be an economical system (requiring a fewer number of genes) that enables the organism to adapt to different environmental necessities (Shatz 1992).

In other words, even if some aspects of emotion are biologically based, the evidence suggests that biological processes never exist in a social or environmental vacuum.

Appraisal Theories of Emotion

That the expression of emotion involves not only biological components, but learned social and cognitive components has been clearly suggested by appraisal theories of emotion. These theories maintain that before we either experience or express a feeling, we interpret our ongoing situation in particular ways. We scan the environment and appraise events to be either novel vs. familiar; pleasant or unpleasant; controllable or uncontrollable; certain or uncertain in outcome; or caused by ourselves or others (Scherer 1984).[4] Each of these interpretations influences the quality of the emotions we experience. Thus, even though people across cultures agree that emotions have at least two major dimensions (valence and intensity), they tend to diverge on the specific situations that evoke emotions because they appraise situations in different ways. For example, Americans have been described humorously as "believing that death is optional"—a belief system quite different from British fatalism. Such a worldview, as farfetched as it sounds, may cause some Americans to blame themselves when contracting a fatal illness to a greater extent than some British, and may lead Americans to feel guilt and regret for failing to take better care of themselves.

When we appraise unpleasant events as being caused by other people, we experience anger; when we appraise negative events as being our own fault, we experience guilt or regret; when we appraise events as being caused by fate, we experience sorrow or despair (Smith and Ellsworth 1985; Moore and Isen 1990). How we perceive and interpret the power, status, and closeness dimensions in our interpersonal relationships, although not usually included in lists of appraisal theory dimensions, are also of critical importance in affecting our emotional expressiveness.

Within the same culture, males and females may appraise situations differently. Women may appraise unfamiliar men as uncontrollable and therefore experience fear, whereas men may appraise unfamiliar men not only as uncontrollable, but also as a threat to their status and therefore experience anger. The emotions males and females experience and express are related to their interpretations of events, which in turn are related to their motives, social roles, power and status, personality characteristics, and cultural values. If women and men differ on any of these dimensions (and in later chapters I will demonstrate that they do), then they will consequently differ in their emotional expressiveness. The point is that the particular emotions that males and females express, as well as the ways in which they express those feelings, emerge partly from the differing life circumstances and roles in which men and women find themselves.

Ultimately, the question of how gender differences in emotional expression develop and emerge cannot be answered without considering how gender roles themselves emerge. For example, why do women become caretakers, and why do men end up in positions of social power? Although there are no clear answers to this immensely complex question, hypothetical answers have interesting implications for the emergence of gender differences in the expression of emotion, which I will consider as I go along.

OVERVIEW.   Emotion is a multifaceted motivational system with behavioral, cognitive, physiological, and experiential components. Although it is biologically rooted, emotional development unfolds as a function of the interaction among biological, social, and cultural processes. I have argued that the inner experience of emotion and the outward expression of emotion can be independent. Emotional experience functions to maintain our well-being by monitoring our motives and needs. Emotional expression communicates those needs to others, and may both influence and be influenced by our emotional experiences.

It is easy to over-generalize when exploring the extent of gender differences in the expression of emotions. Gender differences may vary across different aspects of emotional expression, including the quality, intensity, frequency, and modality in which emotions are expressed. Further, there may or may not be gender differences in the kinds of situations that precipitate emotional expression. There may also be cultural and age differences in the extent to which men and women express dissimilar feelings. How and whether men and women express different emotions depends on their respective ages, social roles, temperaments, cultural values, motives, needs (including their self-esteem), and their power and status in the culture. These factors are all formative for the emergence of gender differences in emotional expression.

3

Words, Faces, Voices, and Behaviors

If I was playing Chutes and Ladders and I got really mad, I'd probably
throw a piece of the board at my friend, you know, probably fling the
directions at him.

—*Dylan, age 6*

If I'm mad it says right across my face that I'm mad. If I am, you
know it.

—*Martha, age 42*

In contrast to our stereotypes, which link the expression of anger with
men, and sadness, fear, and warmth with women, actual gender differences in emotional expressiveness cannot be summarized so quickly and
easily. Gender differences occur in some situations, but not in others,
and similarly, in some modalities of emotional expression, but not in
others. If we attempt to systematically understand the nature of the
situations and modalities in which gender differences occur, but also in
which they do not occur, we will be one step closer to understanding the
meaning of gender differences in emotional expressiveness, one step
closer to understanding why gender differences occur at all.

In this chapter, I will look at how women and men use words, behaviors, and facial and vocal expressions to express emotions. Because gender differences in each of these modalities vary so widely in different
situations, I will emphasize the context in which emotions are expressed.
Much previous research fails to acknowledge the degree to which gender
differences are situationally and culturally based.

There are some other cautions that apply to the studies I am about
to summarize. One is that they often focus on gender differences in

only one modality of emotional expression, for example, facial expressions or behaviors. A second is that some studies investigate the expression of general emotionality, rather than the expression of specific emotions, such as anger or sadness. By ignoring the simultaneous expression of feelings in more than one modality, and by ignoring differences in the expression of specific emotions, researchers fail to capture the complexity of how people actually express emotions in their daily lives.

General emotionality is a misleading concept because people probably express particular positive and negative emotions at differing frequencies and intensities. Some studies have shown that the intensity with which people express emotions does generalize to a modest extent across positive and negative emotions (Gross and John 1998), but Barrett and Russell (in press) have recently pointed out that the relationship between the degree to which people report positive and negative emotions may vary depending on the valence and intensity of the particular emotions being measured. For example, serene and calm are emotions with positive valence and low activation, and people who experience more serenity may experience less jitteriness and tenseness. These are emotions with negative valence and high activation that are polar opposites to serenity. In contrast, the degree to which people report serenity and calmness may bear no relationship to the degree to which they report emotions such as depression, which also has low activation. Although these ideas are based on reports of emotional experience and may or may not apply to emotional expression, they should make us cautious about the concept of general "emotionality." The point is that studying general emotionality becomes nonsensical without distinguishing between particular positive and negative emotions. Other researchers have pointed out that the quality of the relationships between negative and positive emotions may vary over time, showing more inverse relationships within short time periods, and more independent relationships over longer time periods (Diener and Emmons 1984).[1]

Future research should help to clarify the complexity of the relationship between positive and negative emotional intensity expressed over time. At the moment, studies on general emotionality provide us with a necessary, although at times misleading, starting place for understanding gender differences in emotional expression.

Words

Language conveys nuances of emotional experience that cannot be conveyed in any other way. For example, compare the feelings of guilt and chagrin. The two feelings are difficult to distinguish on the basis of facial expressions, physiological responses, or voice quality. In fact, it is difficult to guess that someone is feeling either one of these emotions by looking at their facial expressions, or even by listening to their tone of voice. Only language can clearly demonstrate the subtleties of each feeling.

Some theorists (Stern 1985) have persuasively argued that only by using language can we make our private emotional experiences accessible to others, sharing them in ways that may transform the nature of the experiences. When emotional experiences are not shared with others, they may become inaccessible and unacknowledged even to ourselves. Recent work has indicated that the social sharing of an emotional experience (usually through language) is an integral part of the emotional process. Eighty-eight percent of a sample of individuals interviewed in Belgium reported that they had spoken to someone about emotional episodes they had experienced. Across different cultural groups, women reported sharing their emotional experiences with a wider variety of people than did men. Men limited themselves to sharing emotional experiences with their intimate partners (Rime et al. 1991).

Such social sharing may affect our adaptation to, and perhaps even our biological integration of the initial event. The psychiatrist A. Pontius (1993) has argued that in extreme cases, if early traumatic emotional experiences are not shared using language, communicatory links between the limbic system and the cortex may never develop, leading to a predisposition to experience limbic seizures when the initial event is re-activated. Limbic seizures may result in bizarre (sometimes violent) behaviors and hallucinations. Although this is a rare and extreme situation, it illustrates the importance of verbalizing emotions not only for our social interactions with others, but possibly also for our biological development.

Researchers measure verbal emotional expression in a variety of ways. One way is to ask people what emotions they feel frequently or intensely, using checklists or statements that they must deny or endorse. Another way is to ask people to record their verbal expressions of emotion on daily log sheets as they occur. Researchers also analyze the emotions people write about when asked to produce memories or stories. Or they observe and record the emotion words people use in the course of their social interactions, for example how frequently people state to others, "I'm angry at you." These measures each address somewhat different aspects of verbal expression. All of these measures involve words, and presumably, conscious access to language-emotion relationships, but some involve a spontaneous tendency to talk about feelings, while others involve an acknowledgment in words that emotional experiences have occurred, without necessarily using emotion words as part of the initial experience. Often, researchers blur this distinction.[2]

Self-Report Measures

Across 26 different countries, including countries as diverse as Indonesia, Croatia, and Tunisia, women rate themselves as more verbally expressive than men (Pennebaker, Rime, and Blankenship 1996). Women use words to express both a wider range of feelings and more intense emotions than men do in the United States, Europe, and possibly in Asian countries (Copeland, Hwang, and Brody 1996; Scherer, Wallbott, and Summerfield 1986). In one study, when asked how they would feel in response to emotional scenarios such as, "You and your best friend are in the same line of work. There is a prize given annually to the best performance of the year. The two of you work hard to win the prize. One night the winner is announced—your friend," women used a higher number of differentiated emotion words than men, including happy, sad, and angry, as opposed to undifferentiated words, such as feeling tired, bad, or punching the wall (Barrett et al., n.d.).

Women also consistently report expressing more intense positive and negative emotions than do men on the Affect Intensity Measure (Diener, Sandvik, and Larsen 1985; Barrett et al. 1998). On this measure, people are asked to rate how likely it is that they would express or experience intense feelings, such as "When I'm happy I feel very energetic," or "When I talk in front of a group for the first time my voice gets shaky and my heart races." The items tend to blur emotional experience and expression, and hence the scale should be viewed as a measure of general "emotionality." (It is important to note that the negative items on this scale tend to fall into the sadness/distress/anxious categories and to exclude anger). Participants who have completed the AIM have ranged in age from 16 to 68, and have come primarily from the United States, although recent data have shown the same pattern of gender differences in participants from Asian countries (Diener, Sandvik, and Larsen 1985; Eisenberg et al. 1991b; Fujita, Diener, and Sandvik 1991; Copeland, Hwang, and Brody 1996; Brody, 1997).

Women also report that they express more intense positive and negative emotions in a family or interpersonal context than men (Cassidy et al. 1992; Barrett 1998). And, in a recent study by James Gross and Oliver John (1998) that factor-analyzed six different measures of emotional expressivity and then explored sex differences on the emerging five factors, women reported moderately greater positive and negative expressiveness than men, and much higher impulse intensity than men. Impulse intensity included items measuring the intensity of emotional experience, such as, "I experience my emotions very strongly."

Gender differences are clearer for the intensity with which emotions are expressed, rather than the frequency, with women reporting that they express more intense emotions than men, but not necessarily more frequent emotions (see Brody and Hall 1993). Barrett et al. (1998) found that women rated their *global* emotional intensity and expressiveness to be higher than men, but found no gender differences in the intensity of participants' ratings of *specific* emotional experiences rated immediately after a social interaction.

Barrett and her colleagues' work (in press, a) as well as that of Seidlitz and Diener (1998), suggest that women's reports of higher affective intensity on global self-report measures such as the AIM may not be accurate reflections of sex differences in affective intensity at the time that emotions are initially expressed or evoked. Seidlitz and Diener (1998) found that men actually reported positive events in their lives to be *more* intense than did women when using daily rating forms, but not when subsequently recalling those same events. Self-reports of emotional intensity as reported on the AIM were also not significantly related to the intensity of emotional reactions at the time they occurred. Seidlitz and Diener (1998) speculate that gender differences on measures of general emotionality, such as the AIM, may appear because women's memories of emotion are represented in greater detail than are men's. This then contributes to women's subsequent reports of more intense emotions relative to men's, even in the absence of gender differences in emotional intensity at the time the two sexes initially expressed their feelings.

Alternative explanations for these discrepant results are also possible. One is that scores on the AIM may not concur with women's and men's specific reports of emotional expression because the AIM blurs the distinction between emotional experience and emotional expressiveness. It is also possible that in the time that elapses between an initial event and the memory of the event, women may ruminate over the triggering event more than the men, which may reactivate emotional experiences and result in cumulatively more intense emotional experiences for women than men. However, these new studies suggest a measure of caution when inferring sex differences in emotional expression from global self-report measures.

It is also critical to note that gender differences in self-reported emotional expression vary a great deal depending on the situation. In an intriguing study in which participants recorded their emotions as they were randomly beeped by pagers for a one week period, women reported more positive affect states (happy, cheerful, and friendly as opposed to unhappy, irritable, and angry) while at work rather than while at home. The opposite was true of men (Larson, Richards, and Perry-Jenkins 1994).[3] The authors speculate that people feel more positively about activities they choose to perform, rather than those they feel compelled or obligated to perform. Men may feel that they have more choices about what they do at home than at work (and in reality they engage in more personal and recreational activities at home than women do), whereas women may feel that they have more choices at work than at home, where they feel obligated to care for children or do housework. Women's positive emotionality at work was also related to the perceived friendliness of their coworkers, while men's was not, suggesting that interpersonal relationships are more important to women's emotional experiences than they are to men's, a theme to which I will return.

The reported intensity of emotional expression also changes depending on whether feelings are being expressed to or about men or women. For example, women report expressing more intense fear in situations in which they are threatened by men, rather than by women (Brody 1993). They also express more anger at men than at women (Brody, Lovas, and Hay 1995). And Barrett et al. (1998) found that both male and female college students reported that they experienced more intense emotion and expressed more emotion when interacting with an opposite rather than a same sex partner, possibly because they saw members of the opposite sex as potential romantic involvements.

Cultural Specificity

Although some research indicates that women across cultures report more intense positive and negative emotions than men do (see Brody 1997), this may be too broad of a generalization. For example, several studies suggest that men and women from other cultures do not differ from each other as markedly as American men and women do. One study showed that only among Americans did women score higher than men on the extent to which they reported relying on emotional verbal appeals in their social interactions. Japanese men and women did not significantly differ (Frymier, Klopf, and Ishii 1990).[4] A collaborative research study I did with Anne Copeland and Helen Hwang (1996; Brody 1997) was consistent with these results. Only women of European-American ethnicity reported more intense anger, annoyance, fear, nervousness, and shame than did their male counterparts in response to emotionally laden stories, such as "You've always done favors for your friend, and one day he refuses to do a favor for you in return." Asian-American and Asian international students did not show gender differences in these emotions. Contradicting the typical American gender difference pattern, Asian American men actually reported more intense shame in response to stories than did Asian American women.

It may be that one of the reasons that Americans show greater gender differences than those shown by members of other cultural groups is that America is a highly individualistic culture, in which personal accomplishments are emphasized, as opposed to a collectivistic culture, in which group accomplishments are emphasized. Fischer and Manstead (in press) compared individualistic and collectivistic cultures on the extent to which gender differences were evident. Individualistic countries showed greater gender differences in the intensity of joy, shame, disgust, and guilt than did collectivistic countries. The researchers speculate that males in individualistic cultures are more likely to minimize emotional expressions in an effort to maintain control—an attribute that is critical to their status as independent males.

To understand fully the extent and origins of these gender differences, researchers would need to evaluate different cultures' norms around appropriate emotional expressions for the two sexes, as well as differing patterns of emotional expressiveness for the two sexes in each culture. Very few studies addressing these types of issues have been completed.

Do Self-Report Measures Conform to Stereotypes?

Does the fact that women report more intense emotion than men simply reflect the stereotype that women should be more emotional than men? In other words, do men and women complete emotion checklists with some socially desirable standard in mind, trying to make a good impression? Some research supports this idea. In one study, when children watched a frightening film in which two boys were home alone while a stranger lurked outside, gender differences in reported emotions were limited to those children who scored high on social desirability (that is, who needed to present themselves in a socially acceptable light). Only among those children did boys report feeling less distressed and happier than did the girls (Eisenberg and Fabes 1995).

There is no doubt that, to some extent, stereotypes contribute to self-reports of gender differences in emotional expressiveness. For example, Grossman and Wood (1993) argue that sex differences in self-report measures are the result of social role expectations. Women are expected to be more emotional than men, and therefore report themselves to be more emotional. To test this, they asked male and female college students to rate the frequency with which they experienced and expressed several different emotions. They also asked them to rate the extent to which they believed that the two sexes were different in their emotional expressiveness. The extent to which people endorsed gender stereotypes related to the extent to which they reported experiencing different emotions than the opposite sex. For example, the extent to which the men endorsed stereotypes of greater female emotional intensity related to lowered intensity in their own reported expressions. Women who endorsed stereotypic sex differences in anger reported experiencing subdued anger themselves. Finally, men who believed that men expressed more anger than women reported that they themselves expressed heightened anger.

Another study showed that gender differences in estimates of how much emotion men and women would feel could be reduced or eliminated when specific information about situations was provided. When men and women were asked about emotional reactions to specific situations, such as being diagnosed with a serious disease, rather than about general, "troubling" situations, gender differences in their emotional intensity ratings tended to be lower (Robinson and Johnson 1997).

These data convincingly demonstrate that stereotypes may distort or influence our responses to global self-report measures, or, to be fair, that the reverse may also be true: our experiences influence our global stereotypes. And Seidlitz and Diener's (1998) research suggests that gender differences in reported intensity may be due not only to stereotypes, but also to gender differences in memory processes, with women possibly memorizing more detailed aspects of emotional situations than men.

Yet, even in the face of this evidence, I believe that gender differences in self-reported emotions reflect actual differences in emotional expressiveness, not merely stereotypes or differential memory processes. On what do I base my argument? First, men and women differ in more than self-reported emotional experiences. Women use more emotion words in social interactions and in writing samples than men, and their facial expressions are more expressive than men's. In fact, research by Grossman and Wood (1993) found that not only did women produce more facial activity in response to emotional imagery than men, but they found it difficult to inhibit their facial activity, even when requested to do so. Men had the opposite problem: they were incapable of exaggerating their facial expressivity when they were asked to do so. In other words, the social demands of the situation were not sufficient to override the direction of the gender differences in facial expressivity.

Further arguing against the point that gender differences in self-ratings exclusively reflect gender stereotypes are research findings that indicate that independent observers, such as close friends or family members, tend to corroborate participants' self-ratings of how expressive they are, including such characteristics as the duration of their anger, their emotional intensity, and whether they express anger by withdrawing or exploding (Burrowes and Halberstadt 1987; Larsen and Diener 1987; Lai and Linden 1992). Moreover, people's ratings of themselves also correspond to their actual behaviors as observed by experimenters. For example, Moskowitz (1990) showed that women's self-descriptions of friendliness were related to their actual friendly behaviors; while men's self-descriptions of dominance were related to their actual dominant behaviors.

To conclude this issue: although our sex-role stereotypes undoubtedly influence the way in which gender is socialized, they are not sufficient, in and of themselves, to account for the strong gender differences in emotional intensity consistently obtained when using self-report measures. Gender differences in self-reports of emotional expression reflect more than our social biases, and probably reflect more than gender differences in memory processes as well.

Verbalizing Emotions in Writing Samples and Interpersonal Interactions

Women verbalize more frequent and intense emotions not just on self-report measures, but also in spontaneous interactions and in writing samples. For example, men and women were asked to imagine the following scenario, which I have paraphrased (Girdler et al. 1990): "You are on your way to give an important talk at a professional conference. Upon arriving at the airport, through no fault of your own, you discover that your prebooked seat has been given away and the flight is full." The participants' task was to describe every step that they would take in dealing with the obstructive travel agent, what they thought other people would do in response to their actions, what emotions they would feel, and what they thought the final outcome of their actions would be. They were given three minutes to prepare their scenario, using pencil and paper, and three minutes in which to tell their story. In this task, the women (all graduate, medical, or dental students) talked more about feelings and made more emotional references than did the men. The word feel/felt was used eight times more frequently by women than by men; other emotion words were used about 33 percent more frequently than women.

Another illustration of gender differences in emotional expression comes from writing samples collected from middle-aged mothers and fathers in my research project. Mothers wrote stories with more warmth, empathy, emotional intensity, and positive emotion words, such as "happy" or "glad", than fathers did (Brody, Wise, and Monuteaux 1997).

Women also talk more about feelings with their husbands than vice versa. This has been shown both by asking people what they say and do in their marriages, as well by observing and recording studies of husbands' and wives' interactions. Wives are more willing to tell their husbands when they are feeling tense, they are more apt to disclose their feelings, and they are also more apt to try to explain their feelings than are husbands (Burke, Weir, and Harrison 1976; Parelman 1983).

Observations of marriages indicate that women express more emotion words, especially more negative emotions, in interpersonal interactions than men, including more distress and anger (Shimanoff 1983; Levenson, Carstensen, and Gottman 1994;[5] Gottman and Levenson 1992; Notarius and Johnson 1982). In an intensive study of a single married couple who wore radio transmitters throughout the day, the wife talked more about her feelings and experiences, while the husband gave more information and directions (Soskin and John 1963). In a similar study, the members of several 20- to 54-year-old couples were asked to record all conversations with each other for a complete day using daily log books (Shimanoff 1983). Subsequently, a computer search was done on all the emotion words in their logs. Wives disclosed more hostile emotions than husbands in their conversations. They also reported a more positive attitude toward disclosing vulnerable, hostile, and regretful emotions than did their husbands.

Emotion Words and Development

At least in American samples, gender differences in emotional vocabulary appear to set in very early in development. There is evidence that by age 2, girls have a wider emotional vocabulary than boys do in conversations with family members (Dunn, Bretherton, and Munn 1987). School-aged girls express more sadness and fear than boys in a variety of situations, including self-reports and responses to stories and films (Brody 1984; Brody, Lovas, and Hay 1995; Zahn-Waxler et al. 1995). In particular, greater expressions of fear by school-aged girls have been documented in countries as disparate as China, the United States, and Great Britain (Ollendick et al. 1995). As with adults, it is important to note that the expression of emotion using words by children also varies depending on the situation. For example, although young girls generally report more sadness than boys while watching films of adults having a dispute, boys report more sadness when the disputes are unresolved than girls do (Cummings et al. 1991).

Facial Expressions

Facial expressions vividly convey some emotions, and elicit reliable responses from people who observe them. Mimes and silent comedians dramatically demonstrate how the emotions conveyed in facial expressions shape people's reactions. One such comedian, the British Mr. Bean, creates a scenario in which he carefully selects a delicious-looking chocolate dessert at a fair, his face the picture of delight and anticipation. Unbeknownst to him, his car, parked behind him, is being used in a demolition demonstration and is run over by a huge army tank while he savors his dessert. The audience at first laughs hilariously. Then Mr. Bean turns around, sees his car, and a look that can only be described as pathetic crosses his face. The audience's laughter immediately changes to an empathic, lower-register, drawn-out "Oooh," as one would say to a small child who has been hurt.

Mr. Bean's facial expressions are clear, recognizable, and evocative. They elicit predictable responses from others. His often exaggerated expressions powerfully illustrate how important facial expressions are to our social interactions. Analyses of videotaped conversations show that for many people, the face is constantly generating movements, some lasting for as little as 40 milliseconds (Rinn 1991). We may or may not be aware of our fleeting facial expressions, or even of those that last for several minutes, such as knitting our brows while we concentrate. However, such movements are certainly visible to others and affect their feelings about us, themselves, and the quality of our relationships.

Mr. Bean's clearly recognizable facial expressions are usually more characteristic of women's than of men's facial expressions. Women display more recognizable emotions in their faces than men do, whether in naturalistic or posed situations (Hall 1984). The only possible exception to this is the expression of anger, which I will review at length in Chapter 5. Women have more expressive faces for all other emotions (Hall 1984), although these data are clearest for American women. Emerging studies on European and Japanese men and women show some similar trends as well as some differences (Scherer, Wallbott, and Summerfield 1986; Matsumoto 1992; Biehl et al. 1997). Meta-analyses in 1984, in which effect sizes were calculated across several different studies,[6] indicated that women were more facially expressive than men to a strong degree (see Hall 1984). Meta-analyses also indicated that women smiled moderately more than men (Hall 1984; Hall, Carter, and Horgan, in press) and gazed moderately more than men (Hall 1984). Even in a study of couples discussing and trying to resolve marital conflicts, women have been found to smile more than their husbands (Kiecolt-Glaser et al. 1993).

Let's look more specifically at how gender differences in facial expressions have been measured. One way is to use judges (either naive observers or trained psychologists) who rate men's and women's faces for the intensity and quality of emotional expressions, using such evidence as smiling, frowning, and direction of eye gaze. Observational studies using judges need to be interpreted quite cautiously, since they are apt to be biased. Since women are stereotyped as sadder, more fearful, and less angry than men, the same face is more likely to be interpreted as sad or fearful if described as female, and angry if described as male. In fact, studies using a baby of a sex unknown to the judges have found just that. When told a baby is male, participants are more likely to see it as angry; when told the same baby is female, they are more likely to see it as sad or scared (Condry and Condry 1976).[7]

More systematic coding of facial expressions is provided by measuring facial muscle movements using electromyograph (EMG) assessments. Surface electrodes are placed on the face to record movement in the facial musculature by detecting electrical discharges of contracting muscle fibers (see Manstead 1991). Sometimes EMG recordings can detect facial muscle movements not widely visible to others. For example, Schwartz and his colleagues (1976) found that clinically depressed women had an attenuated or minimized version of the facial muscle patterns shown by nondepressed women when they imagined happy situations. When they imagined sad situations, depressed women had an exaggerated version of the patterns displayed by nondepressed people. And, moreover, when asked to imagine a "typical day," the nondepressed women more reliably generated happy patterns than did the depressed women. None of these patterns would be recognized by casual observers.

There are also four widely used systems that code facial muscle movements, such as eyebrow raises or frowns, by the microsecond. These systems include Ekman and Friesen's Facial Action Coding System (FACS) and Emotion Facial Action Coding System (EMFACS), Izard's Maximally Discriminative Facial Movement Coding System (MAX) and Izard's AFFEX, or the System for Identifying Affect Expression by Holistic Judgment. These systems are not completely identical, but have some overlap (Ekman and O'Sullivan 1991).[8] Because observers are coding movements on a micro-level, they are somewhat less apt to be biased by stereotypes about emotion. The downside of these systems is that they require extensive training to use and they may pick up on aspects of facial expressiveness that are not particularly meaningful in everyday social interactions. However, when EMFACS ratings have been compared to global ratings by observers, studies have shown significant relationships for some emotions (Halberstadt, Fox, and Jones 1993).

These three systems (judges' ratings, micro-analytic coding systems, and EMG recordings) each have been used in several kinds of settings. These have included videotaped naturalistic interactions, posed facial expressions,[9] and a "slide-viewing" paradigm in which men and women watch different kinds of slides (including sexual imagery, car accidents, maternal scenes) and judges guess which slide is being observed on the basis of the viewers' facial expressions. In this paradigm, the facial expressiveness score is measured by how accurate the judges' guesses are.

Gender differences in facial expressions are most likely to be seen when either EMG recordings or judges are used to measure facial expressiveness (Schwartz, Brown, and Ahern 1980; Harper et al. 1981; Dimberg and Lundquist 1990; Wallbott and Scherer 1991; Lang et al. 1993; Grossman and Wood 1993). Women generate larger facial EMG patterns when either posing emotional expressions or responding to emotional stimuli than do men, including when viewing slides of angry and happy faces (Dimberg and Lundquist 1990).[10]

Cultural Specificity

There are, unfortunately, few cross-cultural data on gender differences in facial expressivity. In one suggestive study in Belgium, France, Great Britain, Israel, Italy, Spain, Switzerland, and West Germany, female university students (aged 18–53) reported more nonverbal emotional reactions than did males, including facial reactions, vocal reactions, and body movements. Females also reported more laughing, smiling and movements toward other people for several emotions, including joy, sadness, fear, and anger (Scherer Wallbott, and Summerfield 1986). However, these studies represent reports of facial expressions, and not actual observations of the facial expressions themselves.

In studies comparing American and Japanese college students who were asked to pose emotional expressions, the emotions depicted by women from both cultural groups were sometimes recognized more clearly than those depicted by men (Matsumoto 1992; Matsumoto and

Ekman 1989). In general, both American and Japanese females' facial expressions were more accurately judged than males' by members of six different cultural groups, including Poles, Hungarians, Japanese, Vietnamese, Sumatrans, and Americans (Biehl et al. 1997). Women were also sometimes rated as having more intense emotions, especially more intense sadness, than men (Matsumoto and Ekman 1989).

However, for some emotions, the gender differences in facial expressivity were inconsistent. For example, women posing happiness were seen as happier than their male counterparts by both Japanese and Americans, but only if they were Caucasian. Similarly, only Caucasian and not Japanese men were seen as more surprised than women. This study suggests that gender differences in facial expressivity (or perceptions of facial expressivity) may vary in different cultures for different emotions (Matsumoto and Ekman 1989).

Eye Gaze

Eye gaze, both its duration and its directionality (whether aimed directly at another person's face or lowered, as in humiliation), has been interpreted as expressing emotion. Maintaining eye gaze with others is related to communicating nurturance and warmth (Libby and Yaklevich 1973). A consistent body of research has indicated that women tend to engage in more eye contact, both while listening and speaking, for longer periods of time than do men (Exline, Gray, and Schuette 1965; Libby and Yaklevich 1973). In one study, women maintained eye contact with a female interviewer over twice as often as males, and broke eye contact before the end of the interviewer's questions about half as often as males (Libby and Yaklevich 1973). Even in interviews in which they are asked embarrassing questions, women engage in more mutual glances than men do, regardless of the sex of the experimenter (Exline, Gray, and Schuette 1965). Meta-analyses of gazing indicate a moderate effect size in favor of females of all ages (Hall 1984).

Women tend to signal abasement (accepting blame, giving in, avoiding fights) by looking away to the left, while men do not (Libby and Yaklevich 1973), once again indicating that women may use facial cues to express their feelings more than men do. An alternative explanation is that men don't experience abasement as frequently as women do because of their higher status and power in the culture, and therefore express it less frequently.

Smiling

Several meta-analyses have indicated that European-American women smile more frequently in both social and nonsocial situations than men do, with effect sizes in the moderate range for adults (Halberstadt, Hayes, and Pike 1988; Hall, Carter, and Horgan, in press; see also Hall 1984). Younger children do not show a clear trend for greater female smiling (Hall 1984), nor is there greater smiling among American Black women as compared to American Black men (Halberstadt 1983; Halberstadt and Saitta 1987).

Gender differences in smiling have been related to the idea that women may use smiling to appease or gain approval from more powerful others because they are usually in subordinate or oppressed roles. This "oppression hypothesis," which I will discuss further in Chapter 10, has only weak or mixed evidence to support it at present (Hall and Halberstadt 1996). Smiling may have a number of different additional meanings, including being happy, nervous, apologetic, encouraging, disarming, or welcoming (Frieze and Ramsey 1976). However, studies do indicate that people interpret nonsmiling faces as dominant and smiling faces as friendly, happy, or feminine (Halberstadt and Saitta 1987; Keating et al. 1981).

The Development of Gender Differences in Facial Expressions

INFANTS. There is much contradictory evidence about whether or not there are gender differences in infants' emotional expressiveness. Several studies and reviews of infant characteristics suggest that males express more negative emotions, such as crying, than females during the first two years of life (Landreth 1941; Maccoby and Jacklin 1974; Moss 1974; Kohnstamm 1989; Belsky, Fish, and Isabella 1991). For example, Kohnstamm (1989) reports that when he asked Dutch parents, "How much does your baby cry or get worked up?," parents rated boys as significantly higher than girls between 5 and 22 months. Similarly, an observational study of children both at home and at school found that from 3 to 5 years of age, boys cried more frequently at home (but not at school) and more often over frustrating events than did girls (Landreth 1941). Crying includes both facial expressions and behaviors.

Other studies have found that male infants express both more frequent and more intense emotions than girls. For example, one study controlled for people's stereotypes about gender and emotion by systematically varying the accuracy of the information conveyed about 6-month-old infants' actual sex (Cunningham and Shapiro 1984). In this study, people rated the actual boys as expressing more intense emotions (including negative emotions), regardless of what sex they believed the infants to be. Similarly, an observational study of mother-child interaction using the AFFEX facial expression coding system found that 6-month-old male infants expressed more frequent emotions in three different play settings and at two different time periods than did female infants (Weinberg et al. in press). At least in some studies, gender differences on the part of the infants occurred regardless of the mother's behaviors, which did not differ toward their male and female infants (Weinberg et al. in press).

In contrast, other studies show no or mixed gender differences in infants' expressivity, sometimes depending on how expressivity is measured (see a review of these studies by Cossette et al. 1996). Many studies report no gender differences when infants are either involved in face-to-face interactions with their mothers or when their mothers are instructed to be unresponsive to them (termed the still face paradigm) (Field et al. 1987; Fogel, Toda, and Kawai 1988; Gusella, Muir, and Tronick 1988; Ellsworth, Muir, and Hains 1993). Inconsistent studies show that sometimes males express more negativity in the still face paradigm (Weinberg et al. in press), and sometimes females do (Toda and Fogel 1993). In infants below the age of 6 months, some studies have shown boys to smile more while interacting with mothers (Lasky and Klein 1979; Roe and Beckwith 1992) or when aroused in a variety of circumstances (Kagan et al. 1994), while others have shown, in direct contradiction, that girls smile more than boys (Cossette et al. 1996).

Louise Cossette and her co-authors (1996) point out that one of the primary reasons for these discrepancies may be that the frequency with which some emotions are expressed may not be reliable or stable until about 6 months of age. Infants' expressions of interest, joy, negative expressions, and neutral expressions were found to be relatively inconsistent between 2½ months and 5 months (Cossette et al. 1996). Other researchers find increasing evidence of the consistency of emotional expressiveness after 5 months of age (Malatesta et al. 1989), although Sullivan, Lewis, and Alessandri (1992) report, in contrast, that the expression of anger was stable from 2 to 4 months of age when an expected reward did not materialize.

Other reasons for these contradictory data may be that gender differences in infants' emotional expressiveness are related to the social context. When separating from and subsequently reuniting with their mothers, full and preterm infant girls expressed more anger than did infant boys (Malatesta et al. 1986). This result suggests that girls may be more stressed by the absence of a social relationship than are boys, a point I will return to in Chapter 7. Infant girls have also been found to be more likely to display facial expressions of interest in mother-infant interactions (Malatesta and Haviland 1982; Weinberg et al., in press), while infant boys have been found to display more interest in a toy with moveable parts than girls (Stifter and Grant 1993). Just as in adults, gender differences in infants' emotional expressions may be context-specific.

SCHOOL-AGED CHILDREN.   Many studies of school-aged children in natural social interactions or while watching films show that boys and girls do not differ in their facial expressions of sadness, fear, happiness, and anger (Halberstadt, Fox, and Jones 1993; Yarczower and Daruns 1982; Morency and Krauss 1982; Strayer and Roberts 1997). As noted above, there are also no gender differences in the overall frequency of smiling in young children (Hall 1984). On the other hand, school-aged boys do less well at posing happiness, sadness, anger, and fear than girls, showing a pattern similar to the one found in adult men and women (Shortt et al. 1994).

Just as for adults, gender differences for school-aged children may be specific to certain emotions and situations. Boys displayed more facial expressions of anger in situations in which an adult simulated distress, such as dropping a box on her foot (Zahn-Waxler et al. 1995), while girls exhibited more facial sadness than boys when watching a tape about a girl whose pet had died (Eisenberg et al. 1989).

DEVELOPMENT AND MASKING OR MINIMIZING EMOTIONS.   A clearer pattern emerges in studies that look at how emotional expressions change with development for each sex. Boys' expressions of sadness and affection become less recognizable as they get older. For instance, younger boys expressed more sadness in their facial expressions while watching sad films than older boys did (Buck 1977; Eisenberg et al. 1989). Similarly, according to mother's diaries, boys were increasingly less likely to be openly affectionate as they got older, which was largely measured by the boys' overt behaviors, but may have included their facial expressions as well (Cummings, Zahn-Waxler, and Radke-Yarrow 1984).

Several intriguing studies suggest that by school age, girls are more adept than boys at changing their facial expressions to be appropriate in different social contexts. They may learn to regulate their emotional expressions in the service of being perceived as "good." For example, preschool and early school-aged boys expressed more negative emotions (including facial expressions and behaviors) when receiving an unattractive gift than girls did (Cole 1986; Davis 1995). Preschool girls also tended to substitute smiles for negative emotions, whereas boys tended to minimize their negative expressions without smiling. In other words, girls substituted an unfelt positive expression, pretending to be happy, whereas boys sought to be unaffected (Cole 1986). In another study, first- and third-grade boys did less well than girls when asked to "trick" an experimenter into believing that they actually liked a disappointing gift. Even when motivated to hide their negative feelings by the promise of a prize, the boys did not, or perhaps could not, suppress their negative expressions (Davis 1995).

Social approval may be a more important goal for girls than for boys: girls report that not getting into trouble is important to them; boys are less concerned (Chung and Asher 1996). Girls also inhibit their negative emotional displays more in the presence of an examiner than when alone, again suggesting that social approval is a motivation for masked emotional expressiveness (Davis 1995). Evidence that young boys care less about the consequences of misbehaving than young girls is provided by a study showing that 3-year-old boys were more likely to admit that they deceived an experimenter than were their female counterparts. Children were told not to peek at a toy while the experimenter left the room. The majority of children indeed did peek, and denied it when asked. However, boys were more likely than girls to admit their transgression (Lewis, Stanger, and Sullivan 1989).

Rather than social approval, control seems to be a more important goal for boys. Boys endorse the importance of such items as "It is important for me to have my own toys/space" more than girls do (Chung and Asher 1996). In fact, intriguing developmental research indicates that only male and not female infants show negative responses that are more intense when they can't control a frightening toy than when they can (Gunnar-vonGnechten 1978), suggesting the importance of control for males at a very early age.[11] Boys' control goals may motivate them to conceal their emotion in public settings, for example by minimizing negative emotions in the face of receiving a disappointing gift (Cole 1986), or reporting happiness or lack of distress during frightening or stressful situations (Eisenberg et al. 1989).

Vocal Expressions

Voice patterns play a key role in signalling motivational and emotional states. How many times has someone said, "I'm not angry" in a tone of voice that belies the words?

Research confirms that voices powerfully convey emotional information. Vocal expressiveness may play a powerful role in the socialization process. Parents frequently use their voices to convey emotion to their children, including encouragement and admonishment, because their active children often do not stop long enough to look at their parents' facial expressions (Campos et al. 1994). Voice changes have also been associated with traumatic experiences. When people disclose intimate traumas, their voices may begin to whisper, or they may accelerate their speech dramatically, in many cases sounding like different people (Pennebaker 1989). Further, students who speak about traumatic events into a tape recorder convey more emotion to the outside observers who code the data than students convey who write down their traumatic experiences (Murray and Segal 1994).

Emotion is expressed by a number of vocal parameters, including intensity, frequency (pitch), rate of speech, and quality (Scherer 1986, 1989). There are enormous conceptual and methodological difficulties in the attempt to objectively measure and define vocal characteristics. To take one example, the accurate interpretation of vocal intensity is very problematic because intensity is dependent on factors such as the distance between the speaker and the listener, or between the speaker and the microphone, as pointed out by Pittam and Scherer (1993).

Perhaps because of these and other difficulties, the patterns in the vocal expression of emotion have not been as clearly mapped as have the patterns for the facial expression of emotion. Specific vocal parameters (voice pitch, quality, volume) that are associated with particular emotions have not been clearly identified (Scherer 1989). Despite our rather inadequate understanding of how voices convey emotion, people are relatively accurate in decoding emotional meaning from vocal cues, attaining high accuracy scores when asked to identify particular emotions (Bezooyen 1984).

Researchers have studied gender differences in voice expressivity in several ways. One way is by measuring the physiological determinants of the voice production process, such as by recording respiration rate or by taking EMG measurements of laryngeal muscles. Another way is to analyze the characteristics of the acoustic waveform generated by the voice. Finally, and most relevant for gender differences, researchers have asked people to rate the emotions conveyed in the voices of professional or lay actors who have been asked to simulate specific emotions.

Gender and Vocal Expressions

Do women and men express different emotions, or even the same emotions in dissimilar ways via their voices? The best way to answer these questions would be to disguise the sex of the speaker before judging the emotion conveyed by the speaker's voice characteristics. This is nearly impossible—male and female voices have different fundamental frequencies (or pitch) and are readily identifiable as such. People's awareness of the speaker's gender may influence them in subtle and not so subtle ways to interpret women's and men's voices differently. For example, female voices are judged to be more positive, pleasant, honest, whiney, personal, admiring, respectful, anxious, delicate, and enthusiastic, but less confident, dominant, and tense than males (Hall 1984). These judgments are undoubtedly influenced by general stereotypes about the two sexes.

The interpretation of emotions expressed vocally also depends a great deal on who's listening. For example, Reardon and Amatea (1973) explored college students' evaluations of men and women who were repeating the following sentences: "There is no other answer. You've asked me that question a thousand times and my answer has always been the same; it will always be the same." Each speaker was asked to say this sentence so that it expressed different emotions, including love, happiness, sadness, fear, anger, and indifference. When either sex conveyed an emotion that was non-gender-role stereotypic (e.g., men conveyed sadness and women conveyed anger), college students tended to evaluate them negatively. Female college students evaluated the expression of anger more negatively than did men and reacted especially negatively to a female voice expressing anger. In contrast, the female expression of sadness was evaluated positively.

It is critical to bypass stereotypes in order to evaluate gender differences in vocal expression. One way around these biases is to require judges to rate specific vocal characteristics associated with emotions, rather than to make global judgments about the emotions conveyed by the voice. Some studies have indicated that there are no gender differences in vocal characteristics, such as the loudness, clarity, pitch level, timbre, or rate used to convey emotions (Davitz 1964; Bezooyen 1984).

However, other studies have shown gender differences in specific vocal characteristics. Most of these studies suggest that men convey more vocal characteristics associated with anger than women (see Hall 1984; Siegman 1993). For example, men and women were given ostensibly neutral phrases such as, "there he is again"; or "two months pregnant"; or "such a big American car"; and were asked to speak the phrases expressing different emotions, including disgust, surprise, shame, interest, joy, fear, contempt, sadness and anger (Bezooyen 1984). Judges then coded each emotion for characteristics such as harshness and laxness. Laxness is a sonorous and resonant voice quality associated with shame, interest, and neutral speech. Harshness is a rough and rasping quality, associated with anger, disgust, and joy. Men were judged to be more lax and harsh in their speech than women (Bezooyen 1984).[12]

Men have also been found to speak more loudly and quickly than women in at least two studies (Hall 1984). For both men and women, loud volume is associated with anger, and a slow speech rate is associated with sadness (Siegman and Boyle 1993). These differences suggest that gender differences in vocal volume and speed may underlie perceived gender differences in anger and sadness, with men perceived as expressing relatively more anger and less sadness than women.

Few studies have looked at the development of gender differences in vocal expressiveness. Such studies would be interesting, since the pitch of boys' and girls' voices is similar and thus gender could be disguised. Researchers instead have focused on boys' and girls' abilities to decode, or recognize, the emotions in others' voices, and have found largely inconsistent results (see Bezooyen 1984). In Bezooyen's study (1984) of 3½-year-olds, there were no sex differences in children's abilities to identify the vocal expressions of disgust, interest, joy, fear, sadness, and anger beyond chance levels, although it was interesting that anger was recognized twice as often by boys than by girls.

Gender differences in voice expressivity for both children and adults may be dependent on the content of what is being said, and how gender-role appropriate it is. For instance, in Bezooyen's (1984) study, men had higher laryngeal tension scores than women for the phrase "the big American car," whereas there was equal tension between male and female speakers for "two months pregnant." Men may care more about cars than women do, thus leading to the gender difference in vocal expressivity.

Further, personality characteristics, as well as the context in which emotion is elicited, may affect gender differences in the patterns of vocalization. For example, women who denied being anxious had a tendency to increase the precision of their articulation when they were stressed in a cognitive task. They also decreased the precision of their articulation when their emotional stress increased (Walbott and Scherer 1991).

Gender differences in voice quality may also vary depending on who is being spoken to. For example, women speaking to each other use voices that minimize loudness, dominance, unpleasantness, and anxiety, in contrast to the voices they use with men (Hall 1984).

Emotional Behaviors

Almost any behavior, from abusing drugs to exercising, may convey emotion. For example, people can express emotions by approaching or avoiding others, hitting, or hugging them. Even a behavior such as aggression can be precipitated by many different feelings, such as anger, fear, or competition for resources (Zillmann 1979). Aggression can also be devoid of emotion, instead characterized by deliberation and manipulation. The only way to interpret the emotional meaning conveyed by behaviors is to know a person's history and the context in which the behavior has occurred. When we are close to others, we learn to recognize what behaviors they use to express their feelings. For example, only a husband may know that when his wife goes for a walk by herself, she is expressing anger toward him.

The behavioral expression of emotion has been measured through observation as well as self-report. For example, a self-report measure, the Affective Communication Test (ACT) (Friedman et al. 1980) has items such as "I show that I like someone by hugging or touching that person," and "At small parties I am the center of attention."[13] People's self-ratings on this measure have been corroborated by independent ratings made by friends or relatives (Burrowes and Halberstadt 1987). There are many self-report measures that assess the behavioral expression of anger or hostility, including the Anger Expression Scale (Spielberger et al. 1985); the Cook-Medley Hostility Inventory (Cook and Medley 1954); the Buss-Durkee Hostility Inventory (Buss and Durkee 1957); the Multidimensional Anger Inventory (Siegel 1986); and the Interpersonal Behavior Survey (Mauger et al. 1980). The items on these scales tend to be fairly similar to each other. For example, on the Anger Expression Scale, people report on the frequency with which they "say nasty things," "lose their temper," "boil inside, but don't show it," and "withdraw from people" when they are angry. Similarly, the Buss-Durkee Hostility Inventory asks people to rate themselves on the following items: "When I am mad, I sometimes slam things" and "When I get mad, I say nasty things."

There are also several interview measures in which both the content as well as nonverbal indicators of the participants' behavior are assessed, such as the Hostility Facet Scoring System, the Component Scoring System, and the Interpersonal Hostility Technique (see Barefoot and Lipkus 1994). For example, on the latter scale, participants get high scores if the interviewer determines that they were challenging or had a hostile tone of voice.

When gender differences are reported on either self-report or interview measures, men score higher on hostility than women do (Kopper 1993), especially on items measuring assault and aggressiveness. Women score higher on items measuring indirect hostility and irritability (Kopper 1993; Stoney and Engebretson 1994; Harris and Knight-Bohnhoff 1996).

1

ａｇｇｒｅｓｓｉｏｎ, or behaving in ways that hurt or inflict injuries on others, is perhaps the single most widely studied behavior that has been linked to gender. Anger is one of the chief instigators of aggression, but aggression can also be motivated by many other feelings, including fear, irritation, discomfort, dominance, or deprivation (Zillmann 1979). It is the infliction of physical injury (or the intent to inflict injury) that distinguishes anger expressed via aggression from the expression of anger via nonaggressive means. Evidence from several studies indicates that the expression of verbal anger and perhaps the expression of verbal feelings in general, may be inversely related to the expression of behavioral aggression. For example, adult men who were most likely to engage in abusive and aggressive behaviors toward their wives were those who did not verbalize their feelings (Babcock et al. 1993).

A recent meta-analytic review (Bettencourt and Miller 1996) on verbal and physical aggression indicates that in neutral situations, men are more aggressive than women, with a moderate effect size. However, when men and women are provoked, including such things as having their progress on a task impeded or being verbally insulted or physically attacked, gender differences in aggression become attenuated, with women becoming as aggressive as men. The data showing that women's aggression increases under provocation are especially interesting when looking at violent couples, where wives have been found to be just as contemptuous and belligerent in conflict situations as are their violent husbands (Jacobson et al. 1994).

When physical and verbal aggression are explored separately, the data reveal that it is women's verbal aggression that increases when women are provoked. Men are more apt to be physically aggressive than women even under provocation (Bettencourt and Miller 1996; Eagly and Steffen 1986).

Contributing to women's less frequent physical aggression may be gender differences in perceptions of provocation and attributions of fear. Women are less likely to perceive many different types of events as provocative than men. They also estimate that they would be in more trouble and danger if they expressed aggression than men.

Women and school-aged girls (by age 9) are more likely to use "indirect" or relational aggression than boys and men in several different cultures, including America and Finland (Bjorkqvist, Osterman, and Kaukiainen 1992; Crick and Grotpeter 1995). In relational aggression the aggressor uses social relationships in order to harm the target person without being personally involved, including gossiping, telling bad or false stories, talking behind another's back, or telling others "let's not play with or talk to him/her." Indirect aggression encompasses verbal as well as behavioral strategies and involves complex social relationships. It is important to note that gender differences in relational aggression have not been found to be as pronounced as gender differences in physical aggression. For example, in Crick and Grotpeter's (1995) research with third- through sixth-grade children, the difference between the mean standardized scores in the two sexes' overt aggression was more than twice as large as the difference in their relational aggression. Further, among 8- to 10-year-old Italian children, boys scored higher than girls on both relational and physical aggression (Tomada and Schneider 1997).

AGGRESSION AND DEVELOPMENT. Gender differences in aggression set in early in development. Boys have been found to express more physical aggression than girls by the time they are preschool age (see Whiting and Edwards 1988). Even 1-year-old boys, by both mothers' reports and videotaped observations, have been found to be more aggressive in situations in which they have caused the distress of another, such as taking away a baby's bottle (Zahn-Waxler et al. 1992). In a study of 21-, 27- and 36-month-old children in play groups, boys engaged in more physical aggression than did girls at all three ages (Fagot and Hagan 1985), including behaviors such as hitting, kicking, pushing, and grabbing for objects. However, in a fascinating study, Fagot, Leinbach, and Hagan (1986) found that 2–3-year-old girls who did not label themselves as girls were more likely to be physically aggressive than those who did label themselves as girls. This suggests that the very act of defining oneself as female may decrease the propensity to engage in aggressive behaviors, in conformity with sex-role stereotypes.

Preschool and school-aged boys have been found to be more apt to resolve conflicts using aggression and are more likely to respond to anger by attacking, or by trying to take away possessions than are young girls (Cummings, Iannotti, and Zahn-Waxler 1985). Not only are boys more aggressive in their play than girls, but they are more tolerant of aggression than are girls, being more likely to endorse such items as "It's okay for a boy to hit or scream at another boy or girl" (Huesmann et al. 1992). Boys' tolerance of aggressive peers may serve to facilitate the development of male aggression.

In my own research, boys expressed more aggression than girls in the stories they told (Brody, Wise, and Monuteaux 1997). This result is consistent with other studies of gender differences in preschool children's narratives or puppet enactments, which have shown that boys' stories more often reflect an attempt to cope with aggressive drives and disorder. Girls' stories more often reflect stable family relationships—caretaking and responding to the needs of others (Eisenberg et al. 1994a; Nicoloupou, Scales, and Weintraub 1992; Libby and Aries 1989).

Although some reviews have concluded that males become more physically aggressive than females at puberty, thus implicating hormones, this evidence is largely drawn from the study of animals. In humans, there is no evidence, other than anecdotal, that aggression increases dramatically in males once they attain puberty (see Benton 1992). Instead, research indicates that young children adopt characteristic patterns of aggressive behavior that remain stable in later life (Huesmann et al. 1992; Eron 1992).

If there is a developmental trend toward more pronounced gender differences with increasing age, it appears to take place well before the onset of puberty. Insulting behaviors, playful aggression, and assaulting others show sex differences cross-culturally in a 7–11-year-old age group (with boys showing more) but not in a 3–6-year-old age group (Whiting and Edwards 1973). Again, this implicates socialization practices, since gender differences in physical size, strength, and hormonal functioning are not particularly heightened in 7- to 11-year-olds as distinct from 3- to 6-year-olds.

AGGRESSION AND CULTURE. The relatively higher expression of aggression by boys than girls has been documented across diverse cultures in school-aged children (Lambert 1974). And although Whiting and Edwards (1988) did not find sex differences across all cultures in the category of dominance and aggression, they did find that males were higher than females in a related dimension, which they termed egoistic dominance. Egoistic dominance refers to giving commands that are intended to meet the needs of the self; for example, getting something or going away and breaking off an interaction. Similarly, in response to conflict story situations, such as being shoved by another child, 4–5-

year-old Japanese and American boys did not show more aggression than did girls, but boys from both cultures showed fewer prosocial behaviors and reparative acts, such as fixing a hurt, or returning a stolen object (Zahn-Waxler et al. 1996). The higher prosocial behaviors on the part of girls may serve as a protective factor against girls' future aggression later in development.

Different societies are dissimilar in their levels of aggression.[14] In fact, based on ethnographic records for 31 societies, the differences between cultures in levels of aggression were found to be greater than differences between the sexes in levels of aggression within the same culture (Rohner 1976). These data indicate that cultural influences play a strong role in the development of aggression in both sexes, unless societies are genetically different in their levels of aggressiveness. The latter is a difficult argument to make, especially since societies are often ethnically diverse.

AGGRESSION AND THE PARTICIPANTS' GENDER.   Gender differences in aggression vary a great deal depending on the sex of the participants in the interaction. Interestingly, it's not clear whether interacting with men or women is likely to result in more aggressive behaviors. Some studies have shown that both sexes are more aggressive when interacting with men, rather than women (Sackin and Thelen 1984; Carli 1989). This finding leads to the hypothesis that men tend to be more aggressive than women simply because they interact with other men more than women do.

On the other hand, Bettencourt and Miller's meta-analytic review indicates that whether the two sexes are more aggressive toward men or women changes as a function of whether or not they are provoked. When provoked, both men and women are more likely to be aggressive toward same sex individuals. However, in neutral situations, both men and women appear to be more aggressive toward men (Bettencourt and Miller 1996).

The data on children's aggression are also inconsistent. Although several studies have shown young children to be more aggressive toward males (Lambert 1974), others have shown that there is more aggression, anger, and conflict in same-sex interaction than in opposite-sex interactions for both boys and girls (Lambert 1974; Serbin et al. 1993; Murphy and Eisenberg 1996; Vespo, Pedersen, and Hay 1993).

These results may be inconsistent because neither the extent of the provocation nor the intimacy of the relationship are systematically evaluated. For example, perhaps males and females are more likely to be aggressive toward intimate opposite-sex partners than toward strangers of the opposite sex; but more aggressive toward same-sex strangers than toward opposite-sex strangers.

Crying

Women have been observed to cry more frequently than men across a wide variety of studies (see Frey and Lampseth 1985; De Fruyt 1997), with many situations inducing crying in both sexes, including the death of loved ones, loneliness, helplessness, or disappointment. On the other hand, in specific situations men and women may differ in their likelihood of crying. For example, women have been found to cry more often when angry than men do (Frost and Averill 1982). One study actually showed a negative correlation between anger and crying for men in response to emotionally laden films (Choti et al. 1987). Boys are observed to cry more than girls as infants and preschoolers (Landreth 1941; Kohnstamm 1988) and then anecdotes suggest that boys and girls are equally likely to cry until they are 13 (Frey and Lampseth 1985).

Withdrawal

Both men and women use withdrawal, sometimes in different situations. Men may withdraw or distract themselves with activities, such as sports, when confronted with sad feelings and loss. Men also withdraw from criticism and conflict, especially marital conflict, by "stonewalling" more than their wives do, which involves inhibiting facial action, and minimizing listening and eye contact (Gottman and Levenson 1986). Women also withdraw in the face of potential aggression and conflict. For example, it has been found cross-culturally that in peer conflicts, young girls withdraw more than boys, including hiding, avoiding, acting shy, or breaking off an interaction (Whiting and Edwards 1973; Murphy and Eisenberg 1996).

Recent research has indicated that for women, withdrawal in marital conflict is predicted by high levels of hostility together with low levels of defensiveness (Newton et al. 1995). For men, this same pattern of high hostility and low defensiveness predicts higher engagement in marital conflict, such as expressing criticism and disagreement, and frequently interrupting their wives' conversation. Women's withdrawal when hostile may be related to their fears of retaliation.

Although research has started to look at how hostility is associated with withdrawal, many other emotions, such as fear, contempt, boredom, helplessness, and confusion may also be linked to withdrawal. The particular emotions being expressed through withdrawal undoubtedly vary with the situation and the individual's characteristic mode of emotional response. How withdrawal is interpreted may be biased by gender stereotypes, in that a woman's withdrawal is likely to be interpreted as an expression of fear and a man's withdrawal as an expression of distancing or contempt.

Distraction versus Rumination

Distraction, or engaging in behaviors such as watching films or playing sports, and at an extreme, abusing alcohol or drugs, can serve to draw attention away from painful feelings. It may also serve to communicate feelings (Nolen-Hoeksema 1991). Men have been found to respond to sad or depressing experiences by distracting themselves. Whether the distraction is a way of avoiding or expressing the sadness is debatable. Women are less likely to use distraction in response to sad experiences, and are more likely to ruminate on their sad feelings, meaning that they tend to focus on their moods and the possible causes for them. They are also more likely to blame themselves. Rumination may actually exaggerate existing depressed feelings, especially because the repeatedly evoked negative feelings tend to exaggerate negative thoughts, which in turn escalate negative feelings (Nolen-Hoeksema 1991).

These gender differences may set in quite early. In response to a question about how they could be less worried, 7- to 15-year-old boys endorsed more behavioral avoidance strategies than girls did; whereas girls endorsed more cognitive strategies than boys did (Williams, Vasey, and Daleiden 1995).

OVERVIEW.   There are consistent patterns in how American men and women express their emotions in each of the modalities I've considered, including words, behaviors, and facial and vocal characteristics. At this point in time, gender differences in each of these modalities appear to be clearer for Americans (and perhaps other individualistic countries) than for other cultural groups, although there are relatively few cross-cultural studies.

In general, women are more facially expressive of most emotions than are men, with the possible exception of anger. Although the developmental timetable for this pattern is not well researched, two developmental trends emerge. The first is that boys become less facially expressive of emotions with increasing age, including positive emotions, such as warmth and affection, and emotions connoting vulnerability, such as sadness and fear. The second is that girls increasingly learn to publicly mask the expression of socially inappropriate negative emotions more than boys do, using a combination of facial expressions and behaviors.

Women also use words to express feelings more than men do. They express a wider variety and more intense positive and negative feelings than men do through self-reports, in conversations with others, and in writing samples. They also talk about feelings with a wider group of people than men, who tend to talk about emotions only to intimate others. These differences in the use of emotion language seem to emerge in Western samples at very young ages.

Many aspects of vocal expressiveness do not appear to differ for the two sexes, although there are some recent data, which I will explore more fully in Chapter 5, that men express anger in their voices more clearly than women do.

Men and women often use different behaviors to communicate the same feeling, such as men using aggression instead of crying to communicate anger. On the other hand, the two sexes may use the same behavior, such as withdrawal, to communicate different feelings, such as anger and sadness. The developmental origins of these behaviors, with the exception of aggression, are not clearly researched. Gender differences in physical aggression are seen not only very early in development (some studies report differences in physical aggression at age 1) but are also seen cross-culturally.

I have emphasized that gender differences in each modality—verbal, vocal, facial, and behavioral—may shift depending on the particular circumstances involved (for example, do they involve provocation?) and on the particular emotion being expressed. It is also true that both sexes tend to display emotions in more than one modality at a time. For instance, it is rare that people will convey hostility via their voices without corresponding changes in some other modality, such as their faces, behaviors, words, or even their physiological arousal patterns. What are the patterns by which the two sexes express emotions via more than one modality? In order to fully address this question, I will consider the role of physiological arousal in emotional expression.

4

Physiological Arousal and Patterns of Emotional Expression

When I get mad, I get all hot and I don't talk to anybody. I usually go upstairs and start playing with my toys, because when I do that it calms me down. Sometimes I eat cold stuff like ice cream. I feel mad inside but I don't think about it, and then sometimes I play Barbie dolls and I make the Barbie dolls have a fight and then it makes me forget about it.

—*Katie, age 9*

We don't always say what we feel, but our bodily processes may change. For example, in anxiety-producing situations, we may sweat more, or involuntarily raise our blood pressures. Lie detector tests are based on the premise that if we are anxious about concealing the truth, our skin conductance will change. Skin conductance is a measure of the ease with which our skin conducts or resists electricity based on how wet it is.

Are there gender differences in the physiology of emotional expressions? The answer is yes, but with many qualifications. The patterns of gender differences are complex, because arousal shows so much variability from one situation to another as well as from one measure to another, such as heart rate compared to skin conductance. For example, men sometimes show higher skin conductance than women do in the course of conflictual marital interactions, but women sometimes show higher skin conductance than men when watching other people in distressing situations, such as coping with severe illnesses. Sometimes gender differences in physiological responses do not appear; sometimes they appear only in specific contexts and for specific types of responses.

I will focus on gender differences in the most frequently studied physiological responses, including heart rate, blood pressure, endocrine levels, and skin conductance. It is important to keep in mind that physiological reactions are neither necessary nor sufficient for the experience of an emotion (Cacioppo et al. 1993). Whether or not they occur, and with what intensity they occur, are determined by a combination of many factors, some of which are related to individual differences in physiological reactivity. For example, one person may exhibit a higher heart rate when any intense emotion is experienced, while another may exhibit relatively little heart rate variability.

Moreover, physiological measures do not necessarily relate to each other in predictable ways, even though they are all interpreted to be measures of arousal. In other words, having higher skin conductance is not predictive of having a higher heart rate (see Fox and Calkins 1993; Wallbott and Scherer 1991).[1] The patterns of correspondence among different types of arousal, as well as among different modes of emotional expression, such as arousal, words, and behaviors, have been found to differ from situation to situation, and from individual to individual, making interpretations about the links between arousal and emotional functioning especially difficult.

Studies that explore gender differences in these complex processes provide important clues as to how and why men and women differ in emotional expression. In piecing together these clues, I will make two arguments. First, men and women become physiologically aroused in different types of situations, situations that hold significant meanings for each of them. Second, for women, physiological arousal is more likely to accompany other forms of emotional expression, such as words and facial expressions, than it is for men. In other words, women tend to be generalizers. If they express an emotion in one modality, they tend to express it in three: physiological, facial, and verbal. Men, in contrast, tend to be internalizers, expressing emotions through physiological arousal, but not through words or facial expressions, especially in situations involving marital conflict or stress.

Physiological Changes Accompanying Emotion

Heart rate, blood pressure, skin conductance, and levels of catecholamines (epinephrine and norepinephrine) may each become elevated under some stressful or emotional conditions. For example, when people are angry, their heart rates may become elevated and their blood pressures may rise, which prepare them to lash out in some way. Such physiological arousal responses are mediated by the sympathetic nervous system, nerve pathways that function largely without conscious will and that work to prepare for emergency situations, often termed "fight or flight" responses. The sympathetic nervous system directly innervates the adrenal medulla, which releases the catecholamines (epinephrine and norepinephrine).

A second system, the pituitary adrenal-cortical system, is responsible for the release of ACTH, associated with sadness, depression, separation anxiety, loss, and more passive coping. Levels of cortisol in the bloodstream have been found to be higher when people report feelings associated with depression (see Hooven, Gottman, and Katz 1995; Mayne in press). There are many connections between the adrenal-cortical and the sympathetic adrenal-medullary systems. For example, heightened levels of circulating catecholamines may increase the pituitary release of ACTH, and levels of epinephrine, norepinephrine, and cortisol are often correlated (see discussion by Polefrone and Manuck 1987).

Elevated skin conductance levels (SCL) may be a measure of the extent to which people inhibit their emotional expressiveness, and several investigators construe high skin conductance as a measure of emotional conflict.[2] For example, skin conductance is high when people conceal their feelings (Hughes, Uhlmann, and Pennebaker 1994). Holocaust survivors who had higher skin conductance levels when interviewed about their traumatic experiences paid more post-interview visits to their physicians than did those survivors who had lower skin conductance levels, suggesting that higher skin conductance levels are related to psychological conflict and distress (Pennebaker, Barger, and Tiebout 1989). And in another example, when college students verbally expressed negative emotions in interviews, their SCL levels were raised. In contrast, when they expressed positive ones, their SCL levels were lowered (Pennebaker 1993).

Gender and Arousal: Are Men More Physiologically Reactive?

For some years, reviews of gender differences in physiological arousal have suggested that men are more physiologically reactive than women, especially in systolic blood pressure reactivity and some neuroendocrine responses (see Polefrone and Manuck 1987). Gender differences in the physiological arousal associated with stress have been hypothesized to account for the higher coronary disease rate among men. Men are twice as likely to die from heart disease than are women (Stoney and Engebretson 1994), possibly and in part because men's tendency to secrete hormones such as epinephrine under stress may cause blood pressure elevations, injury to arteries, or cardiac arrhythmias (Polefrone and Manuck 1987).[3]

Newer evidence allows us to re-evaluate the position that men are always, or even usually, the more reactive sex, and to look at the evidence through a new lens. Gender differences in arousal seem to depend on both the nature of the physiological arousal being assessed as well as on what each sex perceives as "stressful."

The evidence that males become more aroused in response to stress and also exhibit slower recovery times following arousal is based almost entirely on research involving responses to achievement, provocation, and specific types of marital conflict. Gender differences in response to these stressful situations are especially strong for systolic blood pressure, but are also found for endocrine responses and heart rate changes. For example, when harassed during a math task, when treated in an aggressive manner, or when performing stressful cognitive tasks, men show greater cardiovascular increases than women (Hokanson and Edelman 1966; Matthews et al. 1991; Lai and Linden 1992; Davidson et al. 1994). Similarly, while taking exams, men show significantly higher epinephrine levels than women (Johansson and Post 1974; Frankenhaeuser et al. 1978; Van Doornen 1986; Rauste-von Wright and Frankenhaeuser 1989). Often in the same samples, there are no gender differences in the levels of cortisol, adrenaline, or noradrenaline associated with ordinary or routine events (Johansson and Post 1974; Frankenhaeuser et al. 1978).

These gender differences appear early in development. Among 3–6-year-olds tested while playing at home and in day-care centers, epinephrine levels were found to be higher among boys than among girls (Lundberg 1983).[4] This was also true among 12-year-olds after an arithmetic test, but not after watching a neutral film (Johansson 1972).[5]

Marital interactions provide the most provocative evidence that men respond to negative situations with physiological arousal to a greater extent than women do (Levenson, Carstensen, and Gottman 1994). Following unrehearsed conversations between wives and husbands that occurred in a laboratory, couples subsequently watched videotapes of the conversations and rated the degree to which they had experienced negative and positive feelings as the interaction progressed. Husbands' self-reports of negative feelings were related to six of the seven physiological variables that were assessed during the interaction, including higher skin conductance, shorter pulse transmission to the ear, higher finger temperatures, and faster heart rates. In contrast, wives showed no significant relationships between their physiological reactions and their self-rated feelings for any of the physiological measures. These patterns were evident for two different types of conversations, including discussions about pleasant topics and discussions about recurring conflicts. In another study performed by different researchers, wives also had fewer skin potential responses than did husbands in the course of a conflictual marital interaction (Notarius and Johnson 1982). This was interpreted as evidence that wives were less physiologically reactive than were their husbands.

The Importance of Context

Yet, countering the evidence that men are more physiologically reactive than women are studies showing that how meaningful a situation is for each sex influences arousal a great deal. For example, one study demonstrated that men's and women's heart rate responses were differentially affected during cooperative and competitive games played with male confederates (Van Egeren 1979). Women displayed greater heart rate changes during the competitive interaction than during the cooperative interaction, while the reverse pattern was true among the men, even though there were no gender differences in the percentage of competitive responses made by men and women. Since competition against men is non-gender-role stereotypic for women, and conversely, cooperation with other men is non-gender-role stereotypic for men, it may be that higher arousal accompanies situations that are less familiar. An alternative explanation is that in the competitive situation, participants were more apt to lose (or to become subordinate in status), which may have stimulated more heart rate responsivity among women. In the cooperative situation, participants were more apt to win or to become dominant, which may have stimulated men's heart rate responsivity.

The importance of context was also highlighted by a series of studies on gender differences in epinephrine levels across several different tasks. Only men exhibited significant increases in epinephrine when their blood was drawn or when they participated in a color–word conflict task (Frankenhaeuser, Dunne, and Lundberg 1976). However, when taking a school examination, both female and male engineering students demonstrated significant elevations in epinephrine and heart rate levels compared to baseline conditions (Collins and Frankenhaeuser 1978). The school exam may simply have been more meaningful for the women than the venipuncture or cognitive task.[6]

Similarly, many studies have shown more consistent links between the expression or suppression of anger and physiological reactivity, especially blood pressure changes, for men than for women. However, this may be because researchers often use the same anger-inducing task for women and men, such as being harassed. The two sexes may differ in how angry they get in response to such situations. In fact, when Frodi (1976) exposed the two sexes to treatments that they designated in advance to be anger-inducing, she found no differences in the physiological arousal they exhibited. For men, anger was induced by being verbally attacked by another person, who made statements such as, "You dummy, I don't want you to be my teacher." For women, anger was induced by being treated in a condescending way by another, who said things such as, "Oh, you really think that psychology course is hard. I don't." Under these conditions, both sexes showed higher heart rates and greater amplitudes in skin conductance when angry, as well as increases in diastolic blood pressure (Frodi 1976). This study underscores the importance of task relevance when assessing gender differences in physiological responses.

Even in some marital conflicts, wives but not husbands have been shown to evidence physiological arousal that varies as a function of the quality of their interaction. For example, when newlywed couples were asked to discuss and resolve two conflict-producing marital issues, wives whose husbands were more likely to withdraw in the face of negative emotions had higher norepinephrine and cortisol levels as compared to other wives. For husbands, marital conflict behavior did not significantly relate to hormone levels (Kiecolt-Glaser et al. 1996).[7] Similarly, wives who displayed a high proportion of negative emotions during a marital discussion and whose husbands also displayed a high proportion of negative affect had significantly higher heart rates than did other women

(Morell and Apple 1990).[8] Finally, in a sample of hypertensive people, women showed more significant relationships between the quality of their marital interaction and blood pressure changes than did men. Women's hostile behaviors and reported low marital quality were related to their blood pressure increases. In contrast, only a fast speech rate predicted men's blood pressure increases (Ewart et al. 1991). Ewart and his colleagues point out that a fast speech rate may be an attempt to influence or control an interaction, and that these processes may have served to raise men's blood pressure.

Several fascinating studies explore the ways in which women's physiological responses are related to the stresses of being a partner in a dual income couple, and in particular, to their partners' willingness to share housework and child care. Newton, Sanford, and Flores (1996) found that wives who put in more hours of housework on working days than their husbands had higher resting systolic blood pressure than did other wives. Wives who perceived that their husbands put in either equivalent or more hours of child care than they themselves did had lower resting systolic blood pressure than did other wives. Interestingly, there was also a trend for husbands whose wives put in more hours of child care on working days to exhibit lower resting systolic blood pressure than other husbands. In another compelling study, a significant positive correlation existed between working wives' general amount of overtime at work and their epinephrine secretion at home (Lundberg and Palm 1989).

These studies indicate that marital quality and stress indeed affect women's physiological functioning to a greater extent than previously acknowledged, especially when the stresses are related to women's changing gender roles.

At times, women become more physiologically aroused than men when empathy is evoked. They have been found to respond with higher skin conductance responses than males when witnessing either horror films (Sparks 1991)[9] or films about the distress of another, such as programs about spina bifida or dangerous hitchhikers (Eisenberg et al. 1991b). Similarly, when parents accompanied their children to a hospital for testing, mothers showed significantly greater norephinephrine secretion than did fathers (Lundberg et al. 1981).[10] This may be related to relatively higher levels of empathy on the part of mothers as compared to fathers. Alternatively, mothers may have felt more responsible for and stressed by the hospital visit than were fathers, since they are more often the primary child care providers.

The jealousy literature provides a clear demonstration of how the meaning of a situation can vary for the two sexes,which in turn may be related to different patterns of physiological arousal. Women respond with higher skin conductance to imagery in which their partners are emotionally involved with another lover than they do to images of sexual infidelity. Men show the opposite pattern. They manifest higher skin conductance, heart rate, and greater brow contraction to images of sexual infidelity (Buss et al. 1992). Other research has indicated that women are more threatened by their partners' emotional attachments to others, while men are more threatened by their partners' sexual attachments to others (White and Mullen 1989). Physiological arousal patterns accompany what is differentially meaningful to the two sexes.

Male and female physiological patterns may also differ depending on the particular physiological measure. In many stressful situations, even when other measures of arousal (such as neuroendocrine functioning or blood pressure) show men to be more aroused than women, women still have higher increases in heart rate than men (Graham, Cohen, and Shmavonian 1966; Collins and Frankenhaeuser 1978). Women have also been found to show greater heart rate responses than men in response to interpersonal tasks, such as generating story solutions to stressful situations (Matthews and Stoney 1988; Girdler et al. 1990).[11]

Developmental Patterns

Gender differences in children's arousal patterns may be as context-specific as adults' are. In response to a Neonatal Behavior Assessment Scale, newborn boys showed higher cortisol responses than did girls, whereas girls showed greater changes in heart rate than did boys (Davis and Emory 1995). Four- to five-year-old girls' skin conductance in response to simulated distress (a confederate pretending to hurt her finger, or hearing a sad story about a dying grandfather) was higher than was boys' (Zahn-Waxler et al. 1995). Girls also showed more heart rate deceleration during exposure to a sad stimulus, such as a dying grandfather, than did boys. On the other hand, another study showed that kindergarten and second-grade boys, rather than girls, showed more arousal in the form of skin conductance to a film involving children who had been injured in an accident and who expressed feelings such as pain, sadness, and boredom (Fabes et al. 1994).

Control and Affiliation

In sum, these studies suggest that men do not necessarily respond with more physiological reactivity to stressful or emotionally laden situations. Rather, male and female physiological reactions appear to be context- and measure-specific. It may be that what matters more to women than to men are affiliation and interpersonal relationships; what matters more to men than to women are issues of control and status, and it is these issues that drive men's and women's patterns of arousal differently. In other words, the situations in which men get aroused, including provocation, achievement, and strained marital interactions, may cause them to feel either threatened or helpless and out of control. This would induce affect because men are expected to be, and perhaps expect themselves to be, in control. In particular, several researchers have shown that women usually initiate marital conflicts, thus producing a pattern in which men find themselves reacting to, rather than initiating, negative affect (Gottman and Levenson 1992). It may be that feeling "out of control" pushes physiological buttons for men.

Women may also become aroused when their expectations for themselves are threatened or violated. However, rather than expecting to maintain control, women may expect to get help from their spouses and may emphasize empathy and affiliation. These expectations would lead to arousal in marital conflicts in which a spouse's empathy or cooperation was not forthcoming, as well as in situations in which others were distressed.

The perceived emotional quality of the situation may be the most relevant aspect of context when exploring gender differences. Research has shown that sympathetic activity can be augmented or diminished depending on the nature of people's explanations for their arousal (Zillmann 1984; 1989). If people attribute their arousal to factors such as exercise, humor, mild sexual arousal, or fear, their arousal diminishes more quickly than if they attribute it to anger. Men may blame angry feelings for their arousal in marital interactions, since anger is a stereotypically masculine emotion. They may also think they need to "do" something to fix their marriages and may maximize "approach" tendencies. These interpretations may serve to maximize certain types of physiological arousal, such as cardiovascular reactivity. Finally, perhaps men attempt to suppress or inhibit the anger they experience more than women do, because they have learned the message that expressing anger results in harmful aggression. As I will show, emotional inhibition is itself related to physiological arousal, especially to cardiovascular reactivity.

In contrast, if women stereotypically interpret their arousal as due to hurt, rather than to angry feelings, in keeping with stereotypes of feminine emotions, it may serve to minimize cardiovascular reactivity and to maximize neuroendocrine secretion. My suggestions here are strictly hypothetical, especially since most research has shown that there is not a one-to-one correspondence between the quality of an emotion and a corresponding physiological arousal pattern, but these ideas suggest directions for future research.

Two Models of Emotional Expression

The Discharge Model

The relationship among different modes of emotional expression, especially between verbal and behavioral or between verbal and physiological modes of expression, has been theorized about extensively. Psychoanalytic theorists assume that if you can label your feelings, you will not respond with physiological arousal, nor will you behave in destructive ways. Selma Fraiberg (1959), writing about young children, calls this "word magic": the idea that once children learn the word for a feeling, they will no longer act it out. For example, my young daughter learned the word for "bite" and no longer bit when she was angry, an opportune lesson for both of us.

Bloom and Capatides' (1987) research on the relationship between early language acquisition and nonverbal behavior suggests that Fraiberg's theory about word magic may be true. Children who learn words later than other children show a significant increase in their level of nonverbal behaviors, including screaming and gesturing, whereas children who learn words earlier don't. In other words, it is possible that once children learn to communicate in words, they don't need to use other types of vocal or bodily gestures to get their needs met.

The model that words may substitute for either actions or physiological expressions, or for that matter, facial expressions, has been termed the "discharge" theory of emotion. This theory posits that emotion is a form of energy that must be gotten rid of—either directly through words or facial expressions, or if these routes are blocked, through internal pathways, including physiological means such as increased heart rate (Notarius et al. 1982).

There is some support for this model as reviewed thoroughly by Manstead (1991; see also Buck, Miller, and Caul 1974; Buck 1977). For example, husbands who are able to communicate their distress to their wives are less physically and verbally abusive than are other husbands (Burke, Weir, and Harrison 1976; Parelman 1983; Babcock et al. 1993). And women who do not display emotions in their faces while they are being criticized have higher heart rate increases than those who are facially expressive (Notarius et al. 1982). Other evidence that words may substitute for the nonverbal expression of feelings is provided by the syndrome alexithymia. In this syndrome, people lack words for feelings, and often have physical health problems, such as ulcers, or engage in aggressive or acting-out behaviors. Interestingly, men are more likely to be alexithymic than are women (Sifneos 1988).

However, Cacioppo et al. (1992) point out that the negative relationship between facial expressiveness and sympathetic activation holds only when groups of participants are compared to each other. In any single individual, there is a weak to moderate positive correlation between sympathetic activation and facial expressiveness: As one rises, so does the other. It seems that for individuals, intensifying the outward expression of feeling (for example, by posing facial expressions) may also intensify the inner experience.

The Arousal or Co-activation Model

The arousal model of emotion asserts that there is a positive relationship between all components of an emotional reaction—people who express emotions facially will also show greater physiological responses and will verbalize more emotions as well. The assumption is that there is a common underlying excitatory mechanism that marshals bodily resources during emotional states. This model is implicit in the facial feedback hypothesis, which posits that once an emotion is expressed on the face, physiological responses and experiences are activated that correspond to the expressed emotion.

The evidence for this theory is especially strong within individuals, since there is a positive relationship between the degree of facial expressiveness and the degree of sympathetic nervous system activation and other types of physiological arousal (Cacioppo et al. 1992). There is also some support for this model when groups of people are compared in situations eliciting pain, as well as in "constraining" contexts, such as when people's reactions are assessed in the presence of other people. For example, some studies have shown that when participants are exposed to electric shocks (Lanzetta et al. 1976), people who exaggerate their facial expressions have higher skin conductance responses than those who conceal their facial expressions. In other words, when people are exposed to electric shocks, their facial expressions, physiological arousal, and self-reported emotions are either all similarly maximized or minimized. Also, when people are asked to respond to interview questions posed in a challenging way, those who display high numbers of positive facial expressions have higher reactive systolic blood pressure than those who do not (Davidson et al. 1994).

However, Cacioppo and his colleagues (1992) point out that the arousal model ultimately fails to account for data showing that in many people, different measures of arousal do not correlate, with heart rate and skin conductance showing different and discordant patterns of excitation.

Whether or not an arousal model or a discharge model holds may be determined by the intensity and context of the arousing event. The discharge model may hold with less intense emotions and in unstructured situations, and the arousal model may hold with more intense emotions and in structured situations (Notarius et al. 1982). It is also possible that some individuals, termed internalizers and externalizers, conform to a discharge model, while others, generalizers, conform to an arousal model, as I will discuss next.

Individual Differences: Externalizers, Internalizers, and Generalizers

The preferred mode in which people express their emotions varies from individual to individual. We have all heard stories about the overtly calm person who is really anxious underneath, perhaps suffering from high blood pressure. Such people are termed "internalizers," and do not overtly express their feelings through words or facial expressions, but instead show significant physiological changes. They are usually contrasted with "externalizers," who express feelings outwardly, either through words or facial expressions, making their feelings obvious to the outside world. They do not manifest arousal with physiological changes. The notion of internalizers and externalizers emerges from a discharge model, with the idea that the expression of feelings in one modality is inversely related to the expression of feelings in other modalities.

In contrast to both are generalizers (Jones 1950, 1960), who respond with similar levels of activation in all modes of emotional expression, both internal and external. They conform to an arousal model.

Cacioppo and his colleagues (1992) suggest that externalizers, internalizers, and generalizers differ in the particular aspects of their physiological and behavioral functioning that become amplified when exposed to stress. For example, with emotional stimulation, internalizers show a greater increase in sympathetic nervous system activation, while externalizers show a greater activation in facial expressiveness. With emotionally arousing events, both groups show some amplification of the two systems, accounting for the positive relationship between the activation of the two systems for individuals in both groups. Generalizers, in contrast, are individuals whose facial expressiveness and sympathetic activation become equally activated with emotionally arousing events. There is hypothesized to be a wide range of responsivity among generalizers, with some showing relatively minimal expressive and sympathetic reactions to stimuli and with others showing more intense reactions across modalities.

Recently, Davidson and her colleagues (1994) proposed yet another pattern for the relationship between physiological and facial expressiveness, depending on the balance between the expression of positive and negative facial expressions. They theorized that an imbalance between the frequency with which positive and negative emotions were expressed would be related to higher levels of physiological arousal. This hypothesis was supported for women's resting systolic blood pressure levels. Women who expressed either frequent positive emotions combined with infrequent negative emotions, or frequent negative emotions combined with infrequent positive emotions, had higher resting systolic blood pressure than did women who expressed positive and negative emotions at equal frequencies (either high or low). In contrast, men who expressed *fewer* positive *and* negative emotions during stressful tasks (thus not showing an imbalance between the two) had higher resting systolic blood pressure than other men, as consistent with an internalizing style. When the researchers turned their attention to reactive, rather than resting, blood pressure levels, members of both sexes who showed increased systolic blood pressure in response to stressful interview questions were those who displayed more positive emotional expressions during those same interviews, as consistent with an arousal model and a generalizing style. This study suggests that especially for women, an imbalance between positive and negative emotional expressions may predict cardiovascular health problems. It also indicates that each of these styles: internalizing, externalizing, and generalizing, may become predominant under different conditions.

Women as Generalizers

Previous reviews of gender differences in emotional expression (Brody 1985; Manstead 1991) have suggested that men are more often internalizers and women are more often externalizers. This conclusion is often based on early work by Buck and his colleagues (Buck 1977), which showed a negative relationship between facial expressiveness and skin conductance responses in preschool boys. This finding did not hold true for preschool girls. Adult males also showed internalizing patterns, while adult females showed externalizing patterns, that is, facial expressivity without physiological arousal (Buck, Miller, and Caul 1974).

My reading of the current literature suggests something different. In some situations, especially those involving marital conflict, men do appear to be internalizers and women externalizers. But in situations involving empathic distress (and possibly in marital conflict as well), women appear to be generalizers, expressing emotions in many modalities simultaneously. When the definition of generalizers is broadened to include not only a correspondence between physiological arousal and facial expressiveness, but also verbal emotional expressions, women especially conform to a generalizing pattern. In other words, women are apt to express a feeling in several modalities at once, including self-reports, physiological changes, and facial expressions.

Let's look at the evidence. First, some researchers have reported more of a discrepancy between the vocalization of affect and corresponding facial expressions for men than for women. For example, Halberstadt, Hayes, and Pike (1988) videotaped students without their knowledge while asking them to discuss sad and happy experiences and found that when judges rated the students' statements from very sad to very happy, female students were judged to make happier statements when they smiled than when they did not smile. In contrast, male students were judged to make less happy statements when they smiled than when they didn't. In other words, women showed facial expressions consistent with the tone of their conversations, as would be true of generalizers. In contrast, men showed inconsistencies between tone and facial expressions, as would be true of the discrepancies between modalities predicted by an internalizer/externalizer model. Similarly, Berenbaum and Rotter (1992) showed that emotional experience and the intensity of facial expressiveness were positively correlated among women who were watching both positive and negative filmclips. In other words, women who reported feeling unhappy, looked unhappy. In contrast, for men, there was either a negative correlation when watching negative filmclips (suggesting an internalizing pattern), or no correlation when the males watched positive filmclips. Men whose facial expressions were rated as *more* intensely unhappy actually reported feeling *less* unhappy.

Finally, data on the expression of empathy, distress, and sympathy across modalities suggests that women as well as school-aged girls express these feelings concurrently using facial expressions, behaviors, words, and physiological arousal more than boys do (Eisenberg et al. 1989; Eisenberg et al. 1991a; Fabes, Eisenberg, and Eisenbud 1993; Grossman and Wood 1993; Strayer and Roberts 1997). In these studies, in which participants watch distressing slides, or are told distressing stories, measures of arousal, facial expressions, and reported distress relate in consistent positive ways more among females than they do among males. If there is any pattern in the male data on empathy (and it is often difficult to discern one), it appears to be an internalizing one.

Similar conclusions are reached in the relations between urine neuroendocrine levels and self-reports of emotions both during and after a stressful exam. For girls, neuroendocrine levels and self-reported emotional experiences (discomfort during exam, distress, anxiety, lack of self-esteem) were positively related. For boys, correlations were negative and low (Rauste-von Wright and Frankenhaeuser 1989). All of these data suggest more of a generalizing pattern for women than for men.

Research on the relationship between cardiovascular reactivity and the expression of anger in men and women also shows a generalizing pattern for women and a rather inconsistent pattern for men. An important caveat to my discussion of this issue is that the relationship between cardiovascular reactivity and anger-related measures, including both anger expression and anger suppression, has been relatively unexplored in women, since very few studies have included women as participants (Houston 1994). Of those that have, several either have not shown any relationship between cardiovascular reactivity and anger in women (Burns and Katkin 1993), or have found relationships that differ in complex ways from those found in men (Siegman, Anderson, and Berger 1990). Some researchers have gone so far as to speculate that "the tendency to express anger may be a psychological trait which has greater pathophysiological implications for men than for women" (Burns and Katkin 1993, pp. 461). Emerging data indicate that this hypothesis may be correct only in specific situations.

The limited data that do exist indicate that women who express their anger or who are hostile tend to show greater cardiovascular reactivity than those who don't, as consistent with a generalizing model (Weidner et al. 1989; Lai and Linden 1992; Siegman 1993; Burns 1995). For example, women who reported that their usual response style was to express anger had slower cardiovascular recovery times (higher levels of systolic blood pressure) after being harassed than did women whose usual style was to inhibit their anger. In other words, women who routinely expressed anger also maximized their physiological arousal. This was in contrast to a mixed pattern in men; sometimes internalizing, sometimes generalizing (Lai and Linden 1992).

Men, Anger, and Patterns of Reactivity

The relationship between anger expression and cardiovascular reactivity in men is a puzzle: Cardiovascular reactivity has been found to increase both when anger is expressed, as conforming to a generalizing pattern, as well as when it is inhibited or suppressed, conforming to an internalizing pattern (Spielberger et al. 1985; Olweus 1986; Girdler et al. 1990; Lai and Linden 1992; Ewart and Kolodner 1994; Burns 1995).

How is it that both the expression and the suppression of anger have been linked to cardiovascular reactivity in men? This has become a frequent subject of discussion in the literature. Burns (1995) points out that suppressors and expressors may represent two different groups with different attitudes toward anger, both of whom are socially incompetent at managing it. For example, men who routinely suppress their anger have relatively quick cardiovascular recovery times when they write positive evaluations of someone who is harassing them. These men may suppress their anger because they believe that anger is both harmful and socially unacceptable, and thus experience arousal when they do express anger. In contrast, men who routinely express their anger show relatively quick cardiovascular recovery times when they write negative evaluations of their harassers (Engebretson, Matthews, and Scheier 1989). These men may believe it is beneficial to express anger. Cognitive interpretations about the acceptability of anger may influence whether anger maximizes or minimizes physiological arousal.

Burns (1995) also posits an alternative hypothesis: the suppression and expression of anger may both be characteristic of individuals who are often angry. Experiencing anger more frequently would result in higher levels of physiological reactivity, regardless of whether the individual chooses to suppress or express the anger at that moment in time.

In any case, the limited evidence suggests that women more often conform to a generalizing pattern in their expression of anger than do men. It may be that some men conform to an internalizing pattern because they are afraid that the expression of anger will result in aggression. Many studies have indicated that in self-reports men more frequently endorse such "anger-in" items as "withdrawing," "boiling inside," and "keeping things in" than women (McConatha et al. 1994; Spielberger et al. 1985; Stoney and Engebretson 1994). Men's fears that the expression of their anger will harm someone may lead them to an internalizing mode.

Patterns of Physiological Arousal in Children

A few studies have suggested that children's physiological arousal patterns may correspond to those of adults, at least in some contexts. For example, preschool boys, but not girls, showed an internalizing pattern while viewing emotionally evocative slides, with facially expressive boys showing less physiological arousal than other boys (Buck 1977). Moreover, elementary school–aged girls displayed a generalizing pattern of emotional expressiveness in response to films evoking sympathy, with their skin conductance corresponding to their facial distress (Eisenberg et al. 1991a) as well as to their self-reported distress (Fabes, Eisenberg, and Eisenbud 1993). Generalizing patterns for school-aged girls were also found when they watched evocative videotapes. Their facial expressions and verbal reports converged above chance levels for happiness, sadness, and fear. In contrast, for boys, facial expressions and verbal reports converged above chance levels only for happiness (Strayer and Roberts 1997). On the other hand, both boys and girls have been found to show higher heart rate responses with higher facial distress (Eisenberg et al. 1991a), as consistent with a generalizing model for both sexes. Gender differences in the development of the relationships among different modalities may be emotion-, measure-, and context-specific.

Socialization and Arousal

Developmental literature indicates that people's socialization history affects the extent and nature of their physiological arousal. When they are angry, children from homes with lower marital satisfaction take longer to recover from heart rate arousal than do children from homes with higher marital satisfaction (Walker and Wilson 1995). This study suggests that the more children are exposed to conflict, the more physiologically reactive they will become in the face of conflict. Thus, physiological reactivity may be learned. (An alternative explanation is that children and parents are genetically similar in their arousal levels, which may account for the high levels of marital conflict in these parents.)

A fascinating series of studies indicates that gender differences in the physiological reactions of adults can be learned and unlearned. Women and men can be taught the opposite sex's normative physiological patterns. People were given an opportunity to administer electric shocks to a confederate "enemy" who had been administering electric shocks to them. The first set of studies demonstrated that people's blood pressure was significantly raised when they were shocked. When they were given an opportunity to counter-attack their "enemies" by shocking them back, males recovered baseline blood pressure functioning (their blood pressure returned to normal levels) more quickly than did men who were not given an opportunity to shock their enemies. This was not true of women. They showed consistent elevations in their blood pressure, whether or not they counter-attacked. In other words, being aggressive did not reduce women's physiological arousal, but being aggressive did reduce men's physiological arousal. These normative gender patterns also showed that the most rapid cardiovascular recovery in women was achieved through ignoring the confederate rather than by returning shocks (Hokanson and Edelman 1966).[12]

However, there was a second part to these studies, which reversed these normative patterns. Women could be conditioned to reduce their cardiovascular arousal by administering shocks (just like the men), whereas men could be conditioned to reduce their arousal by behaving in a friendly, rewarding fashion, more typical of women (Hokanson, Willers, and Koropsak 1968). How did the conditioning take place? Researchers instructed the confederate enemy to respond in a friendly manner when women shocked them and in an aggressive manner when women rewarded them. Under such circumstances, women's blood pressure returned to normal levels faster when they shocked the confederate than when they delivered a reward to the confederate. In other words, the women's physiological arousal was dependent on making the confederate happy. Their arousal went down when the confederate acted in a friendly manner toward them, and if they had to do this by behaving aggressively themselves, a violation of their usual nonaggressive behavior, they did so.

The opposite consequences were used for men. When men behaved in a friendly manner, the confederates were instructed to reciprocate the friendship; when men shocked the confederates, the confederates behaved aggressively. Using this paradigm, men's blood pressure returned to normal levels faster by behaving in a friendly, rather than an aggressive manner toward the confederate.

Thus, different social consequences changed the physiological arousal patterns for women and men. For both sexes, getting an aggressive response back from the confederate, no matter what behaviors they themselves expressed to provoke the aggression, caused heightened physiological arousal. It may be that in the typical situation, women's arousal in the face of their own aggression is a sign that they anticipate, or fear, counter-aggression. In contrast, when men behave aggressively, they may not anticipate that it will be reciprocated.

The mere presence of other people may also be a powerful socialization variable that affects arousal (Geen and Bushman 1989). When people are in potentially embarrassing circumstances, their physiological arousal levels increase more when other people are present than when they are by themselves. Conversely, when people undergo stressful circumstances, the presence of other people decreases their arousal, including their skin conductance levels and heart rates (Kleck et al. 1976). For example, watching a stressful film in the presence of a nurse minimizes increases in skin conductance, as compared to watching a stressful film alone (Davidson and Kelley 1973). It is certainly plausible that men and women may differ in their physiological responses depending on who is present. Since women more often seek social supports when stressed than men do, this may minimize their physiological arousal in stressful circumstances.

OVERVIEW.   As with the expression of emotion via words, behaviors, face and voice, gender differences in physiological reactions depend a great deal on context. Although some studies indicate that males respond with more physiological reactivity when they feel angry or anxious, there is evidence that women may also respond with physiological arousal when the emotional situation is meaningful for them. In particular, it may be the "out of control" aspects of emotional situations that trigger men's arousal, whereas women's arousal may be triggered by situations involving empathy and interpersonal relationships, especially those that concern shifting gender-role expectations.

Women more than men respond with generalizing patterns across different modes of emotional expression. For men, when there is a discrepancy between modes of expression, it seems to be in the direction of internalizing. In other words, men may show heightened physiological reactivity and lowered facial or verbal expressivity when feeling stressed or angry.

Finally, I have reviewed evidence that physiological patterns of arousal, especially those associated with anger and aggression, can be learned and unlearned. This learning may occur within the context of family interactions. The presence or absence of other people may also affect the quality of physiological responses and may be an important variable in future research, since women tend to seek social supports more often than men do.

5

Sad or Mad? The Quality of Emotions

Imagine a situation where a person was gullible and believed some liar who was obviously exaggerating his own power and importance. If I saw a gullible woman, I'd be afraid and sad for her—afraid she'd be taken advantage of. But if I saw a gullible man, I'd be angry—angry that some man would fall into a situation like that. I'd feel ashamed of him, too.

—Steven, age 40

A gullible woman? I'd feel contemptuous and disgusted with her, also sorry for her. If it were a man, I'd feel really annoyed and irritated.

—Martha, age 42

It's time to turn from *how* men and women convey their feelings to an exploration of *what* they convey and to *whom*. The content of emotional expression contributes in powerful ways to interpersonal adaptation. For example, expressing anger versus sadness elicits predictable responses from other people and affects the future course that social relationships take.

In this chapter, I will be reviewing gender differences in particular feelings, such as loneliness and affection, summarizing across all modalities of emotional expression, including words, behaviors, physiological arousal, and facial and vocal expressions. However, most research has centered on either facial or verbal expressions. The reason for this is twofold. First, the complexities of exploring emotions expressed through the voice have perhaps discouraged researchers from venturing forth into this territory (see Chapter 3). Second, the patterns of physiological or behavioral change that accompany specific emotions are often inconsistent and unclear. For example, increased heart rate or behavioral withdrawal may accompany both fear and anger, two very different feelings.

This makes it difficult for researchers to rely on physiological arousal or behavior as a clear sign that a specific emotion has been expressed.

A brief overview indicates that relative to men, women verbalize or use facial expressions to communicate more intense self-conscious emotions, such as sadness, embarrassment, and shame; emotions connoting vulnerability, such as fear and hurt; positive emotions, such as warmth, affection, and joy; and empathic feelings, such as distress. Only the emotions of contempt, pride, guilt, and loneliness are sometimes, but not always, expressed more intensely in words by men than by women. The context in which the emotion is expressed is critical for understanding these patterns.

Anger is expressed by both sexes using different modalities of expression and in different situations. In a surprising violation of stereotypes, women express more intense and frequent anger using words in many situations than men do. Men express anger with more aggression and physical reactivity than women do, and they may express anger using facial and vocal expressiveness more than women do.

Many of these gender differences, especially those for sadness, empathy, and fear, set in quite early in development, at least by school age. For other emotions, such as jealousy, loneliness, and anger, the developmental course is far less clear.

To Whom Are You Expressing Emotion?

Three factors seem to influence the quality of emotions people express toward each other: how well they know each other, their own sex, and the sex of the person to whom they are expressing emotions. Both women and men are more comfortable expressing most emotions, including anger, toward people they know intimately, rather than toward acquaintances. Intimate relationships provide many opportunities for the experience and expression of both positive and negative emotion— close relationships can be both comforting and supportive as well as conflictual and disappointing (see Berscheid 1991). However, within intimate relationships, women verbalize a wider range and more intense feelings than do men, especially angry and critical feelings.

In nonintimate relationships, both men and women are more comfortable disclosing feelings to women than to men (Dosser, Balswick, and Halverson 1983; Dion 1985). The reason for this may be that female friends are more empathic than male friends, willing to listen to feelings and in turn share their own feelings. Timmers et al. (1998) found that both sexes believed that if they expressed fear or disappointment to women, they would be comforted, while they would be criticized by men. Both sexes are also more comfortable expressing affection and love to women than to men (Aries 1976; Dion 1985; Blier and Blier 1989). Men may be constrained from expressing affection toward other men because of homophobia, whereas women may be constrained from expressing affection toward men because they fear that the expression of affection will be misinterpreted as a sexual advance.

Anger may be the only feeling that is verbally disclosed or directed more toward men than toward women (Frost and Averill 1982; Dosser, Balswick, and Halverson 1983; Blier and Blier 1989; Brody, Lovas, and Hay 1995). In my own research, when given identical story situations that had either male or female characters, women were more likely to express anger toward men than toward women (Brody 1993). In one such story, for example, a friend (described as either male or female) unexpectedly refuses to acknowledge the research participant's hurt feelings, and women express more anger toward male than toward female friends. Greater expressions of anger toward men may occur despite the fact that both sexes report feeling more comfortable expressing anger toward same-sex peers than toward opposite-sex peers (Blier and Blier 1989). Bettencourt and Miller's (1996) meta-analysis indicates that in situations in which they are provoked, both men and women do behave more aggressively toward same-sex targets, once again highlighting the importance of context.

When people are expressing emotions to potential sexual partners, they may limit themselves to expressing gender stereotypic feelings, such as sadness for women, but not for men, because they wish to be seen as sexually attractive. In one study, male and female participants were asked to rate their experimentally induced pain in front of experimenters. Men reported significantly less pain in front of female than male experimenters. In contrast, women reported somewhat, although not significantly higher pain in response to male, rather than female experimenters (Levine and De Simone 1991). Another study showed that while watching emotional movies, women cried more when paired with male partners than with female partners (Choti et al. 1987). In order to maintain their attractiveness, men may feel that they need to conceal their fear or pain in front of women; women, in contrast, may feel that they become more attractive when they express or exaggerate feelings of vulnerability, or that men will respond more empathically to their vulnerability than will women. In a study by Barrett and her colleagues (1998), both men and women rated their emotions in opposite-sex interpersonal encounters to be more intense than their emotions in same-sex interpersonal encounters, suggesting that interactions with opposite-sex partners may increase arousal levels.

Integrating all of the data on how expressiveness relates to the sex of one's partner leads to the following hypothesis. Women may express more affection and emotions associated with vulnerability than men do, and men may express more aggression than women do, because each sex interacts more with their own sex than with the opposite sex (Maccoby 1998). In other words, it is possible that if men interacted more with women, they might be just as expressive of affection and vulnerability as women are. If women interacted more with men, they might be just as expressive of aggression as men are.

Anger

Nonaggressive Anger

Even though it is often taken for granted that men express anger using words more than women, research has shown that this isn't quite true. In many situations, when compared to men, women actually express more, or equal levels of anger. Our erroneous stereotypes may be over-generalizations, stemming from data that men are more physically aggressive in unprovoked situations than women (Bettencourt and Miller 1996). Men may also use their faces and voices to express anger more than women do, so their anger is more visible. Gender differences in anger using face, voice, and behavioral aggression may distort our beliefs about gender differences in anger using words.

People may also stereotype women as less angry than men because anger is believed to be inappropriate for women to express (Frost and Averill 1982; Smith et al. 1989). Women judge the personal and relationship costs of anger as higher than men do (Davis, LaRosa, and Foshee 1992); and in particular, as higher for women than for men (Egerton 1988). For example, they believe that if they were to express anger, they ould be more likely to be rejected by others than would men. In a different vein, Harriet Lerner (1980) has argued that women cannot tolerate the sense of separateness and difference inherent in the experience of anger.

Negative beliefs concerning anger may be more true of American women than of women from some other cultures. In a cross-cultural study, 61 percent of the American women reported a preference for concealing anger, whereas not a single younger German woman expressed this preference (Sommers and Kosmitzki 1988). The negative connotations American women ascribe to anger may relate to their reluctance to attribute it to themselves.

Despite our stereotypes, many studies indicate that men and women are equally likely to use words to express nonaggressive anger. Such studies usually rely on self-report questionnaires in which people check off how frequently or intensely they get angry (Houston and Vavak 1991; Grossman and Wood 1993; Ewart and Kolodner 1994). These checklists provide no context for people to think about, for instance, in what circumstances they get angry, or at whom.

In contrast, when people are presented with situations to think about, or when they are interviewed or observed in conversation with others, women actually express more anger and more intense anger than men do (Frost and Averill 1982; Dosser, Balswick, and Halverson 1983; Burrowes and Halberstadt 1987; Thomas 1989; Brody 1993). Women also report more enduring experiences of anger than men do. For example, in a community survey, women reported that when they were more intensely angry, their anger lasted longer, whereas men reported no such relationship between the duration and the intensity of anger (Frost and Averill 1982). Possibly, women ruminate on their anger more than men; or as Frost and Averill suggest, women may give more weight to the duration of a feeling when judging its intensity. Men, in contrast, may place more weight on their behaviors when judging the intensity of their anger.

Women also respond to angry situations differently than men do. They report crying more; talking in a shaky, cracking voice more; and simultaneously experiencing hurt or disappointment (Frost and Averill 1982; Brody 1993). They also report that they would talk incidents over with the instigator of the anger or a third party more than men (Frost and Averill 1982), as well as use manipulative social strategies intended to hurt a person they are angry at (see Chapter 3; Crick and Grotpeter 1995).

Anger and Relationships

Especially in intimate relationships, women express negative feelings more than their partners. They also cry more to get their own way and are viewed as more likely to give their spouses the silent treatment when upset (Kelley et al. 1978; Parelman 1983; Barnes and Buss 1985). Men are more frequently reported to use a logical, nonemotional approach to problems (Kelley et al. 1978).

Detailed observations of husbands and wives interacting with each other, including observational, self-report, and physiological measures, have revealed that wives show more anger, negative affect, and whining than husbands (Gottman and Levenson 1986, 1992). Husbands show more neutral affect than wives (Levenson et al. 1994). Researchers have also identified a demand/withdraw pattern, in which one partner, most often the wife, makes emotional demands, frequently expressing anger. The other partner, usually the husband, withdraws and avoids the anger (see Chapter 3; Gottman and Levenson 1986). Gottman and Levenson (1986) theorize that wives are more likely than husbands to take responsibility for initiating conflicts and for keeping the couple focused on whatever the conflict is.[1]

A study of conflict in Iran has shown a similar pattern of gender differences. Men and women were compared on their feelings of *qahr* (not to be on speaking terms with someone, which is an indirect expression of negative emotions such as hate, anger, dislike, and hurt, sending a signal to correct wrongdoings). Females engaged in *qahr* more often than men did, although men's *qahr*s lasted much longer than women's because men reconciled much less easily (Behzadi 1994).

Anger: Facial and Vocal Expressions

In contrast to the pattern of gender differences for anger expressed in words, research suggests that men's voices may reflect how angry or hostile they are more than women's voices do. In one study, male speakers' expressions of anger while reading a short story were better identified than were their female counterparts' (Bonebright, Thompson, and Leger 1996). Other studies have shown that men's voices may more often be an outlet for communicating anger than are women's voices. For example, men who rated themselves more highly on anger and hostility than other men had faster speech rates, louder speech, longer vocalizations, and made more interruptions than did men who rated themselves less highly. Women who rated themselves more highly on anger and hostility than other women spoke more loudly, but showed no other distinct voice patterns (Siegman 1993).

Men may convey anger more clearly not only in their vocal expressions, but also in their facial expressions. Both men and women have been found to recognize anger expressed by men more clearly than anger expressed by women (Rotter and Rotter 1988). For example, videotapes of men's facial displays of anger as they discussed angry, sad, or happy emotional memories were identified more accurately by a panel of judges than were women's (Coats and Feldman 1996). Other studies have indicated that men show more facial reactivity in response to angry stimuli than women do (Dimberg and Lundquist 1990).

Developmental Patterns

It is difficult to find consistent gender differences in the expression of anger over the course of development. Some studies indicate that boys express more anger than girls. For example, parents rate their sons (ranging in age from 18 months to 8 years) to be higher on anger-proneness than their daughters (Goldsmith, Buss, and Lemery 1997). Consistent with this finding are two studies showing that young girls reported less anger than boys in response to emotionally evocative videotapes or stories (Brody 1984; Strayer and Roberts 1997). Four- to six-year-old boys also displayed significantly more intensity of anger, as well as physical retaliation, than girls of the same age in peer interactions (Eisenberg et al. 1994b), and four- to five-year-old boys expressed more facial anger than girls in reaction to simulated distress, consisting of hypothetical interpersonal conflicts (Zahn-Waxler et al. 1995). Other studies indicate that in response to watching scenarios depicting adults in conflict situations, boys were more likely to respond with anger and aggression (attacking or taking possessions) than were girls, while girls were more likely to respond with distress than were boys (Cummings, Iannotti, and Zahn-Waxler 1985). Boys were also more likely to attribute anger to story characters than were girls when asked to generate and explain the story character's feelings (Gordis, Smith, and Mascio 1991).

In contrast, other studies show no gender differences in facial expressions of anger in 10-month-old infants (Stifter and Grant 1993), or in the expression of anger in school-aged children, either when children are asked about their feelings in questionnaires (Buntaine and Costenbader 1997), are observed in spontaneous interactions, or when questioned about their feelings of anger in relation to peers (Fabes and Eisenberg 1992; Murphy and Eisenberg 1996). However, although naturalistic observations of preschool children showed that there were no differences in the frequency with which boys and girls became angry, there were differences in the ways in which they expressed their anger. Boys were more likely to respond to angry conflicts by venting (expressing emotions such as crying, sulking, or throwing a tantrum), whereas girls were more likely to actively resist the child with whom they were in conflict, by defending their position or possessions (Fabes and Eisenberg 1992).

As in the work with adults, some studies on adolescents show that females report levels of anger that are either similar to, or are higher than those reported by boys (Ewart and Kolodner 1994). For example, a developmental study done by Spielberger et al. (1985) asked 1000 high-school students to report on their levels of anger and found that girls actually reported higher total anger expression than did boys.

More detailed analyses suggest that gender differences in children's and adolescents' expression of anger are specific to the situation being studied. A study of emotions reported in response to situations found that 8-year-old boys reported more intense anger in response to sad situations than did girls, and male adolescents reported more intense anger in response to situations depicting warmth and love than did females. However, in contradiction to these patterns, female adolescents reported more intense anger in sad situations than did males, while the intensity of anger in angry situations was rated equally by the two sexes (Wintre, Polivy, and Murray 1990). And just to highlight the situational specificity of gender differences in the expression of anger, infant girls were found to display more anger toward mothers than were infant boys in a separation–reunion task, perhaps because of closer mother–daughter than mother–son relationships (Malatesta et al. 1989).

Other developmental research indicates that gender differences in the expression of anger may shift with age and as a function of culture. In an interesting cross-cultural study, Sommers and Kosmitzki (1988) found that older American women reported themselves to be irritated and angry more often than older German women; whereas younger German women reported themselves to be angry and irritated more often than

interesting

younger American women. Among schoolchildren, urban youngsters reported significantly higher levels of anger than rural or suburban children (Buntaine and Costenbader 1997), and among urban children, the expression of anger on the part of daughters may be more acceptable, perhaps even encouraged by parents, than it is among nonurban children (Miller and Sperry 1987).

Love, Happiness, and Affection

Women express more positive emotions than men do, reporting more joy, euphoria, happiness, affection, and positive feelings, as well as satisfaction with life (Kanin, Davidson, and Scheck 1970; Dion and Dion 1973; Allen and Haccoun 1976; Dion 1985; Blier and Blier 1989; Wood, Rhodes, and Whelan 1989). In dating relationships, women are more likely than men to express and experience feelings of love, including reports that they are "floating on a cloud: feeling giddy and carefree" (Balswick and Avertt 1977; Dosser, Balswick, and Halverson 1983). In my own work, women responded with more intense warmth and happiness than men to story situations such as the following: "Bob/Barbara is really busy, but has volunteered his/her time to help children in need after work. How do you feel about Bob/Barbara?" (Brody 1993).

Most situations in which women report expressing more positive emotions than men involve interpersonal relationships. When interpersonal relationships are not involved (for example, watching horror films), men and women express equal intensities of "delight" (Zillmann et al. 1986). I will be arguing in future chapters that women's caretaking roles and high intimacy motivation bears directly on the warmth that they express. Expressing warmth and love may help women to maintain close relationships with others.

Affection and Development

The developmental data on the expression of affection indicate that boys become less expressive of affection with age. Using daily logs, mothers report that boys are increasingly less likely to be openly affectionate in their overt behaviors and facial expressiveness as they get older (Cummings, Zahn-Waxler, and Radke-Yarrow 1984).

Shame, Embarrassment, and Guilt

Shame and embarrassment are more likely to be expressed by adolescent and adult females than males (Gonzales 1992; Stapley and Haviland 1989). For example, in hypothetical shame-inducing situations, such as breaking something that belongs to someone else, women report more shame than men (Tangney 1990; Ferguson and Crowley 1997). Women have also been found to try harder to make amends in embarrassing situations than men do (Gonzales 1992).

Although some research and theory suggest that men express more guilt than women, possibly as a way of actively making amends for inappropriate behavior (Lewis 1971), other research shows no gender differences in the intensity of reported guilt (Brody 1996), or that women report more guilt than men do (Ferguson and Crowley 1997). Gender differences in shame and guilt are unlikely to emerge when people are asked to check off the frequency with which they express behaviors related to guilt, such as expressing remorse or blushing (Harder and Zalma 1990). This may be because checklists provide no context in which to understand what men and women feel guilty or ashamed about. Women may express more guilt about disrupting family relationships, since family caretaking is an expected social function for them; men may express more guilt about hurting someone if they behave aggressively or about not fulfilling their expected roles as financial providers. Thus far, researchers have not focused on the importance of these motivational factors, which may be the primary reason that the pattern of results for gender differences in shame and guilt across studies is inconsistent.

In a sophisticated analysis, Ferguson and Crowley (1997) argue that regardless of the actual levels of guilt and shame reported by each sex, guilt is a predominant emotional experience for men that organizes their personality functioning, whereas shame is a predominant emotional experience for women that organizes their functioning. The researchers measured levels of guilt and shame with the Self-Conscious Attribution and Affect Inventory (Tangney 1990), a story measure in which social blunders are committed and participants rate their likelihood of responding in ways that depict shame, such as hiding, or guilt, such as making reparations. Men's levels of guilt and women's levels of shame

erentially found to contribute to the types of defenses they used
her story measure. For example, men's guilt-proneness was re-
attributing less blame to others and engaging in less self-punitive
strategies, but men's shame-proneness did not contribute as clearly to
their defense use. In contrast, shame-proneness in women contributed
more to their defensive style, such as their increased likelihood to punish
themselves and others, than did guilt-proneness.

Shame, Guilt, and Development

Research on the development of gender differences in shame and guilt is
inconclusive. Some developmental data show that even at young ages,
girls are more prone to express embarrassment and shame than are
males. For example, 2-year-old girls were found to display embarrassment more than boys in such situations as looking in a mirror, being
overpraised, or being asked to dance with mothers and experimenters
(Lewis et al. 1989). However, more detailed developmental analyses indicated that by age 3, boys had caught up to the girls in their levels of
embarrassment and no gender differences were apparent (Lewis et al.
1991). Yet another study showed that 3-year-old girls expressed more
shame than boys in situations in which they failed at a difficult task
(Lewis, Alessandri, and Sullivan 1992). Here again, gender differences in
shame and embarrassment may be context-specific.

Sympathy, Empathy, and Distress

Empathy is hypothesized to be an emotional response that emerges from
the perception of another person's emotional state and is similar to that
state. Empathy for another can lead to sympathy, which entails feelings
of sorrow or sadness for the other person. Alternatively, empathy can
lead to personal distress, involving the expression of one's own anxiety
or discomfort. Researchers have found that individuals who express sympathy are likely to actively assist those in need of help; while individuals
who express personal distress are more likely to avoid another person's
suffering (Eisenberg and Fabes 1995). Further, sympathetic feelings are
thought to be facilitated by the ability to regulate emotional arousal and
behaviors (Fabes, Eisenberg, and Eisenbud 1993).

Gender differences in these emotions have been found to vary a great deal depending on the particular measure used to study them. For example, self-report measures, especially questionnaires, in which individuals report their general empathy and sympathy toward others, show that women report more empathy and sympathy than men do (Lennon and Eisenberg 1987; Eisenberg et al. 1991b; Eisenberg and Fabes 1995). In a 1983 meta-analysis of such studies, Eisenberg and Lennon (1983) found an overwhelming effect size in favor of women, and these two researchers continued to find large sex differences in studies they reviewed through 1987 (Lennon and Eisenberg 1987).

Other studies have explored gender differences in personal distress and sympathy after people are exposed to a needy or distressed person through films or stories. Some of these studies find women to report greater distress. For example, women's greater verbal distress has been documented in studies in which they recall distressing experiences in their own lives, or in which they respond to hurt victims depicted in films, stories, or staged interactions (Eisenberg and Lennon 1983; Eisenberg et al. 1988b). Women also report greater distress in response to horror films than men (Sparks 1991).[2]

In contrast to self-report measures, gender differences in facial expressions and physiological measures of empathy are less clear. However, those studies that do find gender differences in facial expressions and arousal generally find that females are more expressive than are males. For example, in one study, males and females talked to a lonely undergraduate, actually a confederate of the experimenter. Females showed more distressed facial expressions, were observed to be more nurturant, and nodded their heads more than men did (Bem, Martyna, and Watson 1976). Females have also been found to show greater skin conductance than males to sympathy-inducing stimuli (Eisenberg et al. 1991b). On the other hand, some studies have shown that young boys evidence more skin conductance than do young girls in response to distressing stories or videotapes (Fabes et al. 1994).

Females' expressions of sympathy and empathy may be facilitated by the fact that females perceive emotions in other people more accurately than males do (Hall 1984; see Brody 1985). Perceiving emotions in others may be a necessary precursor to empathizing with them. Perhaps men are just as empathic as women when the cues for distress are more obvious. In other words, gender differences in empathy may vary depending on how subtle or obvious another person's distress is, a hypothesis that researchers could explore further.

Empathy and Development

Even children as young as one show gender differences in empathic expressions and behaviors, with girls seeking to comfort those who are suffering more than boys do (Zahn-Waxler et al. 1992; Zahn-Waxler, Robinson, and Emde 1992). Compared to boys, toddler girls also look longer at a distressed adult who pretends to hurt her finger with a hammer (Sigman and Kasari 1994; see also Zahn-Waxler et al. 1992; Zahn-Waxler, Robinson, and Emde 1992). One study with toddlers required mothers to record their observations about their children in two types of situations: situations in which the child caused distress (by taking away a baby's bottle); or situations in which the child witnessed a distressing situation (such as mothers and fathers fighting or younger children getting hurt). The researchers also supplemented this with videotaped observations of distress in the home. Spontaneous behavioral efforts to intervene on behalf of the victim appeared with similar frequencies for boys and girls, but girls expressed more empathic concern than boys by asking questions such as, "Are you okay?" This gender difference occurred for situations in which children were bystanders to naturally occurring distress incidents, and had not caused the distress themselves (Zahn-Waxler et al. 1992). Preschool and school-aged children show similar gender differences (Zahn-Waxler et al. 1995), with feelings of sympathy and distress verbally reported more by girls than boys (Eisenberg et al. 1989; Fabes, Eisenberg, and Eisenbud 1993), and with school-aged girls reporting more verbal empathy than boys when watching emotionally evocative videotapes (Roberts and Strayer 1996; Strayer and Roberts 1997).

There are also cross-cultural data that girls express more caring and affection toward others than boys, including seeking physical contact and offering support to others (Whiting and Edwards 1973, 1988). This gender difference does not reliably occur across cultures until age 7 (Whiting and Edwards 1973). Whiting and Edwards (1988) speculate that nurturing behaviors and displays of affection are fostered by having younger siblings who require care. Girls are more often given the role of caring for their siblings than boys, which may maximize their expressions of empathy and sympathy. In cultures in which boys care for their siblings, gender differences in nurturance markedly decrease (Whiting and Edwards 1988). Other research also suggests that boys' caring behaviors may increase as a consequence of being placed in the position of being caretakers. For example, 2- to 4-year-old boys' caring behaviors were found to increase when their mothers were severely depressed, whereas girls' levels of caring remained high regardless of the severity of their mothers' depression (Radke-Yarrow et al. 1994).

Gender differences in facial empathy are more inconsistent, sometimes depending on whether sympathy or distress is measured and in what contexts. When facial empathy was defined as an exact match between the predominant facial expressions of children and the videotaped characters they watched, female school-aged children showed more facial empathy than males (Strayer and Roberts 1997). It is important to note that these children were not aware that their facial expressions were being videotaped while they watched the films. Other studies have also shown that school-aged females exhibit more sympathetic facial expressions than males (Eisenberg et al. 1989). Yet, kindergarten and second-grade boys were found to display greater facial distress than girls in response to distressing films (Fabes et al. 1994), while third- and sixth-grade girls and boys showed no differences in their facial distress in response to films (Fabes, Eisenberg, and Eisenbud 1993).

Fear, Nervousness, Tension, and Worry

Many studies, including cross-cultural studies conducted in the United States, China, Great Britain, and Australia indicate that women express more fear than men do. This gender difference exists in situations ranging from watching horror movies to going to a dentist's office (Brody 1984; Kirkpatrick 1984; Scherer, Wallbott, and Summerfield 1986; Blier and Blier 1989; Gullone and King 1993). Women report more fear even in situations not stereotypically frightening, such as imagining a romantic partner passionately kissing someone else at a party (Hupka and Eshett 1988), or doing cognitive tasks such as serial subtraction or mirror-image tracing (Matthews and Stoney 1988; Matthews et al. 1991). Greater fear by women has also been documented extensively using a self-report questionnaire called the Fear Survey Schedule (Ollendick et al. 1995; Gullone and King 1993), which includes such diverse situations as meeting someone for the first time, failing a test, encountering snakes, or going to bed in the dark.

Some gender differences in the emotions related to fear, such as anxiety or worry, may be culturally specific. For example, there were no gender differences in the amount of worry reported between African-American boys and girls, even though European-American and Hispanic school-aged girls reported more anxiety and worry than boys as measured via interviews and self-report (Silverman, La Greca, and Wasserstein 1995).

Whether or not there are gender differences in vocal expressions of fear remains an open question. In one recent study, male actors' vocal expressions of fear were more readily identified by students than were females actors' (Bonebright et al. 1996). This lone study requires replication before one can conclude that men use their voices to express fear more than women do.

For both sexes, fear is elicited more by males than by females in children and adults (Brody, Lovas, and Hay 1995). It probably comes as no surprise that a hypothetical story in which a man follows you as you walk down the street elicits more intense fear than a scenario in which a woman follows you down the street.

Fear and Development

Although school-aged girls express more fear than boys do, the developmental onset of these differences is not clear. The evidence for infant gender differences in fear is quite inconsistent. Some studies have shown girls to display more wariness than boys do as early as 14 months (Kagan 1994), while others have shown 2-year-old boys to show more wariness to a stranger (defined as behavioral inhibition and gaze aversion) than girls (Lewis et al. 1989). One study showed that in the face of a fear-provoking toy, infant girls displayed wider eyes, more furrowed brows, tenser bodies, and more crying than boys (Gunnar and Stone 1984). However, using similar toys, other studies have found the reverse: girls were less timid than boys (Gunnar 1980; Gunnar-vonGnechten 1978).

The nature of the fear-inducing situation may be the most important factor as to whether or not gender differences emerge. Fears related to danger, death, and safety are more frequent in girls than in boys, based both on self-reports of children as well as parent and teacher reports.

Both school-aged girls as well as adult women report more fear than their male counterparts in situations in which they feel physically vulnerable, particularly when provoked by males, rather than by other females (Brody, Lovas, and Hay 1995). In Britain, women reported fear of strangers, while in Switzerland, they reported fear of physical aggression (Scherer, Wallbott, and Summerfield 1986).

On the other hand, boys report a preponderance of social-evaluative fears, such as being sent to the principal. Lack of control may also elicit fear in boys. For example, although both infant boys and girls smiled more in the face of a frightening toy when they could control its actions than when they couldn't, only boys were less fearful when they could predict the onset of a loud noise than when they couldn't (Gunnar-vonGnechten 1978). In addition to loss of control, issues related to loss of status may be potentially frightening for boys. For example, boys reported more fear in response to actors who were behaving submissively in disputes than they reported in some other situations (Cummings et al. 1991).

Disgust and Contempt

Women report more disgust than do males to noninterpersonal situations, including reactions to body products (feces, urine); death (picking up the dead body of an animal); animals (stepping on an earthworm with your bare feet); sex (incest); hygiene (not changing underwear), food (eating monkey meat), and body violations (accidentally sticking a fishing hook through a finger). This has been found in a broad range of social classes in North American samples (Rozin, Haidt, and McCauley 1993).

Gender differences for contempt, signifying a position of superiority over others, are not as clear as for disgust. Some studies have shown that young adolescent males report more contempt than females, including more frequent, intense, and longer lasting contempt (Stapley and Haviland 1989). Similarly, college women (more than men) frequently identify their partner's contemptuousness toward them in dating relationships, including acting in condescending ways and treating them as if they were inferior (Buss 1989). However, in my own research (Brody 1993), I found no gender differences in the intensity of contempt expressed by adult males and females in response to men and women in a wide range of hypothetical interpersonal situations.

Jealousy

Jealousy is a complex emotion with respect to gender differences. Men express jealousy about the sexual aspects of a rival relationship. In contrast, women express jealousy when they feel that the closeness of an intimate relationship may be disrupted (White and Mullen 1989; Buss et al. 1992). When participants were asked to imagine that they had just discovered their romantic partner passionately kissing another at a party, women were likely to predict they would be more fearful than men, but not more angry, disgusted, surprised, sad, or jealous (Hupka and Eshett 1988).

Sadness, Grief, and Depression

Women in America as well as in a wide range of European countries express sad and distressed feelings for a longer duration and with more intensity than men do, using both words and behaviors (Allen and Haccoun 1976; Scherer, Wallbott, and Summerfield 1986; Burrowes and Halberstadt 1987; Nolen-Hoeksema 1991). Women cry more often than men do (Barnes and Buss 1985), and behave in a hopeless and depressed manner more often than men. That women score more highly on measures of depression (measured as the expression of sadness, crying, and hopelessness) between the ages of 18 and 64 has been documented cross-culturally, with the exception of some developing countries, the Amish, the recently widowed, and college students (Nolen-Hoeksema 1991). Women may also be more aware of their own sadness than are males (Hooven, Gottman, and Katz 1995).

In one study, female college students used more words connoting depression, such as "hopeless," "grief," and "worthless" than did males when asked to write in detail about their earliest, most positive, and most negative memories of their mothers and fathers (Halberstadt, Leslie-Case, and King 1994). Similarly, in my research, women reported more intense sadness than men in response to interpersonal stories, such as the following: "You ask David/Diane to turn down some loud music that you are finding annoying. He/she refuses to do so. How would you feel?"

There is also some evidence that American, Japanese, and Anglo-European women express more sadness, or are perceived to express more sadness, in their facial expressions than men express (Scherer, Wallbott, and Summerfield 1986; Matsumoto and Ekman 1989).

Sadness and Development

Gender differences in the expression of sadness seem to set in quite early. Young girls use both facial expressions and words to express sadness more than young boys. For example, 6-year-old girls report more sadness than boys in response to situations that might elicit either sadness, anger, or hurt (Brody 1984). And in a recent study, 4–5-year-old girls reported that they felt sadder while listening to sad stories than did the boys (Zahn-Waxler et al. 1995). Similarly, in conversations with their mothers about shared past experiences, 40-, 48-, and 70-month-old girls mentioned sadness more often than boys did. And, when watching sympathy-inducing films, preschool and second-grade girls exhibited more facial sadness than did boys (Eisenberg et al. 1988a; Eisenberg et al. 1989), while early school-aged girls reported more sadness than did boys (Eisenberg et al. 1993). These gender differences continue into adolescence. In high-school students, both white and black inner city high-school girls reported more sadness and pessimism than did high-school boys (Ewart and Kolodner 1994).

Boys, in fact, may mute their expressions of sadness increasingly as they get older. For example, second-grade boys were found to exhibit less facial sadness than preschool boys exhibited when they watched evocative films (Eisenberg et al. 1989).

Some gender differences in sadness have been found to be context-specific. Cummings et al. (1991) required 5- and 9-year-old boys and girls to view videotaped interactions between adult actors that consisted of either resolved or unresolved disputes. Children were asked to label their own feelings and that of the actors. Five- and nine-year-old girls reported more sadness than boys did; but 11-, 14-, and 19-year-old boys reported more sadness than girls did in response to unresolved marital disputes.

Pride and Feelings of Success

Studies indicate that men report more pride and feelings of success than women do. For example, when asked to report on their feelings following a 6-hour matriculation examination in Helsinki (which involved writing essays), high-school girls reported higher levels of anxiety and dissatisfaction with their own performance, while boys reported more alertness and concentration as well as a higher sense of success and confidence (Frankenhaeuser et al. 1978). It is important to note that there were no differences in the scores the two sexes obtained. Similarly, among male and female engineering students taking a cognitive-conflict task, in which participants had to ignore a word and name the color in which the word was printed, self-reports of good performance were consistently higher among males, even though they were not reflective of actual performance differences between the two sexes (Collins and Frankenhaeuser 1978). And on the Personality Attributes Questionnaire (Spence, Helmreich, and Stapp 1974), men typically score higher than women on the item, "I think I am better than most people," connoting a sense of pride.

These differences in pride may reflect the gender-stereotypic circumstances and roles being assessed. Perhaps if women were asked to report on their feelings of pride on a stereotypically feminine task or attribute, such as their friendliness, they might score at higher levels than would men. On the other hand, gender differences in the expression of pride may be part of a general picture in which women devalue themselves and report lower self-esteem than men, perhaps related to their social roles and lower power and status in the culture (Wise and Joy 1982; Baruch and Barnett 1986b).

Loneliness

In general, men have been found to express more loneliness than women (Wheeler, Reis, and Nezlek 1983). Schmitt and Kurdek (1985) found that college men reported more loneliness than college women in three types of relationships: family relationships, large group relationships, and friendships. On the other hand, in an inner city population, Ewart and Kolodner (1994) found that high-school girls reported more loneliness (in conjunction with sadness and pessimism) than did high-school boys. The expression of loneliness has been tied to the perception that relationships are not meeting one's social needs, and here again, gender differences may be culturally and situationally specific.

OVERVIEW. I cannot emphasize too strongly that gender differences in any particular emotion vary depending on the type of situation that elicits the emotion and to whom the emotion is being expressed. For example, men express more jealousy at sexual infidelity; women express more jealousy at threats to their emotional relationships. Men express more anger when physically provoked; women express more anger when disappointed in interpersonal relationships. Situational differences indicate that women's and men's dissimilar emotional expressions are linked to their differing motivations and social roles. For example, perhaps women express more warmth and affection because they are more often motivated to be close to others. Perhaps men express more contempt because they are more often motivated to maintain competitive and high status positions.

The expression of feelings also varies depending on who the participants are and what the nature of their relationship is. For example, men are likely to minimize expressions of vulnerability when interacting with potential sexual partners; women are likely to maximize expressions of vulnerability in the same situation. I have also speculated that men and women may express dissimilar emotions because each sex engages in more same-sex than opposite-sex interactions. Women interact with a greater number of women than men do, perhaps leading them to express emotions related to warmth, affection, and vulnerability, and men interact with a greater number of men than women do, perhaps leading them to express emotions related to aggression.

It is noteworthy that three of the emotions sometimes expressed more by men, namely pride, contempt, and loneliness, all have to do with aspects of individualism, or independence from others. Pride signals a personal accomplishment, important for men in the world of competition for resources. Loneliness signals a disconnection from others, possibly related to the fact that men are not socialized to make relationships a priority in their lives. Contempt signifies feelings of superiority with respect to others, which may relate to the importance men place on competition and their relatively higher status with respect to women. Even guilt, which men sometimes express more than women, may be a function of men's relatively higher status and power. All of these emotions reflect the reality of men's social roles.

II

Gender, Biology, and the Family

6

The State of the Art:
Biological Differences?

If a girl was rough and strong, I'd feel like she was kind of mixed up in her wire connections. Because if a girl's brain was switched around and she had the brain of a boy, she would know how to control more muscle than a girl's brain—she would be strong. And a girl's brain would know how to use lips more than a boy's brain, you know, how to kiss [followed by laughter].

—*Josh, age 6*

The role of biological processes in gender differences is intriguing, but dismayingly inconsistent and inconclusive to date. In an effort to explore whether the biological processes associated with emotional functioning are gender-linked, studies have addressed gender differences in several biological structures and processes thought to mediate emotional expression. Most notably, these include the relationships among emotion, cerebral lateralization, and testosterone levels. Despite much publicity to the contrary in publications such as *Newsweek* (March 27, 1995), the role of gender in these brain-emotion relationships and processes is quite unclear (see Fausto-Sterling 1997).

A subtle and unsettling bias permeates much of this research, consisting of the idea that gender differences in brain organization must exist and will eventually be documented, despite the failure of all previous efforts to convincingly do so. For example, in his recent book, *Left Brain, Right Brain*, Iaccino (1993) reviews the inconsistent literature on gender and cerebral lateralization and reassures his readers: "The outcomes have not always been consistent ones, but this should not be a source of discouragement . . ." (pp. 151). The message he conveys is that despite inconsistencies across studies, gender differences in cerebral lateraliza-

101

tion simply must be there and, given enough time and hard work, eventually will be discovered. In fact, he attempts to redeem the existence of gender differences in lateralization by arguing that such differences interact with (or may sometimes be masked by) gender differences in attentional and cognitive strategies, thus serving to keep a biological explanation viable in the face of often weak and inconsistent evidence. The biases of researchers in this area may serve to distort interpretations of their data.[1]

What is clear from research in this area is that males have higher testosterone levels than females (approximately ten times higher). Testosterone, an androgen, is responsible for the development of the male sex organs. Why are differential testosterone levels important for understanding gender differences in emotional expressiveness? Popular impressions and some inconsistent research have tied testosterone levels to the expression of aggression. Yet, I will review evidence that the causal link between testosterone and aggression is questionable. Studies actually show that the direction of causality may go the other way: that is, testosterone levels may be the end result of aggression and competition, not the cause of these processes (Kemper 1990).

Perhaps more interestingly, testosterone is important in understanding gender differences because there are data that early exposure to testosterone affects the organization of the brain in rodents, including the degree to which it is lateralized (Juraska 1991; Collaer and Hines 1995). New and intriguing research with rhesus monkeys has also suggested that neonatal exposure to testosterone may also influence the quality of mother-infant interactions (Wallen, Maestripieri, and Mann 1995). When testosterone levels were experimentally manipulated in newborn rhesus monkeys, those males with the highest neonatal testosterone levels showed the lowest percentage of time interacting in proximity to, or within an arm's reach of, their mothers. Proximity differences were not due to mothers' differential treatment of their offspring, but rather to the interactions initiated by the infants themselves.

Do differing levels of neonatal testosterone exposure in humans produce different patterns of brain organization and differing kinds of mother–infant interactions in the two sexes? At the moment, there is neither convincing evidence that gender differences in human brain organization exist, nor convincing evidence that males and females differ in how their brains mediate emotional expressiveness. While there is evidence that emotional expressiveness is differentially processed by the two hemispheres of the cortex, whether or not there are gender differences in these biological processes remains uncertain.

The research on the biology of gender differences is only in its infancy, and there is some debate among feminists about whether or not it is worthwhile to pursue, given the abuses to which it can be put. Because people erroneously tend to interpret biological differences as immutable, evidence for biological contributions to gender differences in behavior often leads to the neglect of controllable social influences that contribute almost certainly equally, if not more powerfully, to development. Biological research can be misused to contribute to political agendas that limit the opportunities afforded to each sex. Biopsychologists themselves are often apt to ignore the social factors that enter into either emotional functioning or biological development, and thus fail to address or to inform critical issues addressed by social, developmental, or personality psychologists who study emotion.[2]

In light of these concerns, it is important to emphasize that if biological differences are found to underlie the differences in males' and females' emotional expressiveness, they are shaped by and develop in interaction with social processes.

The Interaction between Biological Development and Social Processes

Biological development itself never unfolds within a vacuum: it is always subject to social and environmental inputs. If, in fact, we treat infant boys and infant girls differently from birth, for example, by holding girls more than we do boys, the differential treatment they receive may alter their neurological development. Even those aspects of emotion that may be hard-wired, most probably including some facial expressions and the ability to experience pain and pleasure, develop and change in interaction with the environment.

A compelling example of the interaction between environmental input and biology in determining the very structure of the brain itself comes from a study of infant rats done by Moore, Dou, and Juraska (1992). They were able to experimentally alter the number of spinal cord motor neurons in infant rats by changing the frequency with which the mother rats licked their infants. Here's how the study worked: In infant rats, the number of motor neurons in the spinal cord is determined by a process of initial overproduction followed by selective cell death during early development.[3] Maternal licking behavior provides extensive tactile stimulation to the infant's developing spinal cord throughout the neonatal period. This stimulation turns out to affect the number of motor neurons that survive. The experimenters reduced maternal licking behavior by treating mothers intranasally with zinc sulfate, which eliminated their sense of smell. Although the infants were healthy in all other ways, by 77–82 days of age, anatomical analyses indicated that there was an 11 percent reduction in the number of motor neurons for both male and female rats reared by the zinc sulfate–treated mothers. This reduction was apparently due to increased neonatal cell death, although the precise neurological or hormonal mechanisms that mediate this process remain a mystery. The important point about this study is that social input, in the form of maternal licking behaviors, contributes significantly to the development of brain characteristics, in this case to the number of motor neurons. The complex nature of the interactions between social and biological factors is highlighted by the fact that maternal licking behaviors are promoted by androgen chemosignals carried in the urine of male pups, so that males typically receive more maternal licking than females do.

Social factors may also contribute to human infants' EEG patterns. Dawson and her colleagues (1992) found that 11–17-month-old infants of depressed mothers had different EEG patterns than infants of nondepressed mothers. When they were observed in play situations designed to elicit positive feelings, these infants showed less left frontal EEG activation than did their counterparts with nondepressed mothers. These infants also did not show a typical pattern of greater right frontal EEG activity during a maternal separation condition designed to elicit distress (Dawson et al. 1992). Although these differing EEG patterns may represent an underlying biological marker for depression shared by depressed mothers and their infants, it is also likely that the quality of these infants' social interactions with their unresponsive mothers triggers a pattern of neurological development that differs from the norm. These social interactions may dampen children's positive affect as mediated by hemispheric asymmetry.

Keeping in mind that biological development never occurs in isolation from social processes, I will critically review the data relevant to the biological bases of gender differences in emotional expressiveness. It is not difficult to be critical of this research, since it tends to be contradictory, inconclusive, and puzzling at best.

Types of Studies Addressing the Issue

One of the limitations in studying biological gender differences in emotional processes is that there are few studies that directly explore gender differences in the biology of emotion. There are separate studies looking at the biology of emotional expression and the biology of gender differences. But very few studies put the two topics together, exploring sex differences in the specific brain structures involved in emotional expressiveness. I will attempt to integrate these two topics.

Recent work on gender and the biopsychology of emotions can be divided into two categories. The first are brain lateralization studies, which attempt to identify specific brain regions that mediate emotional expression. The second are studies of hormonal effects on emotional behavior, especially the effects of testosterone. These two kinds of studies overlap because hormones exert organizing influences on the brain, affecting the development of various brain structures (Collaer and Hines 1995).

The conclusions we can draw about these two areas are quite different. The evidence is clear that the levels of some hormones, like testosterone and estrogen, are different in males and females. If the levels of these hormones were the same, there would not be two biologically different sexes, since the presence of testosterone in prenatal development is responsible for the development of male sexual organs. Thus, if a clear relationship between testosterone and the expression of emotion, such as aggression, can be found, then hormonal differences between males and females may be related to gender differences in aggression. I prefaced the previous statement with a rather big "if," however, and will present evidence that the relationship between testosterone and aggression is tenuous at best. Moreover, the relationship between testosterone and aggression may be different for the two sexes, presenting a surprisingly complex picture.

The story is somewhat different for cerebral lateralization. First, unlike testosterone levels, which differ for the two sexes, it's not clear that males and females actually differ in cerebral lateralization, despite the widely publicized and cited evidence to the contrary. Second, we're only beginning to learn how cerebral lateralization is related to emotional expressiveness. Thus, the evidence that gender differences in emotion are linked to gender differences in cerebral lateralization is quite shaky. Any conclusions we may reach about gender, emotion, and gender differences in cerebral lateralization will be speculative at best.

Some Basics

Understanding much of what I will present in this chapter requires knowing some basic brain anatomy. The cerebral cortex is generally what is thought to make us human. Part of the forebrain, it mediates complex conscious behaviors. It consists of left and right hemispheres that are connected by the corpus callosum (Kolb and Whishaw 1996). The largest parts of both left and right hemispheres are the frontal lobes, which receive input from both motor and sensory areas of the cortex and the neocortex. The frontal lobes are believed to mediate all the behaviors we learn as we develop, including abstract thought and behavioral inhibition (Kolb and Whishaw 1996). Other lobes in the cortex are the temporal, parietal, and occipital lobes.

The left hemisphere has been tied to language functioning; the right hemisphere to visual-spatial functioning. The corpus callosum serves as a communication link between the two hemispheres. In "split-brain" patients in which the corpus callosum is severed in order to treat severe cases of epilepsy, the two hemispheres operate independently. Split brain patients, for example, have a hard time naming an object when they feel it with their left hands, because the information is going only to their right hemispheres. However, they can identify it by pointing to a picture of what they have felt (Sperry 1964).

Both cortical and subcortical (below the cortex) processes, especially those in the limbic system, are involved in emotional expression. The limbic system, evolved earlier than the cortex, lies just above the brainstem and consists of several structures, including the amygdala, the hippocampus, and the hypothalamus; all of which are hypothesized to play a role in emotional functioning.

Hormones and Behavior

Testosterone, one of the androgens, has a long history of being viewed as a cause of aggressive behaviors in humans. The popular view is that testosterone is responsible for aggression, and the deliberately exaggerated description, "testosterone poisoning," has been used as a causal explanation for violent or abusive behaviors among men. Archer (1994) quotes a recent British politician who publicly held high levels of testosterone responsible for the violent behaviors of his right-wing followers.

Sociobiologists relate testosterone to both sexual functioning and aggression by arguing that because males compete with other males for sexual access to females, testosterone may have the dual effect of enhancing both sexual motivation and intermale aggression, thus facilitating the goal of reproduction (Archer 1994). There is certainly evidence that testosterone is related to sexual behaviors. For example, administering replacement testosterone to hypogonadal males clearly increases sexual activity (Laschet 1973). The link between testosterone and aggression, on the other hand, is far less clear.

A systematic review of the research indicates that there is very little basis to the widely accepted idea that there is a causal relationship between testosterone levels and human aggression. Albert, Walsh, and Jonik (1993) argue that it is not testosterone that directly mediates aggression in humans, but rather the functioning of particular brain systems, especially the limbic system, including the amygdala and the hypothalamus. (The authors do not explore the possibility that high prenatal testosterone levels may indirectly affect aggression by affecting the early organization of limbic system functioning, a possibility I will explore below; see Collaer and Hines 1995.) Even among rodents, testosterone does not mediate all aggression, but only specific types of aggression, including aggression toward unfamiliar male rats, or aggression toward familiar male rats when dominance is in question. Testosterone-dependent aggression in rats can be identified by ritualized behaviors, including the presence of piloerection and a lateral attack pattern, in which the rat rises up on its toes, arches its back, approaches the target laterally, and pushes against it with its flank or hind foot (Albert, Walsh, and Jonik 1993). When rats kill mice or fight when shocked, they do not display this set of hormone-dependent behaviors.

In humans, we have no idea what kinds of aggression are mediated by testosterone, if any, and which are not. If anything, the aggression that humans engage in is similar to the nonhormone mediated aggression engaged in by rats, because it is present at all age levels, is displayed by both men and women as well as directed at both sexes, and is not dependent on seasonal changes in hormone levels or events such as sexual activity (Albert, Walsh, and Jonik 1993). Further, the testosterone-based aggression seen in rodents does not necessarily have to have an analogue in people. There are many precedents for arguing a lack of continuity between species in the control of a complex behavior such as aggression. For instance, in the case of sexual reproduction, nonprimate females (and even nonhuman primates, such as the great apes), have an estrous cycle, in which they are sexually receptive only during a period of fertility, or in which they exhibit heightened sexual motivation during a period of fertility. In contrast, women can be sexually receptive during any part of their menstrual cycles (Albert, Walsh, and Jonik 1993). There are many discontinuities and differences between the social and biological processes of rats and humans, yet the assumption that testosterone is responsible for aggressive human behavior stems mostly from research with rats. Does this ready assumption about the causal links between testosterone and aggression allow us to ignore the harder-to-address complex social factors that mediate aggression and violence?

Even in research with primates, levels of aggression are heavily dependent on the social, rather than the hormonal environment (Wallen 1996). For example, variability in levels of male rhesus monkeys' rough-and-tumble play and aggression was found to be influenced by the quality of the early rearing environment, while the elimination of neonatally secreted testicular androgen had no detectable effect on levels of threatening behavior or rough-and-tumble play (Wallen, Maestripieri, and Mann 1995; Wallen 1996). Higher levels of aggression among males were related to early rearing environments without mothers as well as to early brief periods of peer interaction (30 minutes per day), in contrast to continuous exposure to peers.

Returning to the evidence in people, there have been several types of studies exploring the links between testosterone and aggression. Some have compared the testosterone levels of high and low aggressive individuals. Others have explored the relationships between testosterone levels and aggression within both clinical (e.g., highly aggressive men) as well as nonclinical samples. The changes in aggression that occur at puberty and when testosterone is increased or decreased relative to normal levels have also been studied. A final group of studies has explored the relations between fetal androgens and aggression (Albert, Walsh, and Jonik 1993). Reviews of many studies exploring all five types of relationships show confusing, inconsistent and in many cases, largely negative results (see Archer 1991, 1994).

Perhaps the most dramatic illustration of the nonsignificant relationship between testosterone and aggression is provided by research on testosterone replacement in hypogonadal males. Although replacing testosterone does increase sexual activity, not one of eleven studies reviewed by Albert, Walsh, and Jonik (1993) shows that replacing testosterone results in a significant increase in anger, irritability, or aggression. Likewise, in males, lowering testosterone levels either via castration or by administering anti-androgens does not consistently decrease aggression. Similarly, levels of aggression in female to male transsexuals who are treated with androgens have not been found to vary after injections of testosterone (Cohen-Kettenis and Gooren 1992).

If there is any evidence to support changes in emotional functioning with androgen administration, it may be in levels of verbal aggression or anger. Athletes who were taking androgenic steroids were found to be more verbally aggressive compared to those who had used steroids in the past, but had discontinued their use (Galligani, Renck, and Hansen 1996). Androgen treatment has also been linked to reported increases in anger proneness among female to male transsexuals, although there were no changes in overt aggressive behaviors. This study is somewhat difficult to interpret, since the self-reported increases in anger proneness could come from an emerging male gender role identity, rather than from the androgen administration directly (Van Goozen, Frijda, and Van de Poll 1994).

Studies looking at whether rising testosterone levels at puberty result in heightened aggression also show no convincing effects. There is a 20–100-fold difference in testosterone levels pre- and post-puberty (Constantino et al. 1993). Yet, levels of aggression in males do not significantly rise at this time (Benton 1992; Halpern et al. 1993). There is, instead, a high degree of long-term stability to aggressive patterns, originating in early childhood (Eron et al. 1974; Eron 1992). A recent well-conducted study showed no relationships among testosterone levels, aggression, and pubertal development in a three-year panel study of 100 adolescent males (see Halpern et al. 1993).

The only studies that support a rather moderate relationship between testosterone and aggression are those that have correlated the two variables in samples of males, and especially within highly aggressive groups of males, who may represent a special group (see Benton 1992; Archer 1994). In particular, several recent studies have taken advantage of the relatively new technique of assaying testosterone levels via saliva, and have shown links between behavioral aggressiveness and testosterone in samples of aggressive children and adults (Dabbs 1993). For example, Scerbo and Kolko (1994) found that within a group of 40 disruptive 7–14-year-old children, aggression as rated by staff and teachers, but not by parents, was moderately related to testosterone levels, even when controlling for the children's age, height, and weight. Other recent studies have shown modest correlations between testosterone levels and levels of aggressive behaviors from childhood to adulthood (Windle and Windle 1995; Dabbs 1993), including the tendency to administer shocks (Berman, Gladue, and Taylor 1993), but have not found testosterone levels to vary among men who abuse their spouses versus those who don't (Lindman et al. 1992).

Higher levels of testosterone have also been related to alcohol and drug abuse, trouble with the law, extramarital affairs, divorce, having tattoos, going AWOL (in a study of over 4,000 military veterans [Dabbs 1993]), as well as to higher self-reported emotional expressiveness in middle-aged men (Julian and McKenry 1989). This research has found such a wide array of behaviors related to testosterone levels that it leads one to wonder how such diverse behaviors from getting tattoos to expressing emotions can be mediated by the same hormone.

The relationship between testosterone levels and aggression in women has been studied to only a limited extent, and the data are inconsistent and puzzling. Androgens are present in women, being released by the adrenal cortex and the ovaries. Although some studies show the same patterns of relationship between testosterone levels and aggression in females as that found in males (see Benton 1992), others show no significant relationships (Susman et al. 1987) or a pattern of negative relationships between testosterone levels and self-reported physical and verbal aggression (Gladue 1991).

Some studies also suggest that researchers have been too narrow in focusing exclusively on testosterone as a potential source for the hormonal origins of aggression. Estradiol levels are significantly higher in females than in males and are rarely a focus of research on human aggression, yet estradiol levels have significant positive correlations with self-reported physical and verbal aggression in both men and women (Gladue 1991). Estrogen has also been found to be related to offensive aggression in laboratory rats (Adams 1992).

What's troubling about the studies that do show links between aggression and testosterone is that they are correlational: that is, the direction of the effect is unknown. Aggressive and dominant behaviors can actually cause testosterone levels to rise. Studies have shown that among both people and animals, winning a competition, which causes a change in status, leads to higher testosterone levels. This may in turn have the effect of maintaining competitive and dominant behavior (Mazur, Booth, and Dabbs 1992). For example, if male rhesus monkeys low on the dominance hierarchy are placed with females they can dominate, their testosterone levels rise markedly. Moreover, when a male rhesus monkey is defeated in a fight, his testosterone level drops and remains low (Rose, Bernstein, and Gordon 1975).

In humans, the testosterone levels of chess players, as well as participants in more physical sports, have been found to be higher in winners than losers, despite equal levels of engagement in the game or sport. Over the course of a game, testosterone levels remain the same or increase in winning players, but drop in losing chess players. Also, in certain circumstances, competitors show rises in testosterone levels before their games, as if in preparation for the contest (Kemper 1990; Mazur, Booth, and Dabbs 1992).

The powerful implications of these data are that social processes may be partly responsible for higher testosterone levels in aggressive as opposed to nonaggressive men, particularly social processes that accord power and status to aggressive men (Kemper 1990). It may be these same social processes that allow men to be more aggressive than women, rather than hormonal influences.

Testosterone and Brain Organization

We have seen that the testosterone-aggression relationship is not a clear cause-effect process. In fact, it's not even clear that testosterone is directly related to aggression. It may only mediate aggressive behaviors indirectly, via at least two different mechanisms. The first possible mechanism is that testosterone may increase muscle size and strength, thus facilitating physical aggression (Albert, Walsh, and Jonik 1993). (In fact, men may be more aggressive than women simply because on average they do have greater muscle size and strength). The second possibility is that testosterone may have organizational effects on the central nervous system, particularly on the limbic system and the extent of cerebral lateralization in the cortex of the brain, which may predispose males and females to behave differently (Benton 1992).

How is testosterone related to brain organization? Based primarily on data from animals, it has been hypothesized that in humans, testosterone may affect the lateralization of the brain. Geschwind and Galaburda (1985) have hypothesized that testosterone actually inhibits the growth of the left hemisphere, allowing the right hemisphere to grow more rapidly.[4] More recent theorists, notably Levy and Heller (1992) have suggested that the development of the right hemisphere is actually stimulated by androgens, and that the maturation of the left hemisphere is both slowed by androgens and stimulated by estrogen.[5]

Rat studies have demonstrated that typical, noncastrated male rats have thicker right corti (outer brain layers) than do females. However, if males are castrated at birth, they have thicker left than right corti by 90 days of age (Diamond 1984), or they show a lack of any hemispheric asymmetries (Stewart and Kolb 1988). A corresponding pattern is seen in newborn females, who display the male pattern of thicker right corti after their ovaries are removed (Diamond, Johnson, and Ehlert 1979; Diamond, Dowling, and Johnson 1981, but also see Stewart and Kolb 1988). Exposure to testicular hormones may suppress the enlargement of the left cerebral cortex, as consistent with Geschwind and Galaburda's (1985) theory. The presence of testosterone at critical developmental periods has also been found to affect the organization of the forebrain, the hypothalamus and possibly the amygdala in rats (Meaney, Dodge, and Beatty 1981; Collaer and Hines 1995).

The effects of testosterone on human brain organization are largely theoretical. Because androgens are elevated in boys during 8–24 weeks of gestation, and again during the first 6 months of life, testosterone is thought to organize male brains differently from female brains (Collaer and Hines 1995). The problem is that, unlike researchers who work with animals, those who work with humans cannot systematically or experimentally alter hormone exposure levels and then examine subsequent brain development. In fact, studies with humans on the effects of testos-

terone on brain organization (such as those exploring the effects of androgen administration on transsexual patients, or the effects of genetic
defects) are quite unconvincing and are plagued with inconsistencies
such as heterogeneous populations who vary in age and background, as
well as confounding genetic, hormonal, and experiential factors (Tobet
and Fox 1992; Levy and Heller 1992). Stewart and Kolb (1988) point out
that even in rats, right-left asymmetries vary as a function of age, rearing
conditions, and part of the cortex measured, with few consistent patterns
of results. Some cortical asymmetries even reverse as a function of age. In
Stewart and Kolb's (1988) work with rats, males who had been exposed
to stress in the form of crowded housing and shipping conditions did not
show typical cortical asymmetries, nor did those raised in enriched environments.

Are there gender differences in human brain structures? If the answer
is yes, then it would follow that the expression of emotions may be
processed differently by the two sexes. We will see, however, that the
evidence is quite equivocal.

Bringing in Gender

The most widely disseminated theory of sex differences in the organization of the brain is that of female bilateralization (see Levy and Heller
1992; McGlone 1986; Iaccino 1993). This theory argues that there is
more symmetrical functional organization between the two hemispheres
in women than in men. This is thought to reflect both a greater bilateral
representation of language in the two hemispheres for women, as well
as less specialized right hemisphere spatial functions for women than
for men. A recent review by Levy and Heller (1992) elaborates on the
theoretical model by positing that men's right hemispheres lack the
emotional specialization of women's right hemispheres, just as women's
right hemispheres lack the spatial specialization of men's right hemispheres.

Many neuropsychologists have marshalled evidence for female bilateralization by pointing out that the corpus callosum is relatively larger in
women than in men. Gender differences in the size of the corpus callosum have been used to suggest greater interhemisphere connectivity in
women than in men (see Driesen and Raz 1995).

Although the popular press has now taken the sex difference in the corpus callosum to be an established fact, the actual data are inconsistent and confusing. The earliest study in this area, conducted by de Lacoste-Utamsing and Holloway in 1982, led to a flurry of interest. Amazingly, the results were based on a post-mortem examination of only 9 male and 5 female brains, and the results, showing an absolute larger corpus callosum size in women than in men, have been largely discounted (see Driesen and Raz 1995). A recent meta-analysis based on 11 studies indicates that the relative size of the corpus callosum, when adjusted for the overall size of the brain, is slightly larger in women than in men, with the effect size being low. When overall brain size is not taken into consideration, based on 36 studies, the opposite is true: the area of the corpus callosum is larger in men than in women, with approximately 21 percent of the distribution of men's and women's corpus callosum sizes being nonoverlapping. However, the authors of the meta-analysis are careful to point out that their analyses are tentative. The studies they review are plagued with measurement difficulties (Driesen and Raz 1995). For example, many studies do not control for the overall size of the brain; do not control for age (the size of the corpus callosum may decrease with age); use inconsistent methods to ascertain and divide the area of the corpus callosum, sometimes varying whether part or total volume of the corpus callosum is measured; and do not report the time from death to autopsy to corpus callosum examination. All of these variables may affect the results. Research results on this topic continue to be inconsistent. One recent study, published in 1995 (and not included in the meta-analysis), shows no significant gender differences in adult corpus callosum size based on magnetic resonance imaging (MRI) (Parashos, Wilkinson, and Coffey 1995), while others do show gender differences in the forebrain or cranial volume-adjusted size of the corpus callosum (Steinmetz et al. 1995; Johnson et al. 1996).

Even if corpus callosum (CC) size did differ for the two sexes, the meaning of this is far from clear, as pointed out by Driesen and Raz (1995). A larger CC size does not necessarily mean more fibers connecting the hemispheres and thus increased bilateralization. For example, in rhesus monkeys as well as in rats, there is no relationship between CC size and the number of axons (Driesen and Raz 1995; Juraska 1991). Some research with rats has indicated that females have *more* axons in the corpus callosum, while males have *larger* axons, suggesting complex gender differences at the ultrastructural level (Juraska and Kopcik 1988).

It is currently unknown how gender differences in the corpus callosum, including its absolute size, its size relative to the rest of the brain, or intrastructural differences interact to affect the emotional, cognitive, or behavioral functioning of the two sexes.

The other noteworthy information about the corpus callosum, as well as related brain structures, is that the type of rearing environment affects its development, both in size and at an ultrastructural level, at least in rats. Janice Juraska and John Kopcik (1988) raised male and female rats in either a complex environment, in which they had stimulating toys and same-sex rats to play with, or in an isolated environment, in which they were housed individually in a standard laboratory cage. Analyses of the rats' brains at 55 days of age indicated that there were no sex differences in corpus callosum size within each type of environment. However, gender differences manifested themselves in the diameter and frequency of unmyelinated and myelinated nerve fibers as a function of the type of environment in which the rats were raised. Males tended to alter their axon size in response to more complex environments; whereas females tended to increase their number of axons in complex environments. The development of the female rats' corpus callosum also showed a greater plasticity of response to the environment than did that of males, in that females from the complex environment had larger corpus callosums (in the anterior two-thirds) than females from the isolated environment, while males exhibited no differences between the environments in that section of their corpus callosums. Here again the evidence suggests that the social environment can affect, or at the very least, interact with gender differences in the development of brain structures.

Female Bilateralization?

The evidence for female bilateralization is based on studies of brain-damaged patients, as well as on tachistoscopic and dichotic listening data, in which visual or auditory stimuli are presented to either the left and right ear or to left and right visual fields. The rate and accuracy of processing between left and right sides is compared to evaluate left versus right hemispheric functioning. Moreover, left and right hemisphere involvement in various tasks have been measured by looking at cerebral blood-flow patterns, EEG activation patterns, auditory evoked potentials, PET (positron emission tomography),[6] or CT (computed tomography) scan patterns in particular locations of the brain in response to stimuli or in response to reported mood.

In some language tasks, men show more of a right-side advantage than women show, meaning that they are relying more on left hemisphere processing. Women sometimes rely on both left and right hemisphere processing for language-related tasks. Female bilateralization is also supported by some studies of brain-damaged patients that have indicated that women are less apt to suffer from speech disorders or aphasia after left hemisphere damage than are men and are also less likely to suffer from nonverbal disorders after right hemisphere damage than are men (see review by Levy and Heller 1992).

However, the results of these studies are task-specific. For example, verbal tasks such as defining vocabulary words support the bilateralization hypothesis because they are affected by both left and right hemisphere damage in women. In contrast, in tasks involving basic speech or oral fluency, such as naming words that begin with a specific letter, left frontal activity occurs in both men and women (Kimura and Harshman 1984), with women being just as asymmetrically organized as men.

Moreover, sometimes studies directly contradict the bilateralization hypothesis, but are interpreted in such a way that bilateralization is supported. For example, a frequently cited study in the literature (Gur et al. 1982) found that during a verbal task, both men and women showed an increase in left hemisphere blood flow. However, during a spatial task, women exhibited greater increases in right hemisphere blood flow relative to left hemisphere blood flow than men did. This seems to contradict the idea that women are less lateralized than men. However, the increased blood flow has been interpreted to mean that women were exerting greater effort at the spatial task because of weaker right hemisphere abilities; in other words, they used right hemisphere abilities in conjunction with left hemisphere abilities (Iaccino 1993). Interestingly, this convoluted argument has not been applied to a recent study that used magnetic resonance imaging (Shaywitz et al. 1995). This study showed gender differences in cerebral blood flow during a task involving judging rhymes for visually presented nonsense words. Activation of the inferior frontal gyrus region of the cortex was lateralized to the left hemisphere in males, but was bilateral in females. No one argued here that the cerebral blood-flow changes in men's left hemispheres were due to a relative weakness and actually reflected a bilateral strategy!

In fact, it is quite common in biopsychological research for researchers to interpret both decreased and increased brain activation in a specific brain region as evidence that the region is weak for a particular skill. Thus, when activation is decreased, it is argued that the region doesn't mediate a skill; but when activation is increased, it is argued that the region is exerting greater effort in mediating a skill and thus also usually doesn't mediate it. What this means, essentially, is that researchers can interpret almost any results they obtain in accordance with their pre-existing biases about gender.

As argued by several researchers, the evidence for the female bilateralization theory is inconsistent and task-dependent (Hahn 1987; Silberman and Weingartner 1986; Bryden, McManus, and Bulman-Fleming 1994). The degree of lateralization differs depending on how stimuli are presented, with subtle variations of stimuli producing differences, as well as factors such as attention, memory, and reporting biases also affecting lateral asymmetries (Hahn 1987). For example, although men have a right-ear preference in approximately half of the dichotic listening tasks, half of the studies show no gender differences and a few report reversed asymmetry (Iaccino 1993). Similarly, some tachistoscopic designs have failed to find the male asymmetrical advantage. Some, using the discrimination of melodies and nonlinguistic sounds, have shown reversed asymmetry, with women demonstrating stronger left-ear advantages and with men showing no asymmetry (Piazza 1980).

A few EEG and CT (computed tomography) studies have also not supported the female bilateralization hypothesis. For example, women were better able than men to maintain asymmetrical patterns of alpha activity in a biofeedback task (Davidson and Schwartz 1976). Kertesz and Benke (1989) argue that there are no gender differences in interhemispheric cerebral organization based on examining CT data concerning the location of lesions causing aphasia. They dismiss previous studies based on EEG and clinical evidence, claiming that such evidence is less reliable than CT evidence.

An alternative to gender differences based on lateralization are localization hypotheses, or hypotheses based on intrahemispheric gender differences (McGlone 1986). Data from Kimura's laboratory (1983) suggest that women may process language using different regions of the left hemisphere than men, thus accounting for sex differences in language recovery following brain damage. Female stroke patients suffer speech problems with damage to the front part of the left hemisphere (anterior regions), whereas male stroke patients suffer similar difficulties if the damage is in either the front or the back regions of the left hemisphere (anterior or posterior parts). Kimura's work places less emphasis on cerebral lateralization gender differences and more on gender differences in intracerebral organization.

It is apparent that the data are not all in on gender differences in cerebral lateralization. Even if gender differences were convincingly demonstrated to exist, there might still be variability in the way individual members of each sex were lateralized for particular functions. Moreover, women and men might still prefer to process tasks either using language or not using language, regardless of what their biological organization was. For example, women might take a visual-spatial task, such as a puzzle, and talk to themselves about the size and shape of each of the pieces, thus bringing in left hemisphere functions. A female preference for using language might be based on the fact that in development, caretakers emphasize language more to girls than they do to boys. Men, on the other hand, might simply use visual cues to guide them through successfully completing the puzzle (Iaccino 1993; Bryden, McManus, and Bulman-Fleming 1994). These differential strategies would not necessarily indicate differences in underlying biological structures. Perhaps the same biological structures can function differently at different times.

Subcortical Gender Differences

In order to fully address the biological bases of gender differences in emotional expression, I also will look at gender differences in subcortical structures. Significant sex differences in various morphological characteristics of the medial nucleus of the amygdala (sexual dimorphisms) have been found in squirrel monkeys, toads, and rats (Tobet and Fox 1992). Although the amygdala has been hypothesized to mediate many sex-specific functions, such as gonadotropic secretion, sexual and play behavior, as well as the onset of puberty, none of these functions has actually been correlated with the observed biological sexual dimorphisms (Tobet and Fox 1992).

Several examples of sexually dimorphic structures within the preoptic anterior region of the hypothalamus have also been identified in several species of animals, including rats, gerbils, ferrets, and guinea pigs. In humans, the third interstitial nucleus of the anterior hypothalamus (INAH-3) has been identified as sexually dimorphic (see Tobet and Fox

1992). This area is involved in the expression of male sexual behavior, and recent studies have shown smaller nuclei in heterosexual men than in presumed heterosexual women; as well as smaller nuclei in homosexual men as compared to heterosexual men (LeVay 1991; Tobet and Fox 1992). However, Tobet and Fox (1992) point out that the INAH-3 differences between homosexual and heterosexual men may be due to circulating levels of androgens, which may decrease in people with AIDS. All of the homosexual men in LeVay's study had AIDS, while only one third of the heterosexual men had AIDS. Confounding issues such as these mean that the studies on people need further replications to be convincing.

Cerebral Lateralization and Emotion

Researchers interested in the question of biological gender differences in emotion assume that if men and women differ in cerebral lateralization, they may process emotions differently. What are the links between cerebral lateralization and the expression of emotion? Studies on how the brain processes emotion have been conducted using three types of populations: normal groups; brain-lesioned groups, who have diagnosable, and often localized, brain impairments; and mood-disordered populations, whose emotional expressiveness may differ from that of normal groups.

Brain-emotion relationships in all three groups vary depending on whether you are talking about expressing emotion through the face, voice, behaviors, physiological processes, or words. It is actually quite difficult to disentangle the underlying biology of these modalities, since people often express emotion using all five. Further, even when you may think that someone is expressing anger merely through facial expressions or behaviors, they may actually be engaged in verbal thought, holding a silent conversation with themselves, a process that would be quite difficult to measure (see Feyereisen 1991). The issue is further complicated because the expression of emotion brings in a multitude of central nervous system functions, is subject to both involuntary and voluntary control, and involves not just mood states and arousal, but also cognitive functioning and attentional processes (Damasio 1994; Kolb and Whishaw 1996).

In general, the right hemisphere of the cortex (especially the right frontal lobes) appears to be specialized for vocal and facial expressiveness, as well as for physiological arousal (Silberman and Weingartner 1986). For example, the left side of the face (mediated by the right hemisphere) typically displays more intense emotional expressions, regardless of valence, than the right. This finding is more consistent when asking people to pose expressions than when analyzing their spontaneous expressions (Silberman and Weingartner 1986). However, even some studies of spontaneous facial expressions, including videotaped recordings of people's facial expressions while eating in restaurants, or discussing emotional experiences in laboratories, have found a left-side bias in facial expression (Moscovitch and Olds 1982; Silberman and Weingartner 1986). Other researchers have taken photographs of people posing particular emotions, cut these photographs down the midline, and then asked judges to rate the intensity of the expression produced by pasting together mirror images of each half. When two left halves of the face are pasted together, a more intense expression results than when two right halves are viewed (Sackeim, Gur, and Saucy 1978).

Several other studies suggest that emotional intensity is mediated by right frontal activation. Individuals with greater right frontal activation during rest periods report more intense fear in response to films than do individuals with greater left frontal activation (Tomarken, Davidson, and Henriques 1990). A similar pattern manifests itself in infancy. Infants with greater right hemispheric activation while resting are more likely to be distressed when separated from their mothers. Inhibited children, who show unusually high levels of fear, also show greater EEG activation in the right than in the left frontal areas (Kagan 1994).[7]

Vocal expressiveness is also mediated by the right hemisphere. For example, patients with right hemisphere lesions who are asked to convey anger, happiness, and sadness while reading content-neutral sentences do so with more monotony in their voice quality than do patients with other types of lesions, or than normal individuals do (Tucker, Watson, and Heilman 1977; Feyereisen 1991). Ross and Mesulam (1979) describe patients with right hemisphere strokes whose speech lost its emotional intonation in the absence of either aphasia or mood disturbance.

On the other hand, the left hemisphere, which is specialized for language functioning, is certainly involved whenever there is verbal mediation in the expression of emotions. For example, Safer and Leventhal (1977) presented spoken sentences to one ear at a time, and found that the right ear (or left hemisphere) judged the emotional tone of sentences by making use of verbal content; the left ear (or right hemisphere) used tone of voice, not the content, to judge the emotional tone of sentences.

The right hemisphere is also involved in mediating physiological arousal in response to stress. For example, right hemisphere–damaged individuals show reduced autonomic responses (skin conductance) in response to electrical stimulation (Kolb and Whishaw 1996). Also, when people view emotionally arousing films selectively with only their right hemispheres, they show more autonomic nervous system activation, as measured by heart rates, than people who view the film exclusively with their left hemispheres (Dimond and Farrington 1977; Wittling and Roschmann 1993). In these studies, films are restricted to either left or right hemispheres using either special contact lenses or a complex film setup in which participants' eye movements are monitored and controlled so that they can perceive the film only in one visual hemifield.

Lateralization and Positive versus Negative Emotions

The expression of positive emotions (cheerful or euphoric) appears to be mediated by the left frontal hemisphere, while the expression of negative emotions (depressed, fearful, sad) appears to be mediated by the right frontal hemisphere (Heller 1990).[8]

Evidence supporting this position comes from several sources, including the hemisphere-restricted film procedure, which showed that normal adults judged films to be more unpleasant when processed exclusively with the right, as compared to the left hemisphere (Dimond, Farrington, and Johnson 1976; Wittling and Roschmann 1993). Studies of brain-damaged people have indicated that left brain-injured patients are more likely to become clinically depressed, while right-brain-injured patients are more likely to become inappropriately cheerful (see Sackeim et al. 1982; Robinson et al. 1984). Other studies have simply asked people to grimace using the left or right sides of their faces, and have subsequently asked them to report on the quality of emotions they experience. Left-sided grimaces resulted in more reports of negative emotion, and right-sided grimaces resulted in more reports of positive emotion (Iaccino 1993).

The same hemispheric pattern has been demonstrated in young infants. In response to separation from mothers, infants' positive moods are accompanied by greater left frontal activation, whereas negative moods show the opposite pattern (Fox and Davidson 1991). That the left hemisphere has a special role in regulating positive mood states is also suggested by the fact that dopamine, thought to be related to reward mechanisms that mediate positive affect, may be more present in the left than the right hemisphere (Oke et al. 1978).

How can we account for the contradiction that the right hemisphere is specialized for general emotional expressiveness, yet the two hemispheres seem to differentially mediate positive and negative emotions? Several possibilities have been raised to account for this incongruity (see Kinsbourne and Bemporad 1984; Silberman and Weingartner 1986). One is the idea that both hemispheres become involved when emotional tasks are complex or detailed. A second idea is that the right hemisphere is responsible for controlling the balance between positive and negative affects, being the more dominant hemisphere in terms of emotional processing. Yet a third possibility is that the studies showing hemisphere emotion specialization, as opposed to those showing right hemisphere unilateral involvement, tend to be newer studies with access to improved technology. Since the range of human emotions includes more negatives than positives, older studies may have assumed that negative emotions and general emotional expressiveness were synonymous (Silberman and Weingartner 1986).

Communication between Brain Regions

Many theorists and researchers make the point that emotional expressiveness depends not only on the integrity of specific brain regions, but also on the quality of communication between the two hemispheres, which takes place through the forebrain commissures, including the corpus callosum, and through subcortical structures. Interhemispheric communication can include both facilitory as well as inhibitory influences. Researchers have suggested that the right hemisphere may modulate the positive emotion associated with the left hemisphere (Heller 1990). They have also suggested that the left hemisphere, using language, may play an inhibitory role with respect to the negative expressiveness of the right hemisphere. In other words, using left hemisphere–based language may help to minimize the experience of right hemisphere–based negative emotional intensity (Silberman and Weingartner 1986; Heller 1990; Fox and Davidson 1991).

Communication between cortical and subcortical structures is also critical to emotional expressiveness. Subcortical structures, such as the amygdala, thalamus, and hypothalamus, all of which have links to the cortex, are involved in the regulation of physiological, autonomic responses linked to emotion, such as changes in blood pressure, heart rate, and respiration (Kolb and Whishaw 1996). They are also involved in emotional behaviors such as fear and aggression (LeDoux 1993). For example, monkeys with missing or damaged amygdalas are less fearful of threatening stimuli than are monkeys with intact amygdalas. Electrical stimulation of the amygdala in rats elicits a pattern of behaviors that mimic natural states of fear, including increased startle responses (Davis 1992). Further, the amygdala is part of the medial temporal lobe region of the brain, and temporal lobe lesions and epilepsy produce changes in emotional behavior, such as increased anger, aggression, and emotionality (Bear and Fedio 1977).

That both cortical and noncortical processes are involved in facial expressions has been extensively demonstrated. Patients with a lesion on the cortical motor strip (part of the frontal lobes) may be unable to pose a smile when asked to do so, but are able to spontaneously smile in response to a humorous situation (Rinn 1991). Conversely, patients with lesions in subcortical systems, especially the basal ganglia, can pose emotional expressions but cannot show spontaneous emotion. This is seen in Parkinson's disease, characterized by a "masked face" syndrome, in which facial expressiveness is quite muted. Parkinson's disease affects the neurotransmitter systems of the basal ganglia (Kolb and Whishaw 1996).

More complex emotional processing that involves higher cognitive functions, such as interpreting the meaning of situations, also involves bidirectional cortical-subcortical connections. For example, the cortex may be involved in inhibiting the amygdala, the thalamus, and hypothalamus, and may also be stimulated by them. Although it is not clear exactly how subcortical systems interact with the cortex to modulate emotion, there are many rich neuroanatomical connections between the frontal lobes and the limbic system, as well as the possibility of many indirect connections via neurotransmitters. These frontal-limbic connec-

tions were the basis of the cottage industry in frontal leukotomies (famil-
iarly known as frontal lobotomies), which presumably had the goal of
managing aggressive behavior.

Gender, Emotion, and Lateralization

It is difficult to know whether or not there are gender differences in any
of the brain-emotion relationships I have discussed. Most researchers
who study the biology of emotions do not report their findings separately
for each sex. Moreover, there are no consistent sex differences in studies
testing the lateralization of emotional functioning. Some studies find
laterality effects in men, but not women, while others find laterality
effects in women, but not men (see Silberman and Weingartner 1986).
An oft-cited study in the literature, that by Moscovitch and Olds (1982),
showed that when men and women were videotaped in restaurants, the
proportion of women who showed more left-sided facial expressions
(implicating the right hemisphere) was significantly greater than the
proportion of men who did so. Yet, the researchers did not replicate this
sex difference in three other studies they did on the same topic.

There are some intriguing suggestions that the biological processes
that mediate emotional functioning may differ in men and women. For
example, in one study, different hemispheric patterns for women and
men were noted in conjunction with pathological (inappropriate and
involuntary) crying and laughing, which occurred subsequent to brain
infections, degenerative diseases, lesions, or seizure disorders. Men were
equally likely to present laughing as crying following left-sided damage,
whereas women were three times as likely to present crying than laughing following left-sided damage. Both sexes were more likely to manifest
laughing rather than crying to right-sided damage, but this effect was
stronger for men than for women (Sackeim et al. 1982). These data raise
the possibility that the two sexes differ in the degree to which negative
and positive emotions are lateralized.

A recent and fascinating study, foreshadowing more sophisticated
studies to come, used positron emission tomography (PET) data to look
at gender differences in brain activation patterns during self-induced
affect states. Ten men and ten women were asked to recall sad, happy, or
neutral life events. It was found that women activated a significantly

wider portion of the limbic system than did men during transient sadness, even though the two sexes reported similar changes in mood during the task (George et al. 1996). (On the other hand, the content of sad memories differed for the two sexes. Both sexes tended to remember deaths, separations, and illnesses, but men remembered more career disappointments and losses than did women). Unfortunately, there are many possible interpretations for the results of this and similar studies that have shown more symmetrical frontal activation on the part of women than men when sadness is induced (see Pardo, Pardo, and Raichle 1993). As Mark George and his colleagues point out (1996), women may have been experiencing more emotion than men even though the two sexes reported similar mood levels. Alternatively, sex differences in brain activation may be because men and women used different methods to induce their sadness, for example visual imagery versus verbal cues. The final possibility, of course, is that the two sexes are characterized by divergent brain processes for similar types of emotional functioning.

In brief, there are few conclusions that can be drawn about how gender differences in brain processes, if indeed they do exist, affect gender differences in emotional expressiveness.

Developmental Processes: Some Hypotheses

Some data suggest that male infants may be *more* intensely expressive of emotions (especially distress) than are female infants, but become relatively *less* expressive as they develop. Although far from conclusive, developmental studies on cerebral lateralization can be used to generate hypotheses about this shift. Some studies indicate that girls may show patterns of lateralization for processing speech and music like those of adults earlier than boys do. Further, both dichotic listening and visual-tactile cross-modal tasks indicate that in boys, the right hemisphere may be relatively more mature than the left; while in girls, the left hemisphere may be relatively more mature than the right (Taylor 1969; see review by Levy and Heller 1992). For example, one study showed that by 6 months, female infants were responding to music and speech stimuli in ways similar to that of adults, with greater EEG left hemisphere activation to speech stimuli and greater right hemisphere activation to musical stimuli. In contrast, unlike adult males, 6-month-old boys had greater right than left hemisphere EEG activation for both speech and musical stimuli (Shucard, Shucard, and Thomas 1984).[9]

If it is true that young males rely more on the right hemisphere, this may be related to their expression of intense emotions, since the right hemisphere seems to mediate emotional intensity (Fox and Davidson 1991). Once the left hemisphere matures in males, gender differences in the pattern of emotional expressiveness may flip, with less intense and dysphoric emotions expressed by males as compared to females.

There is also some evidence that attaining puberty at later ages is associated with greater cerebral asymmetry. Both boys and girls who mature later tend to do better on spatial as opposed to verbal tasks, suggesting greater asymmetry (Waber 1976). The rate of pubertal maturation may also affect emotional functioning, either by affecting bilateralization or by affecting self-esteem and social relationships. Research has shown that girls who are earlier maturers (attaining puberty at a young age) express higher levels of sadness and spend less time with peers than do later maturers (Susman et al. 1985). This leads to the speculation that earlier maturation, bilateralization, and the expression of negative emotions may all be linked. However, this is only a speculation, since it leaves out the obvious social causes for early maturers' negative emotion, including isolation from the peer group.

OVERVIEW. Can the gender differences I have reviewed in the first several chapters be linked to gender differences in the biology of emotional expression? Unfortunately, the role biology plays in these processes and the precise mechanisms through which it operates are still unknown. Men have higher testosterone levels than women, and testosterone has been tied to the expression of aggression in some samples of men. However, even these seemingly indisputable facts are qualified by studies showing that testosterone may be the result and not the cause of aggressive behaviors.

There are plenty of hypotheses about biologically based gender differences in emotional functioning. But at the moment they are only hypotheses. For example, the more intense facial and vocal expression of emotions by women is consistent with several biological sex difference theories, including greater interhemispheric connectivity and a more active role played by the right hemisphere in emotional functioning in females relative to males. Also, the more frequent verbal expression of emotions by women than by men is consistent with the idea that women have better linguistic abilities than men do. Whether or not women's relatively better language abilities are due to bilateralization is ambiguous. Bilateralization alone, even if it does exist in women, is not sufficient to explain their enhanced emotion-language abilities (see Kolb and Whishaw 1996). In fact, bilateralization in men is associated with dyslexia, stuttering, and other language disorders. Even if women are more bilateralized than men, we can easily argue that their greater bilateralization may be caused by the differing social inputs they receive.

Most important, I have emphasized that even if there are biological differences between males and females, these differences may be the result, not the cause, of variations in emotional expressiveness. At the very least, gender differences in emotional expressiveness are the result of complex interactions between biological predispositions and social interactions. The biological underpinnings of emotion tell only a partial story about the origins of gender differences in emotional expressiveness. The rest of the story is told by culturally determined gender roles, socialized by families, peers, and society in interaction with biological predispositions.

7

Transactional Relationships within Families

A little boy baby and a little girl baby act differently. That's what causes you to bring them up in certain ways.

—Sally, age 42

Parents are driven by their kids, who are driven by their environments. You try to treat sons and daughters equally, but you don't. They're definitely different.

—Mark, age 42

In this chapter, I begin to unravel the intertwined family threads that contribute to the development of gender differences in emotional expression. One of these threads weaves together infants' temperament with the differential socialization of emotion for the two sexes. I will argue that during the first several years of life, there are subtle differences in girls' and boys' temperamentally related behaviors that evoke divergent reactions from parents. In turn, this creates different trajectories for the development of emotional expressiveness in girls and boys.

The process by which children with different characteristics and needs elicit different reactions from their parents is known as a reactive or an evocative effect (Scarr and McCartney 1983). I will review evidence that infant girls are more verbal, more sociable, less active, less easily aroused in response to stimulation, and more able to regulate their arousal than are their male counterparts. Parents may express different emotions toward their sons and daughters, such as warmth or anger, because of these early differences.[1]

How parents respond to their children leads to a further divergence in their sons' and daughters' behaviors and in the emotions associated with those behaviors. For example, children who are sociable and who are responded to with warmth will continue to be sociable and may even become more sociable than they were initially. Parents whose children are sociable may themselves become more sociable than they were. In a continuous series of cyclical responses, parents and children influence each other over time, each subtly transforming the others' original characteristics in what is called a transactional model of development (Sameroff 1975).

Children's emotional development is not only influenced by parents' and children's characteristics, but also by strong cultural norms to socialize children in gender-specific ways. Even if boys and girls did not differ in any of their characteristics at birth, parents would feel pressured to socialize their daughters and sons differently in accordance with the values of the family's culture. Cultural expectations in the form of "display rules" dictate when, how, and where it is acceptable to express specific emotions.

Across several different cultures, including Norway, Sweden, Denmark, Finland, England, and the United States, women are stereotyped as more emotionally expressive, especially as more loving, nurturing, empathic, and affectionate than men (Hesselbart 1977; Eagly and Wood 1991; Fabes and Martin 1991; Dember et al. 1993; Roberts, Howe, and Dember 1995). They are believed to have more expressive faces, voices, and hands; to smile, laugh and gaze more; and to be more skilled in understanding nonverbal cues, such as facial expressions (Hall 1984; Briton and Hall 1995). Men are perceived as adventurous, logical, nonemotional, skilled in math and science, and self-confident. They are represented in impersonal, individualistic terms such as assertive, dominating, competitive, and cognitive (Dember et al. 1993; Roberts, Howe, and Dember 1995). For both children and adults, the emotions of sadness, love, and fear are attributed to and are seen as appropriate for females but as inappropriate for males, while anger and aggression are attributed to and are seen as appropriate for males but as inappropriate for females (Kelley et al. 1978; Birnbaum, Nosanchuk, and Croll 1980; Birnbaum 1983; Eagly and Steffen 1984; Fabes and Martin 1991; Karbon et al. 1992).[2]

Parents, consciously or not, are heavily influenced by gender-role stereotypes and are themselves the products of gendered values in the culture, including the values surrounding the power and status differences between men and women. Since most parents want to raise children who are well liked and socially acceptable in the culture in which they live, parents tend to raise children whose emotional expressiveness conforms to the stereotypic views of the larger culture (Ruddick 1982).

In brief, the child's temperament, the parents' culturally based gender-role attitudes, and the parents' own characteristics are crucial to development. In this and the subsequent two chapters, I will develop a transactional model for the emergence of gender differences in emotional expressiveness that integrates the contributions made by these many diverse factors. I will especially emphasize the bi-directional influences between characteristics of parents and their children that form a mutually interdependent feedback system.

Early Differences between Girls and Boys

Infant boys and girls differ in some subtle and some not-so-subtle ways within the first year of life. On average, girls learn expressive language earlier than boys do (Schachter et al. 1978; Huttenlocher et al. 1991). They have better and earlier language skills than boys have, including more extensive and earlier vocabularies, reading abilities, and word fluency (Iaccino 1993).[3] Infant boys exhibit higher activity levels than infant girls exhibit (Eaton and Ennis 1986), a characteristic that remains stable, or even increases, throughout development (Eaton and Yu 1989). In addition to higher activity levels, boys are relatively less mature in some self-control and self-regulatory processes than girls are, learning such processes as fine motor control (for example, managing scissors), toilet training, and the inhibition of inappropriate behaviors later than girls (Barfield 1976; Kochanska et al. 1996). In the realm of emotion, there is evidence that boys are more easily aroused than girls are in certain situations (Fabes 1994). Finally, infant girls may be more sociable than infant boys, as indicated by their early responsiveness to caretakers' social signals as well as to their empathy in response to others' distress (Sigman and Kasari 1994; Zahn-Waxler et al. 1992).

Several of the characteristics that I have identified as displaying early gender differences, including self-control processes, arousal, and activity levels fall under the umbrella of infant temperament. I will elaborate what we know about gender differences in each of these characteristics, including the current state of our knowledge regarding their biological or social bases. My emphasis will be on how these early differences set up qualitatively different parent-child interactions for each sex, ultimately affecting emotional functioning.

Language

Some research suggests that boys and girls differ in their propensity to learn expressive language, with girls acquiring more extensive vocabularies at earlier ages than boys, especially from 14 to 20 months (Schachter et al. 1978; Huttenlocher et al. 1991). It is possible that the differing language acquisition rates of males and females are due to varying amounts of encouragement they receive for communicating through language, and not to any biologically based language capabilities. For example, 12- and 18-month-old boys have been found to receive more negative reactions when attempting to verbally communicate than girls receive (Fagot and Hagen 1991), and mothers have been found to imitate their 10- to 14-month-old daughters' speech-relevant sounds at higher rates than they do their sons' (Masur 1987). A recent meta-analysis concluded that parents, especially mothers, talk moderately more to infant girls than to boys, using a higher quantity of speech but not speech that is longer in duration or higher in complexity (Leaper, Anderson, and Sanders 1998; see also Huttenlocher et al. 1991).

Either in response to their daughters' language abilities, or because of their own gender stereotypes, mothers use a greater variety of emotion words when talking to their preschool daughters than to their preschool sons (Dunn, Bretherton, and Munn 1987; Fivush 1989, 1993; Zahn-Waxler et al. 1993). Parents not only speak more frequently and about more varied emotions to their 18- to 24-month-old daughters than to their sons, but they also elaborate narratives more with daughters, including asking questions and embellishing on the information in the story (Reese, Haden, and Fivush 1996).

By 24 months, girls produce more emotion words than boys produce (Dunn, Bretherton, and Munn 1987), and by 70 months, they mention more emotion words when talking about past events than boys mention (Adams et al. 1995). Between the ages of 3 and 6, when asked to tell stories about past experiences with their parents, girls produce narratives that contribute more internal-state information (about feelings and wishes) and more affect modifiers (emotional responses about people or events; for example, "That was my favorite part," or "I had fun"), and they increase their use of both of these types of language from ages 3 to 6 more than boys (Reese, Haden, and Fivush 1996).

Some studies have found that fathers, too, speak more about emotions with their daughters than with their sons (see Adams et al. 1995). In fact, Schell and Gleason (1989) found that father-daughter dyads used the highest frequency of emotion words compared to mother-son, mother-daughter, and father-son dyads, avoiding only the word "disgust."

The fact that mothers and fathers talk more with their daughters than with their sons about emotion has powerful implications for how girls learn to express their feelings. The use of language can symbolize absent objects and people, and can communicate the abstract and private experience of emotion as well. Talking about something can also substitute for demonstrating it through actions (see Fraiberg 1959; Bloom and Capatides 1987). Emphasizing the verbal expression of feelings may teach girls to use more verbal, rather than behavioral strategies for emotional expression.

In brief, girls' tendency to be particularly receptive to language, and parents' tendencies to view girls as more language-oriented, may result in different kinds of parent-child interactions for boys and girls. This may ultimately lead to a greater verbal expression of feelings by women than by men.

Activity Levels

That boys are more active than girls, play more roughly when toddlers and preschoolers, and use more space playing at any given time than girls use (Barfield 1976; Frieze and Ramsey 1976) are gender differences that were ubiquitously noted among the parents who participated in my research project. One mother in my research study illuminated this perspective as follows: "Boys are different than girls. They're more physical when they're younger so they need a little more control . . . I think people who have both sexes (sons and daughters) are very aware of it."

The research literature confirms that boys have higher activity levels than girls have, from late infancy through the preschool years (Eaton and Ennis 1986; Kohnstamm 1989; Goldsmith, Buss, and Lemery 1997). The average difference for boys and girls on measures on motor activity is estimated to be one half a standard deviation. As Eaton and Ennis (1986) point out, the average boy (at the 50th percentile) is more active than

69 percent of girls. Maccoby (1998) argues that the gender difference in activity levels is primarily manifested not when children are playing alone, but when playing with peers, who are usually same-sex peers. Boys' high activity levels may be partly a consequence of the types of play in which boys engage when interacting with other boys (Maccoby 1998).

Data on over 4,500 infants in the 1959 to 1961 Copenhagen birth cohort revealed that boys reached three milestones significantly earlier than girls (as reported by mothers in diaries), including lifting their heads while lying on their stomachs, standing with support, and crawling independently (Reinisch et al. 1991). They also tended to walk with support somewhat earlier than girls. The timing of these developmental milestones may reflect boys' higher activity levels relative to girls, but in any case, once these milestones are achieved, they enable boys to be increasingly more physically active and independent at earlier ages than girls.

Activity levels have been shown to have significant genetic components, based on observer ratings as well as mechanical measures using actometers (Saudino and Eaton 1991, 1995; Saudino, Plomin, and De-Fries 1996; Goldsmith, Buss, and Lemery 1997). Activity levels compared in members of identical versus fraternal twins, at the ages of 7 months and 3 years in one study and 14, 20, and 24 months in a second, have shown modest evidence of heritability (h^2 ranged from .20 to .28; Saudino, Plomin, and DeFries 1996); while heritability in older children (17 months through 8 years) has been estimated to be as high as .72 based on maternal reports (Goldsmith, Buss, and Lemery 1997). Also interesting is that while activity levels correlate modestly in same-sex fraternal twins, they do not do so in opposite-sex fraternal twins (Goldsmith, Buss, and Lemery 1997). Possible explanations for this finding include the hypotheses that activity levels are influenced by genes that are biologically sex-limited, that people may respond in more divergent ways to opposite-sex twins than to same-sex twins, or, more probably, that biological and social factors interact in affecting activity levels.[4]

The higher activity levels of sons may influence parents to control and restrict their sons' behaviors. High activity levels can be disruptive for social relationships as well as for academic learning, and parents may feel the need to "rein in" their sons. In fact, one study suggested that activity and emotional intensity may be linked—3- to 5-month-old infants with higher activity levels were those who were significantly more likely to cry when a reward that they had been trained to expect did not material-ize (Fagen and Ohr 1985). In the face of such behaviors, parents may feel that their sons need help with emotional regulation and control.

Meta-analyses have shown that parents, particularly fathers, tend to be somewhat more restrictive with their sons than their daughters (Lytton and Romney 1991).[5] For example, Snow, Jacklin, and Maccoby (1983) found that fathers gave twice as many vocal prohibitions to their one-year-old sons than to their daughters. This difference was accounted for by the fact that the boys were attempting to touch more forbidden ob-jects than the girls, perhaps related to boys' higher activity levels. (For both sexes, there was a significant correlation between object touching and the frequency of fathers' prohibitions.)

Mothers also report more punitive responses to their sons' emotional expressiveness than their daughters', including such behaviors as send-ing their sons to their rooms if they express sadness (Eisenberg, Fabes, and Murphy 1996). Mexican fathers also use control strategies more often with their 7- to 12-year-old sons than with their daughters, includ-ing more prohibiting, scolding, criticizing, ordering, threatening, and acting hostile (Bronstein 1984). A recent study showed that when chil-dren were involved in discipline situations, both mothers and fathers of boys rated themselves as angrier than did parents of girls (Garner, Robertson, and Smith 1997). And in turn, these parental reactions of anger or punitiveness may serve to minimize sons' positive emotional expressiveness. For example, Garner, Robertson, and Smith (1997) found that the higher fathers' levels of reported anger were to their sons, the lower their sons' levels of expressed positive emotion were in a play situation, suggesting that fathers' anger may have minimized the expres-sion of their sons' positive emotional expressiveness. (Alternatively, it is also possible that fathers may have expressed more anger toward sons who expressed fewer positive emotions.)

In brief, parents may become controlling, angry, and restrictive in response to boys' activity levels, which may ultimately contribute to the minimization of their sons' positive emotional expressiveness.

Arousal Levels, Emotional Regulation, and Self-Control Processes

There is converging evidence that young boys become highly aroused more quickly than infant girls, and then have difficulty in stabilizing or regulating their arousal levels. Arousal refers to the ease and intensity with which various behaviors and physiological responses become elicited by stimulation, including visual, auditory, motor, or olfactory stimulation (see Kagan et al. 1994). The arousal itself may consist of motor activity, vocalization, smiling, fretting, crying, heart rate reactivity, or other measures of physiological arousal.

Evidence for gender differences in arousal levels comes from a variety of experiments. In one, mothers were instructed to stop smiling, talking, or playing with their infants. In this situation, 6-month-old sons evidenced more negativity, fussiness, and twisting and turning away from their mothers than daughters evidenced (Weinberg et al., in press). In another, preschool boys were found to peak in their skin conductance levels more quickly than girls when watching a film about a child with burns who was teased about her scars. Boys' skin conductance levels also took longer to return to baseline levels than did girls (Fabes 1994). Further, teachers rated preschool boys' emotional intensity and arousal as higher than girls', endorsing such items for boys as "this child gets easily upset; this child can't stand waiting; this child does things vigorously." Since parents did not rate their sons and daughters differently on these dimensions, Fabes (1994) hypothesizes that boys may be particularly likely to respond with increased arousal and intensity within the context of peer interactions occurring in school.

Once arousal occurs, it requires self-regulatory abilities in order to maintain stable functioning (Rothbart 1989). Girls may exhibit self-regulatory abilities at younger ages than boys exhibit (see a review by Bjorklund and Kipp 1996). For example, mothers and their infant daughters were able to repair and change mismatched emotional states (e.g., mother is happy while baby is sad) at faster rates than mothers and their sons (Weinberg et al., in press). One- and three-month-old girls were also found to be able to calm themselves after a fussy period without maternal intervention more often than boys (Moss 1974).

Similarly, caretakers rate toddler girls as being able to regulate their emotions better than toddler boys, including being able to inhibit and control inappropriate behaviors (Goldsmith, Buss, and Lemery 1997). Two- to three-year-old girls have been reported to show higher levels of compliance with their mothers' prohibitions than boys (Kochanska and Aksan 1995). Girls were better able to control behaviors such as waiting turns, slowing down motor activities, and whispering than were boys, as well as better able to perform tasks requiring resistance to temptation, such as holding a piece of candy on one's tongue without eating it (Kochanska et al. 1996). Eleanor Maccoby (1998) suggests that girls' higher self-regulatory abilities may be related to their use of language.

What effects would sons' relatively high arousal levels and relatively poor self-regulatory abilities have on their parents? Some research evidence suggests that parents attempt to help their sons regulate their arousal through the quality of their social interactions. Mothers of infant sons have been found to respond to their sons' expressions with similar expressions of their own. In contrast, they respond to their daughters' facial expressions with expressions different from those their daughters produce. The greater matching between mothers' and sons' affect may help boys to regulate their emotional expressiveness (Tronick and Cohn 1989).

Even in older, elementary school–aged children, mothers have been found to display different emotions to their sons and daughters. While watching a distressing film together about spina bifida, mothers of girls exhibited less facial sadness, but more facial distress, than did mothers of boys (Eisenberg et al. 1992). It may be that the mothers exhibit less distress in an effort to help their sons regulate their arousal, or even to withdraw from emotional stimuli in an effort to decrease arousal.

Perhaps in response to their sons' high arousal and activity levels, parents not only modulate their own facial expressions, but they teach their sons to control their feelings. In contrast, daughters are taught to experience their feelings fully. For example, analyses of conversations between preschoolers and their parents have shown that mothers elaborate more on the causes and consequences of feelings with sons, thus teaching them the importance of controlling feelings. With daughters, they focus and elaborate on the emotion state itself, thus teaching their daughters to be sensitive to the emotional experience and minimizing the importance of control (Fivush 1993). Fathers also emphasize explanations and understanding events for their sons, even when the task is not set up to be about feelings (Bronstein 1988). This may lead to a more analytical, abstract way of expressing feelings by sons than by daughters.

Kochanska and Aksan (1995) found some evidence to indicate that mothers adjust the quality of their disciplinary style (how controlling and demanding they are) according to the extent to which their children comply with their demands. More compliant children elicit less negative forms of control, such as threats and demands, and more gentle guidance, such as polite requests and praise. If boys internalize maternal prohibitions less readily than daughters, then mothers may be motivated to use a more negative and controlling parenting style with their sons, which in turn may induce sons to display decreased positive emotion relative to daughters.

In brief, sons' high arousal levels and relatively weak regulation abilities may drive parents to minimize the emotions they express to their sons, to use a controlling discipline style, and to teach their sons to regulate and contain, rather than to intensely express their feelings. Although it is a big leap to use these socialization patterns as a causal explanation for men's patterns of emotional expressiveness, it is not an unjustified one. The parent-child interaction patterns I have described may partially help to explain adult males' relative minimization of verbal and facial emotional expressions.

Sociability, Social Referencing, and Empathy

Infant girls aged 6 to 18 months are more sociable than infant boys. By sociability I mean relatively high levels of responsiveness to social interactions and social cues, including high levels of empathy for others. For example, research has shown that the extent to which female newborns gaze at pictures of faces and checkerboards is related to the amount of face-to-face interaction they have previously engaged in with their mothers. In contrast, male newborns' gazing behavior is related to the amount of time they have previously spent in quiet and awake states, and is unrelated to their interactions with their mothers. These data suggest that social interactions contribute to girls' visual behaviors more than boys' (Moss 1974), and are consistent with observational studies suggesting that infant girls are better able to make eye contact with their mothers than are boys (Silverman 1987).

From 6 to 12 months, girls initiate more interactions with their mothers than boys do, even though mothers' behaviors toward their sons and daughters have not been found to differ (Gunnar and Donahue 1980). Moreover, 12-month-old infant girls use cues in their mothers' and strangers' faces and voices to guide their own behaviors more than boys do, a behavior termed social referencing. For example, when their mothers display fear, girls stay away from a toy, while boys do not (Rosen,

Adamson, and Bakeman 1992). Similarly, 8-to 30-month-old girls look at an experimenter's face more than boys do when a small moving robot toy enters the room (Sigman and Kasari 1994). Young girls also respond more to their mothers when their mothers speak to them than boys do (Clarke-Stewart 1973; Klein and Durfee 1978; Gunnar and Donahue 1980).

By one to two years of age, young girls also express more sympathy and distress than boys when perceiving someone in pain (Zahn-Waxler et al. 1992; Zahn-Waxler, Robinson, and Emde 1992). They also look longer at a distressed adult who pretends to hurt her finger with a hammer than boys do (Sigman and Kasari 1994). Young girls have also been found to comfort their depressed mothers, no matter how severe their mothers' depression is. In contrast, only those boys who have severely depressed mothers are likely to comfort them. Boys may need stronger cues than girls to elicit empathy and caretaking skills (Radke-Yarrow et al. 1994).

There is no direct evidence that these early gender differences in sociability are biological in origin. We cannot point to one area of the brain and say with certainty, this area of the brain is responsible for sociability, and it functions differently in girls than it does in boys. However, some suggestion that it may be biological in origin comes from behavioral genetics studies. Zahn-Waxler, Robinson, and Emde (1992) studied empathy in monozygotic (identical) and dizygotic (fraternal) twins who were 14 and 20 months old. Twins' reactions were coded when mothers and experimenters pretended to hurt themselves. Not only did the researchers find sex differences, with girls showing more empathic concern, prosocial behavior, and self-distress than boys, but they also found that the children's observed empathic concern and maternal reports of children's prosocial patterns showed evidence of heritability at 14 and 20 months. Unresponsiveness and active indifference also showed genetic influences at both 14 and 20 months. Although the heritability estimates for empathic concern are modest ($h^2 = .23$ at 14 months and $h^2 = .28$ at 20 months) and indicate that strong environmental influences are also likely to be operative, they suggest a partial biological basis to early empathic and prosocial behaviors.

What impact would girls' relatively higher sociability have on their parents' behaviors? Girls may not need to be exposed to exaggerated social or emotional cues, such as facial expressions, in order to understand how others are feeling, or in order for a satisfying interpersonal communication to take place. One study suggests that mothers may actually minimize how much emotion, particularly negative emotion, they express to their young daughters (Rosen, Adamson, and Bakeman 1992). Mothers were trained to make a fear face to a novel toy, and experimenters assessed how the mother's facial cues affected the infant's behaviors. Mothers made less intense fear faces toward their daughters than toward their sons, even though they were not trained to do so. Interestingly, mothers' fear faces, which were stronger for their sons, affected their sons' behavior less than their daughters'. Daughters stayed further away from the novel toy when mothers made fear faces than when they made happy faces. In contrast, sons approached the toy regardless of their mothers' facial cues. Thus, mothers may have tried to exaggerate and emphasize feelings of fear in order to get their bold and somewhat socially unresponsive sons to pay more attention to the warnings conveyed in their facial messages. Differing patterns of social and emotional interaction for mothers and their sons compared to mothers and their daughters may result from gender differences in responsivity to social cues as well as activity levels (Eaton and Ennis 1986).[6]

Other evidence indicates that mothers express more positive emotions to infant daughters than to infant sons, perhaps because their daughters are more sociable than their sons. Mothers of 2–3-year-olds have been found to engage in mutual smiling more often with their daughters than with their sons (Parnell 1991). Also, mothers of preschool girls report expressing more positive emotion in the presence of their children than do mothers of preschool boys (Garner, Robertson, and Smith 1997; see Stifter and Grant 1993 for a similar result with 10-month-olds and their mothers). Engaging in more positive emotional experiences with their mothers may lead girls further down the path of being positively emotionally expressive and sociable toward others.

Mothers of kindergarteners and second-graders have also been found to be significantly more emotionally responsive to their daughters than they are to their sons in the course of telling them stories from wordless picture books. Responsiveness included warmth, physical proximity, physical contact, a pleasant tone of voice, and the extent to which mothers directed their children's attention to the story by saying, for example: "Look at this," or "This is just like what happened to you" (Fabes et al. 1994). Although it is certainly probable that mothers may change their child rearing style with daughters to be consistent with their feminine gender-role stereotypes (see Fabes et al. 1994), it is also possible that mothers alter their child rearing style in response to their daughters' sociability.

Can we use the data on infant girls' relatively higher sociability to formulate hypotheses about why adult females are more verbally and facially expressive of emotions than adult males? First, it may be that females express relatively more intense emotions than males express because they are biologically predisposed to express feelings, to be sensitive to emotional cues, and to be empathically responsive when people are distressed. Alternatively, girls' sociability as well as their heightened emotional expressiveness may be learned, the result of their frequent and positive interactions with others.

Both of these hypotheses are too simplistic, however, since they fail to recognize that development proceeds as a result of complex interactions between biological predispositions and cultural socialization. It is more likely that girls' initial propensity to be sociable facilitates patterns of parent-child interaction that affect girls' later emotional expressiveness. For example, I discussed data that mothers provide less intense and fewer facial cues for girls to follow than they do for boys. Mothers may feel that girls don't need such cues because they are already socially attuned and responsive. In the absence of overt emotional cues from others, girls would be forced to learn two things in order to communicate their needs and to get those needs met. The first would be to recognize quite subtle markers of emotions in others; the second would be to use their own emotions as guides or monitors to their behaviors and relationships. Both of these lessons would be instrumental in promoting gender differences in emotional expression, in which girls both recognize emotions and express them more frequently than boys do, especially using facial expressions and words. This argument is consistent with previous research showing that adults who report their families to be relatively inexpressive have better emotional recognition abilities than do adults who report their families to be more expressive (Halberstadt, 1984).

Maximizing Strengths?

Parents may also socialize their sons and daughters differently because they perceive them as having different vulnerabilities and strengths. Ruddick (1982) points out that parents fear for their children's vulnerabilities. Protecting children is a high parental priority. With their sons, parents see high activity and arousal levels, relatively poor self-control processes, and emotional dysregulation in the face of some stressors. All of these processes may signal relative neurological immaturity. For example, boys' relatively high cortisol levels in response to stress (see Chapter 4) may signal that their adrenocortical systems are more neurophysiologically immature than are girls', because higher cortisol levels are associated with less advanced development as measured by gestational age (see Davis and Emory 1995). Boys' higher activity levels may also be due to their relative immaturity. Eaton and Yu (1989) found that, in 5–8-year-olds, children who were more physically mature (based on the proportion of adult height they had attained) were less active. Girls were more physically mature than boys were, and this difference partly accounted for the gender difference in activity level. (By itself, gender accounted for 25 percent of the variance in activity level; when maturity was accounted for, the variance accounted for by gender decreased to only 15 percent of the variance).[7]

The combined effect of these immature behaviors may be that parents perceive their young sons as relatively more vulnerable than their daughters. Sons can't regulate their own behaviors and may be more dependent on others for a longer period of time. Parents may have an especially strong negative reaction to these vulnerabilities because their sons' perceived vulnerabilities fly in the face of male stereotypes, which depict males as strong, independent, and invulnerable.

In the face of their perceived vulnerabilities, parents may attempt to teach their sons how to protect themselves by maximizing an existing strength, namely high activity levels. Sons may be taught to use rough-and-tumble play to retaliate or defend themselves in situations in which they appear to be at risk of being hurt or harmed. Research shows that parents do emphasize retaliation for their sons, with mothers accepting retaliation as a reasonable response to angry situations (Fivush 1989, 1993).

In contrast to sons, daughters' strengths may be perceived as sociability and verbal skills, while their perceived weaknesses may be their relatively low activity levels. Maximizing their daughters' strengths would mean teaching them not to rely on physical aggression or retaliation when threatened, but to maintain and restore social relationships using words, emphasizing their language skills and sociability (Fivush 1989). The fact that sons and daughters are taught different adaptive behaviors based on their pre-existing strengths and vulnerabilities may then serve to exaggerate very early gender differences, with girls becoming increasingly social and verbal and boys becoming increasingly physically active and interested in controlling their environments.

There is a great deal of evidence to indicate that physical activity and retaliation versus harmonious social relationships are differentially emphasized in the types of play opportunities provided for boys and girls. Whether or not they are emphasized for the reason I am asserting, that is, in an effort to maximize the existing strengths of each sex in response to perceived vulnerabilities, is another question entirely, a question upon which little evidence bears directly. It is also true that these differing emphases for the two sexes are those culturally stereotyped to be differentially acceptable for the two sexes. In all probability, the differing ways parents socialize their sons and daughters reflects an interaction between parents' attempts to shape their children's expressiveness in socially acceptable, gender-stereotypic ways and their reactions to their children's perceived strengths and vulnerabilities.

Cultural Values: Mad versus Sad

So far, I have focused on how boys' and girls' cognitive and behavioral predispositions may influence parents' behaviors. Parents are also influenced by cultural values about gender roles. In American culture, masculine boys are expected to be aggressive and active and to minimize expressions of vulnerability, warmth, and sadness. Feminine girls are expected to minimize aggression and expressions of anger and to maximize expressions of warmth, sadness, and vulnerability (see Block 1973, 1984; Lerner 1980).

How do parents facilitate gender differences in emotional expression in accordance with cultural values? In research that analyzed parent-child conversations, mothers and fathers were found to emphasize different consequences for the expression of sad and angry emotions by their preschool and school-aged daughters and sons (Fuchs and Thelen 1988; Perry, Perry, and Weiss 1989; Brock 1993). They spoke more about sadness, distress, fear, and positive emotional states with daughters than with sons and more about anger with sons than with daughters. They also actively attempted to minimize the extent to which their sons dwelt on sadness and their daughters dwelt on anger (Greif, Alvarez, and Ulman 1981; Fivush 1989, 1993; Brock 1993; Zahn-Waxler et al. 1993; Butler and Kuebli 1994; Adams et al. 1995). For example, mothers never used the word "angry" in creating a storybook for their preschool daughters, but did use it with their sons (Greif, Alvarez, and Ulman 1981).

Mothers also tended to use more positive than negative emotion words with their preschool daughters, but approximately equal numbers of positive and negative emotion words with their same-aged sons. When mothers of daughters did use negative emotion words, they attributed them to other people. In contrast, mothers of sons attributed negative emotions to the children themselves. In so doing mothers gave their daughters the message that it was not okay for them to express negative feelings, and in contrast, gave their sons the message that the expression of anger and negative feelings was okay (Fivush 1989, 1993). Mothers have also been found to respond in gratifying ways (e.g., attentive concern) to their 2 to 3½-year-old sons' expressions of anger. In contrast, they have been found to ignore or to attempt to inhibit their same aged daughters' expressions of anger. Depressed mothers differ in these gender-differentiated interaction patterns, with daughters' anger eliciting more attentive involvement from depressed mothers than sons' anger (Radke-Yarrow and Kochanska 1990).

In a fascinating series of studies, Fagot and Hagan (1985) and Fagot et al. (1985) found that in playgroups, adults paid more attention to 12–18-month-old boys' negative behaviors than they did to girls', even though the frequency of the behaviors did not differ for boys and girls. When the boys were engaged in negative and aggressive behaviors, including being physically aggressive, trying to take objects, verbalizing negative feelings, and verbally and nonverbally demanding attention, they got more attention than the girls got. Adults began to react strictly to both boys' and girls' negative behaviors by the time the children were age 2½, rather than acting differently toward each sex. However, by that time, sex differences in rates of aggression were established, with boys showing higher rates than girls. Boys were also found to receive more positive reactions from their parents for aggression at both 12 and 18 months. These data indicate that American parents and caretakers strongly, and sometimes unknowingly, reinforce boys' aggressiveness. [8]

Gender-Stereotyped Play

Meta-analytic studies have indicated that the most reliable gender difference in American socialization patterns is that both fathers and mothers encourage different activities for boys and girls, for example, doll play for girls and playing with trucks or engaging in team sports for boys, with fathers encouraging different activities for both sexes more than mothers (Lytton and Romney 1991; Rheingold and Cook 1975). Here parents may be responding both to the differing characteristics of each sex (for example, high activity levels versus sociability) as well as to gender-role stereotypes about male aggression and female sociability. These differing socialization practices in turn influence the course of emotional development. Playing with dolls provides more opportunities for learning about relationships and the emotions that accompany them, while playing sports provides more opportunities for developing physical skills.

Parents also encourage achievement, independence, control, cognitive mastery, and locomotor exploration more for boys than for girls (Block 1973, 1984; Weitzman, Birns, and Friend 1985), again perhaps as an adaptation to boys' activity levels. The freedom to explore is given more to boys than to girls throughout development. Girls play nearer to their mothers, are encouraged to follow their mothers around the house, are more closely supervised, and are allowed fewer independent excursions into the neighborhood than are boys (Block 1983, 1984). These patterns continue throughout adolescence. In a study of the types of tasks assigned to high-school students in Canada, Peters (1994) found that sons more often were given permission to use the family car and performed chores outside their homes, while daughters more often were given chores inside their homes. Weekend curfew observance was also perceived to be more stringent for daughters. These gender differences were maintained whether or not mothers worked outside the home.

Two studies illustrate the ways in which girls are encouraged to be sociable and somewhat dependent on others. In one, using memory and puzzle tasks, parents of 5-year-olds were more likely to respond to daughters by giving help and encouragement while they ignored or denied help-seeking requests by boys half the time (Rothbart and Rothbart 1976). Girls may eventually develop the expectation that help from others is necessary for successful achievement. In other words, the importance of relationships is emphasized for girls even in the context of a cognitive task. In the second study, fathers of school-aged children in Vermont were 3½ times more likely to engage in a conversation with their daughters than with their sons; but fathers were 4 times more likely to work on a computer with sons than with daughters (Bronstein 1988).[9]

More freedom to engage in locomotor exploration and cognitive activities may minimize the amount of time that boys spend in close dyadic relationships with others, and intimate relationships may constitute the very heart of where emotional expressiveness is learned.

Transactions in a Cultural Context

Interactions between parents and children occur within a cultural context, and how boys and girls' emotional expressiveness is socialized may differ from culture to culture. While there are very few studies on cross-cultural differences in the socialization of emotion for girls and boys, research has indicated that American parents do not seek to control aggression as much as parents in some European countries (Block 1973, 1984). Perhaps because of the cultural endorsement of aggression, American mothers from Pennsylvania, when talking to their 3-year-old children in unstructured audio taped conversations, referred to a wider range of feelings, and more often to negative feelings, including pain, distress, dislike, and anger than did British mothers from Cambridge. American mothers also referred to emotions more often in the context of disputes than British mothers did (Dunn and Brown 1991). American mothers may thus be more apt to promote the message that the expression of negative feelings is acceptable.

Moreover, not every ethnic or social class group within a single culture promotes the same message about how the two sexes should display emotion. For example, fascinating case-study research on inner city American teenage mothers and their daughters reveals that mothers were very clear that their daughters' reactions of anger and ensuing aggression were acceptable in certain situations, namely those in which their daughters were defending themselves against attacks by others, but were not acceptable in situations in which their daughters were being demanding or self-indulgent (Miller and Sperry 1987). This is a different message than mothers of middle-class daughters may impart, in which even aggressive self-defense strategies may not be encouraged.

Further, in a study of mother-child conflicts with 4–5-year-old children, Ann Eisenberg (1996) compared the interaction of mothers and their sons and daughters in Anglo and Hispanic middle- and working-class families. In general, working-class pairs, regardless of their ethnicity, had longer and more aversive conflicts involving mutual opposition and less clear resolutions than did middle-class pairs. This was especially true of working-class girls and their mothers. It may be that in the middle class, the expression of anger and conflict is viewed as dangerous to interpersonal relationships in jobs (Kohn 1963; Stearns and Stearns 1994) and is therefore prohibited in children to a greater extent than it is among working-class families.

OVERVIEW.   Emotional development unfolds as a result of interactions among the infant's characteristics (some of which may be biologically based), the parents' characteristics, the parents' attitudes and expectations, and the values of the parents' culture, including the parents' ethnicity and social class. A transactional model of development proposes that these interactions influence each other and shift over time.

Parents may interact differently with their sons and daughters because their sons and daughters have dissimilar characteristics and rates of development, as manifested in activity and arousal levels, sociability, self-regulation, and language abilities, and also because parents have different expectations for their sons and daughters in accordance with cultural gender stereotypes. I have suggested that parents may try to maximize their children's strengths in the face of perceived threats and vulnerabilities. Boys are socialized to become physically active and aggressive and to control rather than to express or experience their feelings, except for anger. Girls are socialized to become interpersonally oriented and verbally expressive of emotions that accompany sociability, such as warmth, vulnerability, sadness, and fear. There is a great deal of evidence to suggest that fathers and mothers actually create some of the gender differences in emotional expressiveness by encouraging and discouraging the expression of different feelings in their daughters and sons. They also provide different opportunities for their sons and daughters to learn about emotional expressiveness in the gender-typed play activities they provide.

The emotional development of the two sexes appears to follow divergent pathways very early in life. These pathways are not only a product of the differing ways mothers and fathers interact with their daughters as compared to their sons, but are also a product of the quality of the marital relationship. In the next two chapters, I will take a closer look at the effects of family relationships and interactions on the development of girls' and boys' emotional expression.

8

Gender Identification and
De-identification in the Family

I see my son as very much like me. When he was younger, 90 percent
of the time I could predict what he was thinking, what he was going to
say. And it would happen. My wife would be amazed.

—Bill, age 39

My son is who he is and I see him as separate from myself. Which is a
wonderment and a joy to me. To see a separate individual, who is
capable of different reactions than I have in some situations, I love
that. He's being his own person.

—Elizabeth, Bill's wife, age 38, interviewed separately

I really don't want to be strong. I don't want to be big and have
muscles.

—Sophie, age 7

In this chapter, I will evaluate the intriguing idea proposed by feminist
psychoanalytic theorists such as Chodorow (1978) and Fast (1984), that
the development of emotional functioning differs for sons and daughters
because primary caretakers are most often women. Same-sex identification is theorized to be especially characteristic of and formative for
mother-daughter relationships. And, conversely, mothers and their sons
may de-identify with each other, with sons attempting to become dissimilar from their mothers as a way of consolidating or maintaining their
gender role identities. For boys, differentness from their mothers is theorized to be critical in establishing a masculine, "other" identity, while
sameness with mothers threatens this (Fast 1984).

The most striking and counter-intuitive implication of this theory is
that even if mothers behaved in similar ways toward their sons and
daughters, the sons and daughters themselves might actually respond

147

differently to their mothers. For example, if sons attempt to consolidate a gender identity by becoming different from their mothers, then the more emotionally expressive their mothers are, the less emotionally expressive sons should be. The reverse should be true of daughters—mothers' and daughters' emotional expressiveness should be related to each other in a positive direction. These hypotheses are formulated in a cultural context in which emotional expressiveness is a salient and critical dimension on which the two sexes are stereotyped to be different. In other words, sons do not become different from their mothers on many other conceivable characteristics, such as walking backward instead of forward, because they do not view these characteristics as differentially sex-linked.

In both this and the subsequent chapter, I will be weighing the nature of the evidence that addresses this fascinating theoretical perspective, adding some refinements to the theory as I go along. Newly emerging data indicate that there may well be gender-differentiated interaction patterns between parents and their children that accord with the theory. However, the most striking omission in the theory is its failure to account for data showing that the quality of parent-daughter and parent-son relationships varies depending on how the entire family system functions. Moreover, I will contend that gender-differentiated patterns of interaction between parents and their young children may have more to do with gender differences in infant temperament and with cultural gender stereotypes than with patterns of same-sex identification in the family.

Reviewing the Theory

In order to be able to evaluate these theories, I will first explicate them, in particular the theory advanced by Nancy Chodorow (1978) in her influential book *The Reproduction of Mothering*. Her argument, primarily rooted in a Western cultural context, highlights the fact that mothers are most commonly their children's primary caretakers, and that fathers are often distant and unavailable to their children.

Mother-Daughter Relationships

Interacting primarily with a same-sex caretaker provides girls with a role model and love object with whom they can identify and to whom they can express and disclose feelings. Girls are therefore theorized to internalize a model of empathy, and their primary self-definition is rooted in relation, or connection, to their mothers.

Mothers and daughters have been theorized to have more permeable boundaries than mothers and sons have because of their same-gender identification (Jordan 1991; Chodorow 1978). Chodorow writes: "Because of their mothering by women, girls come to experience themselves as less separate than boys, as having more permeable ego boundaries. Girls come to define themselves more in relation to others" (p. 93). Boundaries refer metaphorically to the processes of differentiation and individuation that take place over the course of development; that is, the degree of closeness or distance between parent and child.

One way to think about boundary permeability is that it represents a continuum reflecting the extent to which two people in a relationship have shared and merged emotional experiences as opposed to distinct and unshared emotional experiences. For example, in a relationship with permeable boundaries, the two participants would be likely to express the same feeling in reaction to the same event, such as sadness in response to a loss. Alternatively, they would be able to ascertain what their partner was feeling, either because they were sensitive to nonverbal emotional cues emitted by their partner, or because the two partners would disclose to each other the feelings they were experiencing. In a relationship with less permeable boundaries, the participants might experience distinctly different feelings, such as relief rather than sadness, or would fail to realize or disclose to each other what each had felt.

When boundaries are permeable between mothers and their children, mothers can temporarily suspend their own emotional experiences in order to empathize with, or mirror and reflect back, their children's experiences (Stern 1985). (Alternatively, because of actual similarities between parents and same-sex children, parents may correctly guess what their children are feeling because their feelings happen to match those of their children.) When parents empathize with their children's feelings, it is hypothesized that their children learn to both fully experience and share their feelings with others. Children learn that their feelings are legitimate, and can allow themselves to experience feelings, even painful feelings, without distorting or denying them (Kohut 1971; Winnicott 1958).

In brief, close relationships with their mothers should allow girls to learn the subtleties of expressing and recognizing emotions in others (Chodorow 1978). The effects of greater rather than lesser boundary permeability would be to maximize intimacy and shared emotional disclosures, resulting in increased emotional expressivity and empathy.

However, boundary permeability in mother-daughter relationships may also have negative consequences. Same-sex identification for mothers and daughters may result in what Chodorow alludes to as "hyper-symbiotic" relationships, in which mothers do not allow their daughters to be separate from themselves, engaging in distorted projections of their daughters' needs (pp. 99–104). Mothers may only think that they understand what their daughters are experiencing. They may assume a false sense of similarity and impose their own feelings, or their gender stereotypes of what daughters "ought" to feel, onto their daughters' experiences. In contrast to empathic parents, "intrusive" parents demand that their children suspend their own emotional experiences in the service of attending to parents, rather than the other way around.

Chodorow notes that this process may lead girls to have a less distinct sense of themselves than boys, and she further states, almost as an aside, that girls may express and experience hostility in an attempt to free themselves from their mothers (see Chodorow 1978). Other theorists have asserted that an overcontrolling or intrusive parent is associated with deficits in the formation of the child's self, most notably the inability to deal with ambivalent feelings, as well as feelings of humiliation, rage, conflict, and fear of losing the parent (Kernberg 1975; Greenspan 1989). Rage and shame would be martialled to defend against the "intrusion" and to push the parent away, while feelings of grandiosity and precocious autonomy might also emerge to protect the integrity of the self (Kohut 1971; Modell 1963). The expression of negative feelings thus serves a communicative function, both protecting the child's sense of self (and the validity of his or her own unique emotional experiences) as well as increasing the distance between parent and child, helping to maintain separation and individuation.[1]

One final aspect of maternal behaviors that is related to the concept of boundary permeability is the degree to which mothers grant their children autonomy, or independence from parental influence. Autonomy requires cognitive/affective differentiation between oneself and others in the form of distinct mental representations and also requires the ability to regulate one's own needs, actions, thoughts, and feelings in the context of relationships (Hill and Holmbeck 1986; Anderson and Sabatelli 1990). In a Western cultural context, mothers who impede their children's autonomy are theorized to subtly communicate to their children that leaving their parents is forbidden and would be viewed as an act of disloyalty or betrayal. It is important to note here that the degree to which parents encourage their children to be autonomous reflects cultural values and varies a great deal among different ethnic groups. I will elaborate on this toward the end of this chapter.

Because of their same-sex identification, mothers should theoretically impede their daughters' autonomy more than their sons', inculcating the message that leaving the family is not acceptable, especially in pursuit of individual goals. The struggles for autonomy and the hostility that accompany them are theorized to be especially pronounced for girls in adolescence, when increased parent-child individuation becomes normative in Western cultures. Perhaps girls struggle partly because they identify with their mothers as same-sex role models who may have difficulty establishing their own autonomy and who also may feel helpless as a result of their low power and status within the culture (Blos 1962). Further, girls' difficulties in being autonomous are compounded by gender-role stereotypes that categorize women as passive and dependent.

When parents do not allow their adolescent children to separate, their children may express intense negative emotions as a way of asserting a sense of self and establishing distance. We have all heard children say, "Leave me alone, Mom," or using more colloquial language, "Get off my back, Mom," both intended to assert autonomy and both accompanied by negative emotion. The commonly used clinical term, "hostile-dependent," implicates the expression of hostility as a way of attempting to regulate, or even reverse, dependency in a parent-child or spousal relationship.

In brief, daughters' difficulties with separation and autonomy should be related to the expression of dysphoric emotions, especially in a Western context, in which autonomy is normative and adaptive. Further, daughters may express more dysphoric emotions than sons because of an identification with powerless mothers, and with gender roles and stereotypes that limit women's cultural and social power.

Mother-Son Relationships

The quality of sons' boundaries with their mothers is theorized to differ in many ways from that of daughters'. Early mother-son interactions provide boys with an opposite-sex role model from whom they are required to differentiate within the first few years of life in order to become male. Boys may communicate their needs for distance by minimizing emotional experiences and the disclosure of feelings, especially because emotions are culturally stereotyped to be "feminine." Further, expressing contempt toward their mothers, and ultimately toward all women, may be adaptive for some boys in their struggle to develop a male identity and to become autonomous (see Chodorow 1978, pp. 182–183). The boy's ambivalent relationship to his mother is also theorized to be overlaid by a competitive, rivalrous, and fearful stance that he develops in relation to his father.

In brief, the son's emerging masculine identity involves distancing from relationships with others, becoming goal-directed in the pursuit of individual, rather than communally shared goals, and expressing emotions that are adaptive for autonomy, competition, and disconnection, such as contempt. Aggression and the minimization of expressions of warmth may also help sons to maintain separation and individuation, as hypothesized by several analytic theorists (Edward, Ruskin, and Turrini 1991).

Other gender theorists have suggested that mothers may not be able to identify as completely with their sons as they do with their daughters, thus failing to provide their sons with the kind of empathic relationship they have with their daughters. In their efforts to raise socially acceptable sons who are assertive and have an independent sense of self, mothers may actively reject their sons' dependency before their sons are developmentally ready to be separate (Block 1984; Betcher and Pollack 1993). Because their intimacy needs are not met, sons may respond defensively by developing motives for control and autonomy as well by using aggression. Behaving aggressively may be a way of forcing recognition and intimacy from others (Benjamin 1988). In light of the research evidence in Chapter 7 that mothers actually mirror or match their infant sons' emotions more than their infant daughters' (Tronick and Cohn 1989), this theory appears to be limited, and may fail to address the complexities of these relationships over time. For example, if mothers do fail to empathize with their sons, it may be when sons are older, rather than younger.

The Father's Role

The distant father in the traditional family plays a critical part in these gender-differentiated outcomes for children. Despite the fact that more and more fathers express an interest in being involved with their children, researchers point out that fathers still spend relatively little time with them. Low estimates indicate that fathers spend ⅕ to ¼ as much time interacting with their children as mothers spend (Lamb and Oppenheim 1989), while even the highest estimates indicate that husbands of employed mothers spend between ⅓ and ⅔ the amount of time interacting with their children as mothers spend (Baruch and Barnett 1986a). The father's relative lack of involvement in child care is theorized to exclude representations of the father in the early organization of the child's self, with father-child identification never having the same potency as mother-child identification.

Distant fathers mean that sons have no male role models with whom they can share and express intimate feelings. Instead, sons may identify with what men are supposed to be like, rather than what they are really like. This process is termed positional identification (Chodorow 1978). Sons fail to internalize and identify with their fathers' unique values, traits, and attitudes, but rather emulate societal "macho" symbols, such as the John Wayne image, which represent bipolar opposites of the attributes stereotypically associated with women. In other words, sons base their gender role on the antithesis of the only relationship that they know intimately, that which they have with their mothers (Chodorow 1978).

For girls, distant fathers mean that girls do not have a relationship with an opposite-sex parent that allows them to differentiate from close relationships with their mothers. If fathers were more involved in family life, daughters might not have to express negative feelings as a way of communicating their needs for distance from mothers.

Evaluating the Theory

Chodorow has been criticized previously (see Rossi 1987) for cultural narrowness, for a lack of empirical evidence to support her propositions, as well as for a lack of specificity in the developmental timetable and processes involved in the emergence of the gendered patterns she proposes. However, in the past decade there has been an explosion of research on children's emotional functioning, and the data that have been generated are relevant for testing and evaluating Chodorow's ideas.

Some studies support parts of Chodorow's theory, at least for Western cultures, while others call for modifications or refinements of the theory.

In particular, emerging data indicate that the quality of same- and opposite-sex relationships within the family is not stable, but shifts as a function of who in the family is present. For example, detailed research has shown that the quality of mothers' relationships with their 13-year-old sons shifts as a function of whether or not fathers are present. Mothers become more positive toward their sons when they are with their husbands compared to when they are alone, becoming more engaged, secure, affective, consistent, and less bored (Gjerde 1986). The quality of father-son relationships changes in the opposite direction: it becomes more negative when mothers are nearby. In the presence of mothers, fathers become less involved, engaged, egalitarian, and more critical and antagonistic toward their sons than when they are alone. The important lesson to be drawn here is that the quality of relationships between any two people in a family is not consistent across contexts.

Parent-child relationships may also vary as a function of the family's composition, such as how many daughters are in the family. For example, some research has indicated that it is only when adolescents have a sibling of the opposite sex that they engage in increasingly divergent experiences from other opposite-sex adolescents. Only when adolescent boys have younger sisters do they show a greater increase over time in joint activities with their fathers. Similarly, only when adolescent girls have younger brothers do they spend increasingly less time with their fathers and increasingly more time in dyadic activities with their mothers (Crouter, Manke, and McHale 1995).[2] A conceptually related study has shown that fathers and mothers rate cross-sex activities for sons, such as playing with dolls, more negatively when they have only sons then when they have both sons and daughters. Interestingly, mothers tended to give their daughters more latitude about same-sex choices when there were no sons present in the family, rating same-sex toy choices for girls more positively in families with both boys and girls (Lansky 1967).

The critical importance of exploring entire family systems, not just dyads, for understanding gender development is also demonstrated by studies showing that birth order, marital status, and marital quality influence the quality of emotional functioning in parent-child interactions. For example, mothers smile more and express more playful affect in face-to-face interactions with their second-born than with their first-born children, regardless of gender, perhaps because they are less anxious around second-born children (Moore, Cohn, and Campbell 1997). And, highlighting the issue of marital status, Leaper and his colleagues (1995) found that single mothers, but not married mothers, were more likely to respond supportively (offering reassurance, affection, or praise) to the collaborative suggestions of their daughters than they were to their sons, such as "let's play together." It may be that single mothers have a more difficult time empathizing with their sons than married mothers.

Related findings have shown that opposite-sex interactions between parents and their preschoolers differ as a function of the parents' level of marital satisfaction. Mothers with low marital satisfaction are more likely than other mothers to respond negatively to their sons' negative verbalizations (Kerig, Cowan, and Cowan 1993). Some parents may relate to their opposite-sex children as if they were miniature versions of their spouses, and may displace both the negative and positive feelings they have about their spouses onto those children.

The fact that sons' and daughters' development differs in families with dissimilar gender composition, structure and marital relationships suggests that Chodorow and other feminist psychoanalytic theorists generalize too broadly across all types of families (see Assiter 1996). These theorists also inappropriately generalize from Western family life to family life in other cultures. There may not be a universal developmental process of establishing increasingly differentiated boundaries between children (especially boys) and their parents. In Eastern cultures, there may be less normative parent-child individuation involved in development, or fewer thoughts, feelings, and fantasies that are uniquely "owned" by the child and different from those of their parents (see Markus and Kitayama 1991). For example, in collaborative work I did with Anne Copeland (Copeland et al. n.d.), Asian and Asian-American families were characterized by having more permeable or merged boundaries than European-American families.

On the other hand, there are some intriguing ideas in Chodorow's theory about the salience of same-sex identification in family dyads, and about how identification relates to the development of emotional expressiveness. The most systematic way to evaluate Chodorow's theory is to specify what kinds of behaviors can be used to measure constructs such as identification, de-identification, and boundary permeability. The next step is to then turn to developmental studies that have explored these measures in relation to children's emotional expressiveness, even if these studies were not initially designed to test Chodorow's hypotheses.

Identification and De-identification

An important assumption that Chodorow makes is that mothers experience their daughters as one with themselves (p. 195). How might this hypothesis be tested? One way to measure perceived "oneness" would be to have mothers list characteristics of themselves, their daughters, and their sons. Researchers would then gauge how similar these descriptors are for mother-daughter versus mother-son dyads. In several elegant studies, Frances Schachter (1982) showed that two siblings in a family, particularly two same-sex siblings, de-identified with each other, attributing different personality characteristics to themselves versus their siblings. She also showed that in families with two same-sex children, each sibling in the family was likely to identify with a different parent. In other words, in a family with two daughters (or two sons), one child would more strongly identify with the mother, the other with the father. Schachter called this phenomenon split-parent identification, and she argued that it tended to supersede, or take precedence over same-sex identification within these families.

Schachter (1982) collected data by asking college students and their parents whether they were alike or different in personality using 13 bipolar items, including achieving-nonachieving, conventional-unconventional, active-passive, and strong-weak. The identification score consisted of the number of traits shared in common by a child and her parents; for example, two points would be given if both child and parent scored as active, rather than passive, and as conventional, rather than unconventional. There were certain types of families and situations in which same-sex parent-child identification, rather than split-parent identification, did prevail. The first was among families with three children, in which the third-born child was found to identify more with the same-sex parent rather than with the opposite-sex parent. The second was in families in which the sex of the child was the salient feature of his or her identity, such as the only boy in a family with three children. And the third was that in all of the families tested, boys identified with the potency attributes of their fathers, as measured by the items strong-weak, rugged-delicate, and deep-shallow. Boys described themselves as more similar to their fathers on these dimensions than would be expected by chance.

The complexity of Schachter's data highlights the importance of looking at gender identification within a family systems context. Same-sex identification, as measured by perceived similarity in personality, did occur, but mostly in families with a particular constellation of children, especially in those three-child families that had children of both sexes. And, in contrast to the hypothesized salience of mother-daughter identification, father-son identification was especially evident in Schachter's data.

In my work, I measured parent-child identification and de-identification by considering the extent to which sons and daughters chose to write about their mothers and fathers in open-ended stories they generated. This research relied on children's stories in response to pictures as windows to their relational and emotional worlds (see Figure 1, Chapter 1). There is accumulating research evidence that children's responses to stories may indeed reflect the reality of their social relationships. For example, Radke-Yarrow et al. (1988) presented 6-year-olds with a picture depicting an older child approaching a younger child while the child's mother entered the room. Children were asked what the mother would do. Those children who said that their mothers would punish them had in reality mothers who were significantly more negative with them (44 percent of the time) than children who interpreted the mothers' entrance in benign ways (18 percent of the time). The children who attributed punitive themes to the picture were also more likely to be rated by psychiatrists as having problems in the relationship domain.[3]

Turning back to my own research with school-aged children, I asked children to write stories in response to a picture of a boy or girl gazing into a mirror. I assumed that children who included parents in their stories (when there was no instruction to do so) were more preoccupied or identified with their parents than were children who did not. For example, typical stories that children write describe how characters feel about themselves, particularly about their appearance. When children integrate significant others, such as parents, into their stories, presumably their self-identities are more connected to (or less differentiated from) their parents than the self-identities of children whose parents do not spontaneously come to mind when they write a story.[4]

Chodorow's theory implies that girls should include mothers in their stories more than boys do. What did the results show? Both boys and girls included their mothers alone or both parents in their stories more frequently than they included their fathers alone.[5] There were no significant differences between the number of girls and the number of boys who included mothers and both parents in their stories (25 out of 85 girls and 18 out of 84 boys referred to mothers, while 13 out of 85 girls and 12 out of 84 boys referred to both parents). Fathers (in the absence of mothers) were included in stories more often by boys than by girls (5/84 boys; 1/85 girls), although this difference was not statistically significant.[6] The infrequent appearance of fathers in both boys' and girls' stories is consistent with Chodorow's (1978) argument that fathers are represented in the child's internal world less often than are mothers. It may also reflect the reality that when children do interact with their fathers, their mothers tend to be present.

In summary, the types of characters children included in their projective stories did not support Chodorow's hypothesized patterns of same-sex identification and opposite-sex de-identification, but did suggest father-son identification patterns that were also found by Schachter (1982). Girls did not include their mothers in their stories more than boys did.

Behavioral Imitation among Same-Sex Pairs

Another measure which can be used to study the extent of same-sex identification within the family is the prevalence of imitation among same-sex family members. It can be argued that imitation is one way in which identification is behaviorally evident. Identification involves transforming aspects of a relationship with another person into inner characteristics, including that person's perceived traits, values, attitudes, and behaviors.[7] When the level of identification is higher, the level of imitation should be higher, too.

It is clear that outside of a family context, children imitate same-sex people more than opposite-sex people when they believe that the same-sex people's behaviors are appropriate for their sex. In a classic study, Perry and Bussey (1979) presented children with 4 male and 4 female adults, who each selected one object from a pair, such as an apple versus a banana. The greater the consistency with which adults of the same sex picked a particular item, the more likely that children of the same sex would pick that item. For example, if only 2 women adults selected an apple instead of a banana, girls would be less likely to pick the apple than if all 4 women selected the apple. Further, when asked to rate their perceived similarity to each adult, both boys and girls were likely to rate themselves as similar to particular adults who behaved in exactly the same ways as other adults of that sex.

Perry and Bussey's (1979) work also showed that boys de-identified with a woman when she exhibited sex-appropriate behavior (that is, she chose items selected by other women). Boys who had seen the woman's behaviors in choosing apples or bananas actually chose fewer of her responses than did boys who had not seen her perform at all. There was no corresponding tendency for girls to de-identify with men. In fact, girls did not inhibit imitation of male-appropriate behavior when it was displayed by either a men or a woman, compared to girls who had no previous exposure to the adults. Bussey and Perry (1982) followed up this work by again showing that third- and fourth-grade boys rejected the preferences of opposite-sex adults more than girls rejected them.

Inside the family, there is surprisingly little research on patterns of imitation in same- and opposite-sex family members, especially research that focuses on the imitation of emotional expressions. One study indicated that mothers and their 10- through 14-month-old daughters were found to imitate each other's motor actions and verbalizations during bath-time and free play at higher rates than mothers and sons (Masur 1987). And Moss (1974) similarly found that mothers imitated their 1- and 3-month-old daughters' vocalizations more than their sons'. However, in direct contrast, mothers have been found to "match" or imitate their infant sons' emotional expressiveness *more* than they imitate their infant daughters' expressiveness (Malatesta and Haviland 1982; Tronick and Cohn 1989).

Many studies do show that levels of parents' and children's emotional expressiveness are similar, suggesting processes of imitation or identification (Halberstadt 1991). However, the evidence does not suggest that mothers and daughters show patterns that are more similar to each other than those shown by mothers and sons. Parents who express high levels of negative affect have sons *and* daughters who also tend to express high levels of negative affect (see also Halberstadt, Fox, and Jones 1993). The specific processes that mediate these family resemblances are not clear—they may be imitation, identification, similarities in parent-child temperament, or all three.

The studies that suggest parent-child similarities in emotional expressions, however, must be evaluated in light of other studies that have shown inverse patterns between levels of parents' and children's emotional expressiveness: that is, parents who are low in emotional expressivity have children who facially and behaviorally express higher levels of positive affect (see Halberstadt 1991; Halberstadt, Fox, and Jones 1993). My own data show that mothers who express more warmth and nurturance have daughters who express *less* intense positive affect than other daughters. They also have sons who, unlike them, minimize the intensity of both positive and negative emotions they report (Brody, in press). These studies suggest that even if imitation and same-sex identification occur in parent-child relationships, they are accompanied by a process of differentiation, in which parents' and children's emotional styles become dissimilar to each other. Differentiation may occur in specific contexts and at specific developmental stages, as I will elaborate below.

Boundary Permeability

Chodorow's argument rests on the idea that same-sex identification between mothers and daughters is accompanied by more permeable boundaries than those boundaries that exist between mothers and sons. Boundary permeability is a difficult and complex construct to measure. Data from the infant literature that capture aspects of the construct include the extent to which mothers "match" or imitate their children's emotional expressions, display emotional expressions toward their infants that may or may not be reciprocated, and shift their emotional expressiveness over time to be either similar to or complementary toward their infants' expressiveness. Findings from these studies are intriguing and encouraging for feminist psychoanalytic theories, but are far from conclusive. My evaluative summary focuses first on gender-differentiated interaction patterns in mother-infant relationships, and subsquently on those same patterns in older children's relationships with their mothers. The quality of daughters' and sons' relationships with their fathers, another critical aspect of feminist psychoanalytic theories, will be my focus in the next chapter.

Several infancy studies have shown that mothers "match" their sons' facial expressions more frequently than they match their daughters' (Malatesta and Haviland 1982; Tronick and Cohn 1989; see also Robinson, Little, and Biringen 1993). One clue as to why this might occur was provided by Moss (1974), who found that mothers of 3-week-old and 3-month-old infants held, attended, stimulated and looked at their infant sons more than their infant daughters—a sex difference that disappeared when the infants' levels of irritability, fussing, and crying were controlled. In other words, it may be that mothers match their sons' expressions in an effort to minimize and contain their sons' irritability and arousal levels.

On the other hand, mothers and daughters are in matching states involving object play (the proportion of time they are each attending to or playing with objects in the same one second interval) more often than mothers and sons, and mothers are able to repair mismatches in affective states with their infant daughters more quickly than with their sons (Weinberg et al. in press). (This may be helped by the daughters' own self-regulatory abilities, see Moss 1974.) Mothers also engage in more mutual smiling with toddler daughters than with sons (Parnell 1991), and mothers of 10-month-old girls report expressing more positive affect than mothers of boys (Stifter and Grant 1993).

Some of these data are confusing with respect to their relevance for the concept of boundary permeability. For example, do more frequent displays of both negative and positive affect on the part of mothers toward their daughters reflect more permeable boundaries? If boundaries are defined as the mutual disclosure of feelings, the answer may be yes, but a thorough answer requires looking at the mutual patterns of emotional expressiveness between mothers and their children, something few researchers have studied.

Further, when mutual patterns of emotional expressiveness have been studied, it is not clear what these data mean with respect to boundary permeability. If mothers match their daughters' emotional expressions less frequently than they match their sons', does this necessarily mean that their boundaries with their daughters are less permeable, or that they are less empathic toward their daughters than toward their sons? Perhaps not. They may be paying close attention to their daughters' emotional expressions, but responding with a different expression of their own—an expression that is still sensitive to their daughters' affective state but provides new emotional input to their daughters.

In a study that tried to tease apart some of these issues, Robinson, Little, and Biringen (1993) videotaped mother-infant interactions when the infants were 18 months old and then again when they were 24 months old. They measured maternal intrusiveness, maternal sensitivity, and maternal-infant matching of positive and negative emotions. Intrusiveness consisted of the degree to which mothers were or were not available for their children's emotional communication, "balancing self-initiated interventions with those signalled by the child." Sensitivity was coded by behaviors such as the mother's responsiveness and her ability to soothe her infant. Also measured was the child's role in regulating maternal emotion, consisting of the proportion of shared mother-child emotional states that the child created.

The results of the study indicated that mothers did not show differences in the levels of intrusiveness or sensitivity they displayed toward their sons and daughters. Yet, there were gender differences in the patterns of mother-infant interaction over time. Overall, a complex set of results suggested that mothers' and sons' emotional interactions were reciprocal, whereas mothers' and daughters' emotional interactions were compensatory. For example, sons who were more positive at 18 months had mothers who were more positive at 24 months. For daughters, the reverse was true: there was a negative association between mothers' and daughters' emotions over time. Also, the degree to which individual daughters could create shared emotion states with their mothers was a predictor of their mothers' emotional sensitivity, their mothers' matching behaviors, and their mothers' positive emotions over time. This was not true of sons.[8] The authors suggested that mothers allow sons to take the lead, thus promoting their autonomous functioning, while they socialize daughters into a more mutual social or affective system. Daughters seem to play a greater role in regulating the quality of shared affective interactions with their mothers than sons do.

These data show that the quality of relationships between mothers and their daughters and sons may take dissimilar trajectories over time, affecting the quality of their emotional expressiveness in different ways. Clarke-Stewart and Hevey (1981) also found gender-differentiated shifts in mother-child patterns of interaction, with mothers and their sons becoming more distant over time, but not mothers and their daughters. In their study, mothers and their 12- to 30-month-old children were observed 12 times (at one- to two-month intervals) in naturally occurring interactions at home. Although mother-son physical contact initiated by mothers started at higher levels than mother-daughter contact, it declined significantly over time more for sons than it did for daughters.

This was particularly notable because physical contact was related to social interactions for boys.

For older children and adolescents, boundary permeability in mother-child relationships has been measured by the degree to which relationships are characterized by the empathic sharing of emotional experiences, feelings of closeness, perceived and observed intrusiveness on the part of mothers, and autonomous functioning on the part of the child. Some studies have indicated that there are gender-differentiated patterns in these processes, as I will highlight below.

SHARING EMOTIONAL EXPERIENCES. Studies have indicated that both mothers and fathers of school-aged children report discussing emotional reactions and experiences more with daughters than with sons when asked questions such as, "How do you respond to your child when she or he is distressed or worried?" (Eisenberg et al. 1991a). Other research has shown that both mothers and fathers of 6–7-year-old children respond more positively when their daughters communicate feelings to them than when their sons do (Russell and Russell 1987). Children's perception of this interaction is revealed in my story data. When writing stories, school-aged daughters created characters who disclosed feelings to both parents significantly more often than did sons (8/85 girls; 1/84 boys).[9]

As discussed in Chapter 7, mothers have been found to be more emotionally responsive to their daughters than to their sons in several studies, including being warmer toward them while telling them stories from wordless picture books (see Russell and Russell 1987; Fabes et al. 1994a). Similarly, in recorded conversations about children's typical school experiences during the first and last months of kindergarten, mothers and daughters more often discussed interpersonal and emotional experiences than did mothers and sons, such as a teacher's relationship with the child, or the child's shared experiences with peers. Mother-son dyads tended instead to emphasize child-peer comparisons (such as a situation in which peer didn't know something the child knew; Flannagan 1996). A recent meta-analysis also indicated that mothers interacted in more verbally supportive ways toward their daughters than toward their sons (such as encouraging, praising, and acknowledging them), particularly in unstructured interactions (Leaper, Anderson, and Sanders 1998).

Other evidence for mother-daughter shared affective communication comes from a study by Eleanor Maccoby (1998), in which parents and their six-year-old children were placed in pairs. They were each asked to describe one out of an array of four hard-to-describe pictures that were not visible to their partners. Partners could ask questions so that they could select the designated picture from a matching set. Mother-child pairs were more successful than were father-child pairs in understanding each other, and there were fewer communication errors between parents and daughters than between parents and sons. Mother-daughter pairs were the most successful at communicating competently and father-son pairs were the least.

Other studies suggest that mothers are more open to hearing about feelings from *both* sons and daughters than are fathers. Mothers report themselves to be or are observed to be more nurturing, affectionate, and empathic toward their preschool or school-aged children than fathers, regardless of their children's gender (Barnett et al. 1980b; Russell and Russell 1987; Brody in press). These data are consistent with observational data indicating that both 6–7-year-old girls and boys communicate feelings more toward mothers than toward fathers (Russell and Russell 1987).

By adolescence, studies suggest that mothers and daughters share feelings to a greater extent than do other family dyads (Moser, Paternite, and Dixon 1996). Adolescent daughters report relating to their mothers in qualitatively different ways than do sons, including being closer and more intimate (Campbell, Adams, and Dobson 1984; Furman and Buhrmester 1985), more attached (White, Speisman, and Costos 1983), more communicative (Campbell, Adams, and Dobson 1984), and more empathic and interested (Olver, Aries, and Batgos 1989; Brody 1996). Daughters in their mid-twenties also feel more connected to mothers than do sons, based on in-depth interviews about family relationships (Frank, Avery, and Laman 1988), and retrospectively rate their mothers as having discussed feelings with them more than sons (Barnett et al. 1980a).

Although adolescent and young-adult daughters perceive themselves to be closer to their mothers than sons do, few studies have explored the mother's own sense of closeness to her adolescent daughters and sons. Just as with younger age groups, when mothers are asked about their closeness to their adolescent children, they often report similar levels of closeness to both sons and daughters; and more closeness to their children than fathers report (Bhushan 1993). Moreover, in America, Thailand, Hong Kong, and mainland China, both male and female young adults retrospectively report that their mothers discussed feelings with them, were warmer, or were more affectionate and empathic than their fathers were (Barnett et al. 1980a; Berndt et al. 1993).

In brief, there are some intriguing suggestions that daughters, especially by adolescence, perceive themselves to be closer to their mothers than sons do. Data on relatively high mother-daughter empathy, mutual emotional disclosure, and closeness are beginning to emerge throughout several developmental stages, although mothers' self-reported perceptions may not be consistent with this view. It is fair to conclude that mother-daughter boundaries may be more permeable than mother-son boundaries according to adolescent daughters' perceptions of their closeness to their mothers, and in researchers' observations of dyadic parent-child emotional interactions.

The studies I have summarized, however, do not speak to one very important aspect of feminist psychoanalytic theories, and that is the question of how gender differences in mutual emotional disclosure are related to patterns of same-sex identification within the family. For example, do adolescent daughters perceive themselves to be closer to their mothers because daughters and mothers see themselves as similar to each other by virtue of sharing the same gender? Or, is same-sex identification irrelevant to the quality of the daughter-mother relationship? We don't as yet have any evidence to answer this question, but the rather weak evidence for the existence of same-sex identification within the family leads me back to the hypothesis that gender-differentiated parent-child interaction patterns may be driven not by same-sex identification, but rather by maternal reactions to both cultural gender stereotypes and to gender differences in children's temperament. The studies showing that not only mothers, but also fathers, share feelings more with daughters than with sons (Eisenberg et al. 1991a; Russell and Russell 1987), support the idea that it may not be same-sex identification that drives emotional disclosures in parent-child relationships. Instead, parents' expectations that their daughters should be sociable, along with possible temperamental strengths in girls' sociability, may make mutual emotional disclosures with daughters more likely. Similar hypotheses also stand in the following discussion of patterns of maternal intrusiveness and the promotion of autonomy in relation to daughters and sons.

INTRUSIVENESS. The construct of maternal intrusiveness is a slippery one: upon close inspection, there turn out to be many different kinds of behaviors that might be considered intrusive. For example, intrusive mothers may impose their own feelings onto their children. Alternatively, they may inhibit, restrict, or ignore their children's emotional expressions (possibly in accordance with their own discomfort with or denial of a particular feeling).[10]

There are also various reasons for being intrusive as a parent, and each of these reasons may relate differently to the quality of children's emotional expressivness. For example, the expression of particular feelings might hurt other people, or it might hurt or disappoint the mother herself (especially the expression of feelings that differ from the mother's own feelings). Alternatively, the mother might lack the ability to take her child's perspective and be unable to validate her child's feelings separate from her own. Regardless of the reasons for the mother's intrusiveness, there may also be many kinds of consequences for a child's noncompliance, including withdrawing maternal love, punishing the child, or inducing guilt by expressing disappointment in the child's behaviors (see Krevans and Gibbs 1996).

The research literature is full of contradictions as to whether mothers (or fathers) are more intrusive toward sons or daughters. These discrepancies may arise precisely because researchers have not specified the types of intrusive or restrictive parental behaviors that are assessed, the types of children's behaviors that are restricted or intruded upon, the parents' motivations for their intrusiveness, or the consequences for the child. For example, some studies indicate that mothers are more involved with their children than are fathers and may use more negative control strategies than fathers use, including threatening their children with loss of love when they misbehave (Parker 1983). Other studies have shown fathers of elementary-school children to be punitive and to minimize responses to their children's emotional expressivity. For example, they might endorse such statements as, "I tell my child that if he or she starts crying, then he or she will have to go to his or her room right away" (Eisenberg, Fabes, and Murphy 1996; see also Lytton and Romney 1991).

Moreover, contradictions about which parent is more intrusive, and with what sex child, may arise because patterns of interaction among all members of the family system are not taken into consideration. For example, Gjerde (1988) found that when parents agreed on child-rearing when their children were 3 years old, mothers were subsequently more permissive, less intrusive, and less competitive toward their 5-year-old sons than were mothers who had had discordant marriages when their children were 3. Here again, the family system may affect the quality of dyadic relationships, including intrusiveness, between mothers and their sons.

On the other hand, the available data on school-aged children and adolescents suggests an intriguing pattern in which mothers become especially involved in their daughters' lives during adolescence. For example, in both my own work (Brody 1993) and the work of Rose Olver and her colleagues (1989), adolescent daughters reported that their mothers were more intrusive than adolescent sons reported. Intrusiveness consisted of behaviors such as mothers commenting on their daughters' appearance, opening their personal mail, and directing their behaviors, as reported on the Permeability of Boundaries Scale (Olver, Aries, and Batgos 1989). Moreover, both adolescent sons and daughters reported that their mothers intruded more than their fathers did. Even in school-aged daughters, when there is more gender-differentiated intrusiveness (comparing intrusiveness toward sons versus daughters) on the part of either parent, it tends to be directed toward daughters, as feminist object-relations theories would suggest. For example, Block (1984) also describes a type of anxious intrusiveness on the part of mothers when interacting with their school-aged daughters: mothers provided help for their daughters even when their help was not needed for daughters to successfully complete the task.

In keeping with my hypothesis that gender differences in the quality of mother-child boundaries are related both to gender-role stereotypes and to differing characteristics of boys and girls themselves, it may be that mothers are more intrusive toward their adolescent daughters because their daughters express more frequent or intense negative emotions than their sons express. Research does support the idea that children's negative affect relates to maternal intrusiveness. Robinson, Little, and Biringen (1993) showed that mothers were more intrusive toward those 24-month-old sons who had expressed less positive emotions at 18 months than they were toward sons who had expressed more positive emotions at 18 months.

Mothers may also feel the need to intrude in order to help their daughters modify their expression of negative emotions, since negative emotions are considered less socially acceptable for women than are positive emotions. Indeed daughters are stereotypically expected to be cheerful, as I will discuss in Chapter 11. This may initiate a futile cycle in which mothers attempt to counter their daughters' negative expressiveness, and their daughters may respond in turn with increased negativity, perhaps causing mothers to intrude at an increased rate.

In contrast, mothers may not feel that they need to intrude in the lives of their sons, since sons are expected to express at least some negative emotions, such as anger, and are also expected to function more independently than are daughters.

AUTONOMY.   Mother-daughter relationships are thought to be characterized by a lack of autonomy on the part of daughters. Research does indicate that in Western contexts, adolescent girls have more conflicts over autonomy, particularly in relation to their mothers, than boys do, which may be related to their increased incidence of eating disorders (Humphrey 1989; Bartle, Anderson, and Sabatelli 1989; Palladino and Blustein 1991; Perosa and Perosa 1993). Adolescent daughters disclose greater conflicts over emotional independence with their mothers than sons disclose (cf. Campbell, Adams, and Dobson 1984), and report lower levels of separation from their parents than sons report (Lopez, Campbell, and Watkins 1986). Moreover, adolescent females display an angry-dependent pattern of relationships with their parents in which they are angry and conflicted, but also emotionally attached and dependent; whereas males display an angry-rebellious pattern of relationships with their parents in which they are more independent and dissimilar in their attitudes (Lopez, Campbell, and Watkins 1988).

Adolescent daughters' difficulties with autonomy may be related to stereotypes of women as helpless, dependent, and vulnerable, as well as to parents' attempts to ensure their daughters' safety and to minimize the risks of their daughters being sexually assaulted. Daughters' relatively lower activity levels and higher levels of sociability than boys' may also impede separation from parents.

In sum, emerging data suggest that mother-child emotional interaction patterns may differ for sons and daughters even in infancy. Mothers and their daughters mutually disclose more feelings to each other in early childhood, and certainly by adolescence, there are indications that, relative to sons, daughters feel closer to their mothers, less autonomous from their mothers, and more intruded upon by their mothers (in the sense that they feel that their mothers closely monitor their feelings). I have argued that these patterns may be due less to same-sex identification between daughters and their mothers than to gender-role stereotypes and to early temperament differences between boys and girls.

My next step in evaluating Chodorow's theory is to explore how gender differences in patterns of parent-child interaction, including empathy, intrusiveness, and autonomy, are related to gender differences in children's emotional expressiveness.

Maternal Sensitivity and Children's Emotional Expressiveness

There appears to be no question that parental nurturance, warmth, and empathy are related to increased positive emotional expressions and decreased distress on the part of both children and adolescents. Empathic, warm, and supportive parents have children who are empathic themselves and who express warmth, sympathy, and low personal distress (see Zahn-Waxler, Radke-Yarrow, and King 1979; Barnett et al. 1980a; Eisenberg et al. 1991a; Eisenberg et al. 1993; Eisenberg, Fabes, and Murphy 1996; Bronstein 1994; Eisenberg and Fabes 1995; Diskin and Heinicke 1986; Robinson, Little, and Biringen, 1993). For example, young girls whose mothers reported having discussions with them in emotionally laden contexts were more apt to comfort a crying infant than were other girls (Eisenberg et al. 1993). And, mothers' discussions of their own sad and sympathetic feelings while viewing a film were associated with their sons' self-reported sympathy for others (Eisenberg et al. 1992).[11]

Children with nonempathic parents who minimized their children's feelings, such as "telling them they were overreacting to an emotional situation," had higher negative emotionality, including expressing more worry, sadness, and fear (Eisenberg, Fabes, and Murphy 1996). And adolescent sons and daughters who reported that their mothers were less respectful of their feelings expressed relatively less intense positive emotions, such as happiness and warmth, and relatively more intense negative emotions, such as anger, sadness, shame, and guilt than did adolescents who reported their parents to be more respectful (Brody 1993; see also Ruebush, 1994).

On the other hand, maternal empathy may also result in children's increased comfort in expressing negative feelings, resulting in heightened expressions of negative emotions on the part of sons and daughters. For example, Robinson, Little, and Biringen's study (1993) showed that mothers who were especially sensitive toward their children in the first year of life had daughters who displayed more negative affects at 24 months. Consistent with this finding, my data with school-aged children showed that relative to other girls, those girls whose mothers scored highly on warmth and nurturance displayed an increased intensity of negative feelings in the stories they wrote (Brody, in press; see also Eisenberg et al. 1992).

One interpretation of these results is that sons and daughters of empathic mothers may be more comfortable expressing negative emotions. An alternative interpretation is that children's heightened negative expressions may reflect not only comfort levels with emotional expression, but may reflect a process of becoming different from their mothers in emotional expressiveness. This differentiation interpretation is supported by data showing that not only children's *negative*, but also their *positive* emotional expressiveness may be opposite in valence to the emotional expressivity of their mothers. For example, in my own work, school-aged daughters expressed *less* intense positive feelings on a story task when their mothers expressed higher warmth and nurturance, in contrast to girls whose mothers scored lower on warmth and nurturance (Brody, in press). Moreover, school-aged sons expressed less intense positive and negative emotions in stories when their mothers scored highly on warmth and nurturance. And sons also scored highly on warmth when their mothers scored highly on expressing anger, fear and hurt in a story task (Brody, in press).[12] Here we see evidence not only that sons differentiate from their mothers in emotional expressiveness (as predicted by theory), but surprisingly, that school-aged daughters do so as well, at least in their levels of positive expressiveness.[13]

These differences in parents' and children's emotional functioning can be interpreted as an effort by children to develop their own identities, or alternatively, as a parental reaction to their children. For example, perhaps mothers of sons who express warmth are uncomfortable because warmth is an atypical emotion for males. They may react by expressing negative emotions themselves. Or perhaps mothers whose sons express minimal emotions, as consistent with male gender-role stereotypes, feel more comfortable in expressing warmth toward their sons. It will be important for future researchers to replicate the pattern of emotional de-identification in mother-son relationships (and even at times, in mother-daughter relationships) and to tease apart these alternative explanations.

To conclude, if mothers are more empathic toward daughters than toward sons (as evidenced by more mutual disclosure of feelings), their daughters may develop higher levels of positive and negative emotional expressiveness. They may become more comfortable expressing emotions and they may use the expression of affect to differentiate from close relationships with their mothers. In contrast, mothers' lower levels of mutual emotional disclosure with their sons may influence sons to minimize their emotional expressiveness. Even when mothers are warm and nurturing toward their sons, including matching their sons' facial expressions, their sons may respond in surprising ways, sometimes minimizing their emotional expressiveness as a way of developing a gender identity that is different from that of their mothers.

Maternal Intrusiveness and Children's Emotional Expressiveness

Do gender-differentiated patterns of maternal intrusiveness relate to gender differences in emotional expression? Research suggests that maternal intrusiveness for both boys and girls has different associations with children's emotional expressiveness depending on the particular emotions parents focus on and for what reasons. For example, focusing children's attention to their victims' perspectives (e.g., "How would your friend feel?") as well as expressing disappointment in children's behaviors have been found to be related to children's increased empathy and prosocial behaviors (Krevans and Gibbs 1996). In fact, parents who restrain their school-aged children from expressing feelings that can potentially hurt other children have children who exhibit increased sympathy in response to watching distressing films (Eisenberg et al. 1991a).

In contrast, parents who punish their children, or who restrict their children's self-related feelings, such as sadness or anxiety, have sons with low levels of sympathy (Eisenberg et al. 1991a; Krevans and Gibbs 1996). Their sons also exhibit increased physiological and facial distress as measured by heart rate acceleration and skin conductance, while simultaneously reporting less distress than other children. This pattern suggests that these sons conform to an internalizing pattern, learning to be emotionally inexpressive in response to parental demands (Eisenberg et al. 1991a).

Children of both sexes express higher levels of anger, hostility, aggression, dysphoric moods, anxiety, depression, and phobias when parents are restrictive of their open emotional expression (Parker 1983; Stafford and Bayer 1993). In a study of both men and women who scored highly on hostility, retrospective reports of their parents' child rearing practices indicated that their parents had interfered more with their desires and controlled their behavior more when they were children (Houston and Vavak 1991). Confirming the trend that parental restrictiveness and intrusiveness relates to the expression of children's negative emotions are data from my own research. Here, both maternal and paternal restrictiveness on the Block Child Rearing Practices Report related to increased expression of intense emotions, especially anger and fear, in both school-aged sons and daughters (Brody, in press). Similarly, intrusiveness on the part of mothers (defined as telling adolescents what they should feel) was found to relate to the expression of intense negative emotions, such as anger, shame, guilt, sadness, and fear on the part of both female and male adolescents, using the Permeability of Boundaries Scale (Brody 1996).

This relationship between restrictiveness or intrusiveness and negative emotional expressions has also been found to true of infant boys, but not girls. In a study by JoAnn Robinson and her colleagues (1993), maternal intrusiveness was measured as frequent and intense behaviors in which the mother failed to balance self-initiated intervention with a behavior or an emotion initiated by the child. Eighteen-month-old boys had increased negative affect expressions and decreased positive affect expressions in relation to their mother's intrusiveness. In contrast, infant daughters whose mothers were more intrusive tended to display more positive affects, not less, in contrast to daughters whose mothers were less intrusive.

In summary, the state of the evidence with respect to the relation between maternal intrusiveness and children's emotional expressiveness is intriguing, but far from conclusive. Researchers need to be much more careful about defining what they mean by intrusiveness and about the underlying reasons for the intrusiveness. It may well be (a) that maternal intrusiveness increases the intensity of children's affect expressions, and

(b) that mothers are more intrusive toward their adolescent daughters than their adolescent sons, thus (c) partially accounting for the subsequent development of women's heightened intensity of emotional expression. However, we don't have enough evidence to state this definitively. As yet, it is unclear which maternal behaviors constitute intrusiveness, which emotions are involved, and which sexes at what developmental stages are affected.

Children's Autonomy and Emotional Expressiveness

Children's lack of autonomy in mother-child relationships has also been found to relate to their increased negative emotional expressiveness. For example, school-aged sons and daughters who were less separate from their mothers, as measured by the Block Child Rearing Practices Report, expressed more intense negative emotions, including anger and hurt, in response to stories they heard (Brody, Wise, and Monuteaux 1997). Mothers of these children tended to endorse items such as, "I don't enjoy spending time by myself, apart from my child." Girls also tended to show a pattern of maximizing negative emotional expressiveness and of minimizing positive emotional expressiveness when their mothers reported themselves to be less separate from them (Brody, in press). Pianta and Caldwell's data (1990) show a similar trend: mothers' failure to grant autonomy to their kindergarten and first-grade children in a block-building task was related to increases in their daughters', but not their sons' externalizing symptoms, including aggressive behaviors. Increasing aggressiveness among the boys was more closely related to the boys' own negativity and anger, regardless of mothers' behaviors.

Among adolescents, boys who had difficulty individuating from their families (who came from more enmeshed families) expressed shame, guilt, sadness, and fear (Brody 1996; Brody et al. 1995). Enmeshment in this study was measured with the Family Characteristics Questionnaire (Bloom 1985), and included items such as, "It is hard for members of my family to be doing separate things." Adolescent girls who had difficulty separating from their families described their own personality traits as being dependent and passive. This dependency was in turn related to the expression of intense negative feelings.

In brief, the data on the relationship between autonomy and emotional expressiveness suggest that in Western cultural contexts, a lack of autonomy is related to increased expressions of distress and dysphoria in adolescence. There is also evidence to suggest that daughters have a harder time in being autonomous than sons have, perhaps creating conflict and heightening negative affect for daughters.

These relationships may be quite different in a non-Western context (Copeland, Hwang, and Brody 1996). Higher levels of separateness between parents and children related to lower levels of depression in European-American adolescents, but not in Asian-American adolescents. Similarly, Fuhrman and Holmbeck (1995) found that when emotional autonomy from mothers was higher, European-American adolescents had fewer internalizing behavior problems, such as anxiety, but African-American adolescents did not. For African-Americans, higher levels of emotional autonomy from mothers had the reverse consequence: they were related to higher levels of internalizing behavior problems. Among Asian- and African-American families, closer parent-child relationships may be more adaptive.

OVERVIEW. Feminist psychoanalytic theorists attempt to explain the relatively greater emotional expressivity of females with respect to patterns of gendered relationships within the family. In particular, Chodorow (1978) has hypothesized that mother-daughter identification and mother-son de-identification may affect the quality of mothers' boundaries with their children, including their empathy, emotional intrusiveness, and separateness from their children. In turn, boundary qualities are theorized to relate to children's emotional expressiveness. In this chapter, I have explored the existing evidence with respect to this theory. My review indicates that although the theory has not as yet been thoroughly or adequately tested, the limited data are encouraging for at least some aspects of the theory. In particular, the most promising data suggest that there are gender-differentiated interaction patterns between parents and their children at several developmental periods (with the clearest during adolescence) that relate to children's emotional expressiveness. Moreover, there is some evidence that patterns of differentiation exist between the emotional expressiveness of parents and their school-aged and adolescent children, especially between mothers and sons.

The weakest link in the theory is the ways in which same-sex gender identification and opposite-sex de-identification relate to these gender-differentiated interaction patterns. To be fair, the hypothesis that same-sex identification relates to differing kinds of parent-child interactions for boys and for girls has not been adequately tested. To do so would require systematically assessing how parent-child identification (perhaps in the form of family perceptions of parent-child similarities and dissimilarities) relates to patterns of family interaction and emotional expressiveness within families. Researchers would also need to explore the extent to which same-sex identification between parents and their children waxes and wanes through different developmental periods. Same-sex identification may intensify at adolescence, when adolescents themselves seek clues as to their appropriate social roles from same-sex role models because their experiences increasingly diverge from those of the opposite sex. Parents also may be more identified with their same-sex children during adolescence, perhaps because they remember their own adolescence as a salient developmental period.

However, the available evidence suggests that same-sex identification is not a prominent feature of family life, especially before adolescence. Instead, the gendered nature of mother-child relationships may be influenced both by gender-role stereotypes as well as by the child's own characteristics. Subtle differences between infant sons and daughters in terms of their sociability, their activity levels, their language abilities, and their abilities to self-regulate their arousal levels (see Chapter 7) may make just as important a contribution to the nature of same-sex parent-child boundaries and relationships as shared gender. For example, boys' higher activity levels in contrast to those of girls may contribute to the relative distance that emerges between mothers and sons in contrast to mothers and daughters. Moreover, the de-identification between sons and their mothers may also be related to boys' high activity levels. Even the direction of the relationship between maternal intrusiveness and children's emotional expressiveness may be driven by children's characteristics, such as sociability and activity levels. The role played by parents' perceptions of these temperamental differences in affecting patterns of interactions with their children is also important. Parents may distort, exaggerate, or de-emphasize the existing temperamental characteristics of their children so that they conform to existing gender-role stereotypes, resulting in shifts in the nature of their interactions and relationships with their children.

Although mothers' characteristics have not been a focus of this chapter, they may also contribute to the quality of parent-child boundaries.

Mothers who express emotions in an intense fashion may be more intrusive toward their children than other mothers. My own data, in fact, suggest that mothers who express intense fear in writing stories are more restrictive toward their children (Brody, Wise, and Monuteaux 1997). Sons and daughters of intrusive mothers may model their mother's intense style of emotional expressiveness. Alternatively, perhaps both mothers and children may be genetically predisposed to intense emotional reactivity.

Finally, I have argued that feminist psychoanalytic theorists and researchers need to pay closer attention to the family and cultural context in which any particular family dyad functions. Researchers have often failed to consider mutual and bi-directional patterns of emotional expressiveness on the part of parents and their children, and the wider family context in which mothers and their children live. In the next chapter, I will explore the pivotal role of fathers in affecting both the mother-child relationship as well as the emotional expressiveness of their sons and daughters.

Fathers and the Family Climate

My father wants the best for us, but he never has the time or the way
of telling this to us.

—Mitch, age 34

Theoretically, fathers play a relatively lesser role in the development of
children's self-representations than mothers play because of their relative
lack of involvement in child care (Chodorow 1978). Yet, research indicates that children's emotional expressiveness is related to many aspects
of the quality of the fathering they receive. How available fathers are,
their empathy, the quality of their relationships with their wives, and
how emotionally expressive they are, all make a difference in children's
emotional expressiveness. In this chapter, I will argue that fathers play a
significant role in affecting the quality of their children's emotional expressiveness. In particular, I will focus on how fathers contribute to the
emergence of gender differences in emotional expressiveness.

Feminist psychoanalytic theorists (Chodorow 1978) predict that
when fathers are involved in child care, their children should be less
rigidly gender-stereotyped. Why? The explanation partially derives from
the functions that fathers serve in the development of their children's
identity (Machtlinger 1981). First, fathers are hypothesized to help
mothers and children to differentiate and to become autonomous. With
increased autonomy, daughters should be able to express emotions that
require the ability to disengage, or distance from others, such as competition and pride. Daughters should also have less of a need to communicate dysphoric emotions, such as guilt or distress, because they would
already be separate from their mothers. Involved fathers should also
allow sons the freedom to express emotions without the fear that by

expressing them, they will become too similar to their mothers. In other words, sons with involved fathers should be under less pressure to de-identify from their mothers because they have their fathers as alternative models for identification. In the context of an ongoing intimate relationship with their fathers, sons should learn about, internalize, and ultimately, express emotions. Finally, fathers are theorized to teach their children about modulating and expressing aggression (see Machtlinger 1981). When fathers are more involved in family life, they should help both sons and daughters to regulate aggression, with girls stimulated to become more aggressive and with boys learning to control their aggression.

In brief, sex differences in children's emotional expressiveness should be minimized in families with involved fathers when compared to families with more traditional fathers. Sons should become more interpersonally skillful, less distant from relationships with others, and more emotionally expressive. Daughters should become more aggressive and competitive, more separate from the family, and less expressive of intense dysphoric feelings.

Are there studies that examine the roles that fathers play in their children's emotional expressiveness? Emerging data suggest that at least some aspects of fathers' theorized roles may be correct. When fathers are involved in child care, for instance, gender differences in their children's emotional expressiveness are minimized.

Father Involvement and Children's Emotions

In my research, school-aged children who had involved fathers expressed emotions in ways that did not conform to typical gender patterns. Girls with involved fathers expressed more aggression, competition, and less intense fear and sadness in stories than did girls with less-involved fathers. Boys with involved fathers expressed more intense feelings of vulnerability, such as warmth and fear, and less aggression in stories than did boys with less involved fathers (Brody 1997). They also described themselves to be more interpersonally oriented than did other boys.

I measured father involvement by asking mothers and fathers independently to complete a questionnaire that listed 15 different child-care tasks, including activities such as taking their children to the doctor, helping their children with schoolwork, and being responsible for their children when they were sick.[1] Both parents agreed that mothers spent significantly more time doing child care than fathers spent, and took more responsibility for child care. Half the mothers in the sample were rated as responsible for all 15 child-care tasks either by themselves or jointly with their spouses. The message is hardly surprising: mothers are responsible for child care in their families, and spend significantly more time with their children than fathers spend (see also Rubin 1994). As one of the mothers from a more traditional family noted, "I wish my husband would 'think' more; he rarely notices that things need to be done on a certain schedule." Another mother in the study agreed: "I'll put it this way: he'll do anything I ask him to do, he just doesn't think of it first. A lot of times I find it faster to do things myself than to go through the whole thing of asking him to do it. It's not that he's resistant, it's that he just doesn't initiate things."

Highly involved fathers did not differ from less-involved fathers on socioeconomic status, the age or sex of their children, their own age, or the age of their wives. On the other hand, they tended to have more feminist attitudes toward men's and women's roles, they reported higher self-esteem and more communal characteristics, they were less restrictive toward their daughters, and their wives were more likely to be employed than were noninvolved fathers (Brody, Wise, and Monuteaux 1997).[2]

However, none of these other variables, including the father's feminist attitudes, his emotions, his child rearing style, or the mother's employment and her feminist attitudes, made as powerful a contribution to children's emotional expressiveness as did the father's time involvement. Very similar results were reported in three other studies that looked at fathers' involvement in child care in relation to their children's empathy (Sagi 1982; Bernadett-Shapiro, Ehrensaft, and Shapiro 1996). In these studies, the more involved fathers were in child care, the more empathic their sons were (Bernadett-Shapiro, Ehrsensaft, and Shapiro 1996), or their sons and daughters were (Koestner, Franz, and Weinberger 1990), or the more stereotypically masculine their daughters were (Sagi 1982). It was the father's level of child care involvement, and not his own empathy that best predicted his son's empathy (Bernadett-Shapiro, Ehrsensaft, and Shapiro 1996).

Research has shown that when their fathers are more involved in child care, children are less gender-stereotypic in many aspects of their functioning, not just in their emotional expressivity (see review by Radin 1994). Studies in this area have been diverse in terms of how old the children are, the reasons fathers are participating in child care, and what kinds of outcome measures are used with the children. What is impressive is that despite the diversity of research methods, children from families with involved fathers are consistently more flexible in their sex roles than are children from more traditional families. For example, daughters with involved fathers have been found to have less stereotypic views of male and female roles (Baruch and Barnett 1981). Highly involved fathers of 3–5-year-old children were found to have children with less traditional views of future employment possibilities when they became adolescents than did less involved fathers (Snarey 1993). Thirty- to 40-year-olds who were more androgynous had parents who were less traditional in their sex roles when their children were growing up (Block 1984). And further evidence is provided by a study that compared children's gender-role stereotypes in shared-parenting families with children's stereotypes in traditional families (Fagot and Leinbach 1995). The children were 16 to 18 months old when the study began and were also observed at ages 2 and 4. Fathers, not mothers, behaved differently in the two samples, with more involved fathers interacting more with their children and having more egalitarian gender-role attitudes than did other fathers. The children in the shared-parenting sample learned gender labels later and knew less about cultural gender stereotypes than did children from the traditional families.

Two Sample Families

Consider the stories told by members of two different families in my study who depicted low versus high levels of father involvement. In both families, the parents are in their mid-thirties. Bill, the first father, is involved in child care at relatively low levels compared to other fathers in the sample. He works as an assistant manager in a retail store and attends school to develop his technical skills. His wife, Cathy, works in two part-time positions, and they have two children, a 10-year-old boy, Carl, and a 7-year-old girl, Robin. Both parents agree that Cathy does most of the child care and housework. Cathy says, "I think I probably do more than I should do. I would like a little more help with nitty-gritty work and mundane tasks. He was brought up the old traditional type, momma

ironed his underwear. I mean it's hard to teach an old dog new tricks."
And her husband agrees: "We try to divide up the tasks; I would say she
does much more than I do; only mainly because, I don't know why, I
guess I really don't like to do them [an embarrassed laugh]. That's not
really fair, I know. I'm not as helpful sometimes as I could be; sometimes
I have to light a fire under myself and I know it."

In response to a picture of a boy and girl facing each other with neutral
expressions on their faces (see Figure 1, Chapter 1), their 10-year-old
son Carl tells a story full of conflict, blame, and anger, a typical pattern
for boys in this group. In his story, wrongdoing is measured primarily by
how much trouble the children get into, and there is no real sense of
negotiation or reconciliation.

> They're arguing. They're arguing about not being able to go outside
> because it was both of their fault and they're saying it wasn't his or her
> fault. It was the other's fault. And they thought both of them were
> wrong and they should go outside but it was too late—they already did
> something wrong. Thinking that they shouldn't be arguing—they're
> already in trouble and it's all over with. They think that they were
> wrong to do something that wasn't right. Thinking they shouldn't have
> to argue anymore about things like this and they feel better.

His father Bill, writing a story about the same picture, tells a story of
competition between boys and girls from the perspective of his children:

> My 10-year-old son and my 7-year-old daughter. A discussion about
> height. A sudden growth spurt by my daughter. Older brother letting
> sister know he's her "big" brother. He is still her big brother but in age
> only. Son is feeling a competitive impulse. Daughter is feeling some
> excitement with her increased stature. Both will continue to grow
> physically and emotionally.

His wife Cathy's story is also about a conflict over a toy told from the
perspective of her children, in which the son is assumed to be at fault.
The issue is resolved only because the daughter is able to take the perspective of her brother, and to believe that he did not take her toy. This
reconciliatory and empathic role for girls is quite traditional:

> This is a picture of a brother and sister having an argument over a
> missing toy. The sister is missing a toy and thinks her brother took it.
> She wants him to tell her where the toy is, he wants her to leave him

alone. They are angry with each other and don't like each other at this moment. She will believe him that he doesn't have the toy and the issue will be resolved.

The second family consists of Michael, a corporate executive; his wife, Alice, a homemaker; and their three children, Rachel, aged 11, Sophie, aged 7, and Nathan, aged 5½. Alice worked as a nurse until shortly after the birth of their third child. Both parents concur that they divide household tasks equally, despite the fact that the wife is a homemaker. Michael states:

> I think that . . . I consider the situation is both ours . . . both our responsibility to get things done. So typically she cooks and I clean the kitchen and the table. She will more than likely put the kids into the bathroom while I'm cleaning. They would play for a while and I would go wash the kids' hair, clean them, and cut nails and clean ears and stuff and my wife, she would go do the laundry while I was doing that and when we get in bed we can both sit down . . . I'm known as the ear washer and toenail clipper and do more of the heavy work, and I do things like making arrangements to pick the kids up and get them back. She [his wife] does most of the grocery shopping. It's just routine; if she can't do it, I go do it.

Alice has little to say except that she is happy with the way they manage their child care. This is in stark contrast to most of the other mothers in the study. Her only complaint about her husband is that "I wouldn't mind if he went grocery shopping every now and then."

Here is Michael's story in response to a picture of a boy and a girl facing each other:

> They are both high-level politicians. They are discussing the situation in South Africa; years of oppression by the minority government and British Colonization. They are thinking of ways to protect the business interests and political stability, yet satisfy civil rights activists. They'd like the problem to go away. They feel frustrated, and compassionate. Justice will prevail.

He portrays both women and men in positions of power, consistent with the finding that men who were higher in child-care involvement were more feminist than were other men. In his story men and women are also working together, rather than engaged in a conflict situation.

Alice's story depicts a girl in a powerful position working together with a boy around an affiliative task:

> The people are a boy and a girl about the same age. They are talking about getting a gift for the teacher. The girl is organizing a collection for a gift for the teacher. She tells the boy that it is a surprise. She tells him how much money she wants every student in their class to bring in. He is thinking about her collection. He wants to contribute. She wants to know if he has any other ideas on specific gifts to buy. He offers some advice. She is happy he is willing to contribute. She appreciates his advice. He feels happy to be of help. They will smile at each other and agree to help.

Their older daughter Rachel depicts a sports competition, quite unusual for most of the girls in the sample, but typical of daughters from families in which fathers are highly involved:

> Two kids, and they're fighting about who's going to be basketball captain. Girl says, "I should be Captain, I shoot better." Boys says, "I should be because I run and dribble better." Another kid comes over and says, "I'll be captain and you can both be on my team." They lost the game. The captain of the team says it's not important whether we win or lose, so everyone stopped fighting. They felt mad at each other.

Daughters with highly involved fathers seem to be concerned with competitive themes without losing the interpersonal themes typically associated with females.

A Puzzle

How can we account for the apparent contradiction that fathers socialize children in sex-role stereotypic ways, as previous research has indicated, and yet, when they are more involved in child care, their children express fewer sex-role stereotypic emotions?

Previous research does indicate that fathers, more than mothers, socialize their children in sex-role stereotypic ways. Studies reaching this conclusion have tended to group all fathers together, and have not routinely explored how a father's level of involvement in child care might change his behavior toward his children (see Lytton and Romney 1991). Since involved fathers tend to have children with more flexible gender roles, it is possible that involved fathers treat their sons more similarly to their daughters than do noninvolved fathers, or they may differ from noninvolved fathers in other aspects of their parenting behaviors, as I will elaborate below.

Data indicate that in general, both fathers and mothers encourage different activities for boys and girls, for example, doll play for girls and sports for boys, with fathers encouraging different activities more than mothers do (Lytton and Romney 1991). Kerig, Cowan, and Cowan (1993) found that fathers of preschoolers rewarded daughters for positive compliant behavior, while they rewarded boys for assertiveness. In fact, girls' assertive responses were more likely to be met with negative responses from their fathers than were boys'. Siegel's review of the literature corroborates these ideas and indicates modest support for the idea that it is fathers who promote sex typing in their children more than mothers do, particularly in the areas of discipline and physical involvement with their children (Siegel 1987).

As parents, fathers generally have a style of child rearing that differs from that of their wives. They tend to tease their children more, to use direct imperatives, to focus on explanations, and to be more physical and action-oriented (Bronstein 1988; Gleason 1989). Leaper et al.'s (1998) meta-analysis indicates that fathers are more likely to verbally direct and inform their children than are mothers. Fathers are also less likely to use words to express their dysphoric or distressed feelings in marital conflict than are mothers, as we have seen. If sons use their fathers as role models, the language that fathers use and their discomfort with emotion may be important contributors to sons' minimization of emotional expression. Perhaps in response to their fathers' discomfort with emotional expressiveness, school-aged children report that they would be less likely to express feelings to their fathers than to their mothers (Fuchs and Thelen 1988).

If fathers are the "carriers" of sex typing (for example, by being models of emotional inexpressivity), why don't families with involved fathers have even more gender-typed children than families with noninvolved fathers? Despite the gender-distinct parenting that fathers seem to do, more-involved fathers actually minimize gender differences in their children's emotional expressiveness.

As I suggested above, one possible answer to this question is that when fathers are more involved in their families, the quality of their parenting behaviors changes. In my data, involved fathers were less restrictive toward their daughters than were less-involved fathers (Brody, Wise, and Monuteaux 1997). Other studies indicate that when fathers are primary caretakers (primarily via divorce), they become more nurturing, more affectionate, more emotionally involved with their children, and disclose their emotions more often (Risman 1987; Hanson 1988). In other words, when fathers become primary caretakers, their characteristics resemble those of the stereotypical mother (Hanson 1988; Pruett and Litzenberger 1992), indicating that style of caretaking has very little to do with biological sex.

There is an important qualification here, though. My data and other studies indicate that it is not fathers' changed parenting style that accounts for how emotionally expressive their children are. Even though involved fathers have been found to differ in parenting style from noninvolved fathers, the time fathers spend in child care has been found to be more predictive of their children's emotional expressiveness than their parenting style. How restrictive, empathic, or nurturant a father is does not contribute as much to his children's emotional expressiveness as does his time involvement with his children (Bernadett-Shapiro, Ehrensaft and Shapiro 1996; Brody, Pfister, and Brennan 1997). Of course, it is always possible that researchers have not as yet measured the aspects of fathers' parenting style that are the most relevant for children's emotional functioning; for example, how intrusive fathers are, or their comfort with close relationships and emotional disclosure.

Are Fathers Responding to Characteristics of their Children?

It is also possible that the reason fathers' involvement relates to their children's emotional expressiveness is that fathers choose to spend more time with daughters and sons who have particular qualities. For example, fathers may feel more comfortable spending time with daughters who are more competitive and less expressive of emotions, i.e., daughters who are more similar to males than to females, thereby resembling the fathers themselves. Fathers may also feel less threatened by and less competitive with sons who are less aggressive and more interpersonally skillful than other sons, thus choosing to spend more time with sons who have such characteristics. Although there is no current evidence to support this line of reasoning, it is consistent with a transactional model of development, suggesting that parents' behaviors are shaped by the characteristics of their children as well as by their gender-stereotypic expectations.

Maternal Employment, Gender, and Emotion

Children with less stereotypic gender characteristics not only have fathers who are more involved, but also have mothers who are more likely to be employed (Baruch and Barnett 1986a). Does the relationship between father involvement and the quality of children's emotional expressiveness mask a critical relationship between maternal employment and children's emotional expressiveness? Is mothers' employment status more important than the extent of fathers' child-care involvement in determining children's emotional expressiveness? Mothers' employment might provide daughters with an autonomous role model, and enhance opportunities for increased father-child closeness as well as increased mother-daughter and mother-son differentiation. Partly consistent with this hypothesis, a study of seventh-graders and their parents indicated that when mothers were employed, sons reported greater closeness to their fathers and daughters reported less closeness to both parents (Paulson, Koman, and Hill 1990).

Mothers in my sample were employed far fewer hours per week than were fathers. The average number of hours mothers in this sample worked was 22 hours per week, with only 37 out of 95 mothers working more than 30 hours per week. When mothers were employed more hours, their daughters tended to minimize the expression of emotions, although these patterns were somewhat weak. Daughters whose mothers worked more hours tended to express less fearfulness, less liking of other people, and more competition themes than did daughters of mothers who worked fewer hours.[3] There were only weak and nonsignificant relationships between the number of hours mothers worked per week and sons' emotional expressiveness.

Did the amount of time fathers spend with their children still relate to their sons' and daughters' emotional expressiveness when the number of hours their mothers were employed each week was controlled? The answer is yes: even when the amount of time mothers were working was controlled, the time fathers spent caretaking remained significantly related to their sons' and daughters' expressiveness. In contrast, mothers' employment continued to play a nonsignificant role in relating to their children's emotional expressiveness when fathers' involvement was controlled. These analyses indicate that fathers' involvement plays a more critical role in minimizing children's gender differences in emotional expression than does mothers' employment, results that are corroborated in other studies (Baruch and Barnett 1981).

Fathers, Identification, and Differentiation

Involved fathers may minimize gender-stereotypic emotional expressiveness in their children because they serve a differentiation function for both sons and daughters. When fathers interact closely with their children, they may provide sons with a male role model with whom to identify and emulate, and may also help sons to differentiate from their mothers. Sons should consequently feel less pressured to become dissimilar from their emotionally expressive mothers. Similarly, involved fathers should enable their adolescent daughters to separate from their mothers, consequently minimizing their daughters' expression of dysphoric emotions, which may otherwise have fulfilled a distancing function.

Is there any evidence to support these ideas? Let's start with evidence relevant to father-son identification and then move to the relationships between fathers' boundaries with their sons and daughters and the quality of their children's emotional expressiveness.

When I explored the evidence for same-sex identification in families in Chapter 8, I considered research concerning the perceived similarity of parents' and children's personality characteristics. Schachter (1982) found that sons described themselves as similar to their fathers on the dimension of potency, including how active and strong they were. In fact, she found more evidence for father-son than for mother-daughter identification in the similarity of attributed personality characteristics. Further, in my data on the kinds of characters included in school-aged children's stories, there were only 6 out of a total of 169 children who chose to write about their fathers in the absence of their mothers, and five of those children were sons. Sons depicted their relationships with their fathers in a variety of ways, including doing something with their fathers, competing with their fathers, or becoming like their fathers, with the latter certainly suggesting a process of identification (see Cramer 1991, for a discussion of identification).

The research evidence relevant to father-son identification should include parallel processes that I explored as evidence of mother-daughter identification, such as the quality of father-son boundaries. In other words, if fathers identify more with their sons than with their daughters, they should be more empathic, intrusive, and merged with their sons than they are with their daughters. Chodorow (1978) doesn't consider the quality of fathers' boundaries with their children. Her argument is that children do not form primary identifications with their fathers because of their fathers' limited involvement in the family. Researchers seem to share her view, because there is very little, if any, evidence on the relationship between fathers' individuation and children's emotional expressiveness. (The assumption is that fathers are more autonomous and therefore less merged with their children than are mothers.)[4]

Perhaps identification between fathers and their sons is manifested through similarity in actions, or behaviors, rather than through patterns of merged emotional expressiveness or experiences. Shared activities, rather than emotions, might better reflect the emphases in men's socialization. For example, one behavioral measure of father-son identification might be whether or not fathers prefer their sons to their daughters. Both mothers and fathers report preferring sons to daughters when asked about which sex children they would like to have, with three or four times as many American men than women preferring boys to girls (Coombs, Coombs, and McClelland 1975; Hoffman 1977), and with even higher ratios estimated in other cultures (see, for example, Chowdury, Bairagi, and Koenig 1993). It could be argued that these preferences reflect the higher cultural status accorded to males, rather than the extent of parent-child identification, although mother-daughter identification is suggested by the finding that female American college students express a slight bias in favor of preferring daughters, and mothers report wishing for girls in pregnancy if they already have sons (Coombs, Coombs, and McClelland 1975; Zucker et al. 1994; see also Chowdury, Bairagi, and Koenig 1993).

Differential preference may also be reflected in the fact that fathers spend more time playing with their sons than with their daughters, as well as performing more basic child-care tasks with them, such as feeding, diapering, looking at, and touching them more than they do their daughters (Bronstein 1988; Lytton and Romney 1991). Especially traditional fathers from single income households spend more time with their school-aged sons than they do with their daughters (Crouter and

Crowley 1990). Husbands and wives are also less likely to divorce when they have sons than daughters (Glick 1988), and after a divorce, fathers are more likely to retain custody of sons than of daughters (Hanson 1988). One cautionary note is that custody decisions may reflect the biases of the courts and the legal system in addition to, or rather than, fathers' own preferences.

Mothers do not engage in similar preferential behavioral practices with their daughters as compared to their sons. This may be partly because child care is a more primary responsibility for mothers than it is for their husbands, allowing mothers less choice about how much time they spend performing particular tasks with different sex infants.

In brief, some of the evidence does suggest that fathers spend more time with sons than with daughters, and report preferring sons to daughters, at least before birth. Some of these preferences may be measures of same-sex identification, or they may be measures of the high status allotted to males in the culture. In either case, the question remains as to whether and how these preferences influence sons' and daughters' emotional expressiveness or their sense of themselves. This question has not been a focus for developmental researchers and is an area for future research.

I will now turn to the few studies that address aspects of father-child boundaries, including paternal empathy and intrusiveness. Whether or not these processes differ for boys and girls, and how they are related to gender differences in children's emotional expressiveness are questions that are only beginning to be seriously considered by researchers.

Father-Child Boundaries and Children's Emotional Expressiveness

Paternal Empathy

There are contradictory data as to whether fathers are more empathic toward their sons or their daughters. For example, one study of Mexican families indicated that parents and their same-sex children engaged in more reciprocally cooperative, warm, and supportive behaviors than parents and their opposite-sex children engaged in (Bronstein 1994). Fathers of 10-month-old sons also reported expressing more positive feelings than did fathers of daughters (Stifter and Grant 1993).

On the other hand, my own research indicates that fathers report more empathy and nurturance toward daughters than toward sons (Brody, Wise, and Monuteaux 1997). Similarly, Snow, Jacklin, and Maccoby (1983) found that fathers and their 12-month-old daughters were more likely to hold each other and to remain in close proximity than fathers and their sons, which may be indicators of empathy, or alternatively, which may reflect fathers' encouragement of stereotypically dependent and nurturing behaviors on the part of their daughters. Other research indicates that fathers are more nonverbally attentive to their adolescent daughters than they are to their sons (Noller and Callan 1989).

There is very little research on paternal empathy in relation to children's emotional expressiveness. As I discussed earlier in this chapter, it is fathers' level of involvement with their children, rather than their own empathy, that seems to predict children's empathy (Koestner, Franz, and Weinberger 1990). In my own data, fathers' empathy related to neither their school-aged sons' nor daughters' emotional expressiveness (Brody, Wise, and Monuteaux 1997). Other researchers have similarly found either very weak or nonsignificant relationships between paternal empathy and school-aged children's emotional functioning (Bernadett-Shapiro, Ehrensaft, and Shapiro 1996).

On the other hand, there is some evidence that empathic fathers heighten their children's expression of positive emotion and reduce their children's expression of negative emotion. For example, both adolescent males and females who reported their fathers to be more warm and respectful expressed more intense positive emotions (Brody 1993). And fathers who minimized their school-aged sons' emotional expressiveness, in a nonempathic way, had sons who were reported to have higher negative emotionality, including fear, sadness, worry, and anxiety (Eisenberg, Fabes, and Murphy 1996).[5]

It may be that fathers' empathy is related to their children's emotional expressiveness in complex interactions with mothers' empathy. For example, 5-year-old daughters were found to be significantly high in empathy only when they had both mothers who were high in empathy and fathers who were low in empathy (Barnett et al. 1980b). In other words, empathy may become particularly characteristic of girls only when *both* parents are strongly gender-stereotyped with respect to empathy. In this same study, 5-year-old sons' empathy related to neither their fathers' nor their mothers' empathy scores.

Paternal Intrusiveness

In Chapter 8, I discussed the lack of precise definitions for the construct of intrusiveness, and reviewed tentative evidence that fathers may be more punitive and restrictive toward their children than mothers, especially toward their sons (see, for example, Eisenberg, Fabes, and Murphy, 1996; Lytton and Romney 1991). Mothers may become more involved in the intimate details of their adolescent children's lives than fathers, with both male and female adolescents reporting that their fathers were less intrusive than their mothers in such things as opening their doors without knocking first (Brody 1993).[6]

A few studies have shown that fathers' restrictiveness about emotional expression relates to increased negative emotional expressiveness on the part of their school-aged sons and daughters (see Garner, Robertson, and Smith 1997). In my work, school-aged sons and daughters with restrictive fathers (as measured by the Block Child Rearing Practices Report) expressed more frequent negative emotions in the stories they wrote, including more aggressive themes for girls, and also expressed more intense fear in response to stories they were told (Brody, Wise, and Monuteaux 1997). Eisenberg, Fabes, and Murphy (1996) also found that punitive fathers, such as those who reported sending their children to their rooms when they cried, had sons who had more negative emotionality, such as fear, worrying and anxiety. Similar patterns were found for adolescent sons who reported that their fathers engaged in intrusive behaviors, such as opening their sons' mail without asking. These sons expressed more intense negative feelings, including anger (Brody 1996).

However, data indicate that adolescent daughters' emotional expressiveness relates differently to intrusiveness by fathers. When daughters reported having intrusive fathers, they expressed not *more,* but *less* emotional intensity, with less intense sadness, anger, and shame reported by these daughters in comparison to daughters who had less intrusive fathers (Brody 1996). Data obtained from Eisenberg, Fabes, and Murphy (1996) on father-daughter relationships in school-aged children bear intriguing similarities to these adolescent data. They found that when fathers encouraged their daughters' emotional expressiveness (for example, endorsing such items as "encouraging my child to talk about her nervous feelings") at low and moderate levels, their daughters had a high likelihood of comforting a crying infant. If fathers encouraged their daughter's expressivity at a high level (which may be the equivalent of being intrusive), daughters were less likely to comfort a distressed infant: their comforting behaviors were minimized.

Unlike intrusive mother-daughter relationships, father's intrusiveness does not seem to result in a cycle of intense emotional expressiveness, especially negative expressiveness, for daughters. This may be because fathers' intrusiveness occurs less frequently and at lower levels than mothers' and is therefore less aversive (Brody 1993). Or perhaps an intrusive opposite-sex parent is a less threatening figure to daughters than is an intrusive same-sex parent, being less likely to threaten the attainment of a separate sense of self.

There are other ways these data can be interpreted. Intrusive fathers may provide an alternative means for daughters to differentiate from their highly involved mothers, and may serve as a buffer in a close mother-daughter relationship. In other words, daughters of intrusive fathers may not need to assert intense emotions as a means of self-expression to the same extent that daughters of nonintrusive fathers do.

The relationship between paternal intrusiveness and daughters' decreased intensity of emotional expression may also reflect a response on the part of fathers to their daughters' emotional characteristics. That is, fathers may become more intrusive toward daughters who are relatively emotionally inexpressive as a way of both eliciting a response from them as well as stimulating them to conform to gender stereotypes. Eisenberg, Fabes, and Murphy (1996) had a similar interpretation of somewhat counterintuitive findings concerning father-daughter relationships in school-aged children. They found that fathers who used more problem-focused reactions with their daughters, such as encouraging their daughters to solve a problem that caused them to be distressed (fixing a broken bicycle), had daughters who had lower social skills and were less popular than did daughters whose fathers helped them less. It may be that less socially and emotionally competent girls elicit fathers' help more than do relatively competent girls—that fathers do not become involved in the emotional lives of their daughters unless they feel that there is something to be "fixed."

The relationship between paternal intrusiveness and daughters' emotional functioning may also reflect a process of opposite-sex de-identification on the part of daughters. In other words, daughters may attempt to become unlike their intrusive fathers, who themselves may be expressing their own feelings in an intense manner. De-identification with fathers may help daughters to consolidate their own female identity.

Although still unknown, how fathers' intrusiveness relates to their own levels of emotional expressiveness will be important for evaluating these differing explanations. Levels of fathers' expressiveness may influence levels of their children's expressiveness independent of fathers' intrusiveness. For example, data obtained from 10-month-old infants indicate that when fathers report that they expressed *more* negative emotions, their infants expressed *less* anger when a toy was removed and *less* distress after the toy was returned than did infants with more positive fathers (Stifter and Grant 1993).The data seem to support a differentiation model—that children (both boys and girls) differ from their fathers in levels of negative emotional expression.

In brief, there are some intriguing findings on the relationships between children's emotional expression and fathers' intrusiveness, including the idea that sons' emotional expressiveness may be maximized and daughters' may be minimized in relation to paternal intrusiveness. Many questions remain to be empirically assessed, such as how fathers' intrusiveness relates to their levels of involvement in child care, to their own levels of emotional expressiveness, and to the interactions among all members of the family system. I now turn to the role of the family system in generating gender differences in emotional expressions.

Fathers, the Family System, and Children's Emotional Expressiveness

Families with involved fathers may function in a different emotional climate than families with uninvolved fathers, characterized by different patterns of emotional interaction. For example, families of involved fathers may be characterized by more mutually expressed positive emotions. Research indicates that when fathers are involved in family life, their own sense of satisfaction and fulfillment are enhanced (Lamb, Pleck, and Levine 1986). Children also have been found to express more appreciation to fathers who serve as primary caretakers than they do to single-parent mothers (Hanson 1988).[7] The gratitude and appreciation that involved fathers may receive would serve to facilitate more empathic and mutually satisfying father-child relationships.

When fathers are involved in child care, the family climate may also shift because there are fewer dyadic relationships in the family, in which only two people are involved, and more triadic interactions, in which both parents simultaneously interact with their child. The constellation of people involved may dramatically change the nature of family relationships. In fact, Gjerde (1986) found that each parent displayed different patterns of interaction when alone with their 13-year-old children than they did when the other parent was also present. Especially interesting is that fathers decreased the extent to which their behaviors differed toward their sons and their daughters when mothers were present, while the reverse was true of mothers. Fathers expressed less boredom, were less reserved, had more emotionally toned interactions, and were more likely to be seductive toward daughters than sons, but only when they spent time alone with either sons or daughters, and not when their wives were present. Mothers expressed more boredom and shared less humor with their daughters than with their sons, but only when their husbands were present, not when they were alone with either sons or daughters. These patterns suggest that involved fathers may shift the nature of gender-differentiated interactions between parents and their children in dramatic ways.

Also contributing to a different family emotional climate is mothers' and fathers' marital satisfaction. In my data, fathers who were more involved in child care had wives who reported being more satisfied with their marriages. Husbands also tended to be more satisfied with their marriages when they were more involved in childcare, but this was not significant.[8]

In turn, both spouses' marital satisfaction may relate to their level of marital conflict, which has been found to directly affect children's emotional expressivity. For example, children respond to intensely angry adult interactions with increased distress, shame, and self-blame (Grych and Fincham 1990, 1993). Children with unhappily married parents show greater heart-rate reactivity when producing facial expressions of emotion than do children with happily married parents (Shortt et al. 1994). In one study, fathers who were less positive about their marriages before their infants were born had babies who changed from low to high negative emotionality from ages 3 to 9 months (in contrast to babies who remained low in negative emotionality). Similarly, babies who exhibited low negative expressions over time had mothers who experienced less conflict and ambivalence in their marriages prenatally (Belsky, Fish, and Isabella 1991).

In other words, I am speculating that father involvement relates to lower levels of family conflict, and that in turn, family conflict may influence children's expressivity. Family conflict may affect children's expressivity because it changes the quality of emotions parents express toward their children. For example, fathers who feel they have happier marriages are warmer toward their children than are other men (Belsky, Fish, and Isabella 1991). Marital harmony in a couples' discussion task has also been found to be related to shared positive affect between parents and their young children (Easterbrooks and Emde 1988).

In marriages with high levels of conflict, defensive processes such as displacement and projection may take place. Parents may be especially likely to direct their negative feelings about their spouses toward their opposite-sex children. For example, fathers in conflictual marriages have been found to be more rejecting, critical, and controlling toward their daughters than toward their sons and to be more responsive, engaged, and creative toward their sons than toward their daughters (Kerig, Cowan, and Cowan 1993). The most dissatisfied fathers were the most negative toward their daughters. Mother-son relationships in troubled marital relationships are also more likely to be negative compared to the same relationships in nontroubled families (Osborne and Fincham 1996).

Children may also become critical of their opposite-sex parents during marital conflicts, identifying with their same-sex parents. For example, when watching videotaped marital conflicts between their parents, 6-year-old girls had more negative emotional reactions toward their fathers than boys had. They were also more likely than boys to report that their fathers were angry, despite objective ratings that fathers of boys and girls did not differ in the anger they expressed (Crockenberg and Forgays 1996). Girls whose parents had lower marital adjustment were more assertive with their fathers than with their mothers (Kerig, Cowan, and Cowan 1993). These patterns of results may be due to the fact that girls in dysfunctional families may identify with and ally with their mothers.

Gender and Family Stress

A review of several studies suggests the hypothesis that family stress and conflict results in increased intensity of emotional expressiveness for girls, and decreased intensity of emotional expressiveness for boys, with the exception of aggression. For example, 5-year-old boys from maritally distressed homes tended to decrease their physiological arousal when angry more quickly than girls did, thus minimizing negative affect (Walker and Wilson 1995). Another study using this same sample (as well as an additional sample) showed that 5-year-old boys from unhappily married families had difficulty making accurate facial expressions for happiness, anger, disgust, fear, and sadness (Shortt et al. 1994), whereas girls did not, supporting the idea that boys may minimize their emotional expressivity in the face of conflict.

Also corroborating this hypothesis is some of my own data, in which adolescent girls' self-reported emotions became more intense as family stress increased, while boys' self-reported emotions became less intense (Brody et al. 1996). Family stress included events such as parental divorce, alcoholism, and illness, and was corroborated by ratings from two siblings in each family.[9] For adolescent girls, more frequent and more intense family stress was related to *more* intense negative and positive emotions and *more* frequent shame and guilt in interpersonal story situations. In contrast, for adolescent boys, more frequent and intense family stress was related to *less* intense warmth, shame, and guilt. Girls may be responding to the stress within their families by attempting to maintain communication and family ties through the expression of feelings. Boys' decreased intensity of emotional expressiveness in the face of family stress may be an attempt to distance themselves from their families, as consistent with male gender roles. It is also possible that boys may simply be less willing to talk about their emotions (becoming more defensive) when there is family stress.

In brief, by looking at how the patterns of conflict in family relationships affect gender differences in emotional expressiveness, several hypotheses emerge about why sons and daughters express emotions differently. Girls may express more intense emotions using words and facial expressions than boys express because of several possibilities: Fathers tend to treat their daughters more negatively than they treat their sons in conflict situations, leading to the expression of more dysphoric emotions on the part of daughters. Girls may identify with their less powerful mothers, becoming angry and expressing anger toward their fathers. And finally, girls may attempt to use emotions as a way of maintaining family ties when their families are stressed, rather than distancing, or minimizing emotional expressivity, as boys may do. When fathers are involved in family life, these patterns shift, perhaps because family conflict is minimized.

OVERVIEW. When fathers are more involved in child care, daughters express relatively less emotional vulnerability and become more competitive and aggressive in comparison to other daughters. Sons express relatively more vulnerability and become relatively less competitive and aggressive in comparison to other sons. These findings are consistent with feminist psychoanalytic analyses of the family.

Some hypotheses as to why involved fathers contribute to the minimization of gender differences in their children's emotional expressiveness include the following: Involved fathers' presence may minimize family conflict; their style of child rearing and relating to their children may differ from that of noninvolved fathers; their involvement may be responsive to the ways in which their children express emotions; their involvement may help mothers and daughters to differentiate; their involvement may change the nature of family and marital interactions; and finally, their involvement may provide children, especially sons, with an alternative role model for emotional expressiveness.

The finding that children of involved fathers do not conform to gender-stereotypic emotional expressiveness has profound implications. It implies that family socialization is a powerful influence on the development of gender differences in emotional expressiveness. Family socialization includes not only direct practices, such as rewarding and punishing children for expressing certain types of feelings, but also processes inherent in the family's structure and mode of functioning, such as which parent cares for the children, or how much conflict exists within the family or marital system. These aspects of family functioning are often unacknowledged as formative for the emergence of gender differences in emotional functioning.

Family functioning also exists within a cultural context. We will see next that cultural values exert powerful influences on men and women to express emotions in gender-stereotypic ways and to socialize their children in accordance with gender-stereotypic norms.

III

Cultural Origins and Consequences
of Gender Differences

Social Motives, Power, and Roles

It's been harder for women to advance in the business world than
men—the pay scale is different. If I were a woman, I think I'd be
envious, too.

—*Andrew, age 42*

Although there is no doubt that families contribute to the emergence of
gender differences in their children, families themselves are subject to
many cultural and societal pressures about gender. In the next few chapters, I will be widening the framework for understanding how gender
differences emerge. If family processes are in the center of a gender
differences picture, cultural and social processes form thick borders
around it, often merging with it and changing its focus.

How are cultural and social processes linked to emotional expressiveness? When people experience emotions, such as anxiety, disappointment, pride, or fear, they know the state of their well being and whether
or not they are close to reaching their goals (Carver and Scheier 1990).[1]
In particular, emotions inform people about their position with respect
to the power, status, and intimacy they expect to attain in interpersonal
relationships (Kemper 1978). Expressing particular emotions also enables people to realize their social and cultural goals by influencing the
quality of their relationships, as consistent with functionalist theories of
emotion (Campos, Campos, and Barnett 1989). For example, people
who are motivated to attain status may express contempt for those they
perceive to be low-status individuals. Expressing contempt may make
them feared or hated by low-status individuals, thus keeping low-status
individuals at a distance. Expressing contempt may also bond them in a
common superiority with others who have high status, thus enhancing
self-esteem.

The relevant point for gender differences in emotional expression is that if females' goals, motives, personality characteristics, or social roles differ from those of their male counterparts, then it follows that the emotional expressiveness of the two sexes will also differ. Expressing particular feelings enables men and women to successfully function in their designated social roles, to bring their motives to fruition, and to adapt to the constraints of how much power and status they are afforded within the culture. In so doing, the expression of feelings serves to enhance well-being, satisfaction, and self-esteem.

In this chapter, I focus on two questions. First, are there gender differences in motives, personality characteristics, social roles, and power and status? The answer to this question ranges from a modest to a resounding yes. Second, how do gender differences in these dimensions relate to gender differences in emotional expressiveness? The answer to this second question is an important piece of the puzzle of why and how gender differences in emotional expressiveness emerge at all. It is critical to point out, as a preface to my discussion, that I speak of *average* differences between women and men within a Western cultural context. Not all individual men and women differ in these ways.

The Importance of Power, Status, and Intimacy

Emotions are closely linked to the interpersonal processes of power, status, and intimacy. Power, status, and intimacy have been theorized to be the basic dimensions of human social interaction, which emerge whenever individuals work together to meet basic needs (Kemper 1978; Fiske 1991). People divide up the workload necessary for survival either by coercing others (through power), or by making a voluntary agreement in which they agree to do something because it benefits and rewards themselves or another person who has high status or to whom they feel close. When individuals have power, they can force others to perform tasks for them; when individuals feel intimate or close to each other, they will voluntarily perform tasks for each other.

The fundamental importance of intimacy and power to the human condition is also emphasized by psychoanalytic theorists, who view these processes as arising in early infancy in interactions with primary caretakers. Some theorists assume that intimacy is an intrinsic need and motive, found in infants across all cultures, that promotes attachments to significant caretakers and thus ensures survival (Bowlby 1988). When intimacy needs are not met by caretakers, power motives may result. Through the use of power people may dominate and coerce others into recognizing them at the very least, and at best, into having a relationship with them (Benjamin 1988).

Power motives may not only be a defensive reaction to unmet intimacy needs, but may be adaptive and rewarding in and of themselves. Psychoanalytic theorists write about early precursors of power, such as simple foot-kicking in the crib, as pleasurable (Lichtenberg 1982). Such actions initially may serve to explore the limits of physical capability, but the feelings associated with such actions, such as pride, are also those that accompany later forms of power, such as figuratively "kicking" others. One's own needs have a better chance of being met if one can control the efforts of others. Research has indicated that being in a more powerful position is associated with feelings of satisfaction and high self-esteem, so much so that more powerful people strive to maintain or to increase their distance to less powerful people (Hofstede 1980; Mulder 1977).

Because power, status, and intimacy are universal processes that are critical to survival, it should come as no surprise that they constitute goals that are people be motivated to attain (Fiske 1991). A power motive is the desire to coerce, dominate, or control others (Winter 1988), whereas an intimacy motive is the preference for warm, close interactions and relationships with others (McAdams et al. 1988). Some people seek to attain power as a way of coercing others to do their work; others seek to attain status or intimacy as a way of getting tasks performed cooperatively. This raises two critical questions: Are men and women differentially motivated to attain power, status and intimacy? And, how are these motives related to emotional expressiveness?

Intimacy Motives and Gender

Do men and women differ in intimacy motives, or motives to be close to others? The short answer is: a modest yes. Some research has indicated that women are higher in intimacy motivation than men and are also more interdependent and relational than men (James et al. 1995; McAdams et al. 1988). These observations frequently come from responses to the Thematic Apperception Test (TAT), in which women and men are asked to compose stories to accompany ambiguous pictures. Women write stories involving characters who have loved or liked each other for a long time more often than men do. Other research has shown that when college student research participants wear beepers, are paged, and then asked what they are thinking about, women report nearly twice as many interpersonal thoughts as men do (McAdams and Constantian 1983). In keeping diaries of their social interactions, more college student women than men note communicating with others because they are motivated by needs for affection, such as "letting others know I care"; or being "concerned about them" (Rubin, Perse, and Barbato 1988). And when completing daily logs of how intimate their interactions are with others, college student women rate their interactions as more intimate than men rate theirs (Barrett et al. 1998).

Women also indicate a higher level of preference for emotional support than men do, endorsing such items as, "If I feel unhappy or depressed, I usually try to be around other people to make me feel better." They also report deriving more pleasure from intimacy than men, stating that, "I think being close to others, listening to them and relating to them on a one-to-one level is one of my favorite and most satisfying pastimes" (Hill 1987). Perhaps most important, women's self-esteem is tied to their connections and attachments to others to a greater extent than is men's self-esteem. When memorized words were associated with other people or with best friends, women with high self-esteem recalled more words than did either men or women with low self-esteem. Moreover, when women were deceptively told that according to a bogus test they were not attuned to and responsive to the needs and feelings of those around them, those women with high self-esteem reacted with defensive and compensatory predictions about their performance on a subsequent test (Josephs, Markus, and Tafarodi 1992).

There may certainly be cultural and ethnic differences in the extent to which gender differences in intimacy and related motives exist and are perceived to exist. For example, African-American women are stereotyped to be less emotional, less dependent on others, and less passive than European-American women (Landrine 1985). On the other hand, a recent study of men and women from Japan, Slovenia, and the United States showed that women from all three countries reported placing greater importance on values associated with intimacy and affiliation, including helping people and spending time with their families, than did men (Morinaga, Frieze, and Ferligoj 1993).

Gender differences in intimacy motives suggest that women should express "relational" or "socially engaged" feelings that facilitate relationships with others, including affection, warmth, shame, and liking. These emotions signal to others that closeness is desired. Shame, for example, is an emotion expressed when feelings or experiences are not acknowledged or validated by others, and communicates to others how important their evaluations are deemed to be (Lewis 1971). Shame functions to restore disrupted or threatened relationships (Zahn-Waxler, Barrett, and Cole 1991), while affection, warmth, and liking communicate wishes for closeness.

People who are higher in intimacy motives are indeed rated by peers to be warmer, more loving, and less dominant than those lower in intimacy motives (McAdams 1980). Using beepers, they record more positive emotions in interpersonal situations (McAdams and Constantian 1983). They also display more nonverbal behaviors indicative of warmth and friendliness, such as smiling and eye contact, than do people who are lower in intimacy motives (McAdams, Jackson, and Kirshnit 1984; McAdams 1984). It seems evident that women's relatively high expressions of warmth, shame, liking, and affection may be related to their relatively high intimacy motivation.

Women's relatively high intimacy motivation may also lead them to suppress the expression of feelings that might threaten close relationships, including aggression and competitive feelings. Research indicates that when women feel angry, they express not only anger, but a wider range of feelings than men express, including sadness, hurt, and disappointment (Brody 1993), that pose less of a threat to disrupting relationships than do direct expressions of anger. Men express anger directly to the person who provoked the angry feeling, whereas women complain about their anger to an uninvolved third party (Timmers, Fischer, and Manstead 1998).

Women may also smile more than men because they want to maintain friendly relationships and to avoid offending others. For example, although young girls and boys smile equally when receiving a wanted gift, young girls smile more when receiving a disappointing gift than young boys smile. Girls may smile in order to avoid hurting the feelings of the gift-giver. Smiling in this case may be motivated by empathy and the motive to maintain harmony in relationships (Cole 1986; Saarni 1988).

In an intriguing study, male and female college students provided information about who they were interacting with as well as about the intimacy of their interactions in daily emotion logs. Their reports of happiness, sadness, surprise, embarrassment, and shame all increased as the reported intimacy of their interactions with others increased. Women, in particular, rated themselves as expressing more intense emotion as the intimacy of their relationships increased. And when the level of intimacy in social interactions was statistically controlled, men and women did not differ in the intensity of their emotional experiences, suggesting that women's perceptions of greater intimacy in their interactions may serve to increase the intensity of their emotional expressiveness (Barrett et al., 1998).

Power Motives and Gender

Power refers to the coercion or domination of others on both social and individual levels (Winter 1988). People with high power motives should express more frequent emotions such as pride, contempt, anger and aggression. These "socially disengaged" emotions focus on maintaining a position of superiority and foster a sense of separateness between self and others (Markus and Kitayama 1991).

Indeed, men with high power motives do express anger and aggression (McClelland 1985), while women with high power motives express anger in writing TAT stories (Malatesta and Culver 1984). Further, people with high power motives take an active, assertive, controlling, or helping role with their friends, and are fearful that others will embarrass them by being boorish or crude (McAdams 1984).

There is no evidence that men are higher in power motives than women, despite popular beliefs and theories to the contrary. There are also no gender differences in the conditions that elicit power or in levels of interest in power (Stewart and Chester 1982; Winter 1988). However, men and women may experience power differently. When college students are asked when they have felt the most powerful, both sexes stress leadership and control over others, but only females label power as the sense of accomplishment at doing something well. Further, only men mention exerting physical force over another person as contributing to feelings of power (Lips 1989, 1994).

There is also a great deal of evidence that shows that the behaviors related to high power motivation differ for men and women. In men, power motives are more closely tied to aggression and impulsive behaviors than they are in women. Men who are high in power motivation are more likely to argue, drink, gamble, use drugs, be physically and verbally aggressive, sexually exploitative, engage in competitive sports, and read sexually oriented or sports magazines. Further, they are more likely to have wives without professional careers and to be divorced. They also express more themes of feminine evil in their fantasies, such as women harming men through physical contact or by exploiting men (McClelland 1975; Stewart and Chester 1982; McAdams 1984).

None of these impulsive behaviors are associated with high power motives in women. In fact, women high in power motivation, relative to women low in power motivation, are actually more likely to have stable relationships, to marry successful men, to have higher marital satisfaction, and to be less likely to divorce. Women are more apt to fulfill power needs by being responsible in relationships. This seems especially true of women who define themselves in traditional ways (McAdams 1984; Stewart and Chester 1982).

Even when women have high power motives, they are reluctant to wield dominance over others. For example, women high in power motivation do not exhibit their usual interpersonal assertiveness when interacting with men who are low in dominance. To a greater extent than men, women may use their power to equalize the size of the rewards they and others get, so that they maintain friendly relationships with others (Major and Adams 1983; Lips 1989, 1994). Although men and women may be equally high in their power motives, women may make the attainment of intimacy a priority, whereas men make the attainment of power a priority.

The link between women's power motives and their responsible, caring behavior (Winter 1988) may be due to their socialization history, with young women often being held responsible for the care of their siblings (Whiting and Edwards 1988). Both men and women who cared for younger siblings have been found to express their power motives in more responsible ways, such as political canvassing, when compared to people who did not care for younger siblings (Winter 1988). As a consequence of their nurturing and interpersonal caretaking roles, women may express their power motives less often in the form of emotions such as anger, aggression, and contempt than men, because such emotions distance them from other people.

Control Motives and Gender

Men appear to value a sense of control in relationships more than women (Rosenfeld 1979). For example, male college students who kept diaries of the reasons they communicated with others explained that they talked to someone because, "I wanted someone to do something for me"; or "To tell others what to do" more often than did female college students (Rubin, Perse, and Barbato 1988). They also reported that they would express their anger because they wanted to be seen as self-confident, a form of control (Timmers, Fischer, and Manstead 1998). Further, they reported that they had more control over their interactions than women reported (Barrett et al., 1998).

Qualitative research exploring the reasons people do not disclose their emotions to others indicates that men avoid disclosures in order to maintain control in relationships and to avoid being vulnerable, whereas women avoid disclosures in order to prevent their relationships from being harmed or hurt in some way (Rosenfeld 1979; Timmers, Fischer, and Manstead 1998). Men are more afraid that in disclosing their feelings, they risk retaliation by others, emphasizing the competitive aspects of relationships (Robison, Stockton and Morran 1990). They also report that disclosing their feelings would affect their self-esteem more than women report, endorsing such items as, "If I expressed my feelings, I would not be able to 'hold myself together' as well as before I made the disclosure" (Robison, Stockton, and Morran 1990).

There is some evidence that even in infancy, control is a more important goal for boys than for girls. When Fagot and Kavanaugh (1990) analyzed 12- and 18-month-olds' behaviors in response to strangers, boys showed more resistance and avoidance to strangers who were directive and gave instructions than did girls. In other words, boys responded more adversely than girls to being controlled. In school-aged children, boys' social goals more often revolved around control than girls', including control over activities, possessions, and personal space. For example, boys were more likely than girls to endorse the statement, "I don't want to be disturbed when I'm doing something" (Chung and Asher 1996).

A higher motive to be in control of relationships and of personal space would lead to lowered expressions of vulnerability, such as hurt and disappointment, and heightened expressions of aggression and anger. The expression of vulnerable emotions would be avoided because such emotions might provoke retaliation, demonstrating weakness to others. Anger and aggression, on the other hand, would serve to protect being in control, sending the message that others should not come close. That feelings of control and emotional expressiveness are systematically related was noted by Barrett and her colleagues (1998), who found that feelings of control in daily interactions were related to lower ratings of experienced surprise, as well as to higher global ratings for how much emotion was expressed in an interaction. Although Barrett and her colleagues did not explore the expression of specific emotions, my prediction is that when people perceive that they have more personal control, they express more intense feelings specifically associated with personal agency, such as pride and anger.

Individualism and Gender

Individualism includes differentiation from others, interpersonal objectivity, competitiveness, and when performing cognitive tasks, engaging in separation and ordering. These are characteristics that have been linked to power, dominant acts, and agency (Wiggins 1991). Although both men and women can score high or low on individualism, there is some evidence that American men are, on average, more individualistic than women. For example, Josephs, Markus, and Tafarodi (1992) found that men's self-esteem was linked to an individuation process in which their personal achievements were emphasized. Men with high self esteem rated themselves as "better than most people" in their abilities (including social, academic, creative, and athletic) to a greater degree than men with low self-esteem did and than women did, regardless of their levels of self-esteem.

How might individualism be related to emotional expressiveness? Wegner and Erber (1993) make the fascinating point that autonomy is signalled by having a secret inner life. The individuality of the self is created by concealing what you're really feeling; distinguishing between private experience and what is publicly expressed. If we apply Wegner and Erber's ideas to gender differences, we can hypothesize that since men have lower intimacy motives and higher motives for individualism than women have, they may express fewer emotions outwardly, as a way of creating a sense of self distinct from others, a self that is private and autonomous.

However, in order to be effective in influencing others, people must appear to be genuine. This requires either being a gifted actor, or developing inner experiences that conform to an outward communication of feeling, so as to actually become genuine. In other words, to be genuine, men must not only *appear* emotionally inexpressive, but also *feel* a lack of emotion. They may do this through what Wegner and Erber term mental control processes. Such mental control strategies include immersing themselves in a distracting task or changing their facial expressions to become impassive. Do men engage in these control strategies more than women do? To some extent, the data I've reviewed previously indicate that they do. Men's faces are relatively more impassive than are women's and they engage in more distracting behaviors, like sports, when they are distressed. These processes are consistent with the idea that men may engage in more emotional control strategies than women do. This may be precisely because they have higher motives for control and individualism.

Personality Characteristics and Emotion

Research has attempted to link not only motives, but individual differences in personality characteristics to the quality of emotional expressiveness. The two personality characteristics of communion (being kind, affectionate, or nurturing) and agency (being goal-directed, independent or worldly) have been widely studied with respect to emotional expression. Both men and women can be high or low on either or both of these characteristics. However, communal characteristics are more often found in women than in men; the reverse is true for characteristics related to agency. Because of their differing frequencies in the two sexes, these two characteristics have been associated with gender roles. It is important to note that the distinction between communal and agentic characteristics vastly oversimplifies the complexities of gender roles and leads to the false assumption that they are dichotomized traits. In fact, research has indicated that both traits vary in individual men and women (see Spence and Buckner 1995).

An accumulating body of literature indicates that having communal or agentic characteristics is related to emotional expressiveness. In general, communal individuals are more emotionally expressive and agentic individuals are less emotionally expressive, with the exception of loneliness, anger, and aggression. Communal individuals (both men and women) have been found to be more empathic, sympathetic, and nurturing; to smile, gaze, and nod their heads more frequently; to express more sadness, guilt, nervousness, fear, jealousy, warmth, hurt, and emotional intensity than those who score as less communal in personality. They also express less loneliness, aggression, and verbal hostility; control the expression of anger more; express more feelings using words to their spouses; and disclose more about themselves in social contexts than do less communal individuals (Bem, Martyna, and Watson 1976; LaFrance and Carmen 1980; Bander and Betz 1981; Parelman 1983; Wheeler, Reis, and Nezlek 1983; Dillon, Wolf, and Katz 1985; White and Mullen 1989; Brody, Hay, and Vandewater 1990; Kopper and Epperson 1991; Shaffer, Pegalis, and Cornell 1991; Kopper 1993; Brody et al. 1995). The emotions expressed by communal individuals may be adaptive for pursuing interpersonal intimacy goals.

People who score higher on agency are less emotionally expressive, particularly around emotions having to do with vulnerability, depression, or dysphoric self-consciousness, including fear and shame, than are those who score lower on agency. They are also less intimate in the content of their self-disclosures than are communal individuals (Parelman 1983; Brody 1993). They are more likely to express emotions connoting individualism, such as disgust and anger, as well as happiness and intense positive emotions than are individuals who score lower on agency (Brody et al. 1995). Some of these relationships have been shown in children as well (Brody, Hay, and Vandewater 1990).

My own research has shown that the extent to which an individual is characterized by levels of communion and agency is more powerful than biological sex in predicting the expression of many emotions, including hurt, guilt, shame, happiness, fear, and sadness (Brody, Hay, and Vandewater 1990; Brody et al. 1995). Using multiple regression statistical analyses, biological sex differences contributed less variance to the expression of feelings than personality characteristics contributed, including how communal or agentic both sexes were. This implies that the characteristics associated with communion may be the keys to understanding women's emotional expressiveness, while the characteristics associated with agency, such as the provider role and control motives, may be the keys to understanding men's emotional expressiveness.

There are two problems with the literature on gender role–related personality characteristics and emotional expression. The first is that communion and emotional expressiveness may be synonymous to some extent. Reporting yourself to be "kind," a communal attribute, may consist of assessing what your habitual emotional expressiveness is. In fact, researchers have measured the concept of communion with items such as "I cry easily," thus partly assuming that one aspect of communion is emotional expressiveness. Any relationships found between communion and emotional expressiveness may be due to the fact that the two constructs are not independent in how they are conceptualized and measured (see Shields 1995).

A second problem with the literature is that researchers often do not explore the relationship between these two variables within each sex, as opposed to across both sexes. Researchers frequently pool both sexes together to explore how emotional expressiveness relates to a personality characteristic, such as agency. Because more men than women score high on agency, and more women than men score high on communion, pooling the two sexes confounds the contribution made by biological gender with that made by personality characteristics, independent of gender. In light of these caveats, this body of work should be interpreted cautiously.

Gender, Cultural Power, and Status

So far, I've focused on how emotional expressiveness is related to motives and personality characteristics located within the individual. But the cultural roles imposed on the individual from the outside are also critical to emotional functioning. Especially relevant for the quality of emotions people express are the power and status dimensions of the social relationships they are involved in. People continually evaluate these dimensions, asking themselves questions such as, "is this a person with more power, with the potential to hurt us, or reward us in some way? Is this a person with less status than we have, whose opinion of us doesn't particularly matter? Is this a person we don't feel particularly close to, whose reactions are unpredictable?" People are less safe in relationships in which they wield lower power and have lower status. When dealing with those who are more powerful, personal freedom and safety may be at risk.

The fact that there are power imbalances between women and men should be systematically related to the feelings they express. In a brilliant theory of how emotions relate to the quality of social interactions, Theodore Kemper (1978) has hypothesized that expressed emotions conform to the appraisals of the status and power differences people perceive. Expressed emotions maximize the likelihood that power and status imbalances will shift or be maintained in a direction that furthers people's well-being. I will review the evidence for this assertion in this next section, and, at the risk of stating the obvious, for the assertion that women have lower status and power than men. I should stress at the outset that the links between cultural values, such as power and status, and gender differences in emotion are largely theoretical. At present, there are few systematic studies that have been undertaken to test these ideas.

Here is a succinct list of the ways in which women have less power and status then men: Women do not hold formal positions that give them the right to influence others. For example, far fewer women than men hold management or political positions. Women tend to be occupationally segregated from men and restricted to lower paying jobs. The economic value of their housework and child care is discounted and they often are poorer. Less money is clearly related to less power, as exemplified by the fact that the amount of decision-making power women wield in their marital relationships is proportional to how much money they make and how highly educated they are (Peplau and Gordon 1985). As the comparative economic resources of spouses become more equal, so does the balance of power between them (Peplau 1984; Lips 1989).[2]

Women's interests tend to be subordinated to men's through social pressures. Married women in our society derive much of their status from their husbands. Very little value is placed on the wife's accomplishments in assessing the social status of the couple. In fact, a woman's status is mostly based on her marital status, her children, and her physical attractiveness, perhaps accounting for the relatively greater importance women place on symbols such as clothing, makeup, and plastic surgery. Women's work tends to be undervalued because a woman has done it rather than because of its quality; women's success is attributed to luck or chance more often than men's success (Lips 1994).

The list goes on. Women are perceived to be less logical and competent than are men (Johnson 1978). They have less physical strength than men, and are less likely to inflict physical harm on others. They have less freedom of movement than men and have to cope with threats of violence when travelling alone, walking alone, or venturing into unknown or dangerous places (Hacker 1951). They more often have less time to themselves than men have, since women are more likely than men to perform two jobs, both as financial providers and child caretakers (Hochschild 1990). Frieze and Ramsey (1976) also document that women command less physical space than men command and are less likely to have a personal area, or special chair, than are their spouses. Space can also be interpreted as a form of personal power.

Women's Emotions, Status, and Power

What do women's lower status and power have to do with their emotional expressiveness? Because of their lower status and power, women may interpret some situations as being uncontrollable and risky. When people feel out of control, they get scared. Interestingly, in parts of West Africa, when women attained independent incomes and more power and control over their lives because of changing male labor migration patterns, men began to express heightened fears of female witchcraft, antifeminism, envy of women, and feelings of sexual inadequacy (LeVine 1966).

Lower status and power may also be related to the fact that young girls are less confident about their abilities to perform unfamiliar and unstructured tasks than boys are (Lind and Connole 1985). Assessing tasks as less controllable may lead girls to express more fear than boys. Not only do girls interpret cognitive tasks to be less controllable, but in interacting with aggressive boys, who are potentially sexually harassing, they are likely to interpret heterosexual relationships to be less controllable as well, leading to fear, anger, dread, and dismay (Lips 1989, 1994).

What about the other feelings that women express more intensely than men, including shame, embarrassment, distress, sympathy, and at times, especially within marital relationships, hostility and anger? How are these related to lower status and power? First, if women believe they deserve to have less status and power than men, they will feel less worthy and more ashamed. If they accept the idea that women should be in positions of low power, then they may express guilt if and when they manage to obtain positions of high power. They may apologize for any power they do wield.

Further, if women feel angry about their lower status and power, but feel too scared or anxious to express their anger, this too may ultimately lower their self-esteem, resulting in shame. Kemper (1978) writes: "When felt hostility is not expressed toward the other when the other has done us injury, we suffer not only from loss of what was denied us, but also from the loss of self-esteem by virtue of cowardice in taking the injury lying down, so to speak . . . we must judge ourselves unworthy on that account" (p. 66). Women's relative lack of behavioral freedom may also contribute to their expressions of anger. When behavioral freedom is threatened, people will try to reassert or regain their threatened freedom through anger, hostility, or other means (Walster and Walster 1975; Walster, Berscheid, and Walster 1973).

Although women have less access to power than men, there are no gender differences in motives to obtain power (see Stewart and Chester 1982). This is an inherently frustrating situation that could potentially precipitate distress and anger, including a sense of righteous indignation. Anger would be particularly likely if women blamed men for their lower status and power, interpreting their plight as the fault of men. Research has shown that women become angry more frequently than men in situations in which they have unwillingly consented to something, a demonstration of their own powerlessness (Biaggio 1989).

Although women may feel more entitled to their anger than men, they may actually feel less free to express it, since expressing negative emotions may make women less safe. As a higher status group, men have greater access to resources and have the potential to harm women. Women may only allow themselves to express their negative feelings, such as anger and envy, in intimate relationships, in which they feel safer. This may be why we are especially likely to see women's anger in marital conflicts.

Expressing distress instead of anger may be a strategy used by women to minimize potential interpersonal hurt and harm while attempting to change an unsatisfying interpersonal relationship. Research has shown that individuals in positions of lower power, regardless of gender, use more indirect power strategies, such as expressing positive and negative affect, than do those with equal or higher power (Kipnis 1976; Howard, Blumstein, and Schwartz 1986). Indirect power strategies used by women include not only the expression of distress as a substitute for anger, but also changes in positive emotion, such as looking appealing, winsome, or innocent. Adolescent girls report using positive emotion strategies to get their own way more than boys (Cowan, Drinkard, and MacGavin 1984).

As opposed to direct demands and the expression of hostility, the expression of positive emotions and distress may actually minimize the risk of competition and retaliation. In fact, some but not all research has shown that in abusive relationships, women who express distress and depression are less likely to be abused than are those who express hostility and anger (Biglan et al. 1985; but also see Jacobson et al. 1994). When men are dissatisfied with their relationships, they can simply issue commands or express their anger directly, because they are usually in a position of relative safety. Research has indicated that husbands directly negotiate or withdraw more than their wives do (Falbo and Peplau 1980; Gottman and Levenson 1986, 1992; Lips 1989).

There is a flip side to the argument about women's lower power and status relating to their emotional expressiveness. With arguably greater social and interpersonal skills than men, women have the power to bestow the recognition and affection needed by their husbands and families. Thus, intimacy and emotional expressiveness become a form of power, a resource that women can bestow or withhold.

However, women's emotional power in relationships may actually be lowered because they are more dependent on affection than are men, as indicated by their higher intimacy motivation. People who are more dependent on relationships, or who are invested in keeping the relationships going, are actually more likely to be exploited by their partners, and to use "weak" power tactics such as manipulation and supplication (Noller and Fitzpatrick 1993). These ideas suggest that relational skills are not a very strong source of power for women, and that women's emotional expressiveness probably does not help them to wield significantly greater amounts of power than men.

WARMTH AND SMILING.   Why might women's expressions of warmth, and in particular, smiling, be related to their low status and power? The "oppression hypothesis" suggests that less dominant groups smile more and are more sensitive to nonverbal cues than are dominant groups for several reasons: to ingratiate themselves with powerful groups, to enhance their own power, and to avoid possible aversive consequences. The emotions adaptive for affiliation, such as warmth and liking, may also be a way for women to increase their self-esteem, because research has indicated that individuals can increase their self-esteem by affiliating with higher status individuals (Tesser, Millar, and Moore 1988). Smiling may also help to appease the powerful, helping women to avoid possible punitive experiences. Hall and Halberstadt (1996) point out that the reverse of this argument may be true: superiors may be motivated to not smile and to be insensitive to the feelings of their subordinates as a way of keeping the power dynamics in place (see also Fiske 1993).

The oppression hypothesis continues to be hotly debated with respect to how power and status imbalances affect emotional sensitivity and smiling (see LaFrance and Henley 1994). Research has indicated that the frequency of smiling does change as a result of some power differentials. For example, levels of smiling are higher when people are assigned the role of job applicants rather than job interviewers (Deutsch 1990). Also, people tend to interpret lack of smiling as dominant behavior. Keating et al. (1981) found that in 11 cross-cultural samples, including Germany, Kenya, Spain, Brazil, and Thailand, people associated smiling faces with happiness, whereas nonsmiling faces were associated with dominance. Women's proclivity to smile more than men do may be interpreted by others as meaning that they are less powerful, which in turn may serve a self-fulfilling prophecy, causing people to interact with them differently and ultimately affecting their actual levels of dominance.

However, some studies have shown the opposite of what the oppression hypothesis might predict. Contrary to the hypothesis, women with higher status and power, that is, with higher salary ranks, were actually better at decoding some emotional cues (sad or regretful) than were women with lower salary ranks (Hall, Halberstadt, and O'Brien 1997). Moreover, lower status individuals do not always smile more than higher status individuals (Hall et al., n.d.; LaFrance and Henley 1994). Further, recent research indicates that in experimentally created situations of power, it is not that subordinates are more sensitive to nonverbal cues than are superiors, but that people in superior positions communicate their feelings more clearly than do those in subordinate positions, making it easier for the subordinates to understand what they are feeling. This is especially true of superiors' feelings about the subordinates themselves, which were obvious even to naive observers of the interactions (Snodgrass, Hecht, and Ploutz-Snyder 1998).

Several studies have also indicated that gender differences in emotional expressions and experiences exist regardless of how much power men or women hold in experimental situations. For example, women smile more than men even when engaged in a stereotypically feminine task in which they wield more power than men wield (Dovidio et al. 1988). Moreover, when men and women are both put in positions of power as interviewers, male interviewers more readily describe themselves as dominant (Deutsch 1990).

Judith Hall (1987) points out that the historical oppression of women may have led to certain role expectations. These in turn may have led to particular emotional expressions, such as increased smiling, or minimized emotional expressions associated with power, such as pride or contempt, regardless of whether or not actual power was at hand. In brief, historical expectations could perpetuate sex differences in emotional expressiveness via modeling, reinforcement, and intergenerational transmission, even if oppression was currently nonexistent, and was not directly responsible for the gender differences we currently see.

The combined effects of both differing power and status as well as the differential motives of the two sexes may account for gender differences in smiling behavior. When low status is accompanied by motives to be affiliative, to be liked by others, or to ingratiate oneself with others, then higher levels of smiling may ensue. For example, more frequent smiling and behavioral output, including head nods, gestures, and speech were found to be characteristic of those seeking the approval of others, in contrast to those wishing to avoid others (Rosenfeld 1966).

Men's Emotions, Status, and Power

Can the emotions men express be explained as arising from power and status differences between the two sexes? I have discussed previously that in some situations men express more pride, contempt, loneliness, and aggression than women do. In particular situations involving active wrongdoing, they also express more guilt than women express.

Contempt, especially the derogation of women, may arise out of a defensive need to justify power imbalances as well as to enhance men's self-esteem (Brickman and Janoff-Bulman 1977; Gruder 1977). Those in positions of higher power have been found to devalue the worth of subordinates' performances, attributing good performance to their own power, not the efforts of the subordinate (Kipnis 1972). In one study, when people saw a woman being mistreated, they derogated her instead of expressing compassion, seeing her as the agent of her own powerlessness (Kipnis 1972; Mulder 1977). This suggests that men would be likely to express contempt and pity toward women, and some research has shown that this is indeed the case (Buss 1989; Brody 1993).

Being in a more powerful position may also be associated with feelings of satisfaction and pride. The mere exercise of power provides satisfaction (Mulder 1977). Pride may also ensue from the rationalization that the power imbalance is fair. Men may convince themselves that they deserve more status and power because they are inherently superior. Even delinquents and confidence men spend time and effort trying to convince others that their behavior is "fair," as pointed out by Walster, Berscheid, and Walster (1973).

Higher status groups may also express some negative feelings related to their high power. For example, they may feel guilty or badly about themselves because being more powerful than others may violate their ethical principles of fairness (Walster, Berscheid, and Walster 1973). Some research indicates that men express more guilt over wrongdoing than women express (Lewis 1971). In the face of such guilt, they can compensate their victims (who, in this case, are women), or they can restore equity through self-deprivation. Alternatively, they can persuade themselves that the act was equitable by devaluing women's inputs, accompanied by either contempt or pity. Or, they can deny responsibility for the harm done, consequently resulting in anger.

Finally, male aggression and loneliness may also be inextricably linked to having higher status and power. Aggression is functional for attaining and maintaining power over others. And toleration of loneliness may be adaptive for maintaining higher status and power, too. In order to avoid loneliness, men would have to be involved in intimate and social relationships, which in turn would demand disclosures of vulnerability and weakness, threatening both power and status.

In brief, emotional expressions shift dramatically depending on the relative power and status of the participants in the interaction. Status and power imbalances exist not only within opposite-sex interactions, but also within same-sex interactions. When people interact with members of their own sex, power and status imbalances are no longer based on gender, but on other attributes, such as personality characteristics, physical strength, race, religion, marital status, appearance, or education. Power imbalances based on these other variables would relate to the quality of emotions expressed by each participant in ways similar to those I have already described.

Cultural Differences

Do the theorized relationships between the expression of emotions and power and status hold true for all cultures? One view is that there are universal emotional reactions linked to having or not having power. Restrictions of behavioral freedom in the form of lower power would be experienced as aversive regardless of cultural context (Walster, Berscheid, and Walster 1973; Walster and Walster 1975). Another view is that the relationships among power, status, and emotional expressiveness are culturally specific. Some cultures may accept a power hierarchy as normative. Women and other lower power groups within such a culture may feel satisfied with their station in life. Particularly in non-Western cultures, the emphasis on collectivism and on established power hierarchies may make anger and resentment less likely on the part of women and others who are low in power.

Hofstede (1980) notes that in cultures in which a power hierarchy is acceptable, having higher power will be interpreted positively and will be associated with positive feelings. In cultures in which a power hierarchy is unacceptable, having higher power will be interpreted negatively, even by those in positions of power, and may be associated with shame or guilt.

These hypotheses are untested and it remains unclear how the relationships among power, status, and emotional expressiveness vary among cultures.

Social Roles and Emotion

Expressing emotions is not just adaptive for fulfilling motives and for adjusting to power and status levels. The expression (or the nonexpression) of specific feelings enables people to maximize the likelihood that they will successfully complete their socially assigned roles. For example, maintaining a cheerful expression enables those in service delivery occupations to maintain good relationships with their customers (Hochschild 1983). In most cultures, women's roles involve child and family caretaking, while men's roles involve protecting and providing for their families. Theories and research indicate that these differing roles, caretaking versus providing, are associated with the expression of dissimilar emotions (Eagly 1987; Gutmann 1987).

The Caretaking Role

Women's caretaking roles should be related to the expression of warmth, fear, vulnerability, distress, and the suppression of aggression. As a child caretaker, it is adaptive to suppress aggression because aggression is potentially destructive to children's survival. And in fact, there is some evidence that during the child rearing years, women's birth and nurturance themes increase in the TAT stories they write, while anger and dominance themes in the same stories diminish (Malatesta and Culver 1984).

The expression of warmth is also adaptive for child caretakers because it helps to establish a relationship with young children. In my data, women who were primarily homemakers expressed more warmth than did other women or men who were not primarily homemakers (Brody 1993). Similarly, the enhanced facial expressiveness that is more characteristic of women than of men would be useful and important in enabling communication with nonverbal infants and young children.

Then, too, caretakers are often anxious about the dangers facing their children, whose welfare they are responsible for, but can never completely control. Such anxieties would maximize the likelihood of expressions of fear and vulnerability, including helplessness. My research has partially confirmed this: both men and women working in caretaking roles, such as nursing, or teaching, expressed increased fear relative to those not working in such roles (Brody 1993).

It should hardly surprise anyone that the responsibilities of child care would also be associated with distress. Minor aversive events occur as often as once every 3 minutes when mothers interact with normal preschoolers; and the younger the child, the more frequent these events are (Patterson 1980). Mothers of young children are prone to expressing high rates of dysphoric feelings (Malatesta and Culver 1984), including stress, depression, anxiety, feelings of isolation, and helplessness. Middle-class wives' expressions of resentment toward their spouses also increases during child rearing years.

Despite these high levels of resentment and distress, Sara Ruddick (1982) argues that a certain level of cheerful optimism (which we can also think of as denial) is part of the caretaking role. In order to survive the daily ups and downs of life with children, caretakers must have some optimistic faith that their long-term goals of enabling children to reach adulthood will be reached. Expressing optimism may serve to reassure children (as well as mothers themselves) that they will thrive, despite fantasies as well as realistic worries about their vulnerability.

Expressing dismay, hurt, or disappointment in frustrating situations, rather than, or in addition to anger, may also stem from women's culturally assigned roles as caretakers. Research has indicated that mothers who use gentle control strategies, such as making polite requests, positive comments, or using reasoning, rather than using power-based negative control strategies, such as threats or direct commands, have children who are more likely to comply with their requests in a positive manner (Kochanska and Aksan 1995). Moreover, mothers who express disappointment in their children have children who are in fact more empathic and prosocial (Krevans and Gibbs 1996). In other words, expressing dysphoric feelings, such as disappointment, or positive feelings rather than angry feelings, may be used by mothers as an effective strategy (perhaps an unconcious one) that changes children's behavior in positive directions.

The argument that the caretaking role relates to the quality of emotional expressiveness is supported by research assessing the emotions expressed by men who are caretakers. If men who are caretakers express more distress, warmth, vulnerability, fear, and optimism, but less aggression than do men who are not caretakers, this is strong support for the idea that the caretaking role itself elicits the expression of specific feelings.

There are indeed some data that support the idea that when men are caretakers, they express more vulnerability and warmth. For example, husbands who do more stereotypically female household tasks, including child care, report greater nervousness than other men do

(Brody 1993). Similarly, when fathers in the United States function as primary caretakers (primarily because of divorce), they are more nurturing, affectionate, and emotionally involved with their children than are fathers who do less caretaking (Risman 1987; Hanson 1988; Pruett and Litzenberger 1992).

Other research has shown that when either sex does more, as opposed to less, child care, they express more warmth and nurturance and less aggression. In their cross-cultural research, Whiting and Edwards (1988) found that both boys and girls who interacted frequently with younger children scored higher on nurturance than those who interacted less frequently. In East African societies where "feminine" work is assigned to boys, there are fewer differences in the aggressive, sympathetic, and helpful behaviors of boys and girls than there are in other cultures.

The question of cause and effect remains a mystery in these data. Do people who are originally more fearful, anxious, and nurturing choose more feminine-stereotyped occupations and tasks to perform, or does performing these caretaking tasks lead to more fear and nurturance or warmth? The evidence based on socialization histories (that is, that caring for younger siblings is related to later behaviors and emotions) suggests that the roles we perform lead us to express specific types of emotions, and not the other way around.

All in all, these data strongly indicate that women may express more vulnerability, fear, and distress than men partly because to express such emotions is adaptive for their role as child caretakers.

The Provider Role

The provider role theoretically should be related to the increased expression of aggression and pride, and the decreased expression of vulnerability and warmth. Being aggressive maximizes your chances of gaining access to scarce resources. Suppressing vulnerability makes you less likely to appear weak to others, and weakness may put you at a disadvantage. Further, expressing warmth and empathy toward your opponents may serve to diminish your goal of winning. An episode of the popular PBS children's cartoon show, *Arthur,* vividly illustrated these issues. One of the female characters, Francine, a talented "tomboy" athlete, was told to treat other players with less anger and more respect and warmth. She did so, only to find out that she began to lose every game because she was being so nice. The episode concluded with Francine reverting back to her former angry and somewhat obnoxious personae in the best interests of her team. Everyone ends the show accepting Francine's aggression, and presumably realizing that being polite is not always helpful. The episode powerfully demonstrates the adaptive links between competition and the expression of anger and hostility, and contrary to stereotypes, it does so with a female character. It is the role the character plays that is crucial to her emotional expressiveness, not her gender.

In my research study, both men and women who worked long hours and reported themselves to be more independent and goal-directed expressed less warmth than did their counterparts who worked fewer hours. Also, women who did more household tasks stereotypically associated with men (for example, yardwork or car repairs, involving autonomous instrumental tasks) reported less nervousness and fear than women who did traditional childcare and housework reported (Brody 1993).

An experimental study provides evidence of the connections between competition, inherent in the provider role, and the expression of counter-empathic responses (the expression of emotions opposite to those your partner is expressing). Lanzetta and Englis (1989) led both men and women to expect that they were involved in either competitive or cooperative relationships with partners who were actually co-actors. Those participants who expected a cooperative interaction responded with empathy to their partners. When their partners grimaced, they exhibited heightened autonomic arousal and facial muscle activation consistent with the grimace. In contrast, when participants expected a competitive interaction (in which the partner's gain signalled their own loss), they showed a reverse pattern of autonomic and facial activity to that of their partners. For example, when the partner was rewarded and expressed pleasure, the participant would respond with negative emotion. If the partner expressed distress or displeasure, the participant might smile. This research suggests that competitive roles facilitate both emotional distancing and hostility in the face of a competitor's pleasure or weakness. Since men are typically expected to play competitive roles, they would be apt to minimize empathy and maximize hostility toward others in many situations. Once a competition has been won, men might experience and express pride in accomplishing a socially expected goal, even in the face of their partner's disappointment.

Situations that Provoke Emotional Expression

Because of their differing social roles, men and women are likely to find different situations meaningful, with the maintenance of interpersonal and family relationships being more meaningful for women than for men, and the pursuit of individual goals being more meaningful for men than for women. Finding different situations meaningful may lead the two sexes to express emotions in dissimilar circumstances. Research supports this idea by showing that women's emotional expressivity is likely to follow an interpersonal social situation, such as relationships with friends, family, separations, reunions, births, or deaths. In contrast, men's emotional expressivity is likely to follow such circumstances as world news, achievement-related events, rituals, and illnesses (Scherer, Wallbott, and Summerfield 1986; Robbins and Tanck 1991).

Even the expression of women's anger may be precipitated by the importance women attach to interpersonal relationships. When interpersonal relationships are threatened or violated, women are more apt to get angry than are men (Frost and Averill 1982). Women report that they become angry when someone's behavior "is not in keeping with the kind of relationship" they would like to have or would expect to have. And young girls, like adult women, report more interpersonal causes and consequences for feelings such as anger than boys do (Whitesell, Robinson, and Harter 1993; Murphy and Eisenberg 1996). School-aged girls cite that being rejected or ignored by friends, being jealous of friends, or violating the principles of friendship are the primary reasons they get angry (Murphy and Eisenberg 1996).

In contrast, men and boys cite issues related to control as precipitants for their anger, which may relate to their competitive roles. Boys report that they get angry when being told what to do or not being allowed to do what they want to do. Adult men's anger is reported to be precipitated by violations of their autonomy, including situations in which they are either physically or verbally antagonized, or their intelligence is insulted, or in which women act condescendingly toward them (Biaggio 1989; Bettencourt and Miller 1996).

In brief, different social roles (caretaker versus provider) as well as motives (intimacy versus control) may be linked to the quality and intensity of emotions that males and females express as well as to the types of situations which elicit or precipitate their expressions of emotion.

OVERVIEW.   Social motives, social roles, power, and status are clearly linked to emotional expressiveness. When people are high in intimacy motives or their role is that of a child caretaker, they express more warmth. When they are high on power or control motives or their role is that of a provider, they express more anger and contempt. They may also show a discrepancy between internal experience and outer behavior. Gender differences in these processes—motives, roles, and relative power and status, are systematically linked to gender differences in emotional expressiveness.

In particular, I have shown that the unequal distribution of power between men and women can be used to account for the kinds of emotions they express. By virtue of their low power, women may express shame, warmth, fear, distress, vulnerability, and negative emotions, including anger, especially toward people with whom they have close relationships. By virtue of their greater power, men may express more pride, loneliness, aggression, contempt, and guilt than women do. These theories are compelling, and more studies are needed to systematically evaluate their accuracy.

The relationships between emotion and social roles, motives, and personality characteristics suggest that gender differences in the expression of emotion are, probably in large part, socially and culturally constructed. Cultures ensure that men and women adapt to their differing roles by formulating rules about how, when, and where men and women can express particular emotions.

Stereotypes and Display Rules

When women get angry, men treat them like they're hysterical. There
was a situation recently where I was dealing with a man and kept
getting no place and was told to call back twice by this man. Finally I
said to my husband, here you take this call, I cannot deal with this
man. My husband took the call and my husband was an angry man. I
was a hysterical woman. The man called my husband back. I was
treated like the secretary: well, call me back in five minutes. That's just
the way it is.

—Anita, age 37

I am going to make a fairly provocative argument in this chapter: To help
women adapt to their lower power and their role as child caretakers,
cultures encourage them to express warmth and discourage them from
expressing aggression. To help men adapt to their higher power and their
role as providers, cultures encourage them to express aggression and
discourage them from expressing vulnerability and warmth.

How do cultures regulate which emotions are appropriate for each sex
to express? Culturally shared values about emotion are transmitted in
the form of display rules, which are culturally shared norms that dictate
how, when, and where we should interpret, experience, and communicate our emotional experiences. For example, display rules may constrain men from crying in public when they feel sad, or they may constrain women from shouting an obscenity when they get angry.

Display rules tend to mirror cultural stereotypes about gender and
emotion. Another way of stating this is that display rules are the prescriptive aspects of stereotypes, conveying the message that certain social
consequences will ensue if we do not conform (Fiske 1993). For example, one display rule might be that women are required to smile when
their friends beat them in a competition; if they don't, they may offend

their friends. This display rule reflects the stereotype that women are friendly, nurturant and noncompetitive, and further, it prescribes the stereotype as a cultural value.

The dissimilar expression of emotions by males and females is actually adaptive for maintaining distinct cultural gender roles. By requiring males and females to express different emotions, cultures maintain power and status imbalances and gender-based divisions of labor. For example, if women can't express anger and aggression, and are further expected to express positive emotions in the face of being defeated, this serves them well in their subordinate role as caretakers and makes it unlikely that they will place themselves in a competitive role. The limitations on the kinds of emotions women are allowed to express make it hard for them to change the status quo and become more powerful. If men are discouraged from expressing vulnerability and warmth, they will be less likely to exhibit weaknesses leading to their own defeat, thus making them more likely to succeed in a competitive role. However, they will also be less likely to be successful at caretaking and intimate relationships. In other words, the expression of particular emotions leads to carrying out particular social functions more easily.

I am asserting that display rules are powerful forces in socializing gender differences in emotional expression and that the function of these rules is to maintain cultural gender roles as well as their accompanying status and power imbalances. I base my argument on several sources of indirect evidence as follows. First, display rules are widely known and shared in a particular culture, affecting social interactions, parent socialization processes, and media portrayals of males and females. The violation of display rules in each of these social arenas leads to severe negative social consequences. Second, display rules tend to be different across different cultures, depending on the values of the particular culture. And third, historical analyses have linked shifts in cultural values over time with corresponding shifts in display rules over the same time periods.

All of these pieces of evidence lead me to conclude that cultural display rules for emotional expression are powerful forces that serve not only to generate gender differences in emotional expression, but that also serve to ensure that gender roles remain bifurcated. My argument would be even stronger if I could point to a study showing that across cultures, divergent gender roles for men and women correspond to predictably different display rules for gender and emotional expression. In a culture in which women were the more powerful sex, display rules might prohibit them, and not men, from crying or displaying vulnerability. In the absence of such a study, I will focus here on the strong convergence of the other lines of evidence I have listed.

Display Rules and Gender: He's Mad, She's Sad

Interestingly, it's hard to know how to identify a display rule. There's no published list of such rules, and their implicit nature may be hard for a newcomer to the culture to learn. Often, newcomers find it difficult to know which particular feelings are appropriate to express, in what circumstances, and to whom, and they frequently run the risk of inadvertently offending someone by attempting to communicate feelings that may have been perfectly acceptable in their own country. For example, the New York–based Yiddish newspaper, the *Forward,* which early in the twentieth century helped Eastern European immigrants adjust to American culture, routinely published articles on the acceptability of emotional expressions in different situations. In one case, immigrant women were admonished not to express anger if someone jostled or bumped into them on the crowded market streets, but instead to exchange apologies. Expressing anger was viewed as inappropriate in America, but would have been entirely appropriate in Eastern European cultures (Booth and Matchan 1988).

Researchers assume that display rules operate based on several fairly indirect sources of evidence. First, they may observe the kinds of emotions people express in public as compared to in private settings. Do men, for example, hide their sadness more in public than when alone? Alternatively, they may ask people about the social consequences of expressing particular emotions in public settings. They may also study the kinds of responses people elicit from others when they express a particular emotion, such as sadness. If people are rated as unpopular or unlikable after they express sadness, an implicit display rule prohibiting the expression of sadness is assumed. Researchers have also asked parents to rate their priorities in socializing their children's emotional expressiveness, with the assumption that their priorities reflect display rules about the expression of feelings. Conversely, children have been asked about their parents', peers', or adults' reactions to their emotional displays. Finally, researchers have analyzed emotion themes in the media, including television, films, children's literature, and magazines, with the assumption that the media reflects as well as shapes cultural display rules about emotional expression.

In brief, how children are raised in the context of families and peers, how men and women are portrayed and idealized in the media, and how adults respond to each other all reflect the workings of both stereotypes and display rules about emotional expressiveness. The reverse is also true: Parents, peers, the media, and the workplace not only transmit display rules, they also play an active role in influencing them. For example, by creating films with male stars who cry, film producers may initiate new cultural norms about the acceptability of male crying.

Using some of the research methods I have listed above, it is clear that there are different display rules for females' emotional expressiveness than there are for males'. These rules tend to parallel the stereotypes about gender and emotion that are widely held, with emotionality and vulnerability associated with females, and with aggression and emotional control associated with males (see Chapter 7).

Child Rearing and Display Rules

Parents want to raise children who are well-liked, and to be well-liked means acting in accordance with the stereotypic norms for one's sex. If children (as well as adults) do not conform to display rules, they may be punished via various social processes, including social rejection and teasing, which may result in a negative self-image, poor functioning, and at an extreme, a lack of success in life. For example, less popular college students are those who are worse at expressing gender-stereotypic emotions, such as happiness for females and anger for males (Coats and Feldman 1996).

Block (1984) looked at parental values concerning emotional expression for boys and girls in several different American samples. The parents in these samples had children who ranged in age from 3 to 20 years and who were heterogeneous with respect to ethnic and socioeconomic backgrounds.[1] Across all samples, mothers and fathers tended to encourage their sons to control the expression of emotion while they encouraged their daughters to express emotion. For example, mothers of boys endorsed, "I teach my child to control his feelings at all times,"[2] whereas mothers of girls did not. Both mothers and fathers said they would express affection by holding, kissing, and hugging their girls more than their boys, and would encourage their daughters to talk about their troubles more than they would their sons.

These values about gender and emotion are consistent with the gender-role stereotype that girls are more emotionally expressive than are boys. Stereotypes have been found to have powerful effects on parents' and children's behaviors as well as on their beliefs. For example, parents' gender role stereotypes concerning math and science abilities have been found to be associated not only with their perceptions of their own children's abilities in math and science, but also with their children's beliefs about themselves (Eccles, Jacobs, and Harold 1990). Parents who thought that boys were better in math than girls had sons who actually believed themselves to be better in math than other sons. This remained true even after statistically controlling for the children's actual levels of competence in math. Another way of putting this: even sons who were not so good in math believed themselves to be good, if they had parents who believed that boys were better in math than girls. These types of self-perceptions may have self-fulfilling prophecies. When children believe they are good at something, they will work harder at it and enjoy it more, thus actually becoming better at it.

One can easily see how this might work in emotional expressivity. If parents believe that girls are naturally inclined to be shy and unaggressive, they may influence their daughters to become shy and unaggressive. For example, in a group of 2- to 5-year-olds, mothers responded quite differently to their shy sons and daughters. When sons were shy, mothers were unhappy and complained that they should grow out of their shyness. When daughters were shy, mothers were tender, affectionate, and sad, or commented with pleasure that their daughters still preferred being at home. Mothers' stereotypes about shyness being acceptable in daughters, but not in sons, may reinforce and actually contribute toward their daughters' subsequent shy behaviors (Radke-Yarrow, Richters, and Wilson 1988; Stevenson-Hinde 1988). An important point to note here was that these boys and girls did not actually differ in their levels of shyness; it was only the mothers' attitudes that differed.

Stereotypes may also alter parents' interactions with their infants. Stereotypes tend to organize and structure experiences, influence perceptions and memories, and at times cause us to distort our own and others' behaviors (Kimball 1986; Fiske and Stevens 1993). For example, people judge a baby to be sadder and more fearful when they believe it is a girl rather than a boy (Condry and Condry 1976). They judge a line drawing of a child to be more aggressive when they are told it is a boy than when told it is a girl (Lyons and Serbin 1986). Such beliefs may powerfully alter how people interact with infant girls versus infant boys.

Stereotypes may particularly affect parents' interactions with their opposite-sex infants, since stereotypes have been found to be more accurate for in-group members (in this case, members of the same sex), than for out-group members (in this case, members of the opposite sex). For example, when asked to judge whether women or men have superior nonverbal recognition abilities, women's judgments were more accurate than were men's (Swim 1994). In contrast, men's judgments were more accurate than women's about the fact that men exhibit helping and leadership skills, which portray men in a more positive light. People's stereotypes about their own sex are more accurate than are their stereotypes about the opposite sex. In fact, their stereotypes about the opposite sex may represent overgeneralizations, devaluations, and exaggerations (Fiske and Stevens 1993). This phenomenon may cause parents to distort the behaviors of their opposite-sex children, and may contribute to a failure of empathy between mothers and sons or fathers and daughters. This perspective highlights social and cognitive processes that contribute to the quality of same- and opposite-sex family relationships, perhaps even to the quality of parent-child boundaries I have previously discussed.

Research has shown that fathers, in particular, may stereotype their young daughters to be more emotionally expressive and emotionally competent than their young sons. For example, fathers of elementary-school children believe that girls develop sympathy at a significantly younger age than sons. Fathers also believe that daughters should use their own resources to overcome negative emotions, whereas sons need more help (Hayden and Carter 1995). On the other hand, fathers also said that they believed a girl should be comforted when upset more than a boy (Block 1984). Fathers may be more apt to stereotype their opposite-sex children than mothers because their actual interactions with their children are less frequent, allowing for categorizations and stereotypes to replace reality. Fathers' beliefs that daughters have more emotional capabilities than sons may become self-fulfilling prophecies, with daughters actually becoming more emotionally expressive and able to regulate their emotions than sons.

It is also possible that fathers are more apt to stereotype their children than are mothers if we assume that fathers wield more power than do mothers. Research has indicated that more powerful individuals are more apt to stereotype less powerful individuals than vice versa (Fiske 1993).

The Consequences of Display Rules for Social Interactions

Lack of conformity to display rules may have powerful consequences for self-esteem and social relationships. One compelling example is the recent legal dispute of Ann B. Hopkins versus the international corporation Price Waterhouse (Fiske 1993; Davis, LaRosa, and Foshee 1992). Ms. Hopkins was denied full partnership in the business advisory firm because she was perceived to have an overbearing and abrasive personality (Davis, LaRosa, and Foshee 1992). Her colleagues stated that she needed a "course in charm school." In other words, she may have failed to conform to expectations that females be nonaggressive.

Consequences for Males

In American culture, males who express sadness, depression, fear, and dysphoric self-conscious emotions such as shame and embarrassment are viewed as "unmanly" and are evaluated more negatively than females (Siegel and Alloy 1990; Stoppard and Gruchy 1993). People are apt to feel angry and resentful when men are depressed, because they believe that men should be able to control their lives (Barbee et al. 1993). High-school boys, in particular, tend to be intolerant of other boys who express feelings (Werrbach, Grotevant, and Cooper 1990).

Men do not anticipate that they will receive comfort if they express sadness or helplessness (Timmers, Fischer, and Manstead 1998). Even school-aged boys believed that their parents would ignore them if they expressed sad feelings to them (Fuchs and Thelen 1988), or would fail to understand and accept their feelings (Zeman and Garber 1996). Eleven- to sixteen-year-old boys also reported that they were not supposed to express their feelings more than girls (Zeman and Shipman 1997; see also Rottenberg and Elsenberg 1997). And, adolescent girls anticipated that they would receive an understanding response for showing their feelings more often than adolescent boys anticipated (Zeman and Shipman 1997).

In fact, men's anticipation that they will receive less comfort when sad is justified—in actuality, they do receive less comfort when sad. When boyfriends were sad in response to task failure, their girlfriends did not attempt to cheer them up. Some were actually cold and critical toward their boyfriends, making them feel worse (Barbee et al. 1993). The stereotype, or expectation that men should have few feelings in response to task failure, may dictate against being soothed. Men are supposed to be "hardened" to such situations. It was more acceptable for men to express sadness at a task not related to gender roles; namely, a depressing movie. In this situation, girlfriends did attempt to cheer up their boyfriends. It is worth noting that when the situation was reversed, and girlfriends were sad, boyfriends made an effort to cheer them up regardless of the cause of the sadness.

Although males are discouraged from expressing sadness and depression, they are encouraged by peers to be aggressive. School-aged boys who are aggressive in their playground behavior are better liked and are judged to be more socially competent than boys who are less aggressive (Hart, DeWolf, and Burts 1993; Serbin et al. 1993).

Consequences for Females

Display rules dictate that the expression of both aggression and verbal anger is unfeminine (Lerner 1980; Shields and Koster 1989). Aggressive girls are less well-liked than nonaggressive girls, and girls who are aggressive tend to have a wide variety of problems in peer relationships (Crick 1997). Women also anticipate more negative social consequences for expressing aggression than men do (Eagly and Steffen 1984). They are especially concerned that the expression of anger and aggression will disrupt their social relationships (Frost and Averill 1982). For example, when reading vignettes about supervisors who became angry, women perceived the episode to have more costs to the supervisor-supervisee relationship than men did (Davis, LaRosa, and Foshee 1992).

Women's roles also encourage them to maintain cheerful expressions (Hochschild 1983). For example, adolescent girls training to be cheerleaders are taught to look happy even when they are uncomfortable or disappointed (Eder and Parker 1987). In fact, the very word "cheerleader," a female role, implies imparting cheer to others. Flight attendants, who are most often female, are under similar pressures to maintain a pleasant demeanor, often in very unpleasant circumstances in which they are treated rudely (Hochschild 1983).

Relative to men, women also anticipate more negative social consequences for not communicating happiness about their friends' accomplishments. For example, when women were told a hypothetical story about a friend's victory, they anticipated that other people might disapprove of them, reject them, or ignore them if they expressed sadness rather than happiness. In other words, women are expected to be cheerful in the face of competitive circumstances. Competitive feelings are less socially acceptable for women than for men (Graham, Gentry, and Green 1981).

Women also anticipate more negative social consequences than men for bragging about their own accomplishments, particularly to a female peer who has not done as well as they have (Daubman and Sigall 1997). In a creative experiment, all participants were told that their superior performance on an anagrams task put them in the 91st percentile. One group of women participants was asked to disclose to unfamiliar female peers that they had indeed scored in the 91st percentile on the anagrams task. This "bragging" group of women was less likely to think that their female peers liked them than did women who were instructed to modestly disclose only that they had scored above the 50th percentile on the task. A parallel group of bragging male participants actually thought that female peers would like them more than did a group of modestly disclosing male participants. When the peers were men, both male and female participants judged that the peers liked them at equal levels regardless of whether or not the participants had bragged or disclosed their achievements modestly. Women who bragged also thought that both male and female peers would be more upset than women who disclosed modestly, whereas men who bragged thought their male and female peers would be less upset than did men who disclosed modestly. (The authors suggest that the women may have been more accurate in assessing their partners' potential reactions of distress to bragging than were the men, although they did not test this idea.) Women may inhibit their expressions of pride in order to protect the feelings of others, especially other women, as well to preserve their relationships with them.

Although the research on gender differences in the expression of guilt is mixed (see Chapter 5), the expression of guilt appears to be socially acceptable, perhaps even socially prescribed more for women than for men. Women who make excuses and concessions following a wrongdoing, and who express guilt and remorse are evaluated more favorably than those who do not. Men with these same characteristics are not evaluated more favorably than are other men (Gonzales 1992). Recent work has shown that when men and women are asked to compose narratives concerning an incident in which someone made them feel guilty, women receive more guilt-inducing messages than men receive. The kinds of strategies that were particularly effective in inducing guilt in women included anger, refusing to accept repairs, such as apologies, and turning the other cheek. Men seemed to be more effective inducers of guilt than were women (Ferguson, Ives, and Eyre 1997).

Display Rules, Stereotypes, and the Media

Display rules are also revealed in portrayals of men and women in the media. These portrayals both reflect and contribute to cultural values concerning gender roles.

How adults and children are affected by media images, especially those depicted on television,[3] is an extremely complex question, and one that is the subject of much debate. Television has the potential to be a powerful socialization factor. It is estimated that children spend more time watching television than performing any other activity except sleeping (Liebert and Sprafkin 1988). Some researchers have argued that the values espoused by television have only limited effects without corresponding values espoused by the culture (Calvert and Huston 1987). Others have taken the position that television shapes and cultivates dominant and pervasive cultural norms (Signorielli 1990; Gerbner et al. 1994).

Evidence suggests that children attend to, prefer, and imitate television characters of their own sex more than the opposite sex (Perry and Bussey 1979; Liebert and Sprafkin 1988). When children are able to choose their own television programs, they select programs in which same-sex characters behave in gender-stereotypic ways (Liebert and Sprafkin 1988).

In fact, television has been found to portray emotional expressions in quite gender-stereotypic ways. Reviews indicate that men are portrayed as more physically and verbally aggressive, dominant, powerful, and intelligent than women; while women are portrayed as more sociable, warm, affectionate, nurturing, sympathetic, happy, rule-abiding, and peaceful, but also more jealous and envious than are men (McArthur and Eisen 1976; Liebert and Sprafkin 1988; Comstock and Strzyzewski 1990; Signorielli 1990; Thompson and Zerbinos 1995). Female television characters are also more likely to be victimized than are male characters

(Sommers-Flanagan, Sommers-Flanagan, and Davis 1993). Especially on MTV, women are portrayed as the objects of aggressive sexual advances, while men are portrayed as the aggressors (Sommers-Flanagan, Sommers-Flanagan, and Davis 1993). Similar gender differences have been found in Japanese television programming (Rolandelli 1991).[4]

In televised sports, studies have shown that when women compete with each other, sportscasters are likely to interpret their failures as due to some combination of nervousness, lack of aggression, and lack of confidence. When men lose, the interpretation is that they failed not because of feelings such as nervousness, but because of the power, strength, and intelligence of their male opponents (Messner, Duncan, and Jensen 1993). Thus, women are portrayed as more expressive of their feelings than men, and their feelings are portrayed as interfering with their successful functioning.

Portrayals of interpersonal conflicts on television indicate that women engage in longer lasting conflicts than men. Women's conflicts tend to involve direct confrontation, whereas men's strategies more often involve trying to avoid the offending party (Comstock and Strzyzewski 1990). Male television characters were also found to be more likely to distance from women than from men, meaning that they moved their heads or bodies away from women more frequently than they did from men. In contrast, women's distancing behavior was not related to the gender of the person with whom they were interacting (Lott 1989). These dramatized patterns on television are similar to the male emotional inexpressivity and distancing behaviors in actual marital conflicts that I have previously discussed.

Television and Cultural Values

The prescriptive aspect of gender stereotypes is quite evident on television—women and men who conform to stereotypes are rewarded; those who do not are punished. An analysis of television cartoons revealed that aggressive and dominant females were depicted in unflattering ways, as large and chunky in appearance, as opposed to others who were depicted as sleek and agile. Further, when a woman was depicted in a position of authority, she got herself into trouble and required rescuing (Busby 1974). On Japanese television, cross-sex behavior by males, for example, deference, was associated with a lack of social power and lower likability (Rolandelli 1991).

The relationship between gender stereotypes portrayed on television and cultural values is highlighted by a study showing that the time of day advertisements are aired makes a difference in the types of gender images that are portrayed. Advertisements that air after work portray nonstereotypical gender roles, such as women in positions of authority or dominance and men in the role of fathers. In contrast, daytime advertisements, typically watched by homemakers, focus on stereotypical images of caretaking and attractiveness for women and authority for men. Weekend advertisements, often associated with competitive sports, depict traditional stereotypical masculine images of aggressiveness, competitiveness, and risk-taking, with women depicted as subservient to men (Craig 1992). These analyses indicate that the gender values depicted by television are linked to the cultural values of the intended audience, with the direction of influence unknown, but probably bidirectional. The gender stereotypes portrayed on television, with their corresponding prescriptive aspects, are probably created to please their audience, but may also insidiously shape the gender values of their audience as well.

Effects of Television on Viewers

It is quite difficult to disentangle the effects of television on gender stereotypes from the influences of the rest of society (Kimball 1986). Several studies have shown positive correlations between television viewing and adherence to gender stereotypes, although not necessarily those related to emotional expressiveness (Ross, Anderson, and Wisocki 1982; Signorielli 1990). Since studies in this field tend to be correlational, it is not clear whether or not people with more sex-typed beliefs simply watch more sex-typed television shows. Some of the studies also do not assess the types of shows being watched. Public television may depict quite different views of gender than cartoons on major networks.

On the other hand, there is some experimental evidence that television exposure increases both levels of sex-typed behaviors as well as aggression. One way to assess the effects of television gender stereotypes on behaviors is to experimentally manipulate the quality of the stereotypes people are exposed to. When people watch counter-stereotypic messages about gender and emotion, it has been shown to have dramatic effects on emotional expression. For example, Jennings, Geis, and Brown

(1980) showed college-aged women either gender-stereotypic ads in which men were dominant and women were subservient, or the same ads in which they reversed the gender of the actors so that women were dominant and men were subservient. Subsequently, the women were asked to express their views about controversial topics. The participants' nonverbal behaviors while expressing their views were judged by experimenters to be significantly more self-confident after having watched the nonstereotypic commercials than the stereotypic ones. For example, participants made frequent eye contact as opposed to avoiding eye contact and had emotionally expressive facial expressions after watching the counter-stereotypic commercials. In contrast, they grimaced or had "frozen" facial expressions after watching the messages in which women were stereotypically subservient rather than dominant.

Another way to experimentally evaluate the effects of television is to study communities before and after television is available. In a naturalistic study of a town two years after television was first introduced there, sixth- and ninth-grade girls became significantly more sex-typed than they were before television was available. (This town was compared to two control towns with different levels of access to television viewing.) There were somewhat similar patterns of results obtained for boys (Kimball 1986). Children in the previously televisionless town also demonstrated increased levels of aggressive behavior during play observations and as rated by teachers and peers. In another study of sixth- through eigth-grade children, the amount of television girls watched affected their sex-role stereotypes one year later as compared to initial levels, even when previous scores and other demographic factors were controlled for (Morgan 1982). This effect was the most powerful for intelligent girls who came from higher socioeconomic families.

Several studies have also shown that when boys and girls are exposed to aggressive characters on television shows, the frequency of aggressive responses in their play increases when compared to children who do not view aggressive television shows (Liebert and Sprafkin 1988). Perhaps the most frightening evidence is that in a 22-year followup, Huesmann and Miller (1994) found that there was a significant relationship between exposure to television violence at age 8 and the seriousness of criminal acts performed at 30, even after controlling for many other variables.

Recent analyses have suggested that television's gender stereotypic messages are differentially utilized by people depending on their age, experiences, attitudes, values, and their other sources of information (Durkin 1985; Weaver and Wakshlag 1986). Imitating television models may be especially prominent when direct experience is lacking or ambiguous (Weaver and Wakshlag 1986), or when children do not have a supportive peer group (Pearl, Bouthilet, and Lazar 1982).

Adults and adolescents seem to create their own interpretations of characters and events portrayed on television. For example, in a fascinating study of gender roles depicted on MTV, Kalof (1993) found that adolescent boys and girls who watched exactly the same tape interpreted the gender images of a woman pursued by Michael Jackson differently. Boys were more likely than girls to see the woman as a tease, or as playing hard to get; whereas girls were more likely than boys to see the woman as helpless, scared, and vulnerable. Further, more girls saw the woman as powerful and independent, mostly because of her physical attractiveness and sensuality, whereas more boys described her as submissive and indecisive because she submitted to Michael Jackson's advances. Interestingly, there were no gender differences in boys' and girls' views of the male pursuer. This study suggests that people may use television images to justify their pre-existing biases about gender roles, power, and status.

Viewers' gender-stereotypic personality traits and behaviors may also affect the extent to which they are influenced by television's messages. Huesmann, Lagerspetz, and Eron (1984) found that the boys who were most likely to increase their aggressive behavior in the 3 years subsequent to watching aggressive television shows were those who identified with violent characters. For girls, the greatest effects of watching television aggression occurred for those who preferred masculine activities.

To conclude, many studies suggest that the stereotypes and display rules portrayed on television contribute to gender-role stereotypes, attitudes, and to levels of aggression. They may also influence gender differences in other types of emotional expression, although there is relatively little research that directly tests this idea. Here again, as with other variables that contribute to gender differences in emotional expression, the influence of the media is probably complex and multidimensional, depending on factors such as the age, values, and personality characteristics of the audience.

Display Rules Maintain Cultural Values

I have shown that display rules about gender and emotional expressiveness influence social relationships, parent socialization practices, and the media. I will now turn to the last part of my argument, that display rules in all of these settings reflect and maintain cultural values, especially those concerning gender roles. In the absence of cross-cultural evidence showing that display rules vary as gender roles vary, my argument is based on cultural and historical analyses showing that the quality of display rules and cultural values are related.

The first bit of evidence in support of my argument is that the kind of emotions people are allowed to express to bosses versus supervisees varies in different cultures, depending on the values the culture places on status. For example, Japanese students are less likely to express distress to a higher status person and more likely to rate anger as an appropriate emotion to express to lower status individuals than are American students (Matsumoto 1990; Matsumoto and Ekman 1989, citing Friesen 1972). These differences probably relate to the fact that the Japanese value distinct status relationships in their culture more than Americans do. The emotions that the Japanese encourage (the expression of anger to low status individuals) or discourage (the expression of distress to high-status individuals) help to maintain status imbalances.

Display rules have also been found to be related to the cultural values of collectivism versus individualism. Cultures that are high on collectivism, such as Asian countries, value group harmony and cohesiveness above the needs of the individual. Such cultures stress the suppression of negative emotions in order to avoid confrontation and conflict, particularly toward higher status individuals (Matsumoto 1989). Individualistic cultures, such as the United States, stress the needs of the individual above those of the social group. Since there is no collective group that would be threatened by the expression of negative emotion, negative emotion is more freely expressed in individualistic as opposed to collectivistic cultures. In support of these ideas, research has indicated that across 15 cultures, the more individualistic a culture is, the better able its members are to judge the intensity of anger and fear in facial expressions, and the less able they are to identify sadness (Matsumoto 1989;[5] see also Russell, Suzuki, and Ishida 1993). Moreover, Americans have been found to express more intense emotions than other cultural groups express. In their factor analysis of measures of emotional expressivity, Gross and John (1998) found that Asian-American college students reported less intense emotional impulsivity; less expressive confidence, including items such as, "I would probably make a good actor"; and more attempts at masking their feelings, including such items as, "I've learned it is better to suppress my anger than to show it" than European-American college students reported. Other studies have similarly shown Americans to report more intense emotions than either Canadians (MacKinnon and Keating 1989) or Japanese (Matsumoto et al. 1988) report.

Consistent with the American emphasis on individualism, American children are more likely than Japanese children to acknowledge anger. American parents, when contrasted to Japanese parents, tend to encourage emotional expressivity in their preschoolers. In contrast, Japanese parents emphasize guilt and anxiety induction in their children, emphasizing both their own disappointment when their children misbehave as well as the consequences for others (Zahn-Waxler et al. 1996). These emphases are consistent with communal values.

Cultural values may also shape the kinds of emotions that are associated with feeling good about oneself. For the Japanese, who value the cohesiveness of the group, feeling good about oneself is associated with warmth, an emotion that emphasizes one's relationships with others. For Americans, who emphasize the needs and achievement of the individual, feeling good about oneself is associated with pride, an emotion that emphasizes one's personal achievements and autonomy (Markus and Kitayama 1991). The quality of emotional expressiveness that the culture allows and encourages helps to reinforce and maintain existing cultural values.

Historical analyses also highlight the associations between cultural values and the content of display rules. A provocative study showed that the rules for emotional expressiveness advocated by popular magazines changed as gender roles for women became transformed (Cancian and Gordon 1988). In the early part of the century, popular magazines advised traditional kinds of emotional expressiveness for women, including self-sacrifice, the avoidance of conflict, and the minimization of anger. Expressing these emotions was adaptive for women's roles as family caretakers. In more recent times, magazines promote a different message. The open communication of negative and positive feelings, including anger, is now viewed as appropriate, and signals a more autonomous role for women.

Similarly, in the eighteenth century, Western display rules increasingly allowed men, but not women, to express angry and assertive feelings, rather than to express sad and submissive feelings. This change in the acceptability of men's anger reflected changing cultural values, in which there were less hierarchical social relationships, and in which men were given more control over their lives. That display rules continued to emphasize the acceptabilty of women's sadness, rather than anger, reflected and promoted women's lower status relative to men's, and continued to enforce women's lack of control over their own lives (Stearns 1988).

Cultural values also dictated that too much anger was risky for both women and men during historical periods when the social goal was peaceable interaction in the workplace. In the twentieth century, as the number of service-sector jobs increased, requiring goodwill among employees and their customers, the expression of anger on the job became less socially acceptable (Stearns and Stearns 1994).

In brief, the needs of the culture at any point in time are related to the quality of existing display rules, which in turn influence how emotions are expressed and how social relationships are managed.

OVERVIEW. I have argued that the prescriptive aspects of stereotypes, namely display rules, have powerful consequences for the socialization of gender differences in emotional expression. Display rules are conveyed through the media, parent socialization practices, and social interactions. The negative consequences that ensue for violating display rules serve as powerful forces not only for maintaining conformity to gender-stereotypic emotional expressions but also for maintaining conformity to other aspects of gender roles in the culture.

I have also suggested that parent socialization practices are affected by parents' tendencies to stereotype and distort the emotional expressiveness of their opposite-sex children more than they distort the expressiveness of their same-sex children. Because of their greater power and distance from the family, fathers should be more likely to stereotype their children's emotional expressivity, especially that of their daughters, than mothers. These stereotypes may have self-fulfilling prophecies for the quality of gender differences in emotional expression that eventually develop.

12

The Power of Peers

If a girl was rough, nobody would play with her. At recess they'd probably leave her alone.

—Leonard, age 6

Whenever the boys see the girls, they always act tougher.

—Emily, age 9

Relationships with peers powerfully contribute to gender differences in emotional expression. Children imitate their peers' emotional expressiveness and are also reinforced and punished by peers for expressing particular emotions. They may be rewarded in the form of social acceptance or popularity when they express emotions that are sex-role stereotypic, and punished in the form of social rejection or teasing when they express emotions that are not sex-role stereotypic, such as when boys cry. For example, the all-too-familiar American taunt, "Baby, baby, stick your head in gravy," is one flung by peers at children who may express their feelings in ways deemed to be inappropriate. Being accepted or ridiculed by peers is an extremely potent socialization influence, since children derive some of their identity and self-esteem from their group membership. Successful relationships with peers may predict future achievements, and at a more basic level, are theorized to be adaptive for survival (Harris 1995).

In fact, Harris (1995) argues that peers are the primary agents of socialization in the child's environment, second only in importance to genetic determinants in contributing to personality development. Contrary to mainstream arguments within developmental psychology, she contests that personality is not directly transmitted from parents to children, but is indirectly transmitted by way of the parents' peer group, who transmit values to the children's peer group. She uses this example: The values of British boys and their fathers are similar despite the fact that British boys are sent away to boarding schools at the age of eight. Why are fathers and sons so similar when they have so little contact with each other? Harris argues that it is because fathers and sons were sent to the same boarding schools. For both fathers and sons, the older peers within the boarding schools may provide the formative developmental experiences for younger peers.

In the area of emotion socialization, there is not enough evidence to say whether or not peers exert a more powerful influence on the expression of children's emotions than their parents do. There is a great deal of evidence, however, to suggest that especially in Western cultures, peers contribute to the emergence of gender differences in emotional expression in powerful ways.

Popularity, Social Acceptance, and Emotional Expression

Studies indicate that children closely monitor the types of emotions they express to their peers because they worry about how they will be perceived. For example, a recent study of first-, third-, and fifth-graders showed that children reported that they would control their expressions of sadness, anger, and pain more when they were in the presence of their medium-best friends than when in the presence of their parents. The primary reason they gave for controlling their emotional expressions was that they expected some negative reaction from their peers following their disclosure, including rejection, ridicule, and reprimands. They worried that other children would think they were babies if they expressed pain; or that other children would get mad at them if they expressed anger. Another frequent reason children gave for not showing their feelings (such as anger) to their peers was prosocial: they wanted to protect their friends' feelings (Zeman and Garber 1996). Similar results were found with 11- to 16-year-old children, who reported that their best friends were more likely to belittle them for expressing feelings than were their parents (Zeman and Shipman 1997).

Peers are most likely to accept those behaviors that conform to sex-role norms. For example, young elementary school-aged boys reported that they most preferred as friends those boys who engaged in exclusively masculine behaviors, such as Superhero fantasy play (Zucker et al.

1995). Similarly, elementary school-aged girls most preferred as friends those girls who engaged in exclusively feminine activities and toy preferences, such as playing house or dressing up in feminine clothes. Even 2-year-old boys gave more positive responses to boys who were engaged in male-preferred activities than they did to other classmates (Fagot 1985).

In a detailed observational study of middle school–aged children, children of either sex who expressed nonstereotypic emotions were less popular with their peers. Boys who cried easily—the so-called "sissies"—were low in popularity. Less popular boys were also the ones who expressed vulnerability, in that they were the most frequently hurt and defeated in athletic games (Adler, Kless, and Adler 1992).

Popular boys were those viewed as "cool." Being "cool" involved not only successful self-presentational skills and impression management techniques, such as wearing the right clothing and accessories, but also a defensiveness about revealing feelings over possible rejection, thereby protecting the boys from vulnerability, especially in cross-gender relationships. In addition, acting "tough" and aggressive, challenging adult authority, boasting and bragging about exploits, and receiving disciplinary action made boys more popular. In other words, popular boys were those who acted in competitive and powerful ways and who suppressed vulnerable feelings (Adler, Kless, and Adler 1992).

In contrast, popular girls were observed to be not only those who were viewed as attractive by their peers and whose parents had high socioeconomic status, but those who were able to express themselves verbally, to understand group dynamics, and to be interested in social relationships, especially with boys (Adler, Kless, and Adler 1992). Aggressiveness in girls actually decreased ratings of their likability and acceptability as well as their adjustment as rated by their teachers and themselves (Serbin et al. 1993; Chung and Asher 1996; Crick 1997).

The studies clearly show that boys and girls become popular for very different kinds of emotional expressions. For boys, popularity is associated with the denial of vulnerable or sad feelings and the expression of moderate amounts of aggression. For girls, popularity is associated with low levels of aggression as well as with the verbal expression of and sensitivity to feelings. Popularity constitutes a powerful reward that may shape the nature of the emotions boys and girls express, as well as the gender-stereotypic behaviors in which they engage.

Among adults, social acceptance is also related to expressing emotions in stereotypic ways. Research has indicated that the degree to which potential mates are perceived as likable or sexually attractive depends on how gender-role stereotypic their expressed emotions are. College-aged women who responded with fear to a horror movie were rated by their male partners as more sexually attractive than those who mastered their fear (Zillmann et al. 1986; Mundorf et al. 1989). Their male partners also reported enjoying the film more. These patterns were similar for male emotional expressions: When men showed mastery of fear, they became more sexually appealing to women, and women were more likely to acquiesce to them, yielding to their erroneous judgments about someone's age, in contrast to women's nondeferential reactions to men who had failed to show mastery of fear (Zillmann et al. 1986). In other words, expressing gender-stereotypic feelings enabled both men and women to become more attractive and also enabled men to wield more power. Sexual attractiveness and power are important motivators that may serve to bifurcate the emotions expressed by the two sexes.

Gender-Differentiated Play Patterns

One of the primary reasons that peers are so influential in the development of gender differences is that children play primarily with members of their own sex. In both this and many other cultures roughly 65 percent of boys' and girls' playtime is spent with same-sex playmates (DesJardins, Worth, and Crombie 1991; Leaper 1994). In elementary schools, boys and girls select classroom seats next to same-sex peers, choose playmates from among same-sex peers, and sit at tables with same-sex peers in the cafeteria (Thorne and Luria 1986; Thorne 1993). In fact, when boys and girls publicly play together, they often risk becoming the objects of ridicule and teasing by other peers (Thorne and Luria 1986).

The tendency to segregate by sex is associated with distinct patterns of play for boys and girls, which in turn may encourage different patterns of emotional expression.

Boys' Play

Some studies have estimated that 25–50 percent of boys' play is inter-competitive, as compared to 1–10 percent of girls' play (DesJardins,

Worth, and Crombie 1991). Boys tend to play outdoors in large organized groups more than girls do, and their activities take up more space than the activities of girls. In general, boys' play tends to build toward heightened and intense moments, moments one can describe in terms of group arousal (Thorne and Luria 1986). A typical boys' game might involve running and chasing in large groups, or engaging in an organized team sport. Many of these games involve control and competition (Chung and Asher 1996). Winning competitions gives boys higher status (in the form of being liked and popular) with respect to their peer group.

Status is also gained by risk-taking (sometimes in the form of rule transgressions), which is exciting to boys and is supported by the peer group. The sociologist Gary Fine (1988) has identified a type of play among pre-adolescent boys that he has termed "dirty play," which includes aggressive pranks, vandalism, sexual games, and racist invectives. He argues that this type of play shapes the boys' identity within the peer group, enabling them to gain a reputation for being daring. "Dirty" play tests boundaries and limits, violates rules of politeness, and more important, violates the power structure and control normally inherent in adult-child relationships. In carrying out their pranks, boys make social and emotional statements about the people who are the objects of their pranks, singling them out for either ridicule or special attention. In other words, "dirty" play enables the boys to "play" at being powerful and in control, motives and goals I have discussed as important for males.

Boys' goals of control and competition would result in maximizing expressions of aggression, pride, anger, and contempt (including insults) and in minimizing expressions of fear, warmth, guilt, and vulnerability. Expressing aggression and suppressing vulnerability would enable boys to win competitive games, engage in risk-taking activities, and gain status within their peer group. For example, mocking, competitive challenges are common in boys' play (Leaper 1994). If and when boys do act vulnerable, they are apt to elicit reactions of horsing around and joking from other boys—in other words, they are publicly shamed for expressing such feelings (Adler, Kless, and Adler 1992). Moreover, boys have been found to engage in direct expressions of anger, as well as in competitive and evaluative confrontations with other boys. Boys from a black working-class neighborhood were found to talk about the wrongdoings of boys in the group who were physically present and to express angry feelings close to the time when the feelings were elicited (Goodwin 1990).

Girls' Play

Girls tend to play for long periods of time in intimate, small groups rather than in large, organized groups of children (Benenson, Apostoleris, and Parnass 1997). Girls' games often involve taking turns, playing with only a minimal number of rules, and competing against a standard rather than competing against each other.

Girls' goals have been found to be focused on affiliation and intimacy, rather than competition and control. In detailed observational studies girls organized themselves in terms of pairs of "best friends," and these pairs were part of larger complex social networks. Girls tended to be preoccupied with which girls were friends with other friends (Thorne and Luria 1986; Adler, Kless, and Adler 1992). Friends frequently commented on each others' physical appearance, monitored each others' emotions, shared secrets, and became mutually vulnerable through self-disclosures.

Girls also place a priority on not getting into trouble with adults, and tend to avoid direct confrontation and risk-taking behaviors (Thorne and Luria 1986; Chung and Asher 1996). The female counterpart of male rule violations may be the giggling sessions in which girls engage to a greater extent than boys (Thorne and Luria 1986). These sessions may be an indirect way for girls to challenge adult-child power hierarchies and avoid direct confrontation.

Girls are also concerned with equality in their relationships; that is, not wanting anyone in their group to have superior or inferior status (Lips 1989, 1994; Tannen 1994; Chung and Asher 1996). Their interactions often involve emotional disclosures, especially expressions of warmth, vulnerability, weakness, and humiliation (one-downsmanship, rather than one-upsmanship). These patterns of emotional expression help girls to accomplish their goals of affiliation, and also help them to equalize status among members of the peer group (Tannen 1994). In Chapter 11, we saw that females judged bragging to be less acceptable than did males, probably for the same reason: they do not want to threaten the equality of their relationships with other females.

irch has also indicated that among girls' peer groups, girls mostly express their anger directly to each other. Girls break off friend- ____,)y either acting mean, such as socially ostracizing their former friends, or by expressing hostility about their former friends behind their backs (Thorne and Luria 1986; Cairns et al. 1989; O'Connell, Peplar, and Kent 1995).

In an observational study of 9–14-year-old children in a black work- ing-class neighborhood in West Philadelphia, girls never directly ex- pressed anger, insults, or commands toward each other. Rather, girls told a large peer group about their anger at girls who were absent. The girls who were the objects of anger later learned that other girls talked about them in their absence, and they committed themselves to future confron- tations. Girls often practiced scenarios with the help of friends as to how to confront the offending parties at a future time. In other words, girls continually re-enacted and re-experienced their initial angry feelings, often over several days (Goodwin 1990).

Girls minimize direct expressions of anger for several reasons. Mini- mizing expressions of anger facilitates girls' affiliation goals and serves to preserve friendships. It also preserves the female group norm of equality among group members. Expressions of anger and insults would commu- nicate unwanted signals of entitlement and status. And, finally, expres- sions of anger also run counter to the value girls place on avoiding trouble with adult authorities.

Some of the patterns of gender differences in childhood peer interac- tions continue on well into late childhood, adolescence, and adulthood. Fifth- and sixth-grade girls report more intimacy and affection in their best friendships than boys do (Furman and Buhrmester 1985). A study of almost 2,000 adolescents in the seventh, eighth, and ninth grades in Quebec City found that girls' peer groups were based on friendships, whereas boys' were based on athletics, antisocial activities or extracur- ricular activities (Caron et al. 1996). Other studies, including one con- ducted in New Zealand, have shown that women's peer groups engage in more emotional self-disclosure than do men's and are based on feel- ings of shared closeness, rather than on common interests or activities. Men's friendships, like those of boys, are often based on participating in or observing competitive sports or other common activities (Aukett, Ritchie, and Mill 1988).

Even the importance of status in peer relationships was found among men. Status similarity among college-aged male friends significantly predicted their long-term friendship patterns over a 4-year period (Griffin and Sparks 1990). Status similarity was defined as the two friends' perceived resemblance on physical attractiveness, intellectual ability, social skills, physical coordination, spiritual maturity, and financial resources. Status was not found to be a determinant of women's long-term friendship patterns.

On Interacting with Females

For both sexes, interacting closely with females may be a key factor in promoting the expression of emotions. For example, my colleagues and I asked both mothers and fathers to report what percentage of time their school-aged children played with same- and opposite-sex children. Boys who frequently played with girls expressed more warmth in responding to stories when compared to boys who played less frequently with girls. Similarly, girls who typically played with other girls expressed more warmth, fear, hurt, anger, pity, and characterized themselves as caring more about interpersonal relationships than girls who played less frequently with other girls (Hay, Brody, and Vandewater 1988). The types of play that both boys and girls engage in when playing with girls may be characterized by more intimate interactions, which would serve to facilitate the mutual disclosure of feelings, especially warmth and vulnerability.

Even for adults, interacting with women may facilitate emotional expressiveness. Women's greater access to friendships with other women (relative to men's) means that women have more opportunities for expressing their feelings than men. In fact, men describe their friendships with women as closer and more satisfying than their friendships with men (Elkins and Peterson 1993). Wheeler, Reis, and Nezlek (1983) found that interacting with women was a key variable in mitigating loneliness for both women and men. Women and men who allocated more of their social time to men were more lonely than those who spent more time with women. To put it simply: women may express more frequent and intense emotions because they interact more frequently and with a greater number of other women than men do.

An alternative hypothesis to the one I have proposed, that is, that relationships with females maximize emotional expressiveness, is that people who are comfortable expressing their feelings seek out females as friends. These hypotheses are not mutually exclusive and both may bear some truth.

The Effect of Boys' Play Behavior on Girls

Girls exert lower power and dominance when playing with boys than when playing with girls (Maccoby 1998). This undoubtedly influences the kinds of emotions they express in opposite sex interactions, such as heightening their fearfulness and anxiety.

There are numerous examples of studies showing that girls wield lower dominance in mixed-sex interactions than boys do. Even among toddlers, girls paired with male playmates behave more passively than girls paired with other girls or than boys paired with either girls or boys (Jacklin and Maccoby 1978). Also, when girls do use direct commands, requests, and prohibitions, such as "Stop! Don't do that!," or "Give me the truck," they are likely to be ignored by boys and effective only when used with other girls (Serbin et al. 1982; Powlishta and Maccoby 1990). In fact, perhaps because of how they are responded to, girls more often use indirect strategies as they get older, such as stating, "I need that toy," or "May I please have that toy?," instead of demands and prohibitions. In contrast, direct strategies are increasingly likely to be used by boys during the preschool years.

Among 3- to 5-year-old children, Powlishta and Maccoby (1990) found that boys gained more access to a choice movie-viewing spot than did girls when an adult was not present. When an adult was present, however, boys and girls shared the viewing spot more equally. Boys became inhibited in the adult's presence, dropping their rate of demands and giving girls longer turns at the spot. Powlishta and Maccoby (1990) suggest that female peer groups maintain proximity to adults more than boys do because they are trying to avoid male dominance.

Several of the gender-interaction patterns noted in 1958 in Zander and van Egmond's classic paper are still extant today. Second- and fifth-grade children were placed in small problem-solving groups. Boys attempted to influence others, made more demands, and were more aggressive than were girls in these small groups. Boys who had higher social power to influence others were described as more threatening by their peers. This was not true of girls. Girls with greater power were rated by their peers as more expert in school activities (Zander and van Egmond 1958).

In more recent studies, adolescent girls have been found to rate them-selves as less powerful than adolescent boys (Calabrese and Seldin 1985/86) and are less likely to perceive themselves as in control of deci-sion-making than boys (Lind and Connole 1985). In a task in which boys and girls were asked to construct an animal together that involved several choice points, 14-year-old girls controlled decisions significantly less than 14-year-old boys. They also rated themselves as "unsure" more frequently than the boys, who rated themselves to be more certain of their decisions (Lind and Connole 1985). Lower power and influence may lead girls to express dysphoric feelings, including hopelessness, fear, envy, and anger.

Observations of the language 4- to 7-year-old children use in a variety of role-playing situations reflects the fact that they are aware of power and status differences between males and females (Andersen 1978). When children played fathers, doctors, and parents, as opposed to moth-ers, nurses, and children, they used more directives and imperatives in their speech, as opposed to polite requests or hints. There were also differences in the way children spoke to mothers as opposed to fathers: they used six times as many imperatives to mothers as to fathers, includ-ing statements such as, "You get the milk"; or "Gimme Jimmy's flash-light," whereas statements addressed to fathers were made with greater respect or deference, such as "Would you button me?" or "I want to paint."

How would these gender differences in power and influence affect emotional expressiveness? Certainly the simple fact that boys are more aggressive than girls would promote the expression of fear and anger among girls, a theme I heard frequently among the children in my re-search sample. A 6-year-old girl stated, "I'm more scared of boys than I am of girls because boys are bigger than girls, so they can beat you up." With lesser power, young girls are likely to feel scared, angry, and de-feated, as well as to blame themselves for their own lack of control. With more power and influence, boys are apt to express pride about them-selves and contempt and pity toward girls. These patterns mirror those we have seen in adult gender differences.

In fact, girls' emotional expressiveness may be comprised of dysphoric feelings whether they attain power or not. Without power, they feel helpless, scared, and angry. However, if girls actually attain positions of power, they risk peer rejection. In first and second grades, boys who hold dominant positions in the group are liked and accepted by their peers, whereas dominant and powerful girls are rejected (Jones 1983). This suggests that girls are in a bind: with or without power, they may express dysphoric feelings.

In-Groups and Out-Groups

Just as children differentiate from their opposite-sex parents to form their gender identity, they also differentiate from opposite-sex peers. They attempt to express emotions that are different in quality and kind from those expressed by the opposite sex. The opposite sex constitutes an "out-group," which is perceived to have distinctly different characteristics from one's own sex, the "in-group." In other words, if girls get scared and cry, then to be a "real" boy means not crying. If boys get angry and hit, then to be a "real" girl means not hitting.

Processes of out-group hostility and de-identification from opposite-sex peers occur simultaneously with processes of identification toward same-sex peers. Children feel positively toward the same sex and attempt to emulate the quality and kind of emotions that same-sex peers express, especially gender-role stereotypic emotions. Imitation of same-sex children has two effects. One is that children's own sex-role stereotypic expressions increase. At the same time, by imitating and attending to particular sex-role stereotypic expressions in their peers, the likelihood that their peers will repeat those expressions is increased because social attention is so rewarding.

These processes of imitation, identification, and differentiation are not neutral in affective tone, but are accompanied by strong feelings. Characteristics of the opposite sex are devalued in a contemptuous way while characteristics of the same sex are favored with a spirit of pride. Each sex enhances its own self-esteem as well as its gender identity by judging its own stereotypic characteristics to be superior to those of the opposite sex (Harris 1995). For example, high-school boys emphasize the emotional nature of women as a liability, while girls emphasize the emotional nature of women as an asset. Boys make such statements as, "Women are much more emotional," or "Women get upset a lot easier," whereas girls state, "Women are more able to express their emotions and understand what is inside." Girls comment on the negative consequences of boys' lack of emotional expression, whereas boys describe men as more rational and as "reasoners" (Werrbach, Grotevant, and Cooper 1990).

These processes of in-group favoritism and out-group hostility undoubtedly contribute to the emergence of polarized gender differences in emotional expression.

Sex Differences in Opposite-Sex Peer Differentiation

Out-group hostility also seems to be greater for boys than it is for girls. For example, one expression of out-group hostility among elementary-school children is a game in which each sex accuses the other of having germs or cooties. Thorne (1993) notes that in these "rituals of pollution," boys perceive girls to be more polluting than the reverse. And Archer (1992) notes that rituals of pollution are more frequently directed against women than against men, with men harassing women, making demeaning comments about them, or treating them as objects. In some cultures women are viewed as "unclean" by men unless they undergo specialized rituals. These rituals of pollution and other similar cross-sex interactions (known as borderwork) serve the function of enhancing gender identity and gender boundaries, particularly for males.

Cross-sex behaviors are also more condemned for boys than for girls by both parents and peers. For example, preschool-aged boys who showed cross-gender preferences (e.g., who engaged in activities such as kitchen and doll play) received more criticism and fewer positive reactions from their peers than other boys did. This criticism continued even when the boys subsequently attempted to play in typical male activities. The negative feedback that boys received included physical responses, such as snatching toys and hitting, as well as verbal negative reactions, such as, "you're silly or dumb; that's for girls." Gender nonstereotypic boys played alone almost three times as often as other children in their group. In contrast, girls with cross-gender preferences did not receive differential peer reactions. It was more acceptable for girls to play in male activities than the reverse (Fagot 1977; see also Fagot 1985; Shell and Eisenberg 1990). And similarly, elementary-school–aged girls' ratings of female peers' likability were less negatively affected by the presence of cross-gender behavior than were boys' ratings of male peers who engaged in cross-gender behavior (Zucker et al. 1995).

Greater pressures on males to conform to male stereotypic behaviors and to de-identify with female stereotypic behaviors suggests that the tendency to devalue the emotional expressiveness of females may be particularly strong among males. This may be a strong socialization influence that contributes to boys' minimization of emotional expression.

Why would these pressures be especially salient for males? One possibility is that out-group hostility for males is related to status and power issues. Archer (1992) argues that because males are a high-status group, they may be more invested than are females (a low-status group) in maintaining their in-group identity. When males engage in any female stereotypic behaviors (including emotional expression), they may lose status. In contrast, females who engage in some male stereotypic behaviors such as expressing pride or contempt, may gain in status, especially with respect to male peers. Thus males would place a great deal more weight than females on not engaging in cross-sex behavior—in fact, in devaluing it to make it less appealing for their membership to engage in.

A second possibility is that males' gender identity may be at greater risk than that of females because their primary caretakers are women. Bonding with male peers may help boys to develop a distinct male gender identity. Being similar to and accepted by male peers may have a significance for boys which has no counterpart for females, at least until adolescence.

Girls may experience especially strong in-group and out-group pressures during adolescence. At this time, they may feel increasingly pressured to take on aspects of a feminine stereotypic gender identity, both because of attempts to enhance their attractiveness to the opposite sex, as well as because of the urgency of individuating from their mothers (Blos 1962). Adolescent girls may increase their intimacy with and emotional expressiveness toward their female peers, decrease their tomboy behaviors, display greater anxiety and self-consciousness, and polarize achievement into perceived masculine (math and science) and feminine (social and artistic) spheres of interest (Adler, Kless, and Adler 1992; Thorne 1993). Further, Archer (1992) argues that in adolescence, girls attain status through engaging in stereotypically feminine characteristics because they are valued by higher status older boys.

Pre-adolescent and adolescent girls report that they actually prefer to show their real feelings to peers rather than to parents, whereas boys are split evenly between preferring to show their feelings to adults and peers (Saarni 1988). This was in contrast to second-, fifth-, and eighth-grade boys and girls, half of whom reported that if children always showed their real feelings, they would risk being rejected by their peers. Adolescent girls' increasing preference for sharing feelings with their peers may be in the service of helping them to consolidate a female gender role and to differentiate from their families.

In brief, in-group pride and out-group contempt serve to consolidate gender identity as well as to maintain status differences between males and females, and sometimes manifest themselves at different developmental periods for the two sexes.

The Whys of Gender Segregation

Why children play in sex-segregated groups is a fascinating and important question. Although I have demonstrated that sex-segregated groups facilitate and encourage gender differences in the expression of emotions, the existence of these peer groups is only partially satisfying as an answer to the question of why gender differences in emotional expression emerge. Would it help us to understand more about the origins of gender differences in emotional expressiveness if we knew the reasons underlying the widespread sex segregation among children's peer groups?

Unfortunately, there are no clear answers as to why children play primarily with members of their own sex. Theories about the whys of sex segregation include dissimilar toy and activity preferences between boys and girls; gender differences in social skill levels; the behavioral incompatibility of boys' and girls' play styles (more rough-and-tumble play and higher arousal levels for boys than for girls); the maintenance of behaviors consistent with ideas about self-labeled gender identity; and greater social dominance by boys, making cross-sex interactions aversive for girls (Maccoby 1998). Fabes (1994) argues that boys' high levels of arousability drive gender segregation. He found that boys who were rated as more arousable by their teachers evidenced greater same-sex play preferences and were less likely to play in mixed-sex groups than were other boys. Girls tended not to like arousable children, regardless of their sex.

Some researchers have suggested that the degree to which children in a particular culture play in sex-segregated groups may vary according to the types of gender roles and gender inequality promulgated in the culture (Archer 1992; Leaper 1994). For example, Whiting and Edwards (1988) observed that young boys seek to more strongly dissociate themselves from females in cultures in which there is more status inequality between the two sexes.

It seems that the reasons children play with same-sex children are just as complex as the reasons they express different emotions in some situations. Recognizably familiar explanations emerge when we try to understand the origins of sex segregation among peers. The same biological, social, and intrapsychic processes appear to be up for grabs. None of these hypothesized explanations shed additional light on the origins of gender differences in children's emotional expressiveness. In fact, nothing prevents us from reversing the argument, and asserting that children may segregate by sex because the two sexes express emotions differently and are more comfortable with the emotional style of their own sex.

The lesson to be learned here is that the origins of gender differences in *any* social/relational characteristic can be used to understand, and are probably related to the origins of gender differences in any other characteristic, whether it be emotional expressiveness, play patterns, or personality traits. While this may all feel very circular (causing us to question, where is the fundamental core that underlies gender differences?), I believe that it truly captures the reality—that the origins of gender differences are multi-dimensional interacting processes. Even if a core exists in the form of neuropsychologically based temperament differences between the two sexes, it is a core that is strongly influenced by, reactive to, and perhaps even defined by cultural and social influences. In fact, we would be hard-pressed to find the "original" core if we were somehow able to peel away the surrounding layers of social and cultural processes, because the core would not appear to be distinct.

OVERVIEW.   Peers provide socialization experiences that at the very least reinforce cultural values concerning stereotypes about gender and emotion, and may in fact create gender differences in emotional expression. Sex-segregated peer interactions that emphasize dyadic, intimate interactions for girls and competitive, arousing interactions for boys serve to maximize expressions of warmth and vulnerability for girls while minimizing the expression of those same emotions for boys. Interactions with peers also provide rewards (in the form of social acceptance and popularity) and punishments (in the form of teasing and rejection) for expressing gender-stereotypic emotions. Further, pressures to consolidate a gender identity, especially for boys during school years and for girls during adolescence, may lead to increased differentiation and distancing from the emotions expressed by the opposite sex, resulting in a polarization of emotional expression for girls versus boys.

Although conforming to gender stereotypic norms for emotional expression may facilitate social acceptance and popularity, there is also a steep price to pay. Conforming to gender-stereotypic norms may constrain and impair self esteem as well as physical and mental health.

13

The Health Consequences of Gender-Stereotypic Emotional Expression

I try to minimize feeling envious because you just can't do anything about it—it just aggravates you.

—Frank, age 48

By talking and discussing things you never get to the point of going to slit your throat or getting angry about some minor thing . . . That's how I deal with all of my negative problems, whether it's death or anger, or anything. I talk and talk and then it's over with.

—Denise, age 44

Is expressing emotions in gender-role stereotypic ways good or bad for each sex? Women tend to express more intense and frequent emotions across many different situations than men do, especially those conveying distress and dysphoria. In many studies, expressing emotions is seen as beneficial. For example, expressing negative feelings (especially those related to traumatic experiences) has been found to be related to better immune functioning. It should follow that women's immune functioning would be bolstered more frequently than men's (Pennebaker 1989, 1993). On the other hand, expressing negative feelings does not benefit people's health in all situations. For example, the negative emotions expressed during marital conflict, including criticizing, disagreeing, interrupting, disapproving, and expressing dysphoric affect, compromise the immune functioning of both sexes, but especially women's (Kiecolt-Glaser et al. 1993, 1996; Mayne et al. 1997).

Contradictory evidence about the effects of emotional expression is especially evident for cardiovascular reactivity. In opposite conclusions, men's minmized expression of anger has been linked to hypertension and coronary heart disease (Siegman 1994; Siegman and Smith 1994), but has also been viewed as promoting better health for men because it reduces cardiovascular reactivity (see Levenson, Carstensen, and Gottman 1994). These confusing and seemingly conflicting conclusions about the health consequences of emotional expression warrant a closer look.

The Positive Consequences of Emotional Expression

Accumulating evidence indicates that expressing feelings associated with traumatic experiences, including fear, anxiety, sadness, and depression relates to better mental and physical health. For example, when male and female college students write or record descriptions of traumatic events, including descriptions of murder, rape, abuse, and parental divorce, their health and immune functioning show long-term positive benefits. At 3 months following their disclosure, they differ significantly from college students who have not disclosed their experiences, including being significantly happier and less distressed, reporting higher self-esteem, visiting the student health center less frequently, and evidencing greater immune responsivity (Pennebaker, Kiecolt-Glaser, and Glaser 1988; Pennebaker 1989, 1993; Donnelly and Murray 1991).

Powerful evidence for the effects of disclosing traumatic feelings on immune functioning comes from a study of medical students. Male and female medical students who wrote about traumatic events and were given hepatitis B vaccinations and booster injections showed significantly higher antibody levels against hepatitis B at 4- and 6-month follow-up periods than did a control group of medical students who wrote about topics that involved less emotional disclosure (Petrie et al. 1995). Petrie et al. (1995) present convincing evidence that these health changes were not due to changes in health-related behaviors such as the amount of drinking or smoking the participants engaged in.

Some research has indicated that the positive health benefits of expressing feelings appear to be due to expressing a moderate level of negative feelings associated with trauma (Pennebaker 1993; Pennebaker, Mayne, and Francis 1997).[1] One reason that the expression of negative emotions benefits health is that negative emotions are associated with attempts to understand and integrate the situation that induced the feelings. For example, in a study that analyzed college students' positive, negative, and neutral memories of their mothers and fathers, the negative memory stories were filled with a significantly higher number of cognitive processing words, such as "insight," "realize," and "accept," than were the positive memory stories, reflecting a need to understand or be understood (Halberstadt, Leslie-Case, and King 1994).

In their exhaustive analysis of the relationships between social information processing and affect, Clore, Schwarz, and Conway (1994) convincingly argue that negative emotions motivate people to use detail-oriented planning strategies because negative emotions signal that there is a problem whose solution requires effort. In contrast, positive emotions are associated with more global, simplifying, and flexible cognitive strategies, because people feel less pressured to act. These studies indicate that expressing negative emotions may be associated with adaptive cognitive consequences that facilitate change.

The health consequences of expressing emotions are also apparent in studies of cancer patients and bereaved individuals. Having a confiding relationship in which one can express feelings puts people at lower risk for physical symptoms, increases the rate of recovery from illness and injury, and decreases the chances of dying (Mayne, in press). Without an intimate partner to whom they can confide feelings, people report more physical symptoms such as breathlessness and palpitations. Interestingly, when helpers respond with supportive listening and emotional expressions of empathy to distressed confederates, they themselves feel less depressed than when they try to give advice or try to distract the confederate from focusing on their negative mood (Notarius and Herrick 1988).

Why would expressing feelings be associated with better health? One idea is that when you express your feelings, you communicate to others what your needs are, and you are more likely to get those needs met. Functionalist theories of emotion argue that expressing emotions provides people with important information about themselves and their relationships, which helps them to adapt to their environments. Once emotions are expressed, changes in behavior and relationships may result (Frijda 1986; Greenberg and Johnson 1986). For example, expressing fear and vulnerability may result in less aggressive behaviors on both your own part as well as on the part of your opponents, which may be adaptive for survival (Greenberg and Johnson 1986; Greenberg 1996).

By expressing emotions, people may also find new meaning in upsetting events and be able to assimilate or integrate them in better ways. Pennebaker (1993) discusses evidence for this, in that some of the participants in his study who wrote daily accounts of their memories of sexual assault gradually changed their perspectives about their experiences. Their feelings changed from embarrassment and guilt to anger, and finally, to acceptance.

Expressing emotions has also been found to result in cortical congruence, in which brainwave activities on the two sides of the brain are correlated with each other (Pennebaker 1989). Pennebaker monitored the brainwave activity of people who were writing essays, and found that writing about traumatic experiences was associated with higher interhemispheric correlations for both frontal and parietal lobes than was writing about superficial topics. When writing about traumas, people who routinely disclosed their feelings showed greater cortical congruence than did people who did not routinely disclose their feelings. Although it is not clear what effects cortical congruence has on health or on other aspects of functioning, this is an intriguing area for future research.

People who express emotions also seem to have better social relationships than those who do not. In some studies, the causal direction of this relationship is unclear. Good social relationships may promote the expression of emotions and may also result from expressing emotions. For example, among adults and children, the ability to express feelings relates to being popular and well-liked (DiMatteo, Hays, and Prince 1986). In group therapy, people who frequently communicate their emotions are perceived more positively by other group members than those who express their feelings infrequently (Robison, Stockton, and Morran 1990). Similarly, physicians who are more emotionally expressive have patients who are more satisfied than patients of nonexpressive physicians (DiMatteo, Hays, and Prince 1986). Clear evidence that emotional expressiveness actually promotes good social relationships is provided by a study of Mexican and American children. This study showed that school-aged children's emotional expressiveness was found to predict their social competence, self-esteem, and psychological adjustment 5 years later, when they were adolescents (Bronstein and Cruz 1985; see also Bryant 1987; Fabes and Eisenberg 1992; and Bronstein et al. 1993, for other developmental studies). The popularity and social acceptance associated with emotional expressiveness may allow expressive individuals to garner social support, facilitating their well-being during times of stress.

In particular, research converges to indicate that for men, the higher their levels of emotional expressivity, the better their marital relationships are, even if their expressivity takes the form of demands and criticism. For example, in a sample of rural Alabama families, husbands' self-rated expressiveness was the most powerful predictor of both husbands' and wives' marital adjustment. Wives' expressiveness did not significantly contribute to either husbands' or wives' marital adjustment (Lamke 1989). Further, in nondistressed marriages, when husbands showed involvement and were demanding, rather than being distancing or withdrawing, their wives were more satisfied with their marriages one year later (Christensen and Heavey 1993). And wives whose husbands expressed affection and caring in an interaction rated themselves to be happier, which in turn related to decreased depression in the wives. The husbands also rated themselves to be happier when their wives expressed caring and affection, although their happiness (as well as their other feelings) were not found to be related to their depressive symptoms (Gruen, Gwadz, and Morrobel 1994).

Perhaps another reason that emotional expressiveness, social competence, and health are related is that being emotionally expressive may enable people to influence the mood and behaviors of other people. In small groups comprised of both expressive and nonexpressive individuals (with expressivity measured using the ACT questionnaire), the expressive people's feelings influenced the nonexpressive people's reported fear, anger, and anxiety. In contrast, the expressive people's feelings were not influenced by those of the nonexpressive people (Friedman and Riggio 1981). Expressive individuals may also influence other people's physiological reactivity. For example, being at the receiving end of negative emotions, such as criticism, anxiety, impatience, or anger, was found to be related to increased heart rate and muscle tension, whereas being at the receiving end of positive emotions, such as praise, was found to be related to decreased speech muscle tension (Malmo, Boag, and Smith 1957). Being emotionally expressive may provide a certain influence and power over other people, perhaps partly accounting for the relationship between emotional expressiveness and health.

The Effects of Inhibiting Emotions

When people fail to express emotions, they may expend energy in the process of inhibition, which may take a toll on health through short-term increases in autonomic activity (Pennebaker 1993; Gross and Levenson 1993; Gross 1998). In one study on the effects of inhibition, participants were shown a film about burns and amputation that routinely elicited strong feelings of disgust. Randomly assigned participants were given the instruction that while they watched the film, they should try to mask their feelings so that observers would not know they were feeling anything. Another group of participants was allowed to watch the film without any inhibition instructions. Relative to the control group, the group who was attempting to suppress the expression of emotions showed evidence of greater sympathetic nervous system activation, including increased skin conductance (Gross and Levenson 1993; Gross 1998).

The stress of short-term autonomic activity associated with inhibition may accumulate over time, leading to long-term stress-related disease (Pennebaker, Kiecolt-Glaser, and Glaser 1988). Unlike the expression of negative emotions, which also initially relates to higher skin conductance levels, but which tends to relate to decreased skin conductance levels over time, it seems likely that the effects of inhibition on arousal may continue to intensify over time and become damaging to both cardiovascular and immune functioning (Pennebaker 1993; Hughes, Uhlmann, and Pennebaker 1994; Petrie et al. 1995).

Inhibiting feelings may also be associated with other maladaptive cognitive and affective consequences. It is worth noting that the participants who were inhibiting their feelings of disgust in response to the burn/amputation film rated themselves as feeling more contemptuous than those who did not (Gross and Levenson 1993). This result leads to the interesting speculation that the higher levels of contempt expressed by men than by women in some studies are due to their greater tendency to suppress feelings. Suppression may serve to distance people from the immediacy of interpersonal relationships, and such distancing may be accompanied by feelings of superiority. Moreover, distancing from interpersonal relationships is not good for one's health. A great deal of research suggests that social supports and relationships can buffer the effects of disease and trauma and increase longevity (Mayne, in press).

There is also evidence that for girls, inhibiting anger may place demands on their attentional processes that interfere with their ability to regulate behaviors in other situations, leading to behavioral problems (Cole, Zahn-Waxler, and Smith 1994). Five-year-old girls without behavioral problems allowed themselves to express more anger in private than in public settings when receiving an unwanted gift. In contrast, girls with behavioral problems suppressed their angry feelings in both public and private settings. They seemed to have overgeneralized the display rule about inhibiting their expression of anger, applying it when it wasn't necessary. This may have taxed their abilities to attend to and regulate their behaviors. (It may also be the case that the girls' attentional problems may have caused them difficulties in distinguishing between public and private settings).

More extreme biological as well as behavioral consequences for inhibiting feelings have been hypothesized by the Harvard Medical School psychiatrist A. Pontius (1993). She speculates that not expressing the feelings that accompany extreme early traumatic experiences, such as the death of a parent, can result in a syndrome termed the "limbic psychotic trigger reaction," involving motiveless homicide. One patient with this hypothesized syndrome murdered a man for no apparent reason. The patient was picnicking with a friend and happened to see his future victim fishing nearby. He experienced strange feelings and hallucinations about this person that culminated in murder. Later, in expressing remorse for the crime, the patient remembered that his father, who had died when he was five, had taken him fishing frequently. He had never mourned his father or discussed him subsequent to his death. Pontius (1993) hypothesizes that repressing feelings of grief and anger does not allow for the appropriate development of links between cortical and limbic structures that regulate the expression of aggression. In later life, an event that reminds the individual of a previously unexpressed trauma kindles a seizure of the limbic system, inducing a severe distortion of emotion and behavior. More work is needed to confirm these intriguing ideas, which are currently based on case studies of 12 men who committed motiveless homicide.

In sum, there is much research to indicate that expressing feelings relates to better physical health, more adaptive social relationships, and more positive mood. Since women tend to have closer and more confiding relationships than men have, and also tend to express a wider range of feelings than men express, women may derive health benefits to a greater extent than men. Yet, gender differences in emotional functioning, and in this case, the relationships between gender-specific ways of expressing emotion and adaptation, are never simple. They vary a great deal depending on which emotion is expressed, in which situation and modality, and using which coping strategies.

The Effects of Expressing Anger

The seemingly straightforward relationship between emotional expressiveness and positive adaptation starts to get complex when the subject is the expression of anger. There are two different perspectives on the relationship between anger and health. The first is that expressing anger is beneficial. Why? The suppression of anger results in negative health consequences, especially cardiovascular reactivity. Expressing anger is also beneficial because communicating dissatisfaction helps to change situations so that people have a greater chance of accomplishing their goals and of increasing their self-esteem (Greenberg 1996). Generating an angry feeling may also be useful as an empathy technique, allowing people to identify with others who have been the objects of injustice, and motivating people to act on their behalf (Tice and Baumeister 1993).

The second perspective is directly opposite: expressing anger may have negative health consequences because it increases cardiovascular reactivity, especially if the anger is expressed with aggression or hostility (Houston 1994). Further, expressing anger may be dysfunctional because it alienates people and leads to more distance in relationships and less social support. In extreme cases, anger can evoke hostile responses in others and can lead to a preoccupation with angry feelings as well as to physical abuse (see Mayne in press; Newton et al. 1995). Further negative consequences of expressing anger emerge from observations showing that expressing anger can sometimes lead to experiencing more anger (Zillmann 1984, 1989). Several studies have shown that when people are given an opportunity to vent their anger, they actually report being more angry than when they are not given such an opportunity (Frodi 1976; Lai and Linden 1992). A preoccupation with aggressive thoughts following the expression of anger may be even more true of men than of women (Frodi 1976).

There are ways in which both of these contradictory positions are true:

the expression of anger is at times and in some people associated with positive health consequences, and at times and in some people associated with negative health consequences.

There are three major reasons that may account for the contradictory conclusions drawn by researchers in this area. The first is that the way in which anger is expressed, and with what intensity, is critical for understanding its effects. For example, the verbal versus the physical expression of anger may have quite different consequences. A second reason is that the context in which the anger is expressed is of the utmost importance in understanding its consequences. Expressing anger toward your superiors may result in negative health consequences, while expressing anger toward your spouse may be beneficial in certain circumstances. And finally, a third reason is that there are individual differences in the consequences of expressing anger. For some individuals, expressing anger may be positive, for others it may be negative. Individual differences in reactivity may depend on how comfortable people are with anger expression as well as on the processes they use to regulate and cope with anger, both of which may be different for the two sexes.

The Importance of Labeling Feelings

One way to understand why the expression of anger is sometimes positive and sometimes negative is to look at the mode in which the anger is expressed. Verbalizing anger, especially in a calm and nonreactive way, may be good for mental health and physical health, whereas the physical expression of anger may not be. For example, when participants speak about anger-arousing events in a soft and slow speech style, they reduce their blood pressure and heart rates to significantly lower levels than when they speak about the same events loudly and quickly (Siegman, Anderson, and Berger 1990; Siegman and Snow 1997; Siegman and Boyle 1992; Siegman 1994).

Moreover, it has been found that 4- to 6-year-old children who express anger using nonhostile verbal reactions (rather than hostile physical reactions) have higher interpersonal coping skills and social competence as rated by adults. They also have higher peer status as rated by their fellow students. This is especially true of boys, for whom the use of physical retaliation is negatively related to social competence (Eisenberg et al. 1994b).

The way in which anger is expressed has also been found to be related to the likelihood of abuse in marriages. When husbands' and wives' ability to communicate their distress was rated for delivery, organization, and content, men who were rated as lower on their communication skills were more physically and verbally abusive than those who had higher communication skills. Wives with lower communication skills were more likely to be psychologically, but not physically abused by their husbands (Babcock et al. 1993).

The positive benefits of labeling feelings, a strategy used more by women than by men, was demonstrated in a study by Keltner, Locke, and Audrain (1993). They asked participants to imagine negative life events, thus inducing sad moods. One randomly selected group of participants was asked where and when the negative event took place, focusing on the cognitive causes and consequences of the event. Another randomly selected group was asked to describe which emotions they currently felt. Those who described and labeled their emotions reported significantly higher life satisfaction and thus were less affected by the sad mood manipulation than those who focused on the causes and consequences of the life events and did not label their feelings. Labeling feelings reduced the impact of sad events on participants' judgments and on their perception of new situations.

It would seem that the more linguistically encoded the expression of anger is, the less likely it is to have negative health consequences and dysfunctional consequences for relationships. Daniel Stern has argued that using language enables feelings to become publicly accessible and shared, rather than remaining private experiences (Stern 1985). Using language, people are able to garner support and legitimacy for their feelings, and social support itself has many positive health consequences. Pennebaker (1989, 1993) further argues that by translating events into language, people can more readily understand and find meaning in their emotional experiences, thus assimilating them.

The most positive health benefits may come when feelings are both labeled and interpreted in some way—when people both acknowledge particular feelings and try to understand why they are occurring. Expressing negative feelings without accompanying cognitive interpretation may actually exacerbate those feelings immediately afterwards, increasing depression, sadness, anger, and guilt over the short term (Pennebaker 1989; Donnelly and Murray 1991). Without interpretation, expressing anger may lead to justifying angry feelings by exaggerating or emphasizing the severity of the offense that produced the anger, thus leading to social relationships based on hostility, status differences, and revenge (Tice and Baumeister 1993).

The Importance of Context

Contradictory results have been reported about the health consequences of expressing negative emotions during marital conflicts for both men and women. One explanation for these contradictory results is that negative affect has not been consistently measured in the same way across different studies (see Morell and Apple [1990] for a distinction between active and passive negative affect). But the explanation I would like to examine is that marital conflicts are not uniformly the same: in fact, they represent many different contexts.

First, I will briefly review the contradictions. For women, as consistent with the idea that the expression of negative emotions is generally health promoting, there is evidence that expressing anger within the context of marriage is good for women's marital satisfaction. Wives' satisfaction with their marriages improves over time if they express anger and contempt during marital conflicts, but decreases if they express sadness or fear (Gottman and Krokoff 1989). Thus, wives who express their anger are happier in their marriages over a 3-year period than wives who do not.

On the other hand, other evidence indicates that the expression of negative feelings in distressed marital relationships involves the short-term risk of evoking husbands' negative affect, whining, and oppositionality, a common pattern displayed by husbands in response to their wives' anger (Gottman and Levenson 1986). Expressing negative feelings also compromises women's immune functioning and increases their physiological arousal, but does not do so for men (Kiecolt-Glaser et al. 1993, 1996; Mayne et al. 1997). For example, after a 45-minute conflict discussion, husbands in distressed couples actually improved in their immune functioning and decreased in their reported levels of hostility and anxiety, while wives did not. Wives' immune functioning became less adaptive, and they became more cardiovascularly aroused than did their husbands (Mayne et al. 1997). The authors suggest that their results explain why marriage is more protective for husbands, increasing their health and well-being, than it is for wives. Another study also found that women were more likely than men to show negative immunological changes after discussing a difficult marital issue (Kiecolt-Glaser et al. 1993).

The same contradictions in the research literature exist for men. Some research notes that men's arousal and cardiovascular reactivity increase when they express negative emotions in marital conflicts, suggesting that the expression of negative emotions is bad for men's health (Levenson, Carstensen, and Gottman 1994). Other research suggests that husbands' general emotional expressivity is related positively to their own as well as to their wives' marital adjustment and satisfaction (Lamke 1989; Christensen and Heavey 1993).

In order to understand the contradictions in the literature, the quality of the marital relationship must be carefully considered. How dysfunctional is the marriage? How frequent, intense, and repeated are the conflicts? Are both negative and positive feelings expressed in a marriage, or only negative? Distressed couples may show gender differences not typical of couples who are functioning more adaptively. Research has indicated that couples who were more negative and hostile during a 30-minute problem discussion showed greater dysfunctional immunological changes than did those couples who were less negative. Further, in highly hostile couples, the discussion of marital problems led to larger increases in blood pressure that remained elevated longer than the blood pressures of less hostile couples. It is noteworthy that both sets of couples did not differ from each other on their baseline functioning (Kiecolt-Glaser et al. 1993).

Both wives and husbands in distressed relationships may be fearful that the expression of anger will result in hurtful or harmful consequences. In a dysfunctional marriage, there is a high likelihood that expressing anger will be reciprocated with anger on the part of the spouse, leading to an escalating cycle of bad feelings (Notarius and Johnson 1982; Gottman and Levenson 1986, 1992). It may not be the expression of anger or distress per se that compromises adjustment, but the chronicity with which anger and distress are expressed with no apparent change in the relationship.

Evidence from parent-child relationships also indicates that distressed families may respond less adaptively to the expression of anger than nondistressed families. In nondistressed families, when preschool children find themselves in conflict with others, or when children express negative feelings, helpful family discussions about the causes and consequences of feelings are likely to ensue (Dunn, Brown, and Beardsall 1991; Dunn and Brown 1994). These discussions may teach family members to make appropriate judgments about other people's emotions (Dunn, Brown, and Beardsall 1991). However, in families who express anger and distress with high frequency, the expression of negative emotions by children is unlikely to be discussed. In these families, children have less of an opportunity to learn about the causes and consequences of their feelings. Research has shown that 33-month-old children from families who frequently express anger and distress perform more poorly on an emotion understanding task 7 months later (Dunn and Brown 1994). Other research has similarly indicated that being in a relationship in which anger is frequently expressed or provoked is negatively related to feelings of well-being (Rook 1984). In brief, the expression of the angry feelings that accompany conflicts can be adaptive when they motivate discussions and attempts to understand and ameliorate the anger. Such discussions are more likely to occur in the context of families who are not frequently distressed and conflict-ridden.

Individual Differences in Emotion Regulation

Another way to reconcile the often contradictory consequences of expressing anger is to consider that there are individual differences in how people regulate and cope with angry experiences. Different coping and regulation strategies may lead to different health consequences.

COMFORT IN EXPRESSING ANGER.   One key index of emotional regulation is how comfortable people are in expressing their anger. Some individuals may feel comfortable expressing anger and accrue health benefits for doing so; others may not. For example, Engebretson, Matthews, and Scheier (1989) studied males who were harassed during a problem-solving task, and who were subsequently told to write either a positive or a negative evaluation of the harassing confederate. When participants expressed feelings in their evaluations that were consistent with their usual expressive style, they had significant reductions in systolic blood pressure. For example, when men who characteristically did not express anger wrote positive evaluations of their harassers, they showed cardiovascular benefits. Similarly, when men who characteristically expressed their anger wrote negative evaluations, they showed cardiovascular benefits. In contrast, men who expressed their anger in a style that was not comfortable for them did not show cardiovascular benefits.

One of the most important variables in determining whether or not expressing anger is comfortable may be gender itself. Since anger is stereotyped to be inappropriate for women, they may be socialized to feel uncomfortable when they do express anger. Consequently, women may accrue fewer health benefits from expressing anger than men do.

REAPPRAISAL VERSUS SUPPRESSION. The two sexes may also cope with angry experiences differently, leading to different consequences. For example, even though two groups of people may both express low levels of anger, one group may have failed to express their experienced anger (that is, they may have suppressed their anger), while another may have reappraised the initial anger-inducing situation, leading to not only a diminished *expression* of anger, but also a diminished *experience* of anger.

James Gross's work (1998) suggests that it is only when people suppress an emotional experience, rather than reappraise it, that their physiological arousal increases. He compared the responses of two groups to a highly evocative burn film. One group was given the instruction to reappraise the film, that is to think about the film in such a way that they would feel nothing. The suppression group, in contrast, was told to behave in such a way that someone watching them would not know what they were feeling. The reappraisal group reported a minimized experience of disgust and did not show physiological arousal. In contrast, the suppression group showed increases in physiological arousal in the form of increased finger pulse amplitude, finger temperature, and skin conductance levels and did not show a minimized experience of disgust. This experiment suggests that it is critical to look at the processes people are using to minimize their expression of anger in order to fully understand its health consequences.

Evidence suggests that in some provocative circumstances, women may reappraise anger-inducing circumstances in a manner that allows them to experience more sadness, hurt, and disappointment than men experience (Brody 1993). Some researchers have studied this process under the rubric of internalizing versus externalizing defenses, suggesting that women are more likely to redirect their feelings, particularly anger, toward themselves, whereas men are more likely to turn against others (Cramer 1991).

It turns out that expressing sadness rather than anger has very different impacts on judgments and self-esteem. For example, research has indicated that people who are asked to pose sad versus angry facial expressions interpret the same social situations differently, with sad people more likely to see situational forces (usually not under their control) as responsible for the event, and with angry people more likely to blame other people for the event (Keltner, Ellsworth, and Edwards 1993). For example, college students were presented with a scenario in which one roommate embarrassed another, publicly exposing the roommate's attraction to someone who was already in another relationship. Participants who posed sad facial expressions (thus inducing sadness) were less likely to blame the offending roommate; those who posed angry facial expressions (thus inducing anger) were more likely to blame him.

Since women express more sadness than men, it suggests that they will be less likely to blame others for negative events and more likely to blame situational factors. Situational factors may seem less controllable than are other people and may lead to feelings of hopelessness, anxiety, and depression (Taylor, Wayment, and Collins 1993). Women's tendency to express sadness and hurt in anger-inducing situations may ultimately jeopardize their health in the form of depression.

The extent to which men and women think about the causes of their feelings may be another emotional coping strategy, or type of reappraisal, that impacts gender differences in self-esteem. Research has indicated that when people can identify clear explanations for their negative moods, it does not affect their self-esteem, but when they cannot identify clear explanations, it results in lowered self-evaluations (Schwarz and Clore 1988). Boys are encouraged to think about the causes and the consequences of their feelings more than are girls (Fivush 1989, 1993). If women are less apt to identify specific causes for their emotional experiences than men, it may serve to make them to feel worse about themselves.

RUMINATION AND GENDER.   Women's tendency to express more sadness in anger-inducing situations than men (as well as more sadness in general) has other consequences for their emotional coping. Women have been found to engage in more rumination than men, particularly when depressed or sad (Nolen-Hoeksema 1991). Rumination is defined as repeatedly thinking or experiencing feelings about a given object or situation for an extended period of time (Rime et al. 1992). Rumination prolongs depression and leads to selectively remembering other sad events, possibly resulting in lowered self-esteem and less optimism. It may also inhibit positive actions. With extreme rumination, people may become desperate to escape their negative thoughts, resulting in reckless behaviors, such as drinking. When men experience painful feelings, they are more likely to distract themselves than are women by engaging in activities such as physical exercise or sports (Nolen-Hoeksema 1991). Distraction tends to disrupt the cycle of negative feelings.

Recent research shows that both rumination and expressiveness increase when events are viewed as disruptive (Rime et al. 1992).[2] This suggests that women may engage in both rumination and verbal emotional expressiveness more than men do because women consider events in their lives to be more disruptive than men (causing more obstacles to their goals). Such feelings may stem from their perceived and actual helplessness, their relatively lower status and power, as well as from socialization processes that emphasize dependence on others.

Recent work also suggests that rumination may evoke stress-related physiological arousal and changes (see the argument made by Baum, Cohen, and Hall 1993; Kiecolt-Glaser et al. 1996). Unwanted and repetitive thoughts, in particular, have been related to increased sympathetic nervous system activity, which in turn may ultimately affect cardiovascular pathology. It is possible that women's tendency to ruminate over unresolved marital conflicts may be one of the reasons that women's immune functioning is more influenced by marital conflict than is men's.

In brief, women's style of expressing sad and dysphoric feelings, sometimes in response to anger-inducing situations, may promote feelings of helplessness, anxiety, and depression, and may also be self-perpetuating. Men's style of expressing anger directly, of distracting themselves from sad feelings, and of coping with their feelings by searching for the causes may promote a sense of agency, control, and high self-esteem. It is also possible that men's tendency to express anger (especially aggression) rather than sadness may promote social relationships in which men fail to take responsibility, blaming others rather than themselves for their problems, and in which distance rather than intimacy is promoted.

I have argued that the consequences of expressing anger may differ for females and males, depending on the extent to which they feel comfortable expressing anger, on the types of processes they use to regulate and cope with their anger, as well as on the extent to which they express other feelings, such as sadness, that accompany anger. Further, the way anger is expressed is critical, whether in words or via other means. And finally, the context in which the anger is expressed affects its health consequences, especially whether it is expressed in distressed versus nondistressed family systems.

Emotional Expressivity and Health in Women

I have reviewed evidence that for women, expressing and labeling feelings, including anger, has many positive benefits, including benefits to physical health, to positive mood, to social relationships, and to long term marital satisfaction. It may be that the lower rate of cardiovascular problems in women rather than men is partly due to the fact that women tend to verbalize a wider range of feelings than men.

However, women are twice as likely to be depressed as men, women's immune functioning seems to be affected by marital conflict more than men's, and marriages protect women's health less than they protect men's. The expression of emotion by women may not have all the benefits for their social relationships or for their physical and mental health that would be expected, perhaps because of women's lower status and power and their circumscribed social roles.[3]

For example, although expressing anger is related to higher marital satisfaction and self-esteem for women over the long term, women who express anger may risk the retaliation of their partners in the short term. Their partners may see them as violating display rules, or as threatening the power and status differential of the relationship. In fact, women may feel punished by the consequences of expressing anger in their marriages because of their husbands' negative reactions, including anger, distancing, and stonewalling (Gottman and Levenson 1986). Especially in distressed marriages, the expression of anger may be related to abuse and to compromised immune functioning.

Men's reactions may also be anxiety-producing or frustrating for wives because men themselves are socialized to be emotionally inexpressive. Research suggests that wives are less depressed in marriages in which husbands express affection and caring, but most men are socialized to minimize their expression of these emotions.

Expressing emotions such as anger may also be maladaptive for many women because the anger fails to achieve the goal of improving relationships. Women may frequently feel compelled to repeat their expressions of anger because their initial expressions of anger do not serve to change the anger-producing situation. In marital relationships, women's anger is likely to be elicited by both an unfair division of gender role–related tasks as well as by their husbands' inexpressivity (Noller and Fitzpatrick 1993). Change may not ensue because both the culture as well as individual husbands may be invested in maintaining the status quo, rather than in attempting to address the gender-role inequities that women may be angry about. Greenberg (1996) claims that when an expected consequence does not ensue after an emotion is expressed, the most positive alternative is to recognize and remove the source of stress. In this case, removing the stress would entail changing the power and status imbalances between the two sexes as well as changing the differences in emotional expressivity between the two sexes. Without these unlikely changes, the expression of anger for women may not accomplish the benefits otherwise expected.

Some of the feelings that women express may also be nonadaptive for their health and well-being because they emerge from, or are distortions of other feelings. Because of their socialization histories, women may feel uncomfortable expressing anger, setting up internal conflicts and self-devaluation when they do express it. They may instead substitute other feelings, such as sadness or distress. The expression of distress does not accurately communicate a woman's motives nor does it enable her to accomplish her goals. Expressing distress instead of anger may also lead to lower self-esteem and feelings of helplessness. This may produce a cycle in which the events that occur in women's lives are experienced as disruptive and defeating, accompanied by both rumination and heightened expressions of distress, and ultimately serve to increase women's risk for depression (Nolen-Hoeksema 1993).

In summary, the expression of emotions for women in accordance with stereotypic gender roles is associated with a number of risks.

Women are in a double bind: if they express anger (and other emotions connoting mastery and power), it may ultimately benefit their relationships and their self-esteem; however, they risk short-term rejection and abuse, with some research showing that such women are viewed as less sexually appealing (Zillmann et al. 1986). If they express sadness and distress instead of anger, they may spare themselves abuse and appear more sexually attractive to men, but they risk feeling more helpless, depressed, and anxious. These are risks that can only be minimized with changes in our cultural values and stereotypes about gender roles.

Emotional Expressivity and Health in Men

There are also both health benefits and risks to the style in which men are socialized to express emotions, including the expression of aggression and the minimization of other feelings. Minimizing the expression of feelings in many situations (especially through suppression, rather than reappraisal) may have cumulative adverse effects for men's physiological functioning. Men may also fail to obtain beneficial social supports in times of stress because of their minimized emotional expressivity. Expressing anger using physical aggression also has a number of adverse consequences for interpersonal relationships as well as for physiological reactivity, especially cardiovascular reactivity.

When men do verbally express negative emotions to their wives, it is adaptive for both their own and their wives' marital satisfaction. In verbally expressing anger, especially in conflict situations, there is some evidence that men may decrease their levels of hostility and improve their immune functioning (Mayne et al. 1997).

Yet men, like women, are socially limited as to the types of emotions they are allowed to express. They are viewed as less likeable and attractive when they express too much vulnerability. And expressing anger using moderate amounts of aggression, although perhaps bad for the cardiovascular system, makes men more likable, and may help them to succeed in a competitive world.

In other words, men, too, are in a double bind: If they express anger via aggression, they risk cardiovascular disease; if they don't, they risk social rejection and failure. If they express vulnerability, they may have more satisfying marriages, but they may risk being seen as weak and effeminate, possibly having negative consequences for their self-esteem as well as for their achievement and careers.

Conforming to Display Rules

The mental and physical health of both sexes may suffer when either sex conforms to display rules to an extreme degree. Women are pressured to minimize expressions of anger; men are pressured to minimize expressions of hurt and vulnerability. Not expressing such feelings may lead to more negative health consequences than when both sexes allow themselves to express the entire range of feelings that accompany frustrating or enraging experiences. Greenberg (1996) has hypothesized that when people attempt to control primary feelings, they wind up feeling badly. Moreover, if people have to expend energy to control feelings, the required energy may take their attention away from where its primary focus should be. Simply expressing the feelings would help them to dissipate. Both men and women are at risk for feeling badly because of attempts to conform to the limiting display rules for their own sex.

The quality of marital functioning is also affected by conformity to display rules. Members of couples have been found to misinterpret their partners' expressions of affection in accordance with gender-stereotypic expectations, perhaps leading to unnecessary conflicts. Men have been found to interpret their partners' failures to express affection as evidence of hostility (perhaps because their female partners are expected to be emotionally affectionate), whereas women interpret their partners' lack of hostility as evidence of affection (perhaps because their male partners are expected to be nonexpressive of affection) (Gaelick, Bodenhausen, and Wyer 1985). These distortions would undoubtedly result in many communication failures and disappointments.

Our current cultural values may lead to a process of mutual projective identification in couples, in which each sex projects onto the other their own unacceptable emotions, and behaves as if the other sex "carried" those emotions, producing a self-fulfilling prophecy. How might this work? If both males and females experience the same feelings, but Western cultural values dictate that only one sex (female) is allowed to express distress, while the other sex (male) is allowed to express aggression and mastery, it may result in a process in which people experience pleasure in their opposite-sex partner's expression of emotions partly because they see their own thwarted emotions expressed and recognized by another.

It is easy to see how gender patterns may be replicated in families using this model. For example, if men are taught that their expression of vulnerable feelings is unacceptable, they may project their own feelings of vulnerability onto their wives and daughters, seeing female family members as vulnerable rather than themselves. If they frequently distort their daughters' and wives' emotional experiences, perceiving them as expressing vulnerability instead of some other emotion such as anger, men may subtly reward or reinforce their wives and daughters for expressing such emotions. Wives and daughters may in reality begin to express more vulnerability. In turn, wives may also subtly reinforce their husbands and sons for expressing aggression in ways that they themselves are not allowed to do.

If men and women were equal in power and status as well as in their culturally assigned gender roles, differences in emotional expressiveness would be minimized and the mental and physical health consequences for both sexes would improve. If changes in gender roles were to take place, both men and women would experience fewer internal conflicts in the form of depression and low self-esteem, fewer relational conflicts in the form of abuse and emotional insensitivity to their partners, and fewer health problems in the form of cardiovascular reactivity and impaired immune functioning.

14

Rethinking Gender and Emotion

> I think the best thing I could give my son is a good impression of what women are and that he would respect women as being intelligent people; that we're not just housekeepers, we're not just mothers, we're not just wives. We are intelligent beings and we have so much to give to children and I'd like to see women out of the roles that children see them in. That my son sees that I'm capable of doing many things, just as he sees his father capable of doing many things. And I'd like to see that all mothers, all women would first be seen as people, individuals, and then as mothers and wives. I hope the next generation that has children will not only be mothers, but they'll be people to their children. Which would be the best gift they could give to their children.
>
> —*Elizabeth, age 38*

> I'd like to see the results of an experiment where boys and girls were not raised differently . . . if you raised them exactly the same, how would they come out? Who knows?
>
> —*Mark, age 42*

Cultural values shape and constrain the socialization of females' and males' emotional expressivity, ultimately affecting the quality of their functioning and interpersonal relationships. Gender differences in emotional expressivity are shaped by cultural agents, such as peers, parents, and the media, who respond to subtle differences in temperament between the two sexes very early in life (the precise causes of which have yet to be specified), as well as to social values and stereotypes about gender. Biological differences between the two sexes matter primarily insofar as they elicit different social responses, especially from parents and peers.

Perhaps the most significant cultural values to influence gender differences in emotional expression are those concerning power and status differences between males and females. In most cultures, females have less power and status than males. Expressing particular emotions helps the two sexes adapt to these power imbalances. For example, expressing contempt toward others has been found to be more typical of males than of females in some contexts, and is often an emotion expressed by higher status groups toward lower status groups, helping to maintain these differences. Gender differences in motives and social roles, which are sometimes linked to gender differences in power and status, also contribute to gender differences in emotional expression.

Yet, exploring these processes unearths other questions: Why do women have lower status and power than men, as well as differing social roles? Are these processes related to gender differences in hormones and cerebral lateralization? Are they genetically determined? Are they related to differing levels of identification in the mother-daughter as opposed to the mother-son relationship? The answers to these questions are just as complex, if not more so, as they are for gender differences in emotional expression, and seem to lead us back to where we started.

One argument that can be made is that the differing social roles to which the two sexes are assigned may create sex differences in motivation, which in turn lead to differing types of emotional expressiveness. For example, women with paid employment have been found to have higher achievement motives than women without paid employment, and women with young children have been found to be more concerned about children's welfare than those without young children (Krogh 1985; see also Friedman et al. 1992; James et al. 1995). It is not inconceivable that assigning different social roles to the two sexes sets up differing trajectories for their subsequent motives, and, in turn, for their emotional expressiveness (see Winter 1988).[1]

However, this argument is less than satisfying because it still leads us back to the question of why men and women are assigned to differing social roles. Some theorists have hypothesized that men have more power than women because they are more aggressive than women (Brody 1985). Men then use the social power they attain to convince women that the feminine role should involve intimacy (Kemper 1974). Those with power use it to create a psychology in which others voluntarily want to work for them, rather than being forced to work for them. One way to accomplish this is to socialize less powerful people to accept their subordinate lot in life, making it part of their identity. Emotionality, warmth, and lovingness are projected onto women and ultimately shape their identities, thus leading to their acceptance of their own powerlessness (Kemper 1974). Such socialization can be accomplished through both family and cultural processes, including the media. For example, American girls are taught early on that the role of women is to look beautiful and fall in love with heroic men. Every Disney film that has mesmerized American children (even relatively recent ones such as *Aladdin*, *The Lion King*, or *Beauty and the Beast*) promotes this message. By making heroic status part of men's identity, and by making beauty and marriage to men with high status part of women's identity, the power struggles between men and women that might otherwise occur are minimized. Social psychological research (Walster, Berscheid, and Walster 1973) shows that both exploiters and victims can and do frequently convince themselves that the most unbalanced of exchanges is perfectly fair.

In brief, there are many provocative theories about why men and women have different motives, social roles, and power and status. No one of these theories can fully explain the complexities of sex differences in these processes, and we are forced to come back around to the idea that the origins of gender differences in emotional expression lie in multidimensional interacting processes, including biological, cultural, and social forces. If we are determined to discover some "core" explanation for gender differences, such as social roles, hormonal differences, or peer-segregated interactions, we will most certainly be disappointed. No one process exists in isolation and all exert influences on others. As with many aspects of human behavior, the truth has many facets, and our attraction to one or another theory is affected by the historical and social context in which we function (see Assiter 1996).

Effects of Traditional versus Nontraditional Values

Whatever the reasons underlying the assignment of differing social roles to men and women, traditional cultural values dictate that mothers should be the primary child caretakers, not fathers, which may set up different trajectories for the emotional development of their daughters and sons. Emerging data suggest that patterns of same-sex identification between mothers and daughters, including empathy, intrusiveness, and lack of separation may facilitate daughters' expressivity, while patterns of opposite-sex de-identification between mothers and sons may minimize sons' expressivity. These patterns are heightened by cultural display rules touted by peers and the media.

When fathers are involved in child caretaking, thus violating traditional masculine gender roles, their children become less sex-role stereotypic in their emotional expressivity. I have explored several hypotheses about why involved fathers shift their children's emotional functioning in less stereotypic directions. One hypothesis is that involved fathers provide boys with a model of male emotional expressivity—a more multidimensional view of masculinity than merely one that is "not" feminine. A second hypothesis is that involved fathers enable girls, especially adolescent girls, to develop an identity separate from their mothers so that the expression of intense emotions is no longer needed in the service of differentiation. In fact, girls may de-identify with the emotional expressiveness of their involved fathers. A third hypothesis is that involved fathers may stereotype their children's emotional expressiveness along gendered lines to a lesser extent than do noninvolved fathers. And yet another hypothesis is that involved fathers change the quality of interactions among all members of the family system, leading to different socialization patterns for girls and boys.

Having an involved father may also change the nature of power and status differences between the two sexes, at least within the family context. Shifts in power and status between husbands and wives may be powerful messages internalized by children. These views may affect children's views of their own power and status and ultimately influence the quality of the emotions they express. For example, one study showed that mothers who made fewer compromises with their husbands had daughters who tended to accept or admire forceful women with strong goals (Werrbach, Grotevant, and Cooper 1992). This study suggests that the equalization of power between mothers and fathers may dramatically alter traditional patterns of gender development in the family.

Recent research also indicates that parents with nontraditional gender roles promote better adjustment on the part of their children. For example, parents who are more accepting of emotions typically associated with the opposite sex, that is, fathers who are more aware of sadness and mothers who are more aware of anger, have children with more positive peer relationships, fewer behavioral problems, and lower levels of stress than children who come from more traditional families (Hooven, Gottman, and Katz 1995).

In sum, when the traditional roles played by the two sexes are changed (including those depicted in the media), patterns of gender differences in emotional expressiveness also shift. Although biological differences between males and females do exist, social and cultural forces have the power to shape them in other directions. Given the power of emotional expressiveness in influencing our health and well-being, we would do well to re-examine our cultural values surrounding gender roles and the structure of the family that we now largely take for granted.

Looking Backward and Forward

When I first started writing this book, I thought I would be able to read everything that had been written in the field of gender and emotion. I was quickly disabused of that idea. The field is vast, interdisciplinary, and each day becoming more voluminous (or at least so it seemed to me!). Not only psychologists and sociologists, but also educators, anthropologists, and an occasional philosopher and historian have all engaged in productive inquiries about gender and emotion. What is particularly frustrating, but probably not unique to this area of study, is that researchers in different disciplines rarely read or refer to each other's work. In their failure to take a broad perspective on their work, researchers often miss opportunities to ask important questions, or to interpret their data in meaningful ways. Many researchers simply ignore gender as a variable of interest or importance, for example, pooling men and women together to study facial feedback effects on emotional experience.

In order to make sense of vast amounts of accumulating data, it is imperative to have a theoretical framework about gender development within which to formulate and test hypotheses. Often, researchers operate with no theoretical framework, interpreting gender differences on a post hoc basis. The theoretical framework I have taken in this book is a transactional one. I do not think the evidence allows us to ignore the combined contributions made by cultural, social, and biological processes to emotional expression. Although that is the framework within which I think future researchers will reap the most exciting new findings, I also believe that other theoretical frameworks (for example, a strictly social or a strictly biological framework) can still be mined.

Several important processes are still frequently overlooked, if not ignored, in the study of gender and emotion, including the effects of situational context, cultural variations, ethnic and socioeconomic differences, and even age differences in affecting the quality of emotional expressiveness. All of these variables affect gender differences, and conclusions about gender differences should never be generalized beyond these specific variables to a universal style of female versus male emotional expressiveness. I do not believe that a general male or female emotional style exists without qualifications as to age, situation, culture, and context.

Perhaps the overarching caveat is that complexity should not be simplified. In simplifying the diverse and multi-faceted processes that produce gender differences, we ultimately fail to capture the reality of people's lives. We risk reducing men and women to cartoon characters, missing an opportunity to see ourselves and others as individuals struggling with our own humanity, rather than as stereotyped versions of ourselves.

Notes

References

Index

Notes

1. Introduction

1. Quotations at the beginning of each chapter are taken from individual interviews conducted with family members who participated in the research project on gender and emotion discussed later in this chapter (see Brody, Lovas, and Hay 1995). Names and some ages of research participants have been changed.
2. The results from this study have been presented or published in the following papers: Brody, Hay, and Vandewater (1990); Brody (1993); Brody, Lovas, and Hay (1995); Brody, Pfister, and Brennan (1997); Brody, Wise, and Monuteaux (1997); Brody (1997); Brody (in press).
3. This household tasks checklist was adapted from one used by Baruch and Barnett (1986a).
4. The children were given a children's version of the Attitudes toward Women Scale.
5. Assiter (1996) points out that biological accounts of gender differences have waxed and waned depending on the state of the economy. When unemployment is high and the need for women employees is low, women's "natural" and biological roles as homemakers and nurturers become emphasized by researchers. Although I would like to believe that my account of gender differences is true regardless of the historical context in which I write, I know that my work is undoubtedly influenced by the values of the culture in which I function.

2. Understanding Emotional Expression

1. Some of these patients suffer from a syndrome called pseudobulbar palsy, in which there are lesions of the pyramidal tract, the circuit through which the cortex exercises volitional control over the face (Rinn 1991).
2. Intensity itself is a murky concept, and it is not clear whether every emotion can range from mild to intense, or whether some, for example, contentment or rage, can be inherently only mild or only intense. An-

289

other question that emerges: are some emotions mild or intense forms of other emotions? For example, is frustration a mild form of anger and rage an intense form of anger, or is each emotion qualitatively distinct? No clear answers for these questions exist based on current knowledge.

3. In twin studies, if identical twins' behaviors are more similar to each other than are fraternal twins' behaviors, a genetic basis for the behavior is assumed. A heritability coefficient (h^2) is calculated based on sources of genetic and environmental variation. The coefficient h^2 can range from 0 to 1, with higher numbers indicating that a larger proportion of the differences among individuals can be attributed to genetic sources. For social fearfulness, $h^2 = .26$, and for anger proneness, $h^2 = .34$. Social fearfulness includes items such as, "When your child was being approached by an unfamiliar adult while shopping or out walking, how often did your child show distress or cry?" These studies focus on emotional expressions rather than experiences, although sometimes the measures are blurred.

   Similarly, a construct related to fearfulness, behavioral inhibition, has also shown modest evidence of heritability (see Kagan 1994). Interestingly, same-sex fraternal twins show significantly higher correlations in their fearfulness than do opposite-sex fraternal twins, suggesting strong environmental pressures (in opposite directions) on each of the two sexes (Goldsmith, Buss, and Lemery 1997).

4. There are many other dimensions of situations that have been related to appraisal theories of emotion, including the significance of a situation to one's goals (motivational state), the potential that one can cope with or control the event, and how compatible the event is with both internal and external norms (see Scherer 1984, 1989; Roseman, Antoniou, and Jose 1996).

3. Words, Faces, Voices, and Behaviors

1. Barrett and Russell (in press) also point out that there is a great deal of measurement error in how positive and negative emotional intensity have been measured, especially using unipolar scales. For example, when people rate their feelings of happiness on a 0- to 5-point scale, some people may interpret the 0 to be neutral, while others may interpret it to be the presence of a negative emotion, such as sadness. Until valence, measurement error, and activation are systematically controlled, how the intensity of positive and negative emotion relate to each other over time will remain unknown.

2. I am indebted to Judith Hall for highlighting this distinction.

3. This study is based on reported emotional experiences, but blurs the distinction between experience and expression because people are asked to overtly rate what they are feeling.

4. Americans of both sexes also reported that they would use emotional appeals more than Japanese of both sexes reported.

5. Although Gottman and his colleagues' work includes emotion words, other emotion modalities, such as behaviors, facial and vocal characteristics, and physiological arousal are also assessed.

6. Meta-analysis statistically integrates the results of a number of related studies (see Glass, McGaw, and Smith 1981). An effect size for a meta-analysis can be measured in many ways, but is often measured as *d*, a standardized mean difference between two groups.

7. Other studies have not consistently upheld this bias (see a review by Stern and Karraker 1989).

8. The FACS codes all perceptible "action units" (AUs) that the face is capable of producing and the muscular basis of these AUs. AUs are discrete movements of some part of the face; for example, upper eyelids raised, or brows lowered and drawn together.

   The MAX describes nine fundamental emotional expressions in terms of appearance changes. It does not catalog all possible facial movements, but only those associated with emotion.

9. Several studies have found modest positive correlations between the accuracy of posed or imitated facial expressions and the accuracy of spontaneous facial expressions (Zuckerman et al. 1976; Berenbaum and Rotter 1992). However, other studies show that posed and spontaneous facial expressions differ in some respects (Fujita, Harper, and Wiens 1980).

10. Schwartz, Brown, and Ahern (1980) report that women exhibit somewhat higher levels of corrugator activity (which lowers the brows and pulls them together, found to be greater in people engaging in negative imagery and negative mood states) and somewhat lower levels of masseter activity (possibly indicative of less anger) during rest. Dimberg and Lundquist (1990) found higher levels of corrugator and zygomatic muscle activity (in which the corners of the mouth are elevated to form a smile) in women than in men in response to viewing smiling or angry faces.

11. However, both infant boys and girls smile more in the face of a frightening toy when they can control its actions than when they cannot (Gunnar-vonGnechten 1978).

12. In this same task, no gender differences were found in lip rounding, laryngeal tension, pitch level, loudness, tempo, pitch range, and the precision of articulation.

13. Burrowes and Halberstadt (1987) adapted this scale by adding items that indicated the expression of negative emotion, such as, "I sometimes show my annoyance even in trivial situations," and "When I am sad my face is like an open book."

    Other self-report measures of emotional expressivity that include behaviors are the Emotional Expressivity Questionnaire (King and Emmons 1990); the Berkeley Expressivity Questionnaire (Gross and John 1995); the Emotional Expressivity Scale (Kring, Smith, and Neale 1994); and the Affect Intensity Measure (Larsen and Diener 1987).

14. American society may value aggression more than some other societies. For example, Zahn-Waxler et al. (1996) showed that 4- to 5-year-old American boys as well as girls enacted more aggressive behavior and language in response to conflict-laden stories than did Japanese boys and girls.

4. Physiological Arousal and Patterns of Emotional Expression

1. As Fox and Calkins (1993) point out, this may be because each autonomic response has a different time course, ranging from milliseconds to minutes before it can be reliably measured. For example, changes in cortisol can only be measured 15 minutes after an emotionally eliciting event has occurred, whereas increased heart rate may occur simultaneously with an emotional event.

2. Skin conductance in response to noxious or painful stimulation may be reduced in undersocialized individuals, or sociopaths, suggesting that they do not become as easily aroused in the face of noxious stimuli. This may help to explain why they are more immune to the rewards and punishments inherent in the normal socialization process (Waid 1976).

3. Pennebaker and Roberts (1992) have also argued that men use physiological cues, rather than situational ones, to detect their emotional state; whereas women use situational and contextual cues, rather than physiological ones, to assess their emotional state.

4. An important caveat is that some, but not all, of these studies relied on levels of urinary epinephrine, which may not be a reliable measure of blood catecholamine levels.

5. Interestingly, the boys performed less accurately than the girls did on the test and also reported more apprehension about schoolwork than the girls did—perhaps they found the arithmetic test more stressful (Johansson 1972).

6. Men still showed larger epinephrine increases when compared to their

baseline levels than women did; and cortisol secretion increased significantly in the male group only. The authors also point out that an alternative explanation for these findings is that women who choose male work roles may have constitutional characteristics that make them respond to stress in the same way men tend to do.

7. This same study showed no significant relationships between each spouse's endocrine levels and their self-rated emotions after the conflict, even though Levenson, Carstensen, and Gottman (1994) had shown relationships between self-reported emotions and other aspects of physiological arousal, especially in males.

8. In this study, systolic blood pressure was also elevated in women who displayed a high proportion of indirect negative affects, such as looking away; while the systolic blood pressures of women with high direct negative affect, such as interrupting, continually increased as the interaction progressed.

9. These films primarily concern violence directed against women, which may impact the nature of the gender differences that emerge.

10. The epinephrine responses of the two parents did not differ.

11. When the context is neutral, females as young as infants also display higher resting heartrates than do males (Kagan 1994; Polefrone and Manuck 1987).

   Much research has also centered around the effects of either menopausal status or the phase of the menstrual cycle on physiological patterns in response to stress. In a review of these studies, Polefrone and Manuck (1987) conclude that female reproductive hormones may be associated with reduced cardiovascular responsivity; on the other hand, no clear association has been found between the variations in hormones occurring as a result of the menstrual cycle with the degree or pattern to which women's cardiovascular systems respond to stress.

12. Frodi (1976) argues that women's recovery times were not affected by the opportunity to vent anger because women may not have been experiencing anger, but rather fear.

5. Sad or Mad? The Quality of Emotions

1. Gottman and his colleagues code marital interaction using the Specific Affect Coding System in which verbal content, voice tone, context, facial expression, gestures, and body movement are all coded (Gottman and Krokoff 1989).

2. These results must be viewed in light of the fact that almost all the horror films shown to the women depicted violence against women.

6. The State of the Art: Biological Differences?

1. Another bias also pervades this research: the interpretation that the process of becoming a biological male is more complex and fraught with dangers than the process of becoming a female. (This interpretation is certainly in line with our stereotypic views of men as conquering dangers as well as being threatened by femininity). In their review of prenatal hormone contributions to sex differences in personality development, June Machover Reinisch and Stephanie Sanders (1992) write that "nature's first intention is to produce a female and something must be added (namely fetal androgens) to produce a phenotypic male. Concomitant to the more complex process of male differentiation is the increased possibility of developmental anomalies." They then go on to quote Alfred Jost (1972), who says that becoming male is "a kind of struggle against inherent trends toward femaleness" (pp. 222–223). Although this statement is technically correct, that is, fetal androgens are necessary to produce phenotypic males, it is arguable whether or not this requires a more complex process than becoming a female. At some point in prenatal development, there is a switchway; two different developmental pathways can occur. Males go in one direction, females in another. There is no factual basis for the idea that the switch is more "complex" for males than it is for females.

2. My concern here is not to evaluate sociobiological theories of emotional expressiveness, which are based on the idea that the two sexes differ in their behavior because women and men invest time and energy in different aspects of sexual reproduction (Buss 1994). Sociobiological theories maintain that men's energy goes toward pursuing sexual partners with whom to mate; women's energy goes toward nurturing their offspring. Women are alleged to prefer monogamy because having a partner with whom to share child care protects their long-term investment in each child and increases the likelihood that their offspring will survive. Men are theorized to prefer mating with many partners because increasing their number of progeny is hypothesized to increase the chances that at least some of their offspring will survive. How does this relate to emotional expressiveness? Buss (1994) suggests that emotionally inexpressive men are apt to father more children and hence are more likely to pass down their emotional inexpressiveness to their sons than are more expressive men. Why? Because emotionally inexpressive men are less likely to invest in a monogamous relationship than are men who express their feelings. Thus, inexpressive men would have more opportunities to procreate. This explanation ignores the complexity of these issues, particularly the social and cultural pressures on men and women. It also implies

that emotional expressiveness is genetically sex-limited to males, since inexpressive fathers don't pass down their inexpressivity to their daughters. Finally, it requires an explanation of how inexpressive men signal their sexual availability to a multitude of women, if not through the expression of feelings.

3. The particular neurons selected for study were those that projected to the bulbospongiosus muscles, which are sexually dimorphic: they require androgens during the perinatal period. In the absence of androgens, these muscles atrophy in females, leading to fewer adult motor neurons.

4. Geschwind and Galaburda (1985) also speculate that higher testosterone levels result in a higher frequency of immune disorders, including allergies, asthma, and autoimmune disturbances, as well as left-handed preferences. The evidence for this theory remains inconclusive (Bryden, McManus, and Bulman-Fleming 1994).

5. The role of testosterone versus estrogen is exceedingly complex as pointed out by Olsen (1992), since research with animals has indicated that testosterone can be aromatized into estrogens within some neural regions.

6. In PET scan studies (positron emission tomography), radioactively labelled blood or glucose in the brain is detected by the PET ring, which circles the participant's head. The radiated patterns are used to generate a three-dimensional image of the brain by computer programs. A brighter hue represents a higher metabolic rate. By comparing brightness of hue across successive images, researchers can specify which areas of the brain are active at specific times and in response to particular tasks (Iaccino 1993).

7. Some alternative theories: Heller (1990) has speculated that emotional intensity or arousal may be mediated by the parietal region of the right hemisphere, which may in turn mediate cortical and autonomic arousal. Dawson et al. (1992) have argued that it is generalized frontal activity, not specifically right, that mediates emotional intensity.

8. Several theorists make a slightly different interpretation of how emotional expressiveness is mediated. Fox and Davidson (1991) posit that the left and right hemispheres may not differentially process positive/negative emotions, but rather, that the left anterior region of the brain mediates an approach system; whereas the corresponding right hemisphere subsystem mediates a withdrawal system. For example, fear entails a withdrawal function in escaping from a threatening stimulus, and would usually be processed by the right hemisphere. However, in those unusual circumstances in which fear would be related to approach, it may be mediated by the left hemisphere instead.

Kinsbourne and Bemporad (1984) maintain that the negative affect associated with the right hemisphere is consistent with an arousal reaction to unfamiliar stimuli when effective action is not an option; left frontal activity is associated with positive states because positive states enhance motivation, approach, the readiness to act, and are associated with control.

Finally, Dawson et al. (1992) argue that the left frontal region is specialized for regulation and coping strategies that involve sequential activities, such as language, and also serve to maintain the continuity of ongoing behaviors, while the right frontal region appears to be specialized for processing novel stimuli that disrupt ongoing activities.

9. Some theorists maintain that both hemispheres may mature faster in girls than in boys, with the resulting consequence that the hemispheres may integrate their functions with limbic and brainstem mechanisms to a greater extent in females than in males (Tucker and Frederick 1989). Adele Diamond's work on infant memory (1985, 1990) also suggests that the dorsolateral prefrontal cortex may mature faster in girls than in boys. She found that in a short-term memory task, infant girls were better able than boys to inhibit a response that had been correct on previous trials but was no longer correct (Diamond 1985). The girls could remember the correct response over longer delays than could the boys, who reverted back to the incorrect response with longer delays (Diamond 1985). For example, by 12 months boys were tolerating an average maximum delay length of 9.8 seconds, which girls had been able to do at 10½ months.

7. Transactional Relationships within Families

1. Eleanor Maccoby's (1998; see Chapter 5) analysis of the nature of early gender differences overlaps with the arguments made in this chapter. I wrote the bulk of this chapter before reading hers, and I cite her work when her analysis added a perspective I had not previously considered.

2. Stereotypes about gender and emotion also vary considerably depending on factors such as the type of emotional situation and the age, ethnicity, and personality characteristics of the people being stereotyped (Brody 1997). I'm not going to review these studies in detail, since these qualifications are not really relevant to my argument. I'll provide just one example here to make the point: if no job description is given, women are perceived to be more communal and emotionally expressive than men (Eagly and Steffen 1984). But when asked about individual men and women in specific jobs, the stereotypes shift. For example, women who are homemakers are seen as more emotionally expressive than women

who are executives, athletes, or "Bunnies" (Clifton, McGrath, and Wick 1976). Men who are homemakers are perceived to be more expressive than employed women and men (Eagly and Steffen 1984). It seems that the more specific information people are given about men and women, including age, profession, and ethnicity, the less they rely on general stereotypes. Unfortunately, in many situations, access to specific information is not easily available, and general stereotypes tend to override our perception of individual differences.

3. These data are consistent with the bilateralization hypothesis discussed in Chapter 6, but may also be due to a combination of social and biological influences.

4. The conclusion that activity levels may be partly biologically based is more complex than it may sound. For example, Eaton and Ennis (1986) demonstrated that gender differences in activity levels diverge with increasing age. As Kohnstamm (1989) questions, do biological gender differences in motor activity become stable only with increasing age? Or do cultural expectations play a role in the increasing divergence of activity levels of the two sexes with age? These complex questions have as yet no clear answers.

5. Although the difference between how fathers treated sons compared to daughters was not significant, the authors note that the difference between mothers and fathers was significant—fathers were more restrictive toward sons compared to daughters than mothers were.

6. See Fabes et al. (1994) for evidence that mothers change their emotional responsivity depending on their children's age and their perceptions of their children's emotional reactivity.

7. However, the relation between maturity and activity levels was further complicated by the finding that when each sex was considered independently, maturity levels significantly predicted males' activity levels, but not females'. The authors suggest that maturity may be related to activity levels only for males.

8. Most of the research I have reviewed looks at how parents and caretakers socialize emotions, using rewards such as responding to or elaborating on particular emotions or using punishments such as ignoring the expression of particular feelings. Parents may also use expressions of their own feelings, such as pride, contempt, or disgust, as rewards or punishments that encourage or discourage the display of particular emotions by their children. For example, parents who express contempt when their sons cry may induce their sons to experience shame and thereby minimize future expressions of sadness (Scheff 1990). Research has indicated that parents who are actively hostile, or who express disappointment in their children, tend to have children who are prone to exhibiting shame (Ferguson,

Stegge, and Thompson 1993; Ferguson and Stegge 1995). Gender differences in patterns such as these have not been explored fully.

9. In contrast, some studies have found no consistent gender differences in how fathers treat their sons and daughters. Snarey (1993), in a multi-generational study, found no gender differences in fathers' encouragement of their sons' and daughters' socio-emotional, intellectual-cognitive, or physical-behavioral development. Some of the discrepant findings in previous studies may be due to the fact that studies have measured fathers' child-rearing practices in different ways, including interviews, observations, and self-report data. Also, researchers have not controlled for the role of marital quality in moderating the father-child relationship. Fathers who are dissatisfied in their marriages treat their sons and daughters differently to a greater extent than those who are satisfied. See Chapter 9 and Kerig, Cowan, and Cowan 1993.

8. Gender Identification and De-identification in the Family

1. According to Winnicott (1958) and Balint (1963), being exposed to this "false empathy" will result in children who fail to develop a "true self," but rather, in a chameleon-like fashion, adapt their emotional responses in a way that is acceptable to whomever they happen to be interacting with at that moment.

2. Gender intensification was also evident when parents divided household chores along traditional gender lines.

3. See also research by Eisenberg et al. (1994a) and Hay et al. (1992) on the content of children's puppet enactments as related to their behavior in interpersonal conflicts.

   My research has also shown that the optimistic or pessimistic nature of the stories that children write in response to pictures (see Figure 1, Chapter 1) is significantly related to their self-esteem on self-report scales such as the Piers-Harris Self-Esteem Scale and the Harter Perceived Competence Scale. The quality of children's stories is also significantly related to their adaptation to school as rated by their teachers (Brody and Hay 1991).

4. I am not ruling out the possibility that levels of parent-child conflict may differ for children who do or do not include their parents in their stories. It may be that children with high levels of conflict choose to distance themselves from their parents by not including them in their stories; or it may be that children with low levels of conflict feel comfortable in distancing themselves from their parents and in not including them in their stories. High levels of conflict may be related to low levels of differentiation, but more research is needed to explore these ideas.

5. $\chi^2(1) = 30.93$, $p < .001$ for representations of mothers versus fathers in the entire sample. These analyses were based on a greater number of children than were in the family sample (85 girls and 84 boys as opposed to 51 girls and 44 boys) because additional children were studied whose parents did not participate as part of the family sample. The additional children did not differ from the original sample of children on any significant demographic characteristics (including age, parents' marital status, or parents' socioeconomic status), nor in the quality of their responses to the emotional story tasks, and so were pooled together for these analyses.

6. $\chi^2(1) = 1.59$, n.s. corrected for continuity.

7. Chodorow (1978) frequently distinguishes between primary and secondary identifications, with primary identifications being developmentally earlier, more intense, less conscious, and more basic to the sense of self than are secondary identifications. Daughters are theorized to have a more continuous primary identification with their mothers than are sons.

8. This may be related to daughters' early sociability, which I reviewed in Chapter 7.

9. Girls significantly represented themselves as disclosing more feelings to both parents than did boys [$\chi^2(1) = 4.14$, $p < .05$, (8/85 girls; 1/84 boys)], but not to mothers alone [(5/85 girls; 1/84 boys), $\chi^2(1) = 1.51$, n.s]. All chi-square analyses were corrected for continuity.

   Gender differences were not found for any of the other activities in which mothers were depicted, including setting limits (8/85 girls; 9/84 boys), comforting them (5/85 girls; 3/84 boys), or giving advice (6/85 girls; 4/84 boys). Girls did depict their parents (and tended to depict their mothers alone) as helping them more than boys did [(both parents: 8/85 girls; 1/84 boys), $\chi^2(1) = 4.14$, $p < .05$; (mothers alone: 5/85 girls; 0/84 boys), $\chi^2(1) = 3.24$, $p < .10$].

10. It is important to note that a parent can be both nurturing and restrictive at the same time; these are not mutually exclusive. And in fact, parents need to be somewhat restrictive with their children in order to keep them safe. Parents who are able to be both nurturing and restrictive can be thought of as having more flexible boundaries, which may result in well-adjusted children. In Western cultures, parents high on both nurturance and restrictiveness have been termed "authoritative." Their children have good outcomes on measures of adjustment (Baumrind 1971). Ideally, researchers should use a large enough sample of families so that they are able to explore all possible combinations of these parenting styles.

11. There is some seemingly contradictory evidence that daughters whose mothers sympathize with them when they are distressed are less likely to

comfort a distressed baby. Perhaps, as Eisenberg and her colleagues suggest, the mother's focus on the daughter's feelings (in contrast to focusing on the feelings of others) may actually discourage the daughter from taking instrumental action toward others (Eisenberg et al. 1993).

12. Mothers' warmth and nurturance were assessed in response to both the Block Child Rearing Practices Report and in the stories they wrote.

13. Mother-son differentiation in emotional functioning was also suggested by Bryant's (1987) work on mothers and their 7- and 10-year-old children. In her work, mothers who responded expressively to stressful events had daughters who exhibited high empathy or emotional responsiveness to others, but had sons who had lower abilities to attribute feelings and motives to other people in appropriate ways.

9. Fathers and the Family Climate

1. A complete list of these tasks follows: taking the child to a birthday party; taking the child to the doctor or dentist; going to a teacher conference; supervising the child's morning routine; putting the child to bed and spending special time at bedtime; taking the child to or from lessons; buying the child's clothes; taking the child on outings; making childcare or babysitting arrangements; disciplining; helping with homework; staying with a sick child, or making alternative arrangements for care when the child is sick; supervising the child's hygiene (baths, brushing teeth, etc.); playing with the child; going to school events like plays. This questionnaire was developed by Baruch and Barnett (1986a) in their work on family roles.

2. Pearson correlations between the amount of time fathers spent with their children and: (a) their scores on the Attitudes toward Women's Scale: $r(90) = .20, p < .06$; (b) their F score (communal characteristics) on the Personal Attributes Questionnaire: $r(90) = .23, p < .03$; (c) their self-esteem on the Rosenberg Self-Esteem Questionnaire: $r(90) = .20, p < .06$; (d) the number of hours their wives were employed: $r(90) = .33, p < .01$; (e) their restrictiveness toward their daughters: $r(46) = -.39, p < .01$.

3. These partial correlations (controlling for the daughters' age) were as follows: between number of hours mothers were employed and (a) daughters' competitive themes in stories they wrote: $r(50) = .23, p < .08$; (b) reported fear in response to emotional stories: $r(50) = -.35, p < .01$; and (c) reported liking of other people in stories: $r(50) = -.25, p < .07$.

4. In fact, in my own research, when parents reported on the extent of their individuation from their children using 4 items from the Block Child Rearing Practices Report, such as "I prefer spending time with my child than time by myself," the items had such low interitem reliability for

fathers that I could not use them. In contrast, the scale had adequate reliability for mothers.

5. Intriguingly, fathers' minimizing and punitive reactions did not significantly relate to their daughters' negative emotionality, with the direction of the relationship actually reversed, although not significantly so; i.e., girls with minimizing fathers tended to be less, not more negative. This inverse relationship supports a differentiation model that I elaborate in the chapter.

6. Intrusiveness was measured with the Permeability of Boundaries Scale (Olver, Aries, and Batgos 1989).

7. Emotions can result when expectations are violated, so the appreciation expressed toward fathers may stem from the fact that when fathers are involved in child care, they are doing something unexpected and out of the ordinary. Further, not expressing appreciation for mothers may reflect the devaluation of mothers that is so rampant in the culture.

8. The Pearson correlation between the level of the father's involvement in the family and his wife's marital satisfaction, rated on a 7 point scale from dissatisfied to satisfied, was $r(90) = .26$, $p < .008$; between the father's involvement in the family and his own marital satisfaction: $r(90) = .16$, $p = .15$.

   In contrast, Baruch and Barnett (1986b) found that husbands who worked more around the house were more critical of their wives than husbands who did not work around the house.

9. The events did not include physical or sexual abuse.

10. Social Motives, Power, and Roles

1. Recent work suggests that people in individualist cultures may rely more on their emotional experiences to judge their well-being than people in collectivist cultures (Suh et al. 1998). Although life satisfaction and the preponderance of positive over negative affects were positively correlated across 41 cultures, they were less significantly correlated in collectivist cultures than in individualist cultures.

2. These results do not necessarily hold true cross-culturally. In some patriarchal cultures, such as India, the husband's economic resources are irrelevant to his power in the family: he has more power regardless of his resources (Rodman 1972). In more egalitarian cultures, such as Scandinavia, the resources of the partners matter a great deal.

11. Stereotypes and Display Rules

1. The samples included: parents of nursery school children aged 3–4; par-

ents of children with physical illnesses aged 3–11; parents of high-school students aged 15–17; and parents of university students aged 17–20; with sample sizes ranging from 44 fathers to 183 mothers.

2. "I sometimes tease and make fun of my child" was also endorsed more by fathers of boys in two samples than by fathers of girls, while "I feel it is good for a child to play competitive games" was endorsed more for boys than for girls by both mothers and fathers.

3. Although I am going to focus on analyses of television, children's books, magazines, and films also tend to portray similar display rules for males and females.

4. In Japanese television shows, women are depicted as emotional, warm, submissive, cheerful, and peaceful, whereas men are depicted as active, intelligent, creative, courageous, and violent. Men are also portrayed with higher occupational status and power than women, and in turn, power is associated with characters' likability. Female characters are portrayed as more deferential than powerful (Rolandelli 1991).

5. Matsumoto (1989) used Hofstede's (1980) rankings for individualism versus collectivism.

13. The Health Consequences of Gender-Stereotypic Emotional Expression

1. In recent work that summarized across several different samples, Pennebaker and his colleagues have modified previous conclusions to indicate that high frequencies of insightful and causal emotion words (such as realize, understand, and consider), moderate frequencies of negative emotion words, and high frequencies of positive emotion words are linked to better physical, but not mental health across studies (Pennebaker, Mayne, and Francis 1997).

2. Any relationship between social expressiveness and rumination was due to their common link with the intensity of the disruptive event (Rime et al. 1992).

3. It is also possible that there are in fact two (or more) different groups of women: those who freely express feelings, including anger, and those who don't, thereby becoming depressed and dissatisfied.

14. Rethinking Gender and Emotion

1. On the other hand, arguments have been made that motives, traits, and behaviors are distinct and separate levels of personality functioning (McAdams 1995; Winter and Stewart 1995).

References

Adams, D. 1992. Biology does not make men more aggressive than women. In K. Bjorkqvist and P. Niemela, eds., *Of Mice and Women: Aspects of Female Aggression*, 17–25. San Diego: Academic Press.

Adams, S., Kuebli, J., Boyle, P., and Fivush, R. 1995. Gender differences in parent-child conversations about past emotions: A longitudinal investigation. *Sex Roles*, 33, 309–323.

Adler, P. A., Kless, S. J., and Adler, P. 1992. Socialization to gender roles: Popularity among elementary school boys and girls. *Sociology of Education*, 65, 169–187.

Albert, D. J., Walsh, M. L., and Jonik, R. H. 1993. Aggression in humans: What is its biological foundation? *Neuroscience and Biobehavioral Reviews*, 17, 405–425.

Allen, J., and Haccoun, D. 1976. Sex differences in emotionality: A multi-dimensional approach. *Human Relations*, 29, 711–720.

Andersen, E. 1978. Will you don't snore please? Directives in young children's role play speech. *Papers and Reports in Child Language Development*, 15, 140–150.

Anderson, S. A., and Sabatelli, R. M. 1990. Differentiating, differentiation and individuation: Conceptual and operation challenges. *American Journal of Family Therapy*, 18, 32–50.

Archer, J. 1991. The influence of testosterone on human aggression. *British Journal of Psychology*, 82, 11–28.

——— 1992. Childhood gender roles: Social context and organization. In H. McGurk, ed., *Childhood Social Development*, 31–56. Hillsdale, N.J.: Erlbaum.

——— 1994. Testosterone and aggression. *Journal of Offender Rehabilitation*, 21, 3–39.

Aries, E. 1976. Interaction patterns and themes of male, female and mixed groups. *Small Group Behavior*, 7, 7–18.

Assiter, A. 1996. *Enlightened Women: Modernist Feminism in a Postmodern Age*. London: Routledge.

Aukett, R., Ritchie, J., and Mill, K. 1988. Gender differences in friendship patterns. *Sex Roles*, 19, 57–66.

Babcock, J., Waltz, J., Jacobson, N., and Gottman, J. 1993. Power and violence: The relation between communication patterns, power discrepancies, and domestic violence. *Journal of Consulting and Clinical Psychology,* 61, 40–49.

Balint, E. 1963. On being empty of oneself. *International Journal of Psychoanalysis,* 44, 470–480.

Balswick, J., and Avertt, C. P. 1977. Differences in expressiveness: Gender, interpersonal orientation, and perceived parental expressiveness as contributing factors. *Journal of Marriage and the Family,* 39, 121–127.

Bander, R., and Betz, N. 1981. The relationship of sex and sex role to trait and situationally specific anxiety types. *Journal of Research in Personality,* 15, 312–322.

Barbee, A., Cunningham, M., Winstead, B., Derlega, V., Bulley, M., Yaneeklov, P., and Druen, P. 1993. Effects of gender role expectations on the social support process. *Journal of Social Issues,* 49, 175–190.

Barefoot, J. C., and Lipkus, I. 1994. The assessment of anger and hostility. In A. Siegman and T. Smith, eds., *Anger, Hostility and the Heart,* 43–66. Hillsdale, N.J.: Erlbaum.

Barfield, A. 1976. Biological influences on sex differences in behavior. In M. S. Teitelbaum, ed., *Sex Differences: Social and Biological Perspectives,* 62–122. New York: Anchor.

Barnes, M., and Buss, D. 1985. Sex differences in the interpersonal behavior of married couples. *Journal of Personality and Social Psychology,* 48, 654–661.

Barnett, M., Howard, J., King, L., and Dino, G. 1980a. Antecedents of empathy: Retrospective accounts of early socialization. *Personality and Social Psychology Bulletin,* 6, 361–365.

Barnett, M., King, L., Howard, J., and Dino, G. 1980b. Empathy in young children: Relation to parents' empathy, affection, and emphasis on feelings of others. *Developmental Psychology,* 16, 243–244.

Barrett, L. F., Lane, R., Sechrest, L., and Schwartz, G. Unpublished. Sex differences in emotional awareness.

Barrett, L. F., Robin, L., Pietromonaco, P., and Eyssell, K. 1998. Are women the more emotional sex? Evidence from emotional experiences in social context. *Cognition and Emotion,* 12, 555–578.

Barrett, L. F., and Russell, J. In press. Independence and bipolarity in the structure of current affect. *Journal of Personality and Social Psychology.*

Bartle, S. F., Anderson, S. A., and Sabatelli, R. M. 1989. A model of parenting style, adolescent individuation and adolescent self-esteem: Preliminary findings. *Journal of Adolescent Research,* 4, 283–298.

Baruch, G., and Barnett, R. 1981. Fathers' participation in the care of their preschool children. *Sex Roles,* 7, 1043–1055.

——— 1986a. Fathers' participation in family work and children's sex-role attitudes. *Child Development,* 57, 1210–1223.

———— 1986b. Consequences of fathers' participation in family work: Parents' role strain and well-being. *Journal of Personality and Social Psychology*, 51, 983–992.

Bates, J. 1989. Concepts and measures of temperament. In G. A. Kohnstamm, J. E. Bates, and M. K. Rothbart, eds., *Temperament in Childhood*, 3–26. New York: Wiley.

Baum, A., Cohen, L., and Hall, M. 1993. Control and intrusive memories as possible determinants of chronic stress. *Psychosomatic Medicine*, 55, 274–286.

Baumrind, D. 1971. Current patterns of parental authority. *Developmental Psychology Monograph*, 4(1), pt. 2. Washington: American Psychological Association.

Bear, D., and Fedio, P. 1977. Quantitative analysis of interictal behavior in temporal lobe epilepsy. *Archives of Neurology*, 34, 454–467.

Behzadi, K. 1994. Interpersonal conflict and emotions in Iranian cultural practice: Qahr and Ashti. *Culture, Medicine and Psychiatry*, 18, 321–359.

Belsky, J., Fish, M., and Isabella, R. 1991. Continuity and discontinuity in infant negative and positive emotionality: Family antecedents and attachment consequences. *Developmental Psychology*, 27, 421–431.

Bem, S., Martyna, W., and Watson, C. 1976. Sex typing and androgyny: Further explorations of the expressive domain. *Journal of Personality and Social Psychology*, 34, 1016–1023.

Benenson, J., Apostoleris, N., and Parnass, J. 1997. Age and sex differences in dyadic and group interaction. *Developmental Psychology*, 33, 538–543.

Benjamin, J. 1988. *The Bonds of Love*. New York: Pantheon.

Benton, D. 1992. Hormones and human aggression. In K. Bjorkqvist and P. Niemela, eds., *Of Mice and Women: Aspects of Female Aggression*, 37–48. San Diego: Academic Press.

Berenbaum, H., and Rotter, A. 1992. The relationship between spontaneous facial expressions of emotion and voluntary control of facial muscles. *Journal of Nonverbal Behavior*, 16, 179–190.

Berman, M., Gladue, B., and Taylor, S. 1993. The effects of hormones, Type A behavior pattern, and provocation on aggression in men. *Motivation and Emotion*, 17, 125–138.

Bernadett-Shapiro, S., Ehrensaft, D., and Shapiro, J. 1996. Father participation in childcare and the development of empathy in sons: An empirical study. *Family Therapy*, 23, 77–93.

Berndt, T., Cheung, P. C., Lau, S., Hau, K., and Lew, W. 1993. Perceptions of parenting in mainland China, Taiwan, and Hong Kong: Sex differences and societal diffrences. *Developmental Psychology*, 29, 156–164.

Berscheid, E. 1991. The emotion-in-relationships model: Reflections and update. In W. Kessen, A. Ortony, and F. Craik, eds., *Memories, Thoughts, and*

Emotions: Essays in Honor of George Mandler, 323–335. Hillsdale, N.J.: Erlbaum.

Betcher, R. W., and Pollack, W. 1993. *In a Time of Fallen Heroes: The Re-creation of Masculinity.* New York: Macmillan.

Bettencourt, B. A., and Miller, N. 1996. Gender differences in aggression as a function of provocation: A meta-analysis. *Psychological Bulletin,* 119, 422–447.

Bezooyen, R. 1984. *Characteristics of Vocal Expressions of Emotion.* Dordrecht, Holland: Foris Publication.

Bhushan, R. 1993. A study of patterns of family communication: Parents and their adolescent children. *Journal of Personality and Clinical Studies,* 9, 79–85.

Biaggio, M. 1989. Sex differences in behavioral reactions to provocation of anger. *Psychological Reports,* 64, 23–26.

Biehl, M., Matsumoto, D., Ekman, P., Hearn, V., Heider, K., Kudoh, T., and Ton, V. 1997. Matsumoto and Ekman's Japanese and Caucasian Facial Expressions of Emotion (JACFEE): Reliability Data and Cross-National Differences. *Journal of Nonverbal Behavior,* 21, 3–21.

Biglan, A., Hops, H., Sherman, L., Friedman, L., Arthur, J., and Osteen, V. 1985. Problem solving interactions of depressed women and their husbands. *Behavior Therapy,* 16, 431–451.

Birnbaum, D. 1983. Preschoolers' stereotypes about sex differences in emotionality: A reaffirmation. *Journal of Genetic Psychology,* 143, 139–140.

Birnbaum, D., Nosanchuk, T., and Croll, W. 1980. Children's stereotypes about sex differences in emotionality. *Sex Roles,* 6, 435–443.

Bjorklund, D., and Kipp, K. 1996. Parental investment theory and gender differences in the evolution of inhibition mechanisms. *Psychological Bulletin,* 120, 163–188.

Bjorkqvist, K., Osterman, K., and Kaukiainen, A. 1992. The development of direct and indirect aggressive strategies in males and females. In K. Bjorkqvist and P. Niemela, eds., *Of Mice and Women: Aspects of Female Aggression,* 51–64. San Diego: Academic Press.

Blier, M., and Blier, L. 1989. Gender differences in self rated emotional expressiveness. *Sex Roles,* 21, 287–295.

Block, J. 1965. The child-rearing practices report. Berkeley: Institute of Human Development, University of California, unpublished manuscript.

———— 1973. Conceptions of sex role: Some cross-cultural and longitudinal perspectives. *American Psychologist,* 28, 512–526.

———— 1983. Differential premises arising from differential socialization of the sexes: Some conjectures. *Child Development,* 54, 1335–1354.

———— 1984. *Sex Role Identity and Ego Development.* San Francisco: Jossey Bass.

Bloom, B. 1985. A factor analysis of self-report measures of family functioning. *Family Process,* 24, 225–239.

Bloom, L., and Capatides, J. D. 1987. Expression of affect and the emergence of language. *Child Development,* 58, 1513–1522.

Blos, P. 1962. *On Adolescence: A Psychoanalytic Interpretation.* New York: Free Press.

Bonebright, T. L., Thompson, J. L., and Leger, D. W. 1996. Gender stereotypes in the expression and perception of vocal affect. *Sex Roles,* 34, 429–445.

Booth, M., and Matchan, L. 1988. *The Forward.* A film from the Jewish Forward Film Project.

Bowlby, John. 1988. *A Secure Base: Parent-child Attachment and Healthy Human Development.* New York: Basic Books.

Brickman, P., and Janoff-Bulman, R. 1977. Pleasure and pain in social comparison. In J. Suls and L. Miller, eds., *Social Comparison Processes,* 149–186. New York: Wiley.

Briton, N., and Hall, J. 1995. Beliefs about female and male nonverbal communication. *Sex Roles,* 32, 79–90.

Brock, S. R. 1993. An examination of the ways in which mothers talk to their male and female children about emotions. Poster presented at the biennial meeting of the Society for Research in Child Development, New Orleans.

Brody, L. 1984. Sex and age variations in the quality and intensity of children's emotional attributions to hypothetical situations. *Sex Roles,* 11, 51–59.

——— 1985. Gender and emotional development: A review of theories and research. *Journal of Personality,* 53, 102–149.

——— 1993. On understanding gender differences in the expression of emotion: Gender roles, socialization and language. In S. Ablon, D. Brown, E. Khantzian, and J. Mack, eds., *Human Feelings: Explorations in Affect Development and Meaning,* 89–121. Hillsdale, N.J.: Analytic Press.

——— 1996. Gender, emotional expressiveness and parent-child boundaries. In R. Kavanaugh, B. Zimmerberg-Glick, and S. Fein, eds., *Emotion: Interdisciplinary Perspectives,* 139–170. Hillsdale, N.J.: Erlbaum.

——— 1997. Beyond stereotypes: Gender and emotion. *Journal of Social Issues,* 53, 369–393.

——— In press. The socialization of gender differences in emotional expression: Display rules, infant tempermant, and differentiation. In A. Fischer, ed., *Gender and Emotion.* Cambridge: Cambridge University Press.

Brody, L., Copeland, A., Leader, J., Guedj, T., and Doron, S. 1996. Gender differences in the associations among family stress, family relationships, and the quality of emotion in late adolescents. Poster presented at the American Orthopsychiatry Convention, Boston.

Brody, L., Copeland, A., Sutton, L., Guyer, M., Richardson, D., and Madden, T.

1995. Family boundaries, gender roles and emotional expressiveness. Poster presented at the biennial meeting of the Society for Research in Child Development, Indianapolis.

Brody, L., and Hall, J. 1993. Gender and emotion. In M. Lewis and J. Haviland, eds., *Handbook of Emotions*, 447–460. New York: Guilford.

Brody, L., and Hay, D. 1991. A projective measure of self esteem based on the TED: An alternative to self-report measures. Presented at the biennial meeting of the Society for Research in Child Development, Seattle.

Brody, L., Hay, D. H., and Vandewater, E. 1990. Gender, gender role identity, and children's reported feelings toward the same and opposite sex. *Sex Roles, 23,* 363–387.

Brody, L., Lovas, G., and Hay, D. 1995. Sex differences in anger and fear as a function of situational context. *Sex Roles, 32,* 47–78.

Brody, L., Pfister, K., and Brennan, R. 1997. Fathers' involvement in child care and gender differences in children's emotional expressiveness. Poster presented at the biennial meeting of the Society for Research in Child Development, Washington, D.C.

Brody, L., Wise, D., and Monuteaux, D. 1997. Children's emotional story themes, gender, and parenting styles. Poster presented at the biennial meeting of the Society for Research in Child Development, Washington, D.C.

Bronstein, P. 1984. Differences in mothers' and fathers' behaviors toward children: A cross-cultural comparison. *Developmental Psychology, 20,* 995–1003.

——— 1988. Father-child interaction: Implications for gender role socialization. In P. Bronstein and C. P. Cowan, eds., *Fatherhood Today: Men's Changing Role in the Family,* 107–124. New York: Wiley.

——— 1994. Patterns of parent-child interaction in Mexican families: A cross-cultural perspective. *International Journal of Behavioral Development, 17,* 423–446.

Bronstein, P., and Cruz, M. 1985. Parent-child relations and adolescent functioning: A study of Mexican families. Paper presented at the annual meeting of the American Psychological Association, Los Angeles.

Bronstein, P., Fitzgerald, M., Briones, M., Pieniadz, J., and D'Ari, A. 1993. Family emotional expressiveness as a predictor of early adolescent social and psychological adjustment. *Journal of Early Adolescence, 13,* 448–471.

Bryant, B. 1987. Mental health, temperament, family, and friends: Perspectives on children's empathy and social perspective taking. In N. Eisenberg and J. Strayer, eds., *Empathy and Its Development,* 245–270. Cambridge: Cambridge University Press.

Bryden, M. P., McManus, I. C., and Bulman-Fleming, M. B. 1994. Evaluating the empirical support for the Geschwind-Behan-Galaburda model of cerebral lateralization. *Brain and Cognition, 26,* 103–167.

Buck, R. 1977. Nonverbal communication accuracy in preschool children: Relationships with personality and skin conductance. *Journal of Personality and Social Psychology*, 33, 225–236.

———— 1980. Nonverbal behavior and the theory of emotion: The facial feedback hypothesis. *Journal of Personality and Social Psychology*, 38, 811–824.

Buck, R., Miller, R., and Caul, W. 1974. Sex, personality, and physiological variables in the communication of affect via facial expression. *Journal of Personality and Social Psychology*, 30, 587–596.

Buntaine, R., and Costenbader, V. 1997. Self-reported differences in the experience and expression of anger between girls and boys. *Sex Roles*, 36, 625–637.

Burke, R. J., Weir, T., and Harrison, D. 1976. Disclosure of problems and tensions experienced by marital partners. *Psychological Reports*, 38, 531–542.

Burns, J. 1995. Interactive effects of traits, states, and gender on cardiovascular reactivity during different situations. *Journal of Behavioral Medicine*, 18, 279–303.

Burns, J., and Katkin, E. 1993. Psychological, situational, and gender predictors of cardiovascular reactivity to stress: A multivariate approach. *Journal of Behavioral Medicine*, 16, 445–465.

Burrowes, B., and Halberstadt, A. 1987. Self- and family-expressiveness styles in the experience and expression of anger. *Journal of Nonverbal Behavior*, 11, 254–268.

Busby, L. 1974. Defining the sex role standard in commercial network television programs directed toward children. *Journalism Quarterly*, 51, 690–696.

Buss, A., and Durkee, A. 1957. An inventory for assessing different kinds of hostility. *Journal of Consulting Psychology*, 21, 343–349.

Buss, D. 1989. Conflict between the sexes: Strategic interference and the evocation of anger and upset. *Journal of Personality and Social Psychology*, 56, 735–747.

———— 1994. *The Evolution of Desire: Strategies of Human Mating*. New York: Basic Books.

Buss, D., Larsen, R., Westen, D., and Semmelroth, J. 1992. Sex differences in jealousy: Evolution, physiology and psychology. *Psychological Science, 3*, 251–255.

Bussey, K., and Perry, D. 1982. Same-sex imitation: The avoidance of cross-sex models or the acceptance of same-sex models? *Sex Roles*, 8, 773–784.

Butler, S., and Kuebli, J. 1994. Gender and the use of specific emotions in mother-child conversations over time. Poster presented at the Conference on Human Development, Pittsburgh.

Cacioppo, J., Klein, D., Berntson, G., and Hatfield, E. 1993. The psychophysiology of emotion. In M. Lewis and J. Haviland, eds., *Handbook of Emotions*, 119–142. New York: Guilford.

Cacioppo, J., Uchino, B. N., Crites, S. L., Snydersmith, M. A., Smith, G., Berntson, G. G., and Lang, P. J. 1992. Relationship between facial expressiveness and sympathetic activation in emotion: A critical review, with emphasis on modeling underlying mechanisms and individual differences. *Journal of Personality and Social Psychology,* 62, 110–128.

Cairns, R., Cairns, B., Neckerman, H., and Ferguson, L. 1989. Growth and aggression: I. Childhood to early adolescence. *Developmental Psychology,* 25, 320–330.

Calabrese, R., and Seldin, C. 1985/1986. Adolescent alienation: An analysis of the female response to the secondary school environment. *High School Journal,* 69, 120–125.

Calvert, S., and Huston, A. 1987. Television and children's gender schemata. *New Directions for Child Development,* 38, 75–88.

Campbell, E., Adams, G. R., and Dobson, W. R. 1984. Familial correlates of identity formation in late adolescence: A study of the predictive utililty of connectedness and individuality in family relations. *Journal of Youth and Adolescence,* 13, 509–525.

Campos, J., Campos, R., and Barnett, K. 1989. Emergent themes in the study of emotional development and emotion regulation. *Developmental Psychology,* 25, 394–402.

Campos, J., Mumme, D. Kermoian, R., and Campos, R. 1994. A functionalist perspective on the nature of emotion. *Monographs of the Society for Research in Child Development,* 59, 284–303.

Cancian, F. M., and Gordon, S. L. 1988. Changing emotion norms in marraige: Love and anger in U.S. women's magazines since 1900. *Gender and Society,* 2, 308–342.

Carli, L. 1989. Gender differences in interaction style and influence. *Journal of Personality and Social Psychology,* 56, 365–376.

Caron, D., Legault, F., Soucy, N., and Vazan, N. 1996. Clique belonging and adolescent's adjustment to school. Poster presented at the meeting of the Society for Research on Adolescence, Boston.

Carver, C. S. and Scheier, M. F. 1990. Origins and functions of positive and negative affect: A control-process view. *Psychological Review,* 97, 19–35.

Cassidy, J., Parke, R., Butkovsky, L., and Braungart, J. 1992. Family-peer connections: The roles of emotional expressiveness within the family and children's understanding of emotions. *Child Development,* 63, 603–618.

Chodorow, N. 1978. *The Reproduction of Mothering: Psychoanalysis and the Sociology of Gender.* Berkeley: University of California Press.

Choti, S., Marston, A., Holston, S., and Hart, J. 1987. Gender and personality variables in film-induced sadness and crying. *Journal of Social and Clinical Psychology,* 5, 535–544.

Chowdury, A., Bairagi, R., and Koenig, M. 1993. Effects of family sex composition on fertility preference and behavior in rural Bangladesh. *Journal of Biosocial Science,* 25, 455–464.

Christensen, A., and Heavey, C. L. 1993. Gender differences in marital conflict: The demand/withdraw interaction pattern. In S. Oskamp and M. Costanzo, eds., *Gender Issues in Contemporary Society. Claremont Symposium on Applied Social Psychology,* v. 6, 113–141. Newbury Park, Calif.: Sage Publications.

Chung, T., and Asher, S. R. 1996. Children's goals and strategies in peer conflict situations. *Merrill-Palmer Quarterly,* 42, 125–147.

Clarke-Stewart, K. 1973. Interactions between mothers and their young children: Characteristics and consequences. *Monographs of the Society for Research in Child Development,* 38, 6–7, serial no. 153.

Clarke-Stewart, K., and Hevey, C. 1981. Longitudinal relations in repeated observations of mother-child interaction from 1 to 2½ years. *Developmental Psychology,* 17, 127–145.

Clifton, A., McGrath, D., and Wick, B. 1976. Stereotypes of women: A single category? *Sex Roles,* 2, 135–148.

Clore, G. L., Schwarz, N., and Conway, M. 1994. Affective causes and consequences of social information processing. In R. S. Wyer Jr. and T. Srull, eds., *Handbook of Social Cognition,* v. 1, 323–417. Hillsdale, N.J.: Erlbaum.

Coats, E., and Feldman, R. 1996. Gender differences in nonverbal correlates of social status. *Personality and Social Psychology Bulletin,* 22, 1014–1022.

Cohen-Kettenis, P., and Gooren, L. 1992. The influence of hormone treatment on psychological functioning of transsexuals. *Journal of Psychology and Human Sexuality,* 5, 55–67.

Cole, P. 1986. Children's spontaneous control of facial expression. *Child Development,* 57, 1309–1321.

Cole, P., Zahn-Waxler, C., and Smith, K. D. 1994. Expressive control during a disappointment: Variations related to preschoolers' behavior problems. *Developmental Psychology,* 30, 835–846.

Collaer, M., and Hines, M. 1995. Human behavioral sex differences: A role for gonadal hormones during early development? *Psychological Bulletin,* 118, 55–107.

Collins, A., and Frankenhaeuser, M. 1978. Stress responses in male and female engineering students. *Journal of Human Stress,* 4, 43–48.

Comstock, J., and Strzyzewski, K. 1990. Interpersonal interaction on television: Family conflict and jealousy on primetime. *Journal of Broadcasting and Electronic Media,* 34, 263–282.

Condry, J., and Condry, S. 1976. Sex differences: A study in the eye of the beholder. *Child Development,* 47, 812–819.

Constantino, J. H., Grosz, D., Saenger, P., Chandler, D. W., Nandi, R., and Earls,

F. J. 1993. Testosterone and aggression in children. *Journal of the American Academy of Child and Adolescent Psychiatry*, 32, 1217–1222.

Cook, W., and Medley, D. 1954. Proposed hostility and pharisaic-virtue scales for the MMPI. *Journal of Applied Psychology*, 38, 414–418.

Coombs, C., Coombs, L., and McClelland, G. 1975. Preference scales for number and sex of children. *Population Studies*, 29, 273–298.

Copeland, A., Brody, L., Deguchi, M., and Yoshioka, I. n.d. Cultural influences on family process and adjustment.

Copeland, A., Hwang, H., and Brody, L. 1996. Asian-American adolescents: Caught between cultures? Poster presented at the Society for Research in Adolescence, Boston.

Cossette, L., Pomerleau, A., Malcuit, G., and Kaczorowski, J. 1996. Emotional expressions of female and male infants in a social and nonsocial context. *Sex Roles*, 35, 693–709.

Cowan, G., Drinkard, J., and MacGavin, L. 1984. The effects of target, age and gender on use of power strategies. *Journal of Personality and Social Psychology*, 47, 1391–1398.

Craig, R. S. 1992. The effect of television day part on gender portrayals in television commercials: A content analysis. *Sex Roles*, 26, 197–210.

Cramer, P. 1991. *The Development of the Defense Mechanisms*. New York: Springer-Verlag.

Crick, N. 1997. Engagement in gender normative versus nonnormative forms of aggression: links to social-psychological adjustment. *Developmental Psychology*, 33, 610–617.

Crick, N., and Grotpeter, J. 1995. Relational aggression, gender and social-psychological adjustment. *Child Development*, 66, 710–722.

Crockenberg, S., and Forgays, D. 1996. The role of emotion in children's understanding and emotional reactions to marital conflict. *Merrill-Palmer Quarterly*, 42, 22–47.

Crouter, A., and Crowley, M. 1990. School-age children's time alone with fathers in single- and dual-earner families: Implications for the father-child relationship. *Journal of Early Adolescence*, 10, 296–312.

Crouter, A., Manke, B., and McHale, S. 1995. The family context of gender intensification in early adolescence. *Child Development*, 66, 317–329.

Cummings, E., Ballard, M., El-Sheikh, M., and Lake, M. 1991. Resolution and children's responses to interadult anger. *Developmental Psychology*, 27, 462–470.

Cummings, E., Iannotti, R., and Zahn-Waxler, C. 1985. Influence of conflict between adults on the emotion and aggression of young children. *Developmental Psychology*, 21, 495–507.

Cummings, E., Zahn-Waxler, C., and Radke-Yarrow, M. 1984. Developmental changes in children's reactions to anger in the home. *Journal of Child Psychology and Psychiatry,* 25, 63–74.

Cunningham, J., and Shapiro, L. 1984. Infant affective expression as a function of infant and adult gender. Unpublished manuscript. Brandeis University.

Dabbs, J. M. 1993. Salivary testosterone measurements in behavioral studies. In D. Malamud and L. A. Tabak, eds., *Saliva as a Diagnostic Fluid. Annals of the New York Academy of Sciences,* v. 694. New York: New York Academy of Sciences.

Damasio, A. 1994. *Descartes' Error: Emotion, Reason and the Human Brain.* New York: G. P. Putnam.

Darwin, C. 1897. *The Descent of Man.* New York: Caldwell.

Daubman, K., and Sigall, H. 1997. Gender differences in perceptions of how others are affected by self-disclosure of achievement. *Sex Roles,* 37, 73–89.

Davidson, K., Prkachin, K., Mills, D., and Lefcourt, H. 1994. Comparison of three theories relating facial expressiveness to blood pressure in male and female undergraduates. *Health Psychology,* 13, 404–411.

Davidson, P., and Kelley, W. 1973. Social facilitation and coping with stress. *British Journal of Social and Clinical Psychology,* 12, 130–136.

Davidson, R., and Schwartz, G. 1976. Patterns of cerebral lateralization during cardiac feedback versus the self regulation of emotion: Sex differences. *Psychophysiology,* 13, 62–68.

Davis, M. 1992. The role of the amygdala in fear and anxiety. *Annual Review of Neuroscience,* 15, 353–375.

Davis, M., and Emory, E. 1995. Sex differences in neonatal stress reactivity. *Child Development,* 66, 14–27.

Davis, M., LaRosa, P., and Foshee, D. 1992. Emotion work in supervisor-subordinate relations: Gender differences in the perception of angry displays. *Sex Roles,* 26, 513–531.

Davis, T. L. 1995. Gender differences in masking negative emotions: Ability or motivation? *Developmental Psychology,* 31, 660–667.

Davitz, J. 1964. *The Communication of Emotional Meaning.* New York: McGraw Hill.

Dawson, G., Frey, K., Panagiotides, H., Osterling, J., and Hessl, D. 1997. Infants of depressed mothers exhibit atypical frontal brain activity: A replication and extension of previous findings. *Journal of Child Psychology and Psychiatry,* 38, 179–186.

Dawson, G., Klinger, L. G., Panagiotides, H., Hill, D., and Spieker, S. 1992. Frontal lobe activity and affective behavior of infants of mothers with depressive symptoms. *Child Development,* 63, 725–737.

De Fruyt, F., 1997. Gender and individual differences in adult crying. *Personality and Individual Differences,* 22, 937–940.

de Lacoste-Utamsing, C., and Holloway, R. 1982. Sexual dimorphism in the human corpus callosum. *Science,* 216, 1431–1432.

Dember, W., Melton, R., Nguyen, D., and Howe, S. 1993. Meta-emotion: Tests of the Lutz hypothesis. *Bulletin of the Psychonomic Society,* 31, 579–582.

de Rivera, J., and Grinkis, C. 1986. Emotions as social relationships. *Motivation and Emotion,* 10, 351–369.

DesJardins, M., Worth, D., and Crombie, G. 1991. The correspondence between children's self-perceived masculinity and femininity and their playground behaviors. Poster presented at the Canadian Psychological Association, Calgary.

Deutsch, F. M. 1990. Status, sex, and smiling: The effect of role on smiling in men and women. *Personality and Social Psychology Bulletin,* 16, 531–540.

Diamond, A. 1985. Development of the ability to use recall to guide action, as indicated by infants' performance on AB. *Child Development,* 56, 868–883.

——— 1990. The development and neural bases of memory functions as indexed by the AB and delayed response tasks in human infants and infant monkeys. *Annals of the New York Academy of Sciences,* 608, 267–317.

Diamond, M. 1984. Age, sex and environmental influences. In N. Geschwind and A. Galaburda, eds., *Cerebral Dominance: The Biological Foundations.* Cambridge, Mass.: Harvard University Press.

Diamond, M., Dowling, G. A., and Johnson, R. E. 1981. Morphologic cerebral cortical asymmetry in male and female rats. *Experimental Neurology,* 71, 261–268.

Diamond, M., Johnson, R., and Ehlert, J. 1979. A comparison of cortical thickness in male and female rats—normal and gonadectomized, young and adult. *Behavioral and Neural Biology,* 26, 485–491.

Diener, E., and Emmons, R. 1984. The independence of positive and negative affect. *Journal of Personality and Social Psychology,* 47, 1105–1117.

Diener, E., Sandvik, E., and Larsen, R. J. 1985. Age and sex effects for emotional intensity. *Developmental Psychology,* 21, 542–546.

Dillon, K., Wolf, E., and Katz, H. 1985. Sex roles, gender, and fear. *Journal of Psychology,* 119, 355–359.

DiMatteo, M., Hays, R., and Prince, L. 1986. Relationship of physicians' nonverbal communication skill to patient satisfaction, appointment noncompliance and physician workload. *Health Psychology,* 5, 581–594.

Dimberg, U., and Lundquist, L. 1990. Gender differences in facial reactions to facial expressions. *Biological Psychology,* 30, 151–159.

Dimond, S., and Farrington, L. 1977. Emotional response to films shown to the right or left hemisphere of the brain measured by heartrate. *Acta Psychologia,* 41, 255–260.

Dimond, S., Farrington, L., and Johnson, P. 1976. Differing emotional responses from right and left hemispheres. *Nature,* 261, 690–692.

Dion, K. L. 1985. Sex, gender and groups: Selected issues. In V. O'Leary, R. Unger, and B. Wallston, eds., *Women, Gender and Social Psychology*, 293–347. Hillsdale, N.J.: Erlbaum.

Dion, K. L., and Dion, K. K. 1973. Correlates of romantic love. *Journal of Consulting and Clinical Psychology*, 41, 51–56.

Diskin, S., and Heinicke, C. 1986. Maternal style of emotional expression. *Infant Behavior and Development*, 9, 167–187.

Donnelly, D., and Murray, E. 1991. Cognitive and emotional changes in written essays and therapy interviews. *Journal of Social and Clinical Psychology*, 10, 334–350.

Dosser, D., Balswick, J., and Halverson, D. 1983. Situational content of emotional expressions. *Journal of Counseling Psychology*, 30, 375–387.

Dovidio, J. F., Brown, C. E., Heltman, K., Ellyson, S. L., and Keating, C. F. 1988. Power displays between women and men in discussions of gender-linked tasks: A multichannel study. *Journal of Personality and Social Psychology*, 55, 580–587.

Driesen, N., and Raz, N. 1995. The influence of sex, age, and handedness on corpus callosum morphology: A meta-analysis. *Psychobiology*, 23, 240–247.

Dunn, J., Bretherton, I., and Munn, P. 1987. Conversations about feeling states between mothers and their children. *Developmental Psychology*, 23, 132–139.

Dunn, J., and Brown, J. 1991. Becoming American or English? Talking about the social world in England and the United States. In M. H. Bornstein, ed., *Cultural Approaches to Parenting: Crosscurrents in Contemporary Psychology*, 155–172. Hillsdale, N.J.: Erlbaum.

———— 1994. Affect expression in the family, children's understanding of emotions, and their interactions with others. *Merrill Palmer Quarterly*, 40, 120–137.

Dunn, J., Brown, J., and Beardsall, L. 1991. Family talk about feeling states and children's later understanding of others' emotions. *Developmental Psychology*, 27, 448–455.

Durkin, K. 1985. Television and sex role acquisition. 2: Effects. *British Journal of Social Psychology*, 24, 191–210.

Eagly, A. 1987. *Sex Differences in Social Behavior: A Social Role Interpretation.* Hillsdale, N.J.: Erlbaum.

Eagly, A., and Steffen, V. 1984. Gender stereotypes stem from the distribution of women and men into social roles. *Journal of Personality and Social Psychology*, 46, 735–754.

———— 1986. Gender and aggressive behavior: A meta-analytic review of the social psychological literature. *Psychological Bulletin*, 100, 309–330.

Eagly, A., and Wood, W. 1991. Explaining sex differences in social behavior: A meta-analytic perspective. *Personality and Social Psychology Bulletin*, 17, 306–315.

Easterbrooks, M., and Emde, R. 1988. Marital and parent-child relationships: The role of affect in the family system. In R. Hinde and J. Stevenson-Hinde, eds., *Relationships within Families: Mutual Influences,* 83–103. New York: Oxford University Press.

Eaton, W., and Ennis, L. 1986. Sex differences in human motor activity level. *Psychological Bulletin,* 100, 19–28.

Eaton, W., and Yu, A. 1989. Are sex differences in child motor activity level a function of sex differences in maturational status? *Child Development,* 60, 1005–1011.

Eccles, J., Jacobs, J., and Harold, R. 1990. Gender role stereotypes, expectancy effects, and parents' socialization of gender differences. *Journal of Social Issues,* 46, 183–201.

Eder, D., and Parker, S. 1987. The cultural production and reproduction of gender: The effect of extracurricular activities on peer group culture. *Sociology of Education,* 60, 200–213.

Edward, J., Ruskin, N., and Turrini, P. 1991. *Separation/Individuation: Theory and Application,* 2nd ed. New York: Gardner.

Egerton, M. 1988. Passionate women and passionate men: Sex differences in accounting for angry and weeping episodes. *British Journal of Social Psychology,* 27, 51–66.

Eisenberg, A. 1996. The conflict talk of mothers and children: Patterns related to culture, SES, and gender of child. *Merrill-Palmer Quarterly,* 42, 438–458.

Eisenberg, N., and Fabes, R. 1995. Children's disclosure of vicariously induced emotions. In K. J. Rotenberg, *Disclosure Processes in Children and Adolescents,* 111–134. Cambridge: Cambridge University Press.

Eisenberg, N., Fabes, R., Bustamante, E., Mathy, R., Miller, P., and Lindholm, E. 1988a. Differentiation of vicariously induced emotional reactions in children. *Developmental Psychology,* 24, 237–246.

Eisenberg, N., Fabes, R., Carlo, G., Speer, A., Switzer, G., Karbon, M., and Troyer, D. 1993. The relations of empathy-related emotions and maternal practices to children's comforting behaviors. *Journal of Experimental Child Psychology,* 55, 131–150.

Eisenberg, N., Fabes, R., Carlo, G., Troyer, D., Speer, A., Karbon, M., and Switzer, G. 1992. The relations of maternal practices and characteristics to children's vicarious emotional responsiveness. *Child Development,* 63, 583–602.

Eisenberg, N., Fabes, R., Minore, D., Mathy, R., Hanish, L., and Brown, T. 1994a. Children's enacted interpersonal strategies: Their relations to social behavior and negative emotionality. *Merrill-Palmer Quarterly,* 40, 212–232.

Eisenberg, N., Fabes, R., and Murphy, B. 1996. Parents' reactions to children's negative emotions: Relations to children's social competence and comforting behavior. *Child Development,* 67, 2227–2247.

Eisenberg, N., Fabes, R., Nyman, M., Bernzweig, J., and Pinuelas, A. 1994b. The relations of emotionality and regulation to children's anger-related reactions. *Child Development,* 65, 109–128.

Eisenberg, N., Fabes, R., Schaller, M., Carlo, G., and Miller, P. 1991a. The relations of parental characteristics and practices to children's vicarious emotional responding. *Child Development,* 62, 1393–1408.

Eisenberg, N., Fabes, R., Schaller, M., and Miller, P. 1989. Sympathy and personal distress: Development, gender differences and interrelations of indexes. In N. Eisenberg, ed., *Empathy and Related Emotional Responses: New Directions for Child Development,* 44, 107–126. San Francisco: Jossey Bass.

Eisenberg, N., Fabes, R., Schaller, M., Miller, P., Carlo, G., Poulin, R., Shea, C., and Shell, R. 1991b. Personality and socialization correlates of vicarious emotional responding. *Journal of Personality and Social Psychology,* 61, 459–470.

Eisenberg, N., and Lennon, R. 1983. Sex differences in empathy and related capacities. *Psychological Bulletin,* 94, 100–131.

Eisenberg, N., Schaller, M., Fabes, R., Bustamante, D., Mathy, R., Shell, R., and Rhodes, K. 1988b. Differentiation of personal distress and sympathy in children and adults. *Developmental Psychology,* 24, 766–775.

Ekman, P., Levenson, R., and Friesen, W. 1983. Emotions differ in autonomic nervous system activity. *Science,* 221, 1208–1210.

Ekman, P., and Oster, H. 1979. Facial expressions of emotion. *Annual Review of Psychology,* 30, 527–554.

Ekman, P., and O'Sullivan, M. 1991. Facial expression: Methods, means, and moues. In R. S. Feldman and B. Rime, eds., *Fundamentals of Nonverbal Behavior: Studies in Emotion and Social Interaction,* 163–199. New York: Cambridge University Press.

Elkins, L. E., and Peterson, C. 1993. Gender differences in best friendships. *Sex Roles,* 29, 497–508.

Ellsworth, C., Muir, D., and Hains, S. 1993. Social competence and person-object differentiation: An analysis of the still face effect. *Developmental Psychology,* 29, 63–73.

Engebretson, T., Matthews, K., and Scheier, M. 1989. Relationships between anger expression and cardiovascular reactivity: Reconciling inconsistent findings through a matching hypothesis. *Journal of Personality and Social Psychology,* 57, 513–521.

Enns, C. 1992. Toward integrating psychotherapy and feminist philosophy. *Professional Psychology Research and Practice,* 23, 453–466.

Eron, L., Walder, L., Huesmann, L., and Lefkowitz, M. 1974. The convergence of laboratory and field studies of the development of aggression. In J. De Wit and W. Hartup, *Determinants and Origins of Aggressive Behavior,* 347–377. The Netherlands: Mouton.

Eron, L. D. 1992. Gender differences in violence: Biology and/or socialization. In

K. Bjorkqvist and P. Niemela, eds., *Of Mice and Women: Aspects of Female Aggression*. San Diego: Academic Press.

Ewart, C., and Kolodner, K. 1994. Negative affect, gender and expressive style predict elevated ambulatory blood pressure in adolescents. *Journal of Personality and Social Psychology*, 66, 596–605.

Ewart, C., Taylor, C., Kraemer, H., and Agras, W. 1991. High blood pressure and marital discord: Not being nasty matters more than being nice. *Health Psychology*, 10, 155–163.

Exline, R., Gray, D., and Schuette, D. 1965. Visual behavior in a dyad as affected by interview content and sex of respondent. *Journal of Personality and Social Psychology*, 1, 201–209.

Fabes, R. 1994. Physiological, emotional, and behavioral correlates of gender segregation. In C. Leaper, ed., *Childhood Gender Segregation: Causes and Consequences. New Directions for Child Development*, 65. San Francisco: Jossey-Bass.

Fabes, R., and Eisenberg, N. 1992. Young children's coping with interpersonal anger. *Child Development*, 63, 116–128.

Fabes, R., Eisenberg, N., and Eisenbud, L. 1993. Behavioral and physiological correlates of children's reactions to others in distress. *Developmental Psychology*, 29, 655–663.

Fabes, R., Eisenberg, N., Karbon, M., Bernzweig, J., Speer, A., and Carlo, G. 1994. Socialization of children's vicarious emotional responding and prosocial behavior: Relations with mothers' perceptions of children's emotional reactivity. *Developmental Psychology*, 30, 44–55.

Fabes, R., and Martin, C. 1991. Gender and age stereotypes of emotionality. *Personality and Social Psychology Bulletin*, 17, 532–541.

Fagen, J., and Ohr, P. 1985. Temperament and crying in response to the violation of a learned expectancy in early infancy. *Infant Behavior and Development*, 8, 157–166.

Fagot, B. 1977. Consequences of moderate cross-gender behavior in preschool children. *Child Development*, 48, 902–907.

——— 1985. Beyond the reinforcement principle: Another step toward understanding sex role development. *Developmental Psychology*, 21, 1097–1104.

Fagot, B., and Hagan, R. 1985. Aggression in toddlers: Responses to the assertive acts of boys and girls. *Sex Roles*, 12, 341–351.

Fagot, B., Hagan, R., Leinbach, M., and Kronsberg, S. 1985. Differential reactions to assertive and communicative acts of toddler boys and toddler girls. *Child Development*, 56, 1499–1505.

Fagot, B., and Kavanagh, K. 1990. Sex differences in responses to the stranger in the strange situation. *Sex Roles*, 23, 123–132.

Fagot, B., and Leinbach, M. 1995. Gender knowledge in egalitarian and traditional families. *Sex Roles*, 32, 513–526.

Fagot, B., Leinbach, M., and Hagan, R. 1986. Gender labeling and the adoption of sex-typed behaviors. *Developmental Psychology,* 22, 440–443.

Fairbairn, W. R. D. 1952. *An Object-Relations Theory of the Personality.* New York: Basic Books.

Falbo, T., and Peplau, L. 1980. Power strategies in intimate relationships. *Journal of Personality and Social Psychology,* 38, 618–628.

Fast, I. 1984. *Gender Identity: A Differentiation Model.* Hillsdale, N.J.: Analytic Press.

Fausto-Sterling, A. 1997. Beyond difference: A biologists' perspective. *Journal of Social Issues,* 53, 233–258.

Ferguson, T. J., and Crowley, S. 1997. Gender differences in the organization of guilt and shame. *Sex Roles,* 37, 19–44.

Ferguson, T. J., Ives, D., and Eyre, H. L. 1997. All is fair in war, but not in love: The management of emotions in dyadic relationships. Poster presented at the biennial meeting of the Society for Research in Child Development, Washington, D.C.

Ferguson, T., and Stegge, H. 1995. Emotional state and traits in children: The case of shame and guilt. In J. Tangney and K. Fischer, eds., *Self Conscious Emotions: The Psychology of Shame, Guilt, Embarrassment and Pride,* 174–197. New York: Guilford.

Ferguson, T., Stegge, H., and Thompson, T. 1993. Socialization antecedents of guilt and shame in young children. Poster presented at the biennial meeting of the Society for Research in Child Development, New Orleans.

Feyereisen, P. 1991. Brain pathology, lateralization, and nonverbal behavior. In S. Feldman and B. Rime, eds., *Fundamentals of Nonverbal Behavior,* 31–65. New York: Cambridge University Press.

Field, T., Vega-Lahr, N., Goldstein, S., and Scafidi, F. 1987. Face to face interaction behavior across early infancy. *Infant Behavior and Development,* 10, 111–116.

Fine, G. A. 1988. Good children and dirty play. *Play and Culture,* 1, 43–56.

Fischer, A., and Manstead, A. (In press). Culture, gender and emotion. In A. Fischer, ed., *Gender and Emotion.* Cambridge: Cambridge University Press.

Fiske, A. 1991. *Structures of Social Life: The Four Elementary Forms of Human Relations: Communal Sharing, Authority Ranking, Equality Matching, Market Pricing.* New York: Free Press.

Fiske, S. T. 1993. Controlling other people: The impact of power on stereotyping. *American Psychologist,* 48, 621–628.

Fiske, S., and Stevens, L. 1993. What's so special about sex? Gender stereotyping and discrimination. In S. Oskamp and M. Costanzo, eds., *Gender Issues in Contemporary Society,* Claremont Symposium on Applied Social Psychology, 6, 173–196. Newbury Park, Calif.: Sage.

Fivush, R. 1989. Exploring sex differences in the emotional content of mother-child conversations about the past. *Sex Roles,* 20, 675–691.

———— 1993. Emotional content of parent-child conversations about the past. In D. A. Nelson, *Memory and Affect in Development: Minnesota Symposia on Child Psychology*, 26, 39–78. Hillsdale, N.J.: Erlbaum.

Flannagan, D. 1996. Mothers' and kindergartners' talk about interpersonal relationships. *Merrill-Palmer Quarterly*, 42, 519–536.

Fogel, A., Toda, S., and Kawai, M. 1988. Mother/infant face-to-face interaction in Japan and the United States: A laboratory comparison using 3 month old infants. *Developmental Psychology*, 24, 307–317.

Fox, N., and Calkins, S. 1993. Multiple-measure approaches to the study of infant emotion. In M. Lewis and J. Haviland, eds., *Handbook of Emotion*, 167–184. New York: Guilford.

Fox, N., and Davidson, R. 1991. Hemispheric specialization and attachment behaviors: Developmental processes and individual differences in separation protest. In J. L. Gewirtz and W. Kurtines, eds., *Intersections with Attachment*, 147–164. Hillsdale, N.J.: Erlbaum.

Fraiberg, S. 1959. *The Magic Years*. New York: Scribner.

Frank, S., Avery, C., and Laman, M. 1988. Young adults' perceptions of their relationships with their parents: Individual differences in connectedness, competence and emotional autonomy. *Developmental Psychology*, 24, 729–737.

Frankenhaeuser, M., Dunne, E., and Lundberg, U. 1976. Sex differences in sympathetic-adrenal medullary reactions induced by different stressors. *Psychosomatic Medicine*, 45, 435–455.

Frankenhaeuser, M., Rauste-von Wright, M., Collins, A., von Wright, J., Sedvall, G., and Swahn, C. 1978. Sex differences in psychoneuroendocrine reactions to examination stress. *Psychosomatic Medicine*, 40, 334–343.

Freud, S. 1915. The unconscious. In M. R. Khan, ed. (1925), *Collected Papers*, 98–136. London: Hogarth.

Frey, W., and Lampseth, M. 1985. *Crying: The Mystery of Tears*. Minneapolis: Winston.

Friedman, A., Tzukerman, Y., Wienberg, H., and Todd, J. 1992. The shift in power with age: Changes in perception of the power of women and men over the life cycle. *Psychology of Women Quarterly*, 16, 513–525.

Friedman, H., Prince, H., Riggio, R., and DiMatteo, M. 1980. Understanding and assessing nonverbal expressiveness: The Affective Communication Test. *Journal of Personality and Social Psychology*, 39, 333–351.

Friedman, H., and Riggio, R. 1981. Effect of individual differences in non-verbal expressiveness on transmission of emotion. *Journal of Nonverbal Behavior*, 6, 96–104.

Friesen, W. 1972. Cultural differences in facial expressions in a social situation: An experimental test of the concept of display rules. Ph.D. diss. San Francisco: University of California.

Frieze, I., and Ramsey, S. 1976. Nonverbal maintenance of traditional sex roles. *Journal of Social Issues*, 32, 133–141.

Frijda, N. 1986. *The Emotions.* Cambridge: Cambridge University Press.

Frodi, A. 1976. Experiential and physiological processes mediating sex differences in behavioral aggression. *Goteberg Psychological Reports*, 6, 18–35.

Frost, W., and Averill, J. 1982. Differences between men and women in the everyday experience of anger. In J. Averill, *Anger and Aggression: An Essay on Emotion*, 281–316. New York: Springer-Verlag.

Frymier, A., Klopf, D., and Ishii, S. 1990. Japanese and Americans compared on the affect orientation test. *Psychological Reports*, 66, 985–986.

Fuchs, D., and Thelen, M. 1988. Children's expected interpersonal consequences of communicating their affective state and reported likelihood of expression. *Child Development*, 59, 1314–1322.

Fuhrman, T., and Holmbeck, G. 1995. A contextual-moderator analysis of emotional autonomy and adjustment in adolescence. *Child Development*, 66, 793–811.

Fujita, B., Harper, R., and Wiens, A. 1980. Encoding-decoding of nonverbal emotional messages: Sex differences in spontaneous and enacted expressions. *Journal of Nonverbal Behavior*, 4, 131–145.

Fujita, F., Diener, E., and Sandvik, E. 1991. Gender differences in negative affect and well-being: The case for emotional intensity. *Journal of Personality and Social Psychology*, 61, 427–434.

Furman, W., and Buhrmester, D. 1985. Children's perceptions of the personal relationships in their social networks. *Developmental Psychology*, 21, 1016–1024.

Gaelick, L., Bodenhausen, G., and Wyer, R. 1985. Emotional communication in close relationships. *Journal of Personality and Social Psychology*, 49, 1246–1265.

Galligani, N., Renck, A., and Hansen, S. 1996. Personality profile of men using anabolic androgenic steroids. *Hormones and Behavior*, 30, 170–175.

Garner, P. W., Robertson, S., and Smith, G. 1997. Preschool children's emotional expressions with peers: The roles of gender and emotion socialization. *Sex Roles*, 36, 675–691.

Geen, R., and Bushman, B. 1989. The arousing effects of social presence. In H. Wagner and A. Manstead, eds., *Handbook of Social Psychophysiology*, 261–281. London: Wiley.

George, M., Ketter, T., Parekh, P., Herscovitch, P., and Post, R. 1996. Gender differences in regional cerebral blood flow during transient self-induced sadness or happiness. *Biological Psychiatry*, 40, 859–871.

Gerbner, G., Gross, L., Morgan, M., and Signorielli, N. 1994. Growing up with television: The cultivation perspective. In J. Bryant and D. Zillmann, eds.,

Media Effects: Advances in Theory and Research, 17–41. Hillsdale, N.J.: Erlbaum.

Geschwind, N., and Galaburda, A. 1985. *Cerebral Lateralization.* Cambridge, Mass.: MIT Press.

Girdler, S., Turner, J., Sherwood, A., and Light, K. 1990. Gender differences in blood pressure control during a variety of behavioral stressors. *Psychosomatic Medicine,* 52, 571–591.

Gjerde, P. 1986. The interpersonal structure of family interaction settings: Parent-adolescent relations in dyads and triads. *Developmental Psychology,* 22, 297–304.

———— 1988. Parental concordance on child rearing and the interactive emphases of parents: Sex differentiated relationships during the preschool years. *Developmental Psychology,* 24, 700–706.

Gladue, B. A. 1991. Aggressive behavioral characteristics, hormones, and sexual orientation in men and women. *Aggressive Behavior,* 17, 313–326.

Glass, G., McGaw, B., and Smith, M. 1981. *Meta-Analysis in Social Research.* Beverly Hills: Sage.

Gleason, J. 1989. Sex differences in parent-child interaction. In S. Philips, S. Steele, and C. Tanz, eds., *Language, Gender and Sex in Comparative Perspective,* 189–199. Cambridge: Cambridge University Press.

Glick, P. 1988. Fifty years of family demography: A record of social change. *Journal of Marriage and the Family,* 50, 861–873.

Goldsmith, H., Buss, K., and Lemery, K. 1997. Toddler and childhood temperament: Expanded content, stronger genetic evidence, new evidence for the importance of environment. *Developmental Psychology,* 33, 891–905.

Gonzales, M. H. 1992. A thousand pardons: The effectiveness of tactics during account episodes. *Journal of Language and Social Psychology,* 11, 133–151.

Goodwin, M. 1990. Tactical uses of stories: Participation frameworks within girls' and boys' disputes. *Discourse Processes,* 13, 33–71.

Gordis, F., Smith, J., and Mascio, C. 1991. Gender differences in attributions of sadness and anger. Presented at the biennial meeting of the Society for Research in Child Development, Seattle.

Gottman, J., and Krokoff, L. 1989. Marital interaction and satisfaction: A longitudinal view. *Journal of Consulting and Clinical Psychology,* 57, 47–52.

Gottman, J., and Levenson, R. 1986. Assessing the role of emotion in marriage. *Behavioral Assessment,* 8, 31–48.

———— 1992. Marital processes predictive of later dissolution: Behavior, physiology and health. *Journal of Personality and Social Psychology,* 63, 221–233.

Graham, J., Gentry, K., and Green, J. 1981. The self-presentational nature of emotional expression: Some evidence. *Personality and Social Psychology Bulletin,* 7, 467–474.

Graham, L., Cohen, S., and Schmavonian, B. 1966. Sex differences in autonomic responses during instrumental conditioning. *Psychosomatic Medicine,* 28, 264–270.

Greenberg, L. 1996. Allowing and accepting of emotional experience. In R. D. Kavanaugh, B. Zimmerberg-Glick, and S. Fein, eds., *Emotion: Interdisciplinary Perspectives,* 315–336. Hillsdale, N.J.: Erlbaum.

Greenberg, L., and Johnson, S. 1986. Affect in marital therapy. *Journal of Marital and Family Therapy,* 12, 1–10.

Greenspan, S. 1989. *The Development of the Ego: Implications for Personality Theory, Psychopathology, and the Psychotherapeutic Process.* Madison, Conn.: International University Press.

Greif, E., Alvarez, M., and Ulman, K. 1981. Recognizing emotions in other people: Sex differences in socialization. Presented at the biennial meeting of the Society for Research in Child Development, Boston.

Griffin, E., and Sparks, G. G. 1990. Friends forever: A longitudinal exploration of intimacy in same-sex friends and platonic pairs. *Journal of Social and Personal Relationships,* 7, 29–46.

Gross, J. 1998. Antecedent and response-focused emotional regulation: Divergent consequences for experience, expression and physiology. *Journal of Personality and Social Psychology,* 74, 224–237.

Gross, J., and John, O. 1995. Facets of emotional expressivity: Three self report factors and their correlates. *Personality and Individual Differences,* 19, 555–568.

———— 1998. Mapping the domain of expressivity: Multimethod evidence for a hierarchical model. *Journal of Personality and Social Psychology,* 74, 170–191.

Gross, J., and Levenson, R. W. 1993. Emotional suppression: Physiology, self-report, and expressive behavior. *Journal of Personality and Social Psychology,* 64, 970–986.

Grossman, M., and Wood, W. 1993. Sex differences in intensity of emotional experience: A social role interpretation. *Journal of Personality and Social Psychology,* 65, 1010–1022.

Gruder, C. 1977. Choice of comparison persons in evaluating oneself. In J. Suls and R. Miller, eds., *Social Comparison Processes,* 21–41. New York: Wiley.

Gruen, R., Gwadz, M., and Morrobel, D. 1994. Support, criticism, emotion and depressive symptoms: Gender differences in the stress-depression relationship. *Journal of Social and Personal Relationships,* 11, 619–624.

Grych, J., and Fincham, F. 1990. Marital conflict and children's adjustment: A cognitive-contextual framework. *Psychological Bulletin,* 108, 267–290.

———— 1993. Children's appraisals of marital conflict: Initial investigations of the cognitive-contextual framework. *Child Development,* 64, 215–230.

Gullone, E., and King, N. 1993. The fears of youth in the 1990s: Contemporary normative data. *Journal of Genetic Psychology,* 154, 137–153.

Gunnar, M. 1980. Control, warning signals and distress in infancy. *Developmental Psychology,* 16, 281–289.

Gunnar, M., and Donahue, M. 1980. Sex differences in social responsiveness between six months and twelve months. *Child Development,* 51, 262–265.

Gunnar, M., and Stone, C. 1984. The effects of positive maternal affect on infant response to pleasant, ambiguous, and fear-provoking toys. *Child Development,* 55, 1231–1236.

Gunnar-vonGnechten, M. 1978. Changing a frightening toy into a pleasant toy by allowing the infant to control its actions. *Developmental Psychology,* 14, 157–162.

Gur, R., Gur, R., Obrist, W., Hungerbuhler, J., Younkin, D., Rosen, A., Skolnick, B., and Reivich, M. 1982. Sex and handedness differences in cerebral blood flow during rest and cognitive activity. *Science,* 217, 659–660.

Gusella, J., Muir, D., and Tronick, E. 1988. The effect of manipulating maternal behavior during an interaction on three- and six-month-olds' affect and attention. *Child Development,* 59, 1111–1124.

Gutmann, D. 1987. *Reclaimed Powers: Toward a New Psychology of Men and Women.* New York: Basic Books.

Hacker, A. 1951. Women as a minority group. *Social Forces,* 30, 60–69.

Hahn, W. K. 1987. Cerebral lateralization of function: From infancy through childhood. *Psychological Bulletin,* 101, 367–392.

Halberstadt, A. 1983. A meta-analysis of race and socioeconomic status differences in nonverbal behavior. Paper presented at the 54th annual meeting of the Eastern Psychological Association, Philadelphia.

——— 1984. Family expression of emotion. In C. Z. Malatesta and C. E. Izard, eds., *Emotion in Adult Development,* pp. 235–252. Beverly Hills, Calif.: Sage.

——— 1991. Socialization of expressiveness: Family influences in particular and a model in general. In R. S. Feldman and B. Rime, eds., *Fundamentals in Nonverbal Behavior,* 106–160. Cambridge: Cambridge University Press.

Halberstadt, A., Fox, N., and Jones, N. 1993. Do expressive mothers have expressive children? The role of socialization in children's affect expression. *Social Development,* 2, 48–65.

Halberstadt, A., Hayes, C., and Pike, K. 1988. Gender and gender role differences in smiling and communication consistency. *Sex Roles,* 19, 589–604.

Halberstadt, A., Leslie-Case, K., and King, J. 1994. How students talk about their parents. Poster presented at the Conference on Human Development, Pittsburgh.

Halberstadt, A., and Saitta, M. 1987. Gender, nonverbal behavior, and perceived dominance: A test of the theory. *Journal of Personality and Social Psychology,* 53, 257–272.

Hall, J. 1984. *Nonverbal Sex Differences: Communication Accuracy and Expressive Style.* Baltimore: Johns Hopkins University Press.

—— 1987. On explaining gender differences. In P. Shaver and C. Hendrick, eds., *Sex and Gender: Review of Personality and Social Psychology,* 7, 177–200. Newbury Park, Calif.: Sage.

Hall, J., Carter, J., Friedman, G., Irish, J., O'Brien, C., and Jacobs, C. n.d. Smiling and subordinate status. Unpublished manuscript.

Hall, J., Carter, J., and Horgan, T. In press. Gender and nonverbal behavior. In A. Fischer, *Gender and Emotion.* New York: Cambridge University Press.

Hall, J., and Halberstadt, A. 1996. Subordination and nonverbal sensitivity: A hypothesis in search of support. In M. R. Walsh, ed., *Women, Men, and Gender: Ongoing Debates.* New Haven: Yale University Press.

Hall, J., Halberstadt, A., and O'Brien, C. 1997. Subordination and nonverbal sensitivity: A study and synthesis of findings based on trait measures. *Sex Roles,* 37, 295–315.

Halpern, C. T., Udry, J. R., Campbell, B., and Suchindran, C. 1993. Relationships between aggression and pubertal increases in testosterone: A panel analysis of adolescent males. *Social Biology,* 40, 8–24.

Hanson, S. 1988. Divorced fathers with custody. In P. Bronstein and C. Cowan, eds., *Fatherhood Today: Men's Changing Role in the Family,* 166–193. New York: Wiley.

Harder, D., and Zalma, A. 1990. Two promising shame and guilt scales: A construct validity comparison. *Journal of Personality Assessment,* 55, 729–745.

Hare-Mustin, R., and Marecek, J. 1994. Asking the right questions: Feminist psychology and sex differences. *Feminism and Psychology,* 4, 531–537.

Harper, R., Wiens, A., Fujita, B., and Kallgren, C. 1981. Affective-behavioral correlates of the test of emotional styles. *Journal of Nonverbal Behavior,* 5, 264–267.

Harris, J. 1995. Where is the child's environment? A group socialization theory of development. *Psychological Review,* 102, 458–489.

Harris, M., and Knight-Bohnhoff, K. 1996. Gender and aggression II: Personal aggressiveness. *Sex Roles,* 35, 27–42.

Harrison, R. H. 1986. The grouping of affect terms according to the situations that elicit them: A test of a cognitive theory of emotion. *Journal of Research in Personality,* 20, 252–266.

Hart, C. H., DeWolf, M., and Burts, D. 1993. Parental disciplinary strategies and preschoolers' play behavior in playground settings. In C. H. Hart, ed., *Children on Playgrounds: Research Perspectives and Applications,* 271–313. Albany: State University of New York Press.

Hay, D., Brody, L. R., and Vandewater, E. 1988. Gender, gender role, and children's play patterns with the same and opposite sex. Poster presented at the Conference on Human Development, Charleston.

Hay, D., Zahn-Waxler, C., Cummings, E., and Iannotti, R. 1992. Young children's views about conflict with peers: A comparison of the daughters and sons of depressed and well women. *Journal of Child Psychology and Psychiatry*, 39, 669–683.

Hayden, L., and Carter, B. 1995. Parents' naive theories of children's emotional development: Gender differences. Poster presented at the biennial meeting of the Society for Research in Child Development, Indianapolis.

Heller, W. 1990. The neuropsychology of emotion. In N. C. Stein, B. Leventhal, and T. Trabasso, eds., *Psychological and Biological Approaches to Emotion*, 167–211. Hillsdale, N.J.: Erlbaum.

Hesselbart, S. 1977. Sex role and occupational stereotypes: Three studies of impression formation. *Sex Roles*, 3, 409–422.

Hill, C. 1987. Affiliation motivation: People who need people . . . but in different ways. *Journal of Personality and Social Psychology*, 52, 1008–1018.

Hill, J., and Holmbeck, G. 1986. Attachment and autonomy during adolescence. In G. Whitehurst, ed., *Annals of Child Development*, 3. Greenwich, Conn.: JAI Press.

Hochschild, A. 1983. *The Managed Heart: Commercialization of Human Feeling*. Berkeley: University of California Press.

———— 1990. *The Second Shift*. New York: Avon.

Hoffman, L. 1977. Changes in family roles, socialization and sex differences. *American Psychologist*, 32, 644–658.

Hofstede, G. 1980. *Culture's Consequences: International Differences in Work-Related Values*. Beverly Hills: Sage Publications.

Hokanson, H., and Edelman, R. 1966. Effects of three social responses on vascular processes. *Journal of Personality and Social Psychology*, 3, 442–447.

Hokanson, J., Willers, K., and Koropsak, E. 1968. The modification of autonomic responses during aggressive interchange. *Journal of Personality*, 36, 386–404.

Hooven, C., Gottman, J., and Katz, L. 1995. Parental meta-emotion structure predicts family and child outcomes. *Cognition and Emotion*, 9, 229–264.

Houston, B. K. 1994. Anger, hostility, and psychophysiological reactivity. In A. Siegman and T. Smith, eds., *Anger, Hostility, and the Heart*, 97–115. Hillsdale, N.J.: Erlbaum.

Houston, B. K., and Vavak, C. R. 1991. Cynical hostility: Developmental factors, psychosocial correlates, and health behaviors. *Health Psychology*, 10, 9–17.

Howard, J., Blumstein, P., and Schwartz, P. 1986. Sex, power, and influence tactics in intimate relationships. *Journal of Personality and Social Psychology*, 51, 102–109.

Huesmann, L., Eron, L., Lefkowitz, M., and Walder, L. 1984. The stability of aggression over time and generations. *Developmental Psychology*, 20, 1120–1134.

Huesmann, L., Guerra, N. G., Zelli, A., and Miller, L. 1992. Differing normative beliefs about aggression for boys and girls. In K. Bjorkqvist and P. Niemela, eds., *Of Mice and Women: Aspects of Female Aggression.* San Diego: Academic Press.

Huesmann, L., Lagerspetz, K., and Eron, L. 1984. Intervening variables in the TV violence-aggression relation: Evidence from two countries. *Developmental Psychology,* 20, 746–775.

Huesmann, L., and Miller, L. 1994. Long-term effects of repeated exposure to media violence in childhood. In L. R. Huesmann, ed., *Aggressive Behavior: Current Perspectives,* pp. 153–186. New York: Plenum.

Hughes, C. F., Uhlmann, C., and Pennebaker, J. 1994. The body's response to processing emotional trauma: Linking verbal text with autonomic activity. *Journal of Personality,* 62, 565–585.

Humphrey, L. L. 1989. Observed family interactions among subtypes of eating disorders using structural analysis of social behavior. *Journal of Consulting and Clinical Psychology,* 57, 206–214.

Hupka, R., and Eshett, C. 1988. Cognitive organization of emotion: Differences between labels and descriptors of emotion in jealousy situations. *Perceptual and Motor Skills,* 66, 935–949.

Huttenlocher, J., Haight, W., Bryk, A., Seltzer, M., and Lyons, T. 1991. Early vocabulary growth: Relation to language input and gender. *Developmental Psychology,* 27, 236–248.

Iaccino, J. 1993. *Left Brain Right Brain Differences: Inquiries, Evidence and New Approaches.* Hillsdale, N.J.: Erlbaum.

Jacklin, C., and Maccoby, E. 1978. Social behavior at thirty-three months in same sex and mixed sex dyads. *Child Development,* 49, 557–569.

Jacobson, N., Gottman, J., Waltz, J., Rushe, R., Babcock, J., and Holtzworth-Munroe, A. 1994. Affect, verbal content, and psychophysiology in the arguments of couples with a violent husband. *Journal of Consulting and Clinical Psychology,* 62, 982–988.

James, J., Lewkowicz, C., Libhaber, J., and Lachman, M. 1995. Rethinking the gender identity crossover hypothesis: A test of a new model. *Sex Roles,* 32, 185–207.

James, W. 1952. *The Principles of Psychology.* In R. M. Hutchinson, ed., *Great Books of the Western World.* Chicago: Encyclopedia Britannica (1890).

Jennings, J., Geis, F. L., and Brown, V. 1980. Influence of television commercials on women's self-confidence and independent judgment. *Journal of Personality and Social Psychology,* 38, 203–210.

Johansson, G. 1972. Sex differences in the catecholamine output of children. *Acta Physiologica Scandinavica,* 85, 569–572.

Johansson, G., and Post, B. 1974. Catecholamine output of males and females over a one-year period. *Acta Physiologica Scandinavica,* 92, 557–565.

Johnson, P. 1978. Women and interpersonal power. In I. Frieze, J. Parsons, P. Johnson, D. Ruble, and G. Zellman, eds., *Women and Sex Roles: A Social Psychological Perspective,* 301–320. New York: Norton.

Johnson, S., Pinkston, J., Bigler, E., and Blatter, D. 1996. Corpus callosum morphology in normal controls and traumatic brain injury: Sex differences, mechanisms of injury, and neuropsychological correlates. *Neuropsychology,* 10, 408–415.

Jones, D. 1983. Power structures and perceptions of power holders in same sex groups of young children. *Women and Politics,* 3, 147–164. New York: Haworth.

Jones, H. E. 1950. The study of patterns of emotional expression. In M. Reymert, ed., *Feelings and Emotions,* 161–168. New York: McGraw-Hill.

———— 1960. The longitudinal method in the study of personality. In I. Iscoe and H. Stevenson, eds., *Personality Development in Children,* 3–27. Chicago: University of Chicago Press.

Jordan, J. 1991. Empathy and self boundaries. In J. V. Jordan, A. Kaplan, J. B. Miller, I. P. Stiver, and J. L. Surrey, eds., *Women's Growth in Connection: Writings from the Stone Center,* 67–80. New York: Guilford.

Josephs, R., Markus, H., and Tafarodi, R. 1992. Gender and self-esteem. *Journal of Personality and Social Psychology,* 63, 391–402.

Jost, A. 1972. Becoming a male. In G. Raspe and S. Bernhard, eds., *Advances in the Biosciences,* 10, 3–13. New York: Pergamon.

Julian, T., and McKenry, P. C. 1989. Relationship of testosterone to men's family functioning at mid-life: A research note. *Aggressive Behavior,* 15, 281–289.

Juraska, J. 1991. Sex differences in cognitive regions of the rat brain. *Psychoneuroendocrinology,* 16, 105–119.

Juraska, J., and Kopcik, J. 1988. Sex and environmental influences on the size and ultrastructure of the rat corpus callosum. *Brain Research,* 450, 1–8.

Kagan, J. 1994. *Galen's Prophecy.* New York: Basic Books.

Kagan, J., Arcus, D., Snidman, N., Feng, W., Hendler, J., and Greene, S. 1994. Reactivity in infants: A cross national comparison. *Developmental Psychology,* 30, 342–345.

Kalof, L. 1993. Dilemmas of femininity: Gender and the social construction of sexual imagery. *Sociological Quarterly,* 34, 639–651.

Kanin, E., Davidson, K., and Scheck, S. 1970. A research note on male-female differentials in the experience of heterosexual love. *Journal of Sex Research,* 6, 64–72.

Karbon, M., Fabes, R., Carlo, G., and Martin, C. 1992. Preschoolers' beliefs about sex and age differences in emotionality. *Sex Roles,* 27, 377–390.

Katz, L. C., and Shatz, C. J. 1996. Synaptic activity and the construction of cortical circuits. *Science,* 274, 1133–1138.

Keating, C., Mazur, A., Segall, M., Cysneiors, P., Divale, W., Kilbride, J., Komin, S., Leahy, P., Thurman, B., and Wirsing, R. 1981. Culture and the perception of social dominance from facial expression. *Journal of Personality and Social Psychology,* 40, 615–626.

Kelley, H. H., Cunningham, J. D., Grisham, J. S., Lefebvre, L., Sink, C., and Yablon, G. 1978. Sex differences in comments made during conflict within close heterosexual pairs. *Sex Roles,* 4, 473–492.

Keltner, D., Ellsworth, P., and Edwards, K. 1993. Beyond simple pessimism: Effects of sadness and anger on social perception. *Journal of Personality and Social Psychology,* 64, 740–752.

Keltner, D., Locke, K., and Audrain, P. 1993. The influence of attributions on the relevance of negative feelings to personal satisfaction. *Personality and Social Psychology Bulletin,* 19, 21–29.

Kemper, T. 1974. On the nature and purpose of ascription. *American Sociological Review,* 39, 844–853.

——— 1978. *A Social Interactional Theory of Emotion.* New York: Wiley.

——— 1990. *Social Structure and Testosterone: Explorations of the Socio-bio-social Chain.* New Brunswick, N.J.: Rutgers University Press.

Kerig, P., Cowan, P., and Cowan, C. 1993. Marital quality and gender differences in parent-child interaction. *Developmental Psychology,* 29, 931–939.

Kernberg, O. 1975. *Borderline Conditions and Pathological Narcissism.* New York: Jason Aronson.

Kertesz, A., and Benke, T. 1989. Sex equality in intrahemispheric language organization. *Brain and Language,* 37, 401–408.

Kiecolt-Glaser, J., Malarkey, W., Chee, M., Newton, T., Cacioppo, J., Mao, H., and Glaser, R. 1993. Negative behavior during marital conflict is associated with immunological down regulation. *Psychosomatic Medicine,* 55, 395–409.

Kiecolt-Glaser, J., Newton, T., Cacioppo, J. T., MacCallum, R. C., Glaser, R., and Malarkey, W. 1996. Marital conflict and endocrine function: Are men really more physiologically affected than women? *Journal of Consulting and Clinical Psychology,* 64, 324–332.

Kimball, M. M. 1986. Television and sex-role attitudes. In T. M. Williams, ed., *The Impact of Television: A Natural Experiment in Three Communities,* 265–301. Orlando: Academic Press.

Kimura, D. 1983. Sex differences in cerebral organization for speech and praxic functions. *Canadian Journal of Psychology,* 37, 19–35.

Kimura, D., and Harshman, R. 1984. Sex differences in brain organization for verbal and nonverbal functions. In G. DeVries, J. De Bruin, H. Uylings, and M. Corner, eds., *Progress in Brain Research: Sex Differences in the Brain.* Vol. 61, 423–441. Amsterdam: Elsevier.

King, L., and Emmons, R. 1990. Conflict over emotional expressiveness: Psychological and physical correlates. *Journal of Personality and Social Psychology*, 58, 864–877.

Kinsbourne, M., and Bemporad, B. 1984. Lateralization of emotion: A model and the evidence. In N. A. Fox and R. J. Davidson, eds., *The Psychology of Affective Development*, 7, 259–291. Hillsdale, N.J.: Erlbaum.

Kipnis, D. 1976. *The Powerholders*. Chicago: University of Chicago Press.

Kirkpatrick, D. 1984. Age, gender and patterns of common intense fear among adults. *Behaviour Research and Therapy*, 22, 141–150.

Kleck, R., Vaughan, R., Cartwright-Smith, J., Vaughan, K., Colby, C., and Lanzetta, J. 1976. Effects of being observed on expressive, subjective and physiological responses to painful stimuli. *Journal of Personality and Social Psychology*, 34, 1211–1218.

Klein, R., and Durfee, J. 1978. Effects of sex and birth order on infant social behavior. *Infant Behavior and Development*, 1, 106–117.

Kochanska, G., and Aksan, N. 1995. Mother-child mutually positive affect, the quality of child compliance to requests and prohibitions, and maternal control as correlates of early internalization. *Child Development*, 66, 236–254.

Kochanska, G., Murray, K., Jacques, T., Koenig, A., and Vandegeest, K. 1996. Inhibitory control in young children and its role in emerging internalization. *Child Development*, 67, 490–507.

Koestner, R., Franz, C., and Weinberger, J. 1990. The family origins of empathic concern: A 26-year longitudinal study. *Journal of Personality and Social Psychology*, 58, 109–171.

Kohn, M. 1963. Social class and parent-child relationships. *American Journal of Sociology*, 68, 471–480.

Kohnstamm, G. 1989. Temperament in childhood: Cross-cultural and sex differences. In G. A. Kohnstamm, J. E. Bates, and M. K. Rothbart, eds., *Temperament in Childhood*, 483–508. New York: Wiley.

Kohut, H. 1971. Analysis of self: A systematic approach to the psychoanalytic treatment of narcissistic personality disorders. *Psychoanalytic Study of the Child*, monograph 4. New York: International University Press.

Kolb, B., and Whishaw, I. 1996. *Fundamentals of Neuropsychology*. New York: Freeman.

Kopper, B. 1993. Role of gender, sex role identity, and type A behavior in anger expression and mental health functioning. *Journal of Consulting Psychology*, 40, 232–237.

Kopper, B., and Epperson, D. 1991. Women and anger: Sex and sex role comparisons in the expression of anger. *Psychology of Women Quarterly*, 15, 7–14.

Krevans, J., and Gibbs, J. 1996. Parents' use of inductive discipline: Relations to children's empathy and prosocial behavior. *Child Development*, 67, 3263–3277.

Kring, A., Smith, D., and Neale, J. 1994. Individual differences in dispositional expressiveness: Development and validation of the Emotional Expressivity Scale. *Journal of Personality and Social Psychology,* 66, 934–949.

Krogh, K. M. 1985. Women's motives to achieve and to nurture in different life stages. *Sex Roles,* 12, 75–90.

LaFrance, M., and Carmen, B. 1980. The nonverbal display of psychological androgyny. *Journal of Personality and Social Psychology,* 38, 36–49.

LaFrance, M., and Henley, N. 1994. On oppressing hypotheses; or differences in nonverbal sensitivity revisited. In H. L. Radtke and H. J. Stam, eds., *Power/Gender: Social Relations in Theory and Practice,* 287–311. London: Sage.

Lai, J., and Linden, W. 1992. Gender, anger expression style, and opportunity for anger release determine cardiovascular reaction to and recovery from anger provocation. *Psychosomatic Medicine,* 54, 297–310.

Laird, J. 1974. Self attribution of emotion: The effects of expressive behavior on the quality of emotional experience. *Journal of Personality and Social Psychology,* 29, 475–486.

Lamb, M., and Oppenheim, D. 1989. Fatherhood and father-child relationships. In S. Cath, A. Gurwitt, and L. Gunsberg, eds., *Fathers and their Families,* 11–16. Hillsdale, N.J.: Analytic Press.

Lamb, M., Pleck, J., and Levine, J. 1985–1986. Effects of paternal involvement on fathers and mothers. *Marriage and Family Review,* 9, 67–83.

Lambert, W. 1974. Promise and problems of cross cultural exploration of children's aggressive strategies. In J. De Wit and W. W. Hartup, eds., *Determinants and Origins of Aggressive Behavior,* 437–457. The Netherlands: Mouton.

Lamke, L. K. 1989. Marital adjustment among rural couples: The role of expressiveness. *Sex Roles,* 21, 579–590.

Landreth, C. 1941. Factors associated with crying in young children in the nursery school and at home. *Child Development,* 12, 81–97.

Landrine, H. 1985. Race * class stereotypes of women. *Sex Roles,* 13, 65–75.

Lang, P., Greenwald, M., Bradley, M., and Hamm, A. 1993. Looking at pictures: Affective, facial, visceral, and behavioral reactions. *Psychophysiology,* 30, 261–273.

Lansky, L. 1967. The family structure also affects the model: Sex role attitudes in parents of preschool children. *Merrill-Palmer Quarterly,* 13, 139–150.

Lanzetta, J., Cartwright-Smith, J., and Kleck, R. 1976. Effects of nonverbal dissimulation on emotional experience and autonomic arousal. *Journal of Personality and Social Psychology,* 33, 354–370.

Lanzetta, J., and Englis, B. G. 1989. Expectations of cooperation and competition and their effects on observers' vicarious emotional responses. *Journal of Personality and Social Psychology,* 56, 543–554.

Larsen, R. J., and Diener, E. 1987. Affect intensity as an individual difference characteristic: A review. *Journal of Research in Personality,* 21, 1–39.

Larson, R., Richards, M., and Perry-Jenkins, M. 1994. Divergent worlds: The daily emotional experience of mothers and fathers in the domestic and public spheres. *Journal of Personality and Social Psychology,* 67, 1034–1046.

Laschet, U. 1973. Antiandrogen in the treatment of sex offenders: Mode of action and therapeutic outcome. In J. Zubin and J. Money, eds., *Contemporary Sexual Behavior: Critical Issues in the 1970s,* 311–319. Baltimore: Johns Hopkins Press.

Lasky, R., and Klein, R. 1979. The reactions of five month old infants to eye contact of the mother and of a stranger. *Merrill-Palmer Quarterly,* 25, 163–164.

Leaper, C. 1994. Exploring the consequences of gender segregation on social relationships. In C. Leaper, ed., *Childhood Gender Segregation: Causes and Consequences.* San Francisco: Jossey-Bass.

Leaper, C., Anderson, K., and Sanders, P. 1998. Moderators of gender effects on parents' talk to their children: A meta-analysis. *Developmental Psychology,* 34, 3–27.

Leaper, C., Leve, L., Strasser, T., and Schwartz, R. 1995. Mother-child communication sequences: Play activity, child gender, and marital status effects. *Merrill-Palmer Quarterly,* 41, 307–327.

LeDoux, J. 1993. Emotional networks in the brain. In M. Lewis and J. Haviland, eds., *Handbook of Emotion,* 109–118. New York: Guilford.

Lennon, R., and Eisenberg, N. 1987. Gender and age differences in empathy and sympathy. In N. Eisenberg and J. Strayer, eds., *Empathy and Its Development,* 195–217. Cambridge: Cambridge University Press.

Lerner, H. 1980. Internal prohibitions against female anger. *American Journal of Psychoanalysis,* 40, 137–148.

LeVay, S. 1991. A difference in hypothalamic structure between heterosexual and homosexual men. *Science,* 253, 1034–1037.

Levenson, R., Carstensen, L., and Gottman, J. 1994. The influence of age and gender on affect, physiology, and their interrelations: A study of long-term marriages. *Journal of Personality and Social Psychology,* 67, 56–68.

Levine, F. M., and De Simone, L. L. 1991. The effects of experimenter gender on pain report in male and female subjects. *Pain,* 44, 69–72.

LeVine, R. 1966. Sex roles and economic change in Africa. *Ethnology,* 5, 186–193.

Levy, J., and Heller, W. 1992. Gender differences in human neuropsychological function. In A. Gerall, H. Moltz, and I. L. Ward, eds., *Handbook of Behavioral Neurobiology,* 11, 245–274. New York: Plenum Press.

Lewis, H. B. 1971. *Shame and Guilt in Neurosis.* New York: International University Press.

Lewis, M., Alessandri, S., and Sullivan, M. 1992. Differences in shame and pride as a function of children's gender and task difficulty. *Child Development,* 63, 630–638.

Lewis, M., Stanger, C., and Sullivan, M. 1989. Deception in 3-year-olds. *Developmental Psychology,* 25, 439–443.

Lewis, M., Stanger, C., Sullivan, M., and Barone, P. 1991. Changes in embarrassment as a function of age, sex and situation. *British Journal of Developmental Psychology,* 9, 485–492.

Lewis, M., Sullivan, M., Stanger, C., and Weiss, M. 1989. Self development and self-conscious emotions. *Child Development,* 60, 146–156.

Libby, M., and Aries, E. 1989. Gender differences in preschool children's narrative fantasy. *Psychology of Women Quarterly,* 13, 293–306.

Libby, W., and Yaklevich, D. 1973. Personality determinants of eye contact and direction of gaze aversion. *Journal of Personality and Social Psychology,* 27, 197–206.

Lichtenberg, J. 1982. Frames of reference for viewing aggression. *Psychoanalytic Inquiry,* 2, 213–231.

Liebert, R., and Sprafkin, J. 1988. *The Early Window: Effects of Television on Children and Youth.* New York: Pergamon.

Lind, P., and Connole, H. 1985. Sex differences in behavioral and cognitive aspects of decision control. *Sex Roles,* 12, 813–823.

Lindman, R., von der Pahlen, B., Öst, B., and Eriksson, C. P. 1992. Serum testosterone, cortisol, glucose, and ethanol in males arrested for spouse abuse. *Aggressive Behavior,* 18, 393–400.

Lips, H. 1989. Gender role socialization: Lessons in femininity. In J. Freeman, ed., *Women: A Feminist Perspective* (4th ed.), 121–137. Palo Alto, Calif.: Mayfield.

———— 1994. Female powerlessness. In H. L. Radtke and H. J. Stam, eds., *Power/Gender: Social Relations in Theory and Practice,* 89–107. London: Sage.

Lopez, F. G., Campbell, V. L., and Watkins, C. E. 1986. Depression, psychological separation, and college adjustment: An investigation of sex differences. *Journal of Counseling Psychology,* 33, 52–66.

———— 1988. Family structure, psychological separation, and college adjustment: A canonical analysis and cross-validation. *Journal of Counseling Psychology,* 35, 402–409.

Lott, B. 1989. Sexist discrimination as distancing behavior: II. Primetime television. *Psychology of Women Quarterly,* 13, 341–355.

Lundberg, U. 1983. Sex differences in behavior pattern and catecholamine and cortisol excretion in 3–6 year old day-care children. *Biological Psychology,* 16, 109–117.

Lundberg, U., de Chateau, P., Winberg, J., and Frankenhaeuser, M. 1981. Catecholamine and cortisol excretion patterns in three year old children and their parents. *Journal of Human Stress,* 7, 3–11.

Lundberg, U., and Palm, K. 1989. Workload and catecholamine excretion in parents of preschool children. *Work and Stress,* 3, 255–260.

Lykken, D., and Tellegen, A. 1996. Happiness is a stochastic phenomenon. *Psychological Science,* 7, 186–189.

Lyons, J., and Serbin, L. 1986. Observer bias in scoring boys' and girls' aggression. *Sex Roles,* 14, 301–313.

Lytton, H., and Romney, D. 1991. Parents' differential socialization of boys and girls: A meta-analysis. *Psychological Bulletin,* 109, 267–296.

Maccoby, E. 1998. *The Two Sexes.* Cambridge, Mass.: Harvard University Press.

Maccoby, E., and Jacklin, N. 1974. *The Psychology of Sex Differences.* Stanford, Calif.: Stanford University Press.

Machtlinger, V. J. 1981. The father in psychoanalytic theory. In M. E. Lamb, ed., *The Role of the Father in Child Development,* 113–154. New York: Wiley.

MacKinnon, N., and Keating, L. 1989. The structure of emotions: Canada–United States comparisons. *Social Psychology Quarterly,* 52, 70–83.

Major, B., and Adams, J. 1983. Role of gender, interpersonal orientation, and self-presentation in distributive-justice behavior. *Journal of Personality and Social Psychology,* 45, 598–608.

Malatesta, C., and Culver, C. 1984. Thematic and affective content in the lives of adult women: Patterns of change and continuity. In C. Z. Malatesta and C. E. Izard, eds., *Emotion in Adult Development,* 175–193. Beverly Hills, Calif.: Sage.

Malatesta, C., Culver, C., Tesman, J., and Shepard, B. 1989. The development of emotion expression during the first two years of life. *Monographs of the Society for Research in Child Development,* 50, serial no. 219.

Malatesta, C., Grigoryev, P., Lamb, D., Albin, M., and Culver, C. 1986. Emotion socialization and expressive development in preterm and full term infants. *Child Development,* 57, 316–330.

Malatesta, C., and Haviland, J. 1982. Learning display rules. *Child Development,* 53, 991–1003.

Malmo, R., Boag, T., and Smith, A. 1957. Physiological study of personal interaction. *Psychosomatic Medicine,* 19, 105–119.

Manstead, A. 1991. Expressiveness as an individual difference. In R. S. Feldman and B. S. Rime, eds., *Fundamentals of Nonverbal Behavior,* 285–328. Cambridge: Cambridge University Press.

Markus, H., and Kitayama, S. 1991. Culture and the self: Implications for cognition, emotion, and motivation. *Psychological Review*, 98, 224–253.

Martin, L. L., Harlow, T. F., and Strack, F. 1992. The role of bodily sensations in the evaluation of social events. *Personality and Social Psychology Bulletin*, 18, 412–419.

Masur, E. 1987. Imitative interchanges in a social context: Mother-infant matching behavior at the beginning of the second year. *Merrill-Palmer Quarterly*, 33, 453–472.

Matsumoto, D. 1989. Cultural influences on the perception of emotion. *Journal of Cross-Cultural Psychology*, 20, 92–105.

———— 1990. Cultural similarities and differences in display rules. *Motivation and Emotion*, 14, 195–214.

———— 1992. American-Japanese cultural differences in the recognition of universal facial expressions. *Journal of Cross-Cultural Psychology*, 23, 72–84.

Matsumoto, D., and Ekman, P. 1989. American-Japanese cultural differences in intensity ratings of facial expressions of emotion. *Motivation and Emotion*, 13, 143–157.

Matsumoto, D., Kudoh, T., Scherer, K., and Walbott, H. 1988. Antecedents of and reactions to emotions in the United States and Japan. *Journal of Cross-Cultural Psychology*, 19, 267–286.

Matthews, K., Davis, M., Stoney, C., Owens, J., and Caggiula, A. 1991. Does the gender relevance of the stressor influence sex differences in psychophysiological responses? *Health Psychology*, 10, 112–120.

Matthews, K., and Stoney, C. 1988. Influences of sex and age on cardiovascular responses during stress. *Psychosomatic Medicine*, 50, 46–56.

Mauger, P., Adkinson, D., Zoss, S., Firestone, G., and Hook, D. 1980. *Interpersonal Behavior Survey (IBS)*. Los Angeles: Western Psychological Services.

Mayne, T. J. In press. Negative affect and health: The importance of being earnest. *Cognition and Emotion*.

Mayne, T. J., O'Leary, A., McCrady, B., Contrada, R., and LaBouvie, E. 1997. The differential effects of acute marital distress on emotional physiological and immune functions in maritally distressed men and women. *Psychology and Health*, 12, 277–288.

Mazur, A., Booth, A., and Dabbs, J. M. 1992. Testosterone and chess competition. *Social Psychology Quarterly*, 55, 70–77.

McAdams, D. 1980. A thematic coding system for the intimacy motive. *Journal of Research in Personality*, 14, 413–432.

———— 1982. Intimacy motivation. In A. Stewart, ed., *Motivation and Society*, 133–171. San Francisco: Jossey-Bass.

———— 1984. Human motives and personal relationships. In V. D. Derlega, ed.,

Communication, Intimacy, and Close Relationships, 41–70. Orlando, Fla.: Academic Press.

———— 1995. What do we know when we know a person? *Journal of Personality,* 63, 365–396.

McAdams, D., and Constantian, C. 1983. Intimacy and affiliation motives in daily living: An experience sampling analysis. *Journal of Personality and Social Psychology,* 45, 851–861.

McAdams, D., Jackson, R. J., and Kirshnit, C. 1984. Looking, laughing, and smiling in dyads as a function of intimacy motivation and reciprocity. *Journal of Personality,* 52, 261–273.

McAdams, D., Lester, R., Brand, P., McNamara, W., and Lensky, D. 1988. Sex and the TAT: Are women more intimate than men? Do men fear intimacy? *Journal of Personality Assessment,* 52, 397–409.

McArthur, L. Z., and Eisen, S. V. 1976. Television and sex-role stereotyping. *Journal of Applied Social Psychology,* 6, 329–351.

McClelland, D. 1975. *Power: The Inner Experience.* New York: Irvington.

———— 1985. *Human Motivation.* Glenview, Ill.: Scott, Foresman.

McConatha, J., Lightner, E., and Deaner, S. 1994. Culture, age and gender as variables in the expression of emotions. *Journal of Social Behavior and Personality,* 9, 481–488.

McGlone, J. 1986. The neuropsychology of sex differences in human brain organization. In G. Goldstein and R. Tarter, eds., *Advances in Clinical Neuropsychology,* 3, 1–30. New York: Plenum.

Meaney, M., Dodge, A., and Beatty, W. 1981. Sex dependent effects of amygdaloid lesions on the social play of prepubertal rats. *Physiology and Behavior,* 26, 467–472.

Messner, M., Duncan, M., and Jensen, K. 1993. Separating the men from the girls: The gendered language of televised sports. *Gender and Society,* 7, 121–137.

Miller, P., and Sperry, L. 1987. The socialization of anger and aggression. *Merrill-Palmer Quarterly,* 33, 1–31.

Modell, A. 1963. Primitive object relationships and the predisposition to schizophrenia. *International Journal of Psycho-Analysis,* 44, 282–292.

Moore, B., and Isen, A. 1990. Affect and social behavior. In B. Moore and A. Isen, eds., *Affect and Social Behavior,* 1–21. New York: Cambridge University Press.

Moore, C., Dou, H., and Juraska, J. 1992. Maternal stimulation affects the number of motor neurons in a sexually dimorphic nucleus of the lumbar spinal cord. *Brain Research,* 572, 52–56.

Moore, G., Cohn, J., and Campbell, S. 1997. Mothers' affective behavior with infant siblings: Stability and change. *Developmental Psychology,* 33, 856–860.

Morell, M., and Apple, R. 1990. Affect expression, marital satisfaction and stress reactivity among premenopausal women during a conflictual marital discussion. *Psychology of Women Quarterly,* 14, 387–402.

Morency, N., and Krauss, R. 1982. Children's nonverbal encoding and decoding of affect. In R. S. Feldman, ed., *Development of Nonverbal Behavior in Young Children,* 181–199. New York: Springer-Verlag.

Morgan, M. 1982. Television and adolescents' sex-role stereotypes: A longitudinal study. *Journal of Personality and Social Psychology,* 43, 947–955.

Morinaga, Y., Frieze, I. H., and Ferligoj, A. 1993. Career plans and gender-role attitudes of college students in the United States, Japan, and Slovenia. *Sex Roles,* 29, 317–334.

Moscovitch, M., and Olds, J. 1982. Asymmetries in spontaneous facial expressions and their possible relation to hemispheric specialization. *Neuropsychologica,* 20, 71–82.

Moser, M., Paternite, C., and Dixon, W. 1996. Late adolescents' feelings toward parents and siblings. *Merrill-Palmer Quarterly,* 42, 537–553.

Moskowitz, D. 1990. Convergence of self-reports and independent observers: Dominance and friendliness. *Journal of Personality and Social Psychology,* 58, 1096–1106.

Moss, H. 1974. Early sex differences and mother-infant interaction. In R. C. Friedman, R. M. Richart, and R. L. Van de Wiele, eds., *Sex Differences in Behavior,* 149–163. New York: Wiley.

Mulder, M. 1977. *The Daily Power Game.* Leyden: Martinus Nijihoff.

Mundorf, N., Weaver, J., and Zillmann, D. 1989. Effects of gender roles and self perceptions on affective reactions to horror films. *Sex Roles,* 20, 655–673.

Murphy, B., and Eisenberg, N. 1996. Provoked by a peer: Children's anger related responses and their relations to social functioning. *Merrill-Palmer Quarterly,* 42, 103–124.

Murray, E., and Segal, D. 1994. Emotional processing in vocal and written expression of feelings about traumatic experiences. *Journal of Traumatic Stress,* 7, 391–405.

Newsweek. 1995. The new science of the brain, 48–54. March 27.

Newton, T., Kiecolt-Glaser, J., Glaser, R., and Malarkey, W. 1995. Conflict and withdrawal during marital interaction: The roles of hostility and defensiveness. *Personality and Social Psychology Bulletin,* 21, 512–524.

Newton, T., Sanford, J., and Flores, A. 1996. Child care, housework, and cardiovascular responses of men and women in dual-earner couples. Presented at the 2nd Annual American Psychological Association's Meeting on Psychosocial Factors in Women's Health, Washington, D.C.

Nicolopoulou, A., Scales, B., and Weintraub, J. 1992. Gender differences and symbolic imagination in the stories of four year olds. In A. H. Dyson and C. Genishi, eds., *The Need for Story: Cultural Diversity in Classroom and Community.* Urbana, Ill.: National Council of Teachers of English.

Nolen-Hoeksema, S. 1991. *Sex Differences in Depression.* Stanford, Calif.: Stanford University Press.

———— 1993. Sex differences in control of depression. In D. Wegner and J. Pennebaker, *Handbook of Mental Control,* 306–324. Englewood Cliffs, N.J.: Prentice-Hall.

Noller, P., and Callan, V. 1989. Nonverbal behavior in families with adolescents. *Journal of Nonverbal Behavior,* 13, 47–64.

Noller, P., and Fitzpatrick, M. 1993. *Communication in Family Relationships.* Englewood Cliffs, N.J.: Prentice-Hall.

Notarius, C., and Herrick, L. 1988. Listener response strategies in response to a distressed other. *Journal of Social and Personal Relationships,* 5, 97–108.

Notarius, C., and Johnson, J. 1982. Emotional expression in husbands and wives. *Journal of Marriage and the Family,* 44, 483–489.

Notarius, C., Wemple, C., Ingraham, L., Burns, T., and Kollar, E. 1982. Multichannel responses to an interpersonal stressor: Interrelationships among facial display, heart rate, self-report of emotion, and threat appraisal. *Journal of Personality and Social Psychology,* 43, 400–408.

O'Connell, P. D., Peplar, D., and Kent, D. 1995. Gender and age differences in types of aggressive behavior. Poster presented at the biennial meeting of the Society for Research in Child Development, Indianapolis.

Oke, A., Keller, R., Mefford, I., and Adams, R. 1978. Lateralization of norepinephrine in human thalamus. *Science,* 200, 1411–1413.

Ollendick, T., Yang, B., Dong, Q., Xia, Y., and Lin, L. 1995. Perceptions of fear in children and adolescents: The role of gender and friendship status. *Journal of Abnormal Child Psychology,* 23, 439–452.

Olsen, K. 1992. Genetic influences on sexual behavior differentiation. In A. Gerall, H. Moltz, and I. L. Ward, eds., *Handbook of Behavioral Neurobiology,* 11, 1–40. New York: Plenum.

Olver, R., Aries, E., and Batgos, J. 1989. Self-other differentiation and the mother-child relationship: The effect of sex and birth order. *Journal of Genetic Psychology,* 150, 311–322.

Olweus, D. 1986. Aggression and hormones: Behavioral relationship with testosterone and adrenaline. In D. Olweus, J. Block, and M. Radke-Yarrow, eds., *Development and Antisocial and Prosocial Behavior.* New York: Academic Press.

Osborne, L., and Fincham, F. 1996. Marital conflict, parent-child relationships, and child adjustment: Does gender matter? *Merrill-Palmer Quarterly,* 42, 48–75.

Palladino, D. E., and Blustein, D. L. 1991. Self and identity in late adolescence: A theoretical and empirical integration. *Journal of Adolescent Research,* 6, 437–453.

Parashos, I., Wilkinson, W., and Coffey, C. E. 1995. Magnetic resonance imaging of the corpus callosum: Predictors of size in normal adults. *Journal of Neuropsychiatry and Clinical Neurosciences,* 7, 35–41.

Pardo, J. V., Pardo, P. J., and Raichle, M. 1993. Neural correlates of self-induced dysphoria. *American Journal of Psychiatry,* 50, 713–719.

Parelman, A. 1983. *Emotional Intimacy in Marriage: A Sex Roles Perspective.* Ann Arbor: University of Michigan Research Press.

Parker, G. 1983. *Parental Overprotection: A Risk Factor in Psychosocial Development.* New York: Grune and Stratton.

Parnell, K. 1991. Toddler interaction in relation to mother and peers. Ph.D. diss., Boston University.

Patterson, G. 1980. Mothers: The unacknowledged victims. *Monographs of the Society for Research in Child Development,* 45(5), serial no. 186.

Paulson, S., Koman, J., and Hill, J. 1990. Maternal employment and parent-child relations in families of seventh graders. *Journal of Early Adolescence,* 10, 279–295.

Pearl, D., Bouthilet, L., and Lazar, J. 1982. Socialization and conceptions of social reality. In D. Pearl, L. Bouthilet, and J. Lazar, eds., *Television and Behavior: Ten Years of Scientific Progress and Implications for the Eighties,* chapter 6. Rockville, Md.: National Institute of Mental Health.

Pennebaker, J. 1989. Confession, inhibition and disease. In L. Berkowitz, ed., *Advances in Experimental Social Psychology,* 22, 211–244. New York: Academic Press.

——— 1993. Putting stress into words: Health, linguistic, and therapeutic implications. *Behaviour Research and Therapy,* 31, 539–548.

Pennebaker, J., Barger, S., and Tiebout, J. 1989. Disclosure of traumas and health among Holocaust survivors. *Psychosomatic Medicine,* 51, 577–589.

Pennebaker, J., and Chew, C. 1985. Behavioral inhibition and electrodermal activity during deception. *Journal of Personality and Social Psychology,* 49, 1427–1433.

Pennebaker, J., Kiecolt-Glaser, J., and Glaser, R. 1988. Disclosure of traumas and immune infection: Health implications for psychotherapy. *Journal of Consulting and Clinical Psychology,* 56, 239–245.

Pennebaker, J., Mayne, T., and Francis, M. 1997. Linguistic predictors of adaptive bereavement. *Journal of Personality and Social Psychology,* 72, 863–871.

Pennebaker, J., Rime, B., and Blankenship, V. E. 1996. Stereotypes of emotional expressivenesss of Northerners and Southerners: A cross-cultural test of

Montesquieu's hypotheses. *Journal of Personality and Social Psychology,* 70, 372–380.

Pennebaker, J., and Roberts, T. 1992. Toward a his and hers theory of emotion: Gender differences in visceral perception. *Journal of Social and Clinical Psychology,* 11, 199–212.

Peplau, L. 1984. Power in dating relationships. In J. Freeman, ed., *Women: A Feminist Perspective,* 3rd ed. Palo Alto, Calif.: Mayfield.

Peplau, L., and Gordon, S. 1985. Women and men in love: Gender differences in close heterosexual relationships. In V. O'Leary, R. Unger, and B. Wallston, eds., *Women, Gender and Social Psychology,* 257–291. Hillsdale, N.J.: Erlbaum.

Perosa, S. L., and Perosa, L. M. 1993. Relationships among Minuchin's structural family model, identity achievement and coping style. *Journal of Counseling Psychology,* 40, 479–489.

Perry, D., and Bussey, K. 1979. The social learning theory of sex differences: Imitation is alive and well. *Journal of Personality and Social Psychology,* 37, 1699–1712.

Perry, D., Perry, L., and Weiss, R. 1989. Sex differences in the consequences that children anticipate for aggression. *Developmental Psychology,* 25, 312–319.

Peters, J. 1994. Gender socialization of adolescents in the home: Research and discussion. *Adolescence,* 29, 913–934.

Petrie, K. J., Booth, R. J., Pennebaker, J. W., Davison, K. P., and Thomas, M. G. 1995. Disclosure of trauma and immune response to Hepatitis B vaccination program. *Journal of Consulting and Clinical Psychology,* 63, 787–792.

Pianta, R., and Caldwell, C. 1990. Stability of externalizing symptoms from kindergarten to first grade and factors related to instability. *Development and Psychopathology,* 2, 247–258.

Piazza, D. 1980. The influence of sex and handedness in the hemispheric specialization of verbal and nonverbal tasks. *Neuropsychologia,* 18, 163–176.

Pittam, J. and Scherer, K. 1993. Vocal expression and communication of emotion. In M. Lewis and J. Haviland, eds., *Handbook of Emotions,* pp. 185–197. New York: Guilford.

Polefrone, J., and Manuck, S. 1987. Gender differences in cardiovascular and neuroendocrine response to stressors. In R. Barnett, L. Biener, and G. Baruch, eds., *Gender and Stress,* 13–38. New York: Free Press.

Pontius, A. 1993. Neuropsychiatric update of the crime profile and signature in single or serial homicides: Rule out limbic psychotic trigger reaction. *Psychological Reports,* 73, 875–892.

Powlishta, K. K., and Maccoby, E. E. 1990. Resource utilization in mixed-sex dyads: The influence of adult presence and task type. *Sex Roles,* 23, 223–240.

Pruett, K., and Litzenberger, B. 1992. Latency development in children of primary nurturing fathers: Eight-year follow-up. *The Psychoanalytic Study of the Child*, 47, 85–101.

Radin, N. 1994. Primary-caregiving fathers in intact families. In A. E. Gottfried and A. W. Gottfried, eds., *Redefining Families: Implications for Children's Development*, 11–54. New York: Plenum.

Radke-Yarrow, M., and Kochanska, G. 1990. Anger in young children. In N. Stein, B. Leventhal, and T. Trabasso, eds., *Psychological and Biological Approaches to Emotion*, 297–310. Hillsdale, N.J.: Erlbaum.

Radke-Yarrow, M., Richters, J., and Wilson, W. E. 1988. Child development in a network of relationships. In R. A. Hinde and J. Hinde, eds., *Relationships within Families: Mutual Influences*, 48–67. Oxford: Clarendon Press.

Radke-Yarrow, M., Zahn-Waxler, C., Richardson, D., Susman, A., and Martinez, P. 1994. Caring behavior in children of clinically depressed and well mothers. *Child Development*, 65, 1405–1414.

Rauste-von Wright, M., and Frankenhaeuser, M. 1989. Females' emotionality as reflected in the excretion of the dopamine metabolite HVA during mental stress. *Psychological Reports*, 64, 856–858.

Reardon, R., and Amatea, E. 1973. The meaning of vocal emotional expressions: Sex differences for listeners and speakers. *International Journal of Social Psychiatry*, 19, 214–219.

Reese, E., Haden, C., and Fivush, R. 1996. Mothers, fathers, daughters, sons: Gender differences in autobiographical reminiscing. *Research on Language and Social Interaction*, 29, 27–56.

Reinisch, J., Rosenblum, L., Rubin, D., and Schulsinger, M. 1991. Sex differences in behavioral milestones during the first year of life. *Journal of Psychology and Human Sexuality*, 4, 19–36.

Reinisch, J., and Sanders, S. 1992. Prenatal hormonal contributions to sex differences in human cognitive and personality development. In A. Gerall, H. Moltz, and I. L. Ward, eds., *Handbook of Behavioral Neurobiology*, 11, 221–243. New York: Plenum Press.

Rheingold, H., and Cook, K. 1975. The contents of boys' and girls' rooms as an index of parents' behavior. *Child Development*, 46, 459–463.

Rime, B., Mesquita, B., Philippot, P., and Boca, S. 1991. Beyond the emotional event: Six studies on the social sharing of emotion. *Cognition and Emotion*, 5, 435–465.

Rime, B., Philippot, P., Boca, S., and Mesquita, B. 1992. Social sharing and rumination. In W. Stroebe and M. Hewstone, eds., *European Review of Social Psychology*, 3. New York: Wiley.

Rinn, W. 1991. Neuropsychology of facial expression. In R. Feldman and B. Rime, eds., *The Nonverbal Expression of Emotion*, 3–30. New York: Cambridge University Press.

Risman, B. 1987. Intimate relationships from a microstructural perspective. *Gender and Society,* 1, 6–32.

Robbins, P., and Tanck, R. 1991. Gender differences in the attribution of causes for depressed feelings. *Psychological Reports,* 68, 1209–1210.

Roberts, J., Howe, S., and Dember, W. 1995. Further evaluation of the Lutz hypothesis. Poster presented at the annual meeting of the American Psychological Society, New York.

Roberts, W., and Strayer, J. 1996. Empathy, emotional expressiveness and prosocial behavior. *Child Development,* 67, 449–470.

Robinson, J., Little, C., and Biringen, Z. 1993. Emotional communication in mother-toddler relationships: Evidence for early gender differentiation. *Merrill-Palmer Quarterly,* 39, 496–517.

Robinson, M., and Johnson, J. 1997. Is it emotion or is it stress? Gender stereotypes and the perception of subjective experience. *Sex Roles,* 36, 235–257.

Robinson, R., Kubos, K., Starr, L., Rao, K., and Price, T. 1984. Mood disorders in stroke patients: Importance of location of lesion. *Brain,* 107, 81–93.

Robison, F., Stockton, R., and Morran, D. 1990. Anticipated consequences of self-disclosure during early therapeutic group development. *Journal of Group Psychotherapy, Psychodrama, and Sociometry,* 43, 3–18.

Rodman, H. 1972. Marital power and the theory of resources in cultural context. *Journal of Comparative Family Studies,* 3, 50–67.

Roe, M., and Beckwith, L. 1992. Gender differences in infant smiling to mother and stranger at two and three months. Paper presented at the 8th International Conference on Infant Studies, Miami.

Rohner, P. 1976. Sex differences in aggression: Phylogenetic and enculturation perspectives. *Ethos,* 4, 57–72.

Rolandelli, D. 1991. Gender role portrayal analysis of children's television programming in Japan. *Human Relations,* 44, 1273–1299.

Rook, K. 1984. The negative side of social interaction: Impact on psychological well-being. *Journal of Personality and Social Psychology,* 46, 1097–1108.

Rose, R., Bernstein, I., and Gordon, T. 1975. Consequences of social conflict on plasma testosterone levels in rhesus monkeys. *Psychosomatic Medicine,* 37, 50–62.

Roseman, I., Antoniou, A., and Jose, P. 1996. Appraisal determinants of emotions: Constructing a more accurate and comprehensive theory. *Cognition and Emotion,* 10, 241–277.

Rosen, W. D., Adamson, L. B., and Bakeman, R. 1992. An experimental investigation of infant social referencing: Mothers' messages and gender differences. *Developmental Psychology,* 28, 1172–1178.

Rosenfeld, H. 1966. Approval-seeking and approval-inducing functions of verbal and nonverbal responses in the dyad. *Journal of Personality and Social Psychology,* 4, 597–605.

Rosenfeld, L. B. 1979. Self-disclosure avoidance: Why I am afraid to tell you who I am. *Communication Monographs, 46*, 63–74.

Ross, E., and Mesulam, M. 1979. Dominant language functions of the right hemisphere? Prosody and emotional gesturing. *Archives of Neurology, 36*, 144–148.

Ross, L., Anderson, D. R., and Wisocki, P. A. 1982. Television viewing and adult sex-role attitudes. *Sex Roles, 8*, 589–592.

Rossi, A. 1987. No: On "The Reproduction of Mothering": A methodological debate. In M. R. Walsh, ed., *The Psychology of Women: Ongoing Debates*, 265–277. New Haven: Yale University Press.

Rotenberg, K., and Eisenberg, N. 1997. Developmental differences in the understanding of and reaction to others' inhibition of emotional expression. *Developmental Psychology, 33*, 526–537.

Rothbart, M. 1989. Temperament in childhood: A framework. In G. A. Kohnstamm, J. E. Bates, and M. K. Rothbart, eds., *Temperament in Childhood*, 59–76. New York: Wiley.

Rothbart, M., and Rothbart, M. 1976. Birth-order, sex of child and maternal help giving. *Sex Roles, 2*, 39–46.

Rotter, N., and Rotter, G. 1988. Sex differences in the encoding and decoding of negative facial emotions. *Journal of Nonverbal Behavior, 12*, 139–148.

Rozin, P., Haidt, J., and McCauley, C. R. 1993. Disgust. In M. Lewis and J. M. Haviland, eds., *Handbook of Emotions*, 575–594. New York: Guilford.

Rubin, L. 1994. *Families on the Fault Line.* New York: Harper Collins.

Rubin, R. B., Perse, E. M., and Barbato, C. A. 1988. Conceptualization and measurement of interpersonal communication motives. *Human Communication Research, 14*, 602–628.

Ruddick, S. 1982. Maternal thinking. In B. Thorne and M. Yalom, eds., *Rethinking the Family*, 76–94. New York: Longman.

Ruebush, K. 1994. The mother-daughter relationship and psychological separation in adolescence. *Journal of Research on Adolescence, 4*, 439–451.

Russell, G., and Russell, A. 1987. Mother-child and father-child relationships in middle childhood. *Child Development, 58*, 1573–1585.

Russell, J. 1991. Culture and the categorization of emotions. *Psychological Bulletin, 110*, 426–450.

Russell, J., Suzuki, N., and Ishida, N. 1993. Canadian, Greek, and Japanese freely produced emotion labels for facial expressions. *Motivation and Emotion, 17*, 337–351.

Saarni, C. 1984. An observational study of children's attempts to monitor their expressive behavior. *Child Development, 55*, 1504–1513.

——— 1988. Children's understanding of the interpersonal consequences of dissemblance of nonverbal emotional expressive behavior. *Journal of Nonverbal Behavior, 12*, 275–294.

Sackeim, H., Greenberg, M., Wieman, A., Gur, R., Hungerbuhler, J., and Geschwind, N. 1982. Hemispheric asymmetry in the expression of positive and negative emotions: Neurological evidence. *Archives of Neurology,* 39, 210–218.

Sackeim, H., Gur, R., and Saucy, M. 1978. Emotions are expressed more intensely on the left side of the face. *Science,* 202, 434–436.

Sackin, S., and Thelen, E. 1984. An ethological study of peaceful associative outcomes to conflict in preschool children. *Child Development,* 55, 1098–1102.

Safer, M., and Leventhal, H. 1977. Ear differences in evaluating emotional tones of voice and verbal content. *Journal of Experimental Psychology: Human Perception and Performance,* 3, 75–82.

Sagi, A. 1982. Antecedents and consequences of various degrees of paternal involvement in childrearing: The Israeli project. In M. E. Lamb, ed., *Nontraditional Families: Parenting and Child Development,* 205–232. Hillsdale, N.J.: Erlbaum.

Sameroff, A. 1975. Transactional models in early social relations. *Human Development,* 18, 65–79.

Sandler, J., and Sandler, A. M. 1986. On the development of object relationships and affects. In P. Buckley, ed., *Essential Papers on Object Relations,* 272–292. New York: New York University Press.

Saudino, K. J., and Eaton, W. O. 1991. Infant temperament and genetics: An objective twin study of motor activity level. *Child Development,* 62, 1167–1174.

——— 1995. Continuity and change in objectively assessed temperament: A longitudinal twin study of activity level. *British Journal of Developmental Psychology,* 13, 81–95.

Saudino, K. J., Plomin, R., and DeFries, J. 1996. Tester-rated temperament at 14, 20, and 24 months: Environmental change and genetic continuity. *British Journal of Developmental Psychology,* 14, 129–144.

Scarr, S., and McCartney, K. 1983. How people make their own environments: A theory of genotype → environment effects. *Child Development,* 54, 424–435.

Scerbo, A. S., and Kolko, D. J. 1994. Salivary testosterone and cortisol in disruptive children: Relationship to aggressive, hyperactive, and internalizing behaviors. *Journal of the American Academy of Child and Adolescent Psychiatry,* 33, 1174–1184.

Schachter, F. 1982. Sibling deidentification and split-parent identification: A family tetrad. In M. E. Lamb and B. Sutton-Smith, eds., *Sibling Relationships,* 123–151. Hillsdale, N.J.: Erlbaum.

Schachter, F., Shore, E., Hodapp, R., Chalfin, S., and Bundy, C. 1978. Do girls talk earlier? Mean length of utterance in toddlers. *Developmental Psychology,* 14, 388–392.

Scheff, T. J. 1990. Socialization of emotions: Pride and shame as causal agents. In T. Kemper, ed., *Research Agendas in the Sociology of Emotions*, 281–304. Albany: State University of New York Press.

Schell, A., and Gleason, J. B. 1989. Gender differences in the acquisition of the vocabulary of emotion. Paper presented at the annual meeting of the American Association of Applied Linguistics, Washington, D.C.

Scherer, K. 1984. Emotion as a multicomponent process: A model and some cross cultural data. *Review of Personality and Social Psychology*, 5, 37–63.

——— 1986. Vocal affect expression: A review and a model for future research. *Psychological Bulletin*, 99, 143–165.

——— 1989. Vocal correlates of emotional arousal and affective disturbance. In H. Wagner and A. Manstead, eds., *Handbook of Social Psychophysiology*, 165–197. London: Wiley.

Scherer, K., Wallbott, H., and Summerfield, A. 1986. *Experiencing Emotion: A Cross Cultural Study*. Cambridge: Cambridge University Press.

Schmitt, J., and Kurdek, L. 1985. Age and gender differences in and personality correlates of loneliness in different relationships. *Journal of Personality Assessment*, 49, 485–496.

Schwartz, G., Brown, S., and Ahern, G. 1980. Facial muscle patterning and subjective experience during affective imagery. *Psychophysiology*, 17, 75–82.

Schwartz, G., Fair, P., Salt, P., Mandel, M., and Klerman, G. 1976. Facial muscle patterning to affective imagery in depressed and nondepressed subjects. *Science*, 192, 489–491.

Schwarz, N., and Clore, G. 1988. How do I feel about it? The informative function of affective states. In K. Fiedler and J. Forgas, eds., *Affect, Cognition, and Social Behavior*. Toronto: Hogrefe International.

Seidlitz, L., and Diener, E. 1998. Sex differences in the recall of affective experiences. *Journal of Personality and Social Psychology*, 74, 262–271.

Serbin, L., Marchessault, K., McAffer, V., Peters, P., and Schwartzman, A. 1993. Patterns of social behavior on the playground in 9 to 11 year girls and boys: Relation to teacher perceptions and to peer ratings of aggression, withdrawal, and likability. In C. Hart, ed., *Children on Playgrounds: Research Perspectives and Applications*, 162–183. Albany: State University of New York Press.

Serbin, L., Sprafkin, C., Elman, M., and Doyle, A. 1982. The early development of sex differentiated patterns of social influence. *Canadian Journal of Behavioral Science*, 14, 350–363.

Shaffer, D. R., Pegalis, L., and Cornell, D. P. 1991. Interactive effects of social context and sex role identity on female self-disclosure during the acquaintance process. *Sex Roles*, 24, 1–19.

Shatz, C. J. 1992. The developing brain. *Scientific American*, 61–67.

Shaywitz, B., Shaywitz, S., Pugh, K., Constable, R. T., Skudlarski, P., Fulbright,

R., Bronen, R., Fletcher, J., Shankweiler, D., Katz, L., and Gore, J. 1995. Sex differences in the functional organization of the brain for language. *Nature,* 373, 607–609.

Shell, R., and Eisenberg, N. 1990. The role of peers' gender in children's naturally occurring interest in toys. *International Journal of Behavioral Development,* 13, 373–388.

Shields, S. 1995. The role of emotion beliefs and values in gender development. In N. Eisenberg, ed., *Social Development: Review of Personality and Social Psychology,* 15, 212–232. Thousand Oaks, Calif.: Sage.

Shields, S., and Koster, B. 1989. Emotional stereotyping of parents in child rearing manuals, 1915–1980. *Social Psychology Quarterly,* 52, 44–55.

Shimanoff, S. 1983. The role of gender in linguistic references to emotive states. *Communication Quarterly,* 31, 174–179.

Shortt, J., Bush, L., McCabe, J., Gottman, J., and Katz, L. 1994. Children's physiological responses while producing facial expressions of emotions. *Merrill-Palmer Quarterly,* 40, 40–59.

Shucard, D., Shucard, J., and Thomas, D. 1984. The development of cerebral specialization in infants. In R. Emde and R. Harmon, eds., *Continuities and Discontinuities in Development,* 293–314. New York: Plenum.

Siegal, M. 1987. Are sons and daughters treated more differently by fathers than by mothers? *Developmental Review,* 7, 183–209.

Siegel, J. 1986. The Multidimensional Anger Inventory. *Journal of Personality and Social Psychology,* 51, 191–200.

Siegel, S., and Alloy, L. 1990. Interpersonal perceptions and consequences of depressive-significant other relationships: A naturalistic study of college roommates. *Journal of Abnormal Psychology,* 99, 361–373.

Siegman, A. 1993. Paraverbal correlates of stress: Implications for stress identification and management. In L. Goldberger and S. Breznitz, eds., *Handbook of Stress: Theoretical and Clinical Aspects,* 274–299. New York: Free Press.

———— 1994. Cardiovascular consequences of expressing and repressing anger. In A. Siegman and T. Smith, eds., *Anger, Hostility, and the Heart,* 173–197. Hillsdale, N.J.: Erlbaum.

Siegman, A., Anderson, R., and Berger, T. 1990. The angry voice: Its effects on the experience of anger and cardiovascular reactivity. *Psychosomatic Medicine,* 52, 631–643.

Siegman, A., and Boyle, S. 1992. The expression of anger and cardiovascular reactivity in men and women: An experimental investigation. Paper presented at the 50th anniversary International meeting of the American Psychosomatic Society, New York.

———— 1993. Voices of fear and anxiety and sadness and depression: The effects of speech rate and loudness on fear and anxiety and sadness and depression. *Journal of Abnormal Psychology,* 102, 430–437.

Siegman, A., and Smith, T., eds. 1994. *Anger, Hostility, and the Heart.* Hillsdale, N.J.: Erlbaum.

Siegman, A., and Snow, S. 1997. The outward expression of anger, the inward experience of anger and CVR: The role of vocal expression. *Journal of Behavioral Medicine,* 20, 29–45.

Sifneos, P. 1988. Alexithymia and its relationship to hemispheric specialization, affect and creativity. *Hemispheric Specialization,* 11, 287–292.

Sigman, M., and Kasari, C. 1994. Social referencing, shared attention, and empathy in infants. Paper presented at the International Conference on Infant Studies, Paris, France.

Signorielli, N. 1990. Children, television, and gender roles: Messages and impact. *Journal of Adolescent Health Care,* 11, 50–58.

Silberman, E., and Weingartner, H. 1986. Hemispheric lateralization of functions related to emotion. *Brain and Cognition,* 5, 322–353.

Silverman, D. 1987. What are little girls made of? *Psychoanalytic Psychology,* 4, 315–334.

Silverman, W., La Greca, A., and Wasserstein, S. 1995. What do children worry about? Worries and their relation to anxiety. *Child Development,* 66, 671–686.

Smith, C., and Ellsworth, P. 1985. Patterns of cognitive appraisal in emotion. *Journal of Personality and Social Psychology,* 48, 813–838.

Smith, K., Ulch, S., Cameron, J., Cumberland, J., Musgrave, M., and Tremblay, N. 1989. Gender-related effects in the perception of anger expression. *Sex Roles,* 20, 487–499.

Snarey, J. 1993. *How Fathers Care for the Next Generation: A Four-Decade Study.* Cambridge, Mass.: Harvard University Press.

Snodgrass, S., Hecht, M., and Ploutz-Snyder, R. 1998. Interpersonal sensitivity: Expressivity or perceptivity? *Journal of Personality and Social Psychology,* 74, 238–249.

Snow, M. E., Jacklin, C. N., and Maccoby, E. 1983. Sex-of-child differences in father-child interaction at one year of age. *Child Development,* 54, 227–232.

Sommers, S., and Kosmitzki, C. 1988. Emotion and social context: An American-German comparison. *British Journal of Social Psychology,* 27, 35–49.

Sommers-Flanagan, R., Sommers-Flanagan, J., and Davis, B. 1993. What's happening on music television? A gender role content analysis. *Sex Roles,* 28, 745–753.

Soskin, W., and John, V. 1963. The study of spontaneous talk. In R. Barker, ed., *The Stream of Behavior,* 228–281. New York: Irvington.

Sparks, G. 1991. The relationship between distress and delight in males' and females' reactions to frightening films. *Human Communication Research,* 17, 625–637.

Spence, J., and Buckner, C. 1995. Masculinity and femininity: Defining the undefinable. In P. Kalbfleisch and M. Cody, eds., *Gender, Power, and Communication in Human Relationships,* 105–138. Hillsdale, N.J.: Erlbaum.

Spence, J., and Helmreich, R. 1972. The Attitudes toward Women's Scale. *Journal Supplement: Abstract Service Catalog of Selected Documents in Psychology,* 2, 66–67.

Spence, J., Helmreich, R., and Stapp, J. 1974. The Personal Attributes Questionnaire. *Journal Supplement: Abstract Service Catalogue of Selected Documents in Psychology,* 4, 43.

Sperry, R. 1964. The great cerebral commissure. *Scientific American,* 210, 42–52.

Spielberger, C., Johnson, E., Russell, S., Crane, R., Jacobs, G., and Worden, T. 1985. The experience and expression of anger: Construction and validation of an anger expression scale. In M. Chesney and R. Rosenman, eds., *Anger and Hostility in Cardiovascular and Behavioral Disorders,* 5–30. New York: McGraw Hill/Hemisphere.

Stafford, L., and Bayer, C. L. 1993. *Interaction between Parents and Children.* Newbury Park, Calif.: Sage.

Stapley, J., and Haviland, J. 1989. Beyond depression: Gender differences in normal adolescents' emotional experience. *Sex Roles,* 20, 295–309.

Stearns, C. 1988. "Lord help me walk humbly": Anger and sadness in England and America, 1570–1750. In C. Stearns and P. Stearns, eds., *Emotion and Social Change,* pp. 39–68. New York: Holmes and Meier.

Stearns, P., and Stearns, D. 1994. Historical issues in emotions research: Causation and timing. *Social Perspectives on Emotion,* 2, 239–266.

Steinmetz, H., Staiger, J., Schlaug, G., and Huang, Y. 1995. Corpus callosum and brain volume in women and men. *Neuroreport: An International Journal for the Rapid Communication of Research in Neuroscience,* 6, 1002–1004.

Stern, D. 1985. *The Interpersonal World of the Infant.* New York: Basic Books.

Stern, M., and Karraker, K. 1989. Sex stereotyping of infants: A review of gender labelling studies. *Sex Roles,* 20, 501–522.

Stevenson-Hinde, J. 1988. Individuals in relationships. R. A. Hinde and J. Stevenson-Hinde, eds., *Relationships within Families: Mutual Influences,* 68–82. Oxford: Clarendon.

Stewart, A., and Chester, N. 1982. Sex diffferences in human social motives: Achievement, affiliation and power. In A. Stewart, ed., *Motivation and Society,* 172–218. San Francisco: Jossey-Bass.

Stewart, J., and Kolb, B. 1988. The effects of neonatal gonadectomy and prenatal stress on cortical thickness and asymmetry in rats. *Behavioral and Neural Biology,* 49, 344–360.

Stifter, C., and Grant, W. 1993. Infant responses to frustration: Individual differences in the expression of negative affect. *Journal of Nonverbal Behavior,* 17, 187–204.

Stoney, C., and Engebretson, T. 1994. Anger and hostility: Potential mediators of the gender difference in coronary heart disease. From A. Siegman and T. Smith, eds., *Anger, Hostility and the Heart,* 215–237. Hillsdale, N.J.: Erlbaum.

Stoppard, J. M., and Gruchy, C. G. 1993. Gender, context, and expression of positive emotion. *Personality and Social Psychology Bulletin,* 19, 143–150.

Strayer, J., and Roberts, W. 1997. Facial and verbal measures of children's emotions and empathy. *International Journal of Behavioral Development,* 20, 627–649.

Suh, E., Diener, E., Oishi, S., and Triandis, H. 1998. The shifting basis of life satisfaction judgments across cultures: Emotions versus norms. *Journal of Personality and Social Psychology,* 74, 482–493.

Sullivan, M., Lewis, M., and Alessandri, S. 1992. Cross age stability in emotional expressions during learning and extinction. *Developmental Psychology,* 28, 58–63.

Susman, E., Inoff-Germain, G., Nottelmann, E., Loriaux, D., Cutler, G., and Chrousos, G. 1987. Hormones, emotional dispositions, and aggressive attributes in young adolescents. *Child Development,* 58, 1114–1134.

Susman, E., Nottelmann, E., Inoff-Germain, G., Dorn, L., Cutler, G., Loriaux, D., and Chrousos, G. 1985. The relation of relative hormonal levels and physical development and social-emotional behavior in young adolescents. *Journal of Youth and Adolescence,* 14, 245–264.

Swim, J. 1994. Perceived versus meta-analytic effect sizes: An assessment of the accuracy of gender stereotypes. *Journal of Personality and Social Psychology,* 66, 21–36.

Tangney, J. P. 1990. Assessing individual differences in proneness to shame and guilt. *Journal of Personality and Social Psychology,* 59, 102–111.

Tannen, D. 1994. *Gender and Discourse.* New York: Oxford University Press.

Taylor, D. 1969. Differential rates of cerebral maturation between sexes and between hemispheres. *The Lancet,* 2, 140–142.

Taylor, S., Wayment, H., and Collins, M. 1993. Positive illusions and affect regulation. In M. Wegner and J. W. Pennebaker, eds., *Handbook of Mental Control,* 325–343. Englewood Cliffs, N.J.: Prentice-Hall.

Tesser, A., Millar, M., and Moore, J. 1988. Some affective consequences of social comparison and reflection processes: The pain and pleasure of being close. *Journal of Personality and Social Psychology,* 54, 49–61.

Thomas, S. 1989. Gender differences in anger expression: Health implications. *Research in Nursing and Health,* 12, 389–398.

Thompson, T., and Zerbinos, E. 1995. Gender roles in animated cartoons: Has the picture changed in 20 years? *Sex Roles,* 32, 651–673.

Thorne, B. 1993. *Gender Play: Girls and Boys in School.* New Brunswick, N.J.: Rutgers University Press.

Thorne, B., and Luria, Z. 1986. Sexuality and gender in children's daily worlds. *Social Problems,* 33, 176–190.

Tice, D., and Baumeister, R. 1993. Controlling anger: Self-induced emotion change. In D. Wegner and J. W. Pennebaker, eds., *Handbook of mental control,* 393–409. Englewood Cliffs, N.J.: Prentice-Hall.

Timmers, M., Fischer, A., Manstead, A. 1998. Gender differences in motives for regulating closeness. *Personality and Social Psychology Bulletin,* 24, 974–985.

Tobet, S., and Fox, T. 1992. Sex differences in neuronal morphology influenced hormonally throughout life. In A. Gerall, H. Moltz, and I. Ward, eds., *Handbook of Behavioral Neurobiology,* 11, 41–83. New York: Plenum.

Toda, S., and Fogel, A. 1993. Infant response to the still face situation at 3 and 6 months. *Developmental Psychology,* 29, 532–538.

Tomada, G., and Schneider, B. 1997. Relational aggression, gender, and peer acceptance: Invariance across culture, stability over time, and concordance among informants. *Developmental Psychology,* 33, 601–609.

Tomarken, A., Davidson, R. J., and Henriques, J. B. 1990. Resting frontal brain asymmetry predicts affective responses to films. *Journal of Personality and Social Psychology,* 59, 791–801.

Tomkins, S. 1984. Affect theory. In K. R. Scherer and P. Ekman, eds., *Approaches to Emotion,* 163–195. Hillsdale, N.J.: Erlbaum.

Tronick, E., and Cohn, J. 1989. Infant-mother face-to-face interaction. *Child Development,* 60, 85–92.

Tucker, D., and Frederick, S. 1989. Emotion and brain lateralization. In N. H. Wagner and A. Manstead, eds., *Handbook of Social Psychophysiology,* 27–70. London: Wiley.

Tucker, D., Watson, R., and Heilman, K. 1977. Discrimination and evocation of affectively intoned speech in patients with right parietal disease. *Neurology,* 27, 947–950.

Turner, B., and Turner, C. B. 1994. Social cognition and gender stereotypes for women varying in age and race. In B. F. Turner and L. E. Troll, eds., *Women Growing Older: Psychological Perspectives,* 94–139. Thousand Oaks, Calif.: Sage.

Van Doornen, L. 1986. Sex differences in physiological reactions to real life stress and their relationship to psychological variables. *Psychophysiology,* 23, 657–662.

Van Egeren, L. 1979. Cardiovascular changes during social competition in a mixed-motive game. *Journal of Personality and Social Psychology,* 37, 858–864.

Van Goozen, S., Frijda, N., and Van de Poll, N. 1994. Anger and aggression in women: Influence of sports choice and testosterone administration. *Aggressive Behavior,* 20, 213–222.

Vespo, J., Pedersen, J., and Hay, D. 1993. Young children's conflicts with peers and siblings: Gender effects. Poster presented at the biennial meeting of the Society for Research in Child Development, New Orleans.

Waber, D. 1976. Sex differences in cognition: A function of maturation rate. *Science,* 192, 572–573.

Waid, W. 1976. Skin conductance response to both signaled and unsignaled noxious stimulation predicts level of socialization. *Journal of Personality and Social Psychology,* 34, 923–929.

Walker, K., and Wilson, B. 1995. Children's recovery from expressions of emotion: Effects of gender and parent marital satisfaction. Poster presented at the biennial meeting of the Society for Research in Child Development, Indianapolis.

Wallbott, H., and Scherer, K. 1991. Stress specificities: Differential effects of coping style, gender, and type of stressor on autonomic arousal, facial expression, and subjective feeling. *Journal of Personality and Social Psychology,* 61, 147–156.

Wallen, K. 1996. Nature needs nurture: The interaction of hormonal and social influences on the development of behavioral sex differences in rhesus monkeys. *Hormones and Behavior,* 30, 364–378.

Wallen, K., Maestripieri, D., and Mann, D. 1995. Effects of neonatal testicular suppression with a GnRH antagonist on social behavior in group-living juvenile rhesus monkeys. *Hormones and Behavior,* 29, 322–337.

Walster, E., Berscheid, E., and Walster, G. W. 1973. New directions in equity research. *Journal of Personality and Social Psychology,* 25, 151–176.

Walster, E., and Walster, G. W. 1975. Equity and social justice. *Journal of Social Issues,* 31, 21–43.

Weaver, J., and Wakshlag, J. 1986. Perceived vulnerability to crime, criminal victimization experience, and television viewing. *Journal of Broadcasting and Electronic Media,* 30, 141–158.

Wegner, D., and Erber, R. 1993. Social foundations of mental control. In D. Wegner and J. Pennebakker, eds., *Handbook of Mental Control,* 36–56. Englewood Cliffs, N.J.: Prentice Hall.

Weidner, G., Friend, R., Ficarrotto, T. J., and Mendell, N. 1989. Hostility and cardiovascular reactivity to stress in women and men. *Psychosomatic Medicine,* 51, 36–45.

Weinberg, K., Tronick, E. Z., Cohn, J. F., and Olson, K. L. In press. Gender differences in emotional expressivity and self-regulation during early infancy. *Developmental Psychology.*

Weitzman, N., Birns, B., and Friend, R. 1985. Traditional and nontraditional mothers' communication with their daughters and sons. *Child Development,* 56, 894–898.

Werrbach, G., Grotevant, H., and Cooper, C. 1990. Gender differences in adolescents' identity development in the domain of sex role concepts. *Sex Roles,* 23, 349–362.

Wheeler, L., Reis, H., and Nezlek, J. 1983. Loneliness, social interaction and sex roles. *Journal of Personality and Social Psychology,* 45, 943–953.

White, G., and Mullen, P. 1989. *Jealousy: Theory, Research, and Clinical Strategies.* New York: Guilford.

White, K., Speisman, J., and Costos, D. 1983. Young adults and their parents: Individuation to mutuality. *New Directions for Child Development,* 22, 61–76.

Whitesell, N., Robinson, N., and Harter, S. 1993. Coping with anger-provoking situations: Young adolescents' theories of strategy use and effectiveness. *Journal of Applied Developmental Psychology,* 14, 521–545.

Whiting, B., and Edwards, C. 1973. A cross cultural analysis of sex differences in the behavior of children aged 3 through 11. *Journal of Social Psychology,* 91, 171–188.

——— 1988. *Children of Different Worlds: The Formation of Social Behavior.* Cambridge, Mass.: Harvard University Press.

Wiggins, J. 1991. Agency and communion as conceptual coordinates for the understanding and measurement of interpersonal behavior. In W. Grove and D. Cicchetti, eds., *Thinking Clearly about Psychology,* 89–113. Minneapolis: University of Minnesota Press.

Williams, L., Vasey, M., and Daleiden, E. 1995. Age and gender differences in children's regulation of worrisome thoughts. Poster presented at the biennial meeting of the Society for Research in Child Development, Indianapolis.

Windle, R., and Windle, M. 1995. Longitudinal patterns of physical aggression: Associations with adult social, psychiatric, and personality functioning and testosterone levels. *Development and Psychopathology,* 7, 563–585.

Winnicott, D. 1958. *Collected Papers: Through Pediatrics to Psychoanalysis.* London: Tavistock Publications.

Winter, D. 1973. *The Power Motive.* New York: Free Press.

——— 1988. The power motive in women—and men. *Journal of Personality and Social Psychology,* 54, 510–519.

Winter, D., and Stewart, A. 1995. Commentary: Tending the garden of personality. *Journal of Personality,* 63, 711–727.

Wintre, M., Polivy, J., and Murray, M. 1990. Self predictions of emotional response patterns. *Child Development,* 61, 1124–1133.

Wise, P., and Joy, S. 1982. Working mothers, sex differences, and self-esteem in college students' self-descriptions. *Sex Roles,* 8, 785–790.

Wittling, W., and Roschmann, R. 1993. Emotion related hemisphere asymmetry: Subjective emotional responses to laterally presented films. *Cortex,* 29, 431–438.

Wood, W., Rhodes, N., and Whelan, M. 1989. Sex differences in positive well-being: A consideration of emotional style and marital status. *Psychological Bulletin,* 106, 249–264.

Yarczower, M., and Daruns, L. 1982. Social inhibition of spontaneous facial expressions in children. *Journal of Personality and Social Psychology,* 43, 831–837.

Zahn-Waxler, C., Barrett, K., and Cole, P. 1991. Guilt and empathy: Sex differences and implications for the development of depression. In J. Garber and K. Dodge, eds., *The Development of Emotion Regulation and Dysregulation.* New York: Cambridge University Press.

Zahn-Waxler, C., Cole, P., Welsh, J., and Fox, N. 1995. Psychophysiological correlates of empathy and prosocial behaviors in preschool children with behavior problems. *Development and Psychopathology,* 7, 27–48.

Zahn-Waxler, C., Friedman, R., Cole, P., Mizuta, I., and Hiruma, N. 1996. Japanese and United States preschool children's responses to conflict and distress. *Child Development,* 67, 2462–2477.

Zahn-Waxler, C., Radke-Yarrow, M., and King, R. 1979. Child-rearing and children's prosocial initiations toward victims of distress. *Child Development,* 50, 319–330.

Zahn-Waxler, C., Radke-Yarrow, M., Wagner, E., and Chapman, M. 1992. Development of concern for others. *Developmental Psychology,* 28, 126–136.

Zahn-Waxler, C., Ridgeway, D., Denham, S., Usher, B., and Cole, P. 1993. Pictures of infants' emotions: A task for assessing mothers' and young children's verbal communications about affect. In R. Emde, J. Osofsky, and P. Butterfield, eds., *The IFEEL pictures: A New Instrument for Interpreting Emotions, Zero to Three,* 5, 217–236. Madison, Conn.: International University Press.

Zahn-Waxler, C., Robinson, J., and Emde, R. 1992. The development of empathy in twins. *Developmental Psychology,* 28, 1038–1047.

Zander, A., and Van Egmond, E. 1958. Relationship of intelligence and social power to the interpersonal behavior of children. *Journal of Educational Psychology,* 49, 257–268.

Zeman, J., and Garber, J. 1996. Display rules for anger, sadness, and pain: It depends on who is watching. *Child Development,* 67, 957–973.

———— 1997. Social-contextual influences on expectancies for managing anger and sadness: The transition from middle childhood to adolescence. *Developmental Psychology,* 33, 917–924.

Zillmann, D. 1979. *Hostility and Aggression.* Hillsdale, N.J.: Lawrence Erlbaum.

———— 1984. Transfer of excitation in emotional behavior. In J. T. Cacioppo and R. E. Petty, eds., *Social Psychophysiology: A Sourcebook,* 215–240. New York: Guilford.

———— 1989. Aggression and sex: Independent and joint operations. In H. Wagner and A. Manstead, eds., *Handbook of Social Psychophysiology,* 229–259. London: Wiley.

Zillmann, D., Weaver, J., Mundorf, N., and Aust, C. 1986. Effects of an opposite-gender companion's affect to horror on distress, delight, and attraction. *Journal of Personality and Social Psychology,* 51, 586–594.

Zucker, K., Green, R., Garofano, C., and Bradley, S. 1994. Prenatal gender preference of mothers of feminine and masculine boys: Relation to sibling sex composition and birth order. *Journal of Abnormal Child Psychology,* 22, 1–13.

Zucker, K. J., Wilson-Smith, D. N., Kurita, J. A., and Stern, A. 1995. Children's appraisals of sex-typed behavior in their peers. *Sex Roles,* 33, 703–725.

Zuckerman, M., Hall, J., DeFrank, R., and Rosenthal, R. 1976. Encoding and decoding of spontaneous and posed facial expressions. *Journal of Personality and Social Psychology,* 34, 966–977.

Index

Activity levels, 5; gender differences in, 130, 132–134; genetics of, 133; and immaturity, 141; parental responses to, 133–134, 141–142, 175

Affect Intensity Measure (AIM): gender differences in, 29; relation to other measures, 30–31

Affection, 44, 79, 86, 205, 223. *See also* Warmth

Affective Communication Test (ACT), 49

AFFEX (System for Identifying Affect Expression by Holistic Judgment), 38, 42

Agency, 210–212

Aggression: in boys' play, 246, 248; conditioning of, 75–76; and control, 209; cultural differences in, 52–53, 223; definition of, 50; display rules for, 234; environmental influences on, 108, 143, 173; fathers' role in, 178; gender differences in, 49, 50–54, 84, 108, 143; gender of targets, 53–54; health effects of, 278; and hormones, 107–111; and individuation, 152; and limbic seizures, 28, 266; media depictions of, 236–237; in mixed-sex play, 252; peers' reactions to, 246; and power differences, 219; and provider roles, 223–224; television influences on, 239, 240. *See also* Anger; Relational aggression; Testosterone

Alexithymia, 68

Amygdala, 118, 123. *See also* Limbic system

Anger: appraisals of, 24; in boys' play, 248–249; comfort with, 272–273; and control, 208; cultural differences in, 145–146; developmental patterns, 84–86; display rules for, 4; distressed families' expressions of, 271–272; facial expressions of, 84; in father-son relationships, 134; functions of, 3; gender differences in, 1, 56, 63, 79, 81–86; gender of targets, 80; in girls' play, 250; health effects of, 267–278; historical trends in, 242–243; and individualism, 242; inhibition of, 266; in marital relationships, 83; measures of, 82; peers' reactions to, 245; and physiological reactivity, 63, 73–74, 260–261, 267; power influences on, 215–216; situations evoking, 225; and social competence, 268; socialization of, 142–143; stereotypes, 81–82; suppression of, 74; vocal expressions of, 47, 83–84, 268. *See also* Aggression; Relational aggression

Anger Expression Scale, 49

Appraisal Theories, 23–24

Arousability: gender differences in, 5, 130, 134–137; parents' responses to, 136–137, 141–142; and play patterns, 257. *See also* Arousal levels; Physiological arousal

Arousal levels, 5, 134–137, 141, 175. *See also* Arousability; Physiological arousal

Arousal model, 68–69, 70

Assiter, A., 11

Attitudes Toward Women Scale, 9

Autonomy, 150–151, 152, 168–169, 173–174, 210. *See also* De-identification; Differentiation

Biological development, as affected by environment, 3, 23–25, 103–105, 127

Birth order, effect on family interaction, 154–155

Block Child Rearing Practices Report, 9

Boundary permeability, 149–151, 160–169, 174–176, 176, 232; in fathers, 188–193. *See also* Chodorow, N.

Bragging, 235
Buss-Durkee Hostility Inventory, 49

Cardiovascular reactivity. *See* Physiological arousal
Cerebral cortex, 106
Cerebral lateralization: development of, 125–126; gender differences in, 101–102, 106, 113–118, 124–125; role in emotional expression, 119–122
Child caretaking role, 221–223, 282; and power motives, 207–208. *See also* Fathers; Mothers
Chodorow, N., 6, 147–153, 155, 156, 157–158, 160, 177–178
Collectivism, and emotions, 220, 241–242, 301n1
Communal characteristics, 210–212
Competition. *See* Context; Gender roles; Provider role
Contempt: in boys' play, 248; gender differences in, 79, 93; and out-groups, 254, 257; and power, 201, 218–219, 253, 282; and roles, 97; and suppression, 265
Context, 2, 20–21, 31, 96–97, 225–226, 268, 270–272, 286; and anger, 85–86; and physiological arousal, 61, 62–65, 66, 77; and vocal expressions, 48
Control. *See* Motives
Cook-Medley Hostility Inventory, 49
Cooperation. *See* Context; Gender roles
Corpus callosum, 106, 113–115, 122
Cortical congruence, 263
Crying: development of, 41–42, 54; gender differences in, 54
Cultural differences: in autonomy, 174; in child rearing, 145–146; and Chodorow's theory, 155; collectivist vs. individualist, 32; in empathy, 90–91; in facial expressions, 39–40; in relationship between power and emotion, 220; in sadness, 94; in self-reports, 32. *See also* Collectivism; Cultural values; Individualism
Cultural values, 4, 142; as affecting child rearing, 142–146; as affecting display rules, 241–243; as affecting marital relationships, 279; as affecting motives, 204–205; as affecting socialization,

281–282. *See also* Cultural differences; Display rules

De-identification, 6, 147–148, 159, 175, 178, 284. *See also* Autonomy; Differentiation
Depression, 60, 94, 138, 172, 216, 275, 276, 277, 278. *See also* Sadness
Differentiation, 149, 151–152, 153, 160, 174, 187, 254. *See also* Autonomy; De-identification
Discharge model, 67–68, 70
Disgust, 93
Display rules, 4, 129, 227–231; and child rearing, 230–233; and cultural values, 241–243; for females, 234–236; and gender roles, 228–229; and health, 279–280; for males, 233–234; in marital relationships, 276; measures of, 229–230; and peer interaction, 233–236. *See also* *specific emotions*; Stereotypes
Distraction, 55. *See also* Reappraisal; Suppression
Distress: and anger, 216, 277; and child caretaking, 221–222; definition of, 88; development, 90–91; gender differences in, 79, 88; and power strategies, 215–216; and skin conductance, 60

Embarrassment, 87
Emotional behaviors: gender differences in, 49–55, 56; meaning of, 48–49; measures of, 49. *See also* Aggression; Crying; Withdrawal
Emotional expressions: definition of, 15; dimensions of, 19–20, 22; experiences compared to, 16, 18–19; functions of, 15–17, 201–202, 262; hard-wiring of, 21–23; health effects of, 260–278; measurement of, 16, 19; and motives, 24, 202, 205–209; and personality characteristics, 210–212; and roles, 24, 202; socially engaged and disengaged, 22. *See also* Facial expressions; Self-report measures; Verbalization; Vocal expressiveness
Emotional intensity, 22, 289n2; gender differences in, 30, mediated by right hemisphere, 120

Emotionality, 27, 30
Emotional regulation, 18, 19, 44, 134–137, 272–276
Emotional valence, 15, 22; and cerebral lateralization, 121–122
Emotion Facial Action Coding System (EMFACS), 38
Empathy: definition of, 88; facial expressions, 89–90, 91; in father-child relationships, 189–190; gender differences in, 89–91; genetics of, 138; in mother-child relationships, 148–150, 161–165; and physiological arousal, 64–65, 72; self report measures of, 89; in socialization of emotions, 169–171, 189–190; and social roles, 223, 224
Envy, 251, 253. *See also* Jealousy
Essentialism, 11
Estradiol levels, 110–111
Externalizers, 70, 71

Facial Action Coding System (FACS), 38
Facial expressions: brain mediation of, 123; functions of, 37; gender differences in, 34, 37, 39–45, 56; measures of, 38–39; and physiological arousal, 68–74; stereotypes of, 38. *See also* Cultural differences
Facial feedback hypothesis, 17–18, 68–69
Fairbairn, W. R. D., 5
Family stress. *See* Marital conflict
Family systems interactions, 5, 157, 193–195; effects on dyadic interactions, 154–155, 194. *See also* Marital conflict
Fathers: child rearing involvement, 152–153, 183–186, 187–190; gender preferences, 188–189; involved compared to noninvolved, 179–183, 184–185, 193–195, 197; role in children's development, 143–144, 153, 154, 177–178, 183–187; role in children's emotions, 7, 178–183, 189–195, 197, 232–233, 284–285
Father-son identification. *See* Identification
Fear: and appraisal theories, 24; in boys' play, 248; display rules, 233; gender differences in, 36, 79, 91–93; in peer interactions, 251, 253; and power differences, 214, 253; and restrictiveness, 172, 176; and situational context, 92–93;

and social acceptance of, 247; and social roles, 221, 224
Female bilateralization, 113–118, 127
Functionalist theories, 3, 201, 262

Gazing, 37, 40
Gender roles: and appraisal theories, 24; and emotions, 4, 221–226, 282; father's role in development of, 179–180, 183–185; and identity, 283; in marital relationships, 277–278; measures of, 8; and motives, 282–283; and physiological arousal, 64–65, 66. *See also* Child caretaking role; Nontraditional gender roles; Provider role
Gender Roles Study, 8
Generalizers, 59, 70, 71–73, 74, 75, 77
Geschwind, N., 112
Guilt: and appraisal theories, 24; display rules for, 235–236; gender differences in, 87–88; and power, 219

Happiness, 38, 169, 206. *See also* Affection; Warmth
Health. *See* Emotional expressions; Immune functioning; Physiological arousal
Heritability: definition of, 290n3
Hostility, 49, 172, 216, 224
Hurt, 1, 79, 80, 82, 83, 95, 205, 209; and child care, 222; and peer interactions, 251

Identification: in marital conflicts, 195; in parent-child relationships, 148–151, 155–158, 165, 175, 187–189, 283; in peer relationships, 254–255; with television characters, 236. *See also* Chodorow, N.; De-identification
Imitation, 158–160, 236, 254
Immune functioning, 260–261, 270–271
Individualism, 209–210, 241–242, 301n1. *See also* Cultural differences
Individuation. *See* Autonomy; De-identification; Differentiation
In-groups, 232, 254–257
Inhibition, 34, 44, 54, 265–266. *See also* Suppression
Internalizers, 59, 69–71, 77; development of, 74–75, 171–172
Interpersonal Behavior Survey, 49

Intimacy, 202–203; and emotion, 79–80, 83, 206; in girls' play, 249
Intimacy motives. *See* Motives
Intrahemispheric gender differences, 117–118
Intrusiveness, in parent-child relationships, 150, 162, 166–168, 171–173, 191–193

Jealousy, 65, 94

Language abilities, 131–132, 141–142
Limbic system, 106, 118–119, 123–124, 125
Loneliness, 79, 96, 97, 219
Love. *See* Affection; Warmth

Marital conflict: children's reactions to, 75, 194–197; communication skills in, 269; gender differences in emotions, 2, 37; gender differences in physiological arousal, 61–62, 63–64; health consequences of, 270–271, 276–278; power strategies in, 215–216. *See also* Marital relationships; Marital satisfaction
Marital relationships: children's reactions to, 5; and emotional expression, 264, 276–278; gender differences in emotions, 35–36; gender-stereotypic expectations, 279. *See also* Marital conflict; Marital satisfaction
Marital satisfaction: and anger, 270, 276; and men's expressivity, 264, 278; and parent-child relationships, 155. *See also* Marital conflict; Marital relationships
Matching, parents' and children's emotions, 136, 152, 159, 160–161, 171
Maximally Discriminative Facial Movement Coding System (MAX), 38
Media, 4, 236–240
Memory, as related to emotional expression, 30
Menstrual cycle, 293n11
Mother-daughter identification. *See* Identification
Mothers: interactions with daughters compared to sons, 139–146, 147–152, 154–169, 174–176; role in children's emotions, 7, 8, 157, 169–176. *See also* Autonomy; Boundary permeability; Empathy; Intrusiveness; Restrictiveness

Mothers' employment, effects on children's emotions, 186–187
Motives: affiliation, 66; control, 32, 45, 66, 152, 208–209, 210, 225; in boys' play, 248–249; in girls' play, 249–250; intimacy, 86, 152, 203–206, 210, 216; power, 203, 206–208; social approval, 44, 218
Multidimensional Anger Inventory, 49

Nontraditional gender roles, 284–285; and fathers, 179–180, 182–183, 184–185, 193–195, 197. *See also* Mothers' employment

Object relations theories, 5–7. *See also* Chodorow, N.
Oppression hypothesis, 41, 217–218
Out-groups, 232, 254–257

Parent-child interactions. *See* Boundary permeability; De-identification; Fathers; Identification; Mothers
Peer relationships, adults: emotions expressed in, 79–81, 97; gender differences in, 247, 250–252
Peer relationships, children: effects on emotion, 4, 244–247, 252–255; expressions of anger in, 268. *See also* In-groups; Out-groups; Play patterns
Personality characteristics, related to emotion, 210–212
Physiological arousal: and anger, 63, 73–74, 260–261, 267; and facial expressions, 68–73; gender differences in, 59, 60–67, 70–75; and gender roles, 64–65; response patterns, 59, 78; right hemisphere mediation of, 121; socialization of, 75–76; and social support, 77. *See also* Context
Pituitary adrenal-cortical system, 60
Play patterns: boys', 133, 247–249; girls', 249–250; mixed-sex, 252–254; parents' socialization of, 143–145; in relation to gender identity, 255–257; sex-segregated, 247, 257–258. *See also* Peer relationships, children
Popularity, 245–246, 263–264
Power, 3, 6, 24, 202, 206–208, 212–220, 247, 253–254, 264, 280, 282, 284
Power motives. *See* Motives

Power strategies, indirect compared to direct, 215–216
Pride, 79, 95–96, 97, 209, 219, 242, 253, 257; and boys' play, 248
Provider role, 223–225
Puberty: and aggression, 52; and emotions, 126
Punitiveness. *See* Restrictiveness

Reappraisal, 273–274, 278
Relational aggression, 50–51, 250. *See also* Aggression
Restrictiveness, 134, 171–173, 176
Ruddick, S., 4
Rumination, 31, 55, 274–276

Sadness: appraisal theories, 24, 274; display rules for, 4, 233–234; facial expressions of, 38; gender differences in, 36, 44, 79, 94–95, 205; historical acceptance of, 243; speech rate for, 47
Self Conscious Attribution and Affect Inventory, 87
Self-control processes, 130, 135–136, 137. *See also* Emotional regulation
Self-esteem, 179, 203, 204, 209, 215, 218–219, 254, 263, 298n3
Self-report measures, 19, 33–34. *See also* Verbalization
Sexually dimorphic structures, 118–119
Shame, 79, 87–88, 169, 172, 205, 206, 214–215
Skin conductance, 58, 60, 77, 265
Smiling, 37, 41, 72, 139, 205–206, 217–218
Sociability: gender differences in, 137–140; genetics of, 138; parental responses to, 138–140, 141–142, 165; socialization of, 144
Social competence, and emotional expressiveness, 263
Social referencing, 137–138
Social support, 77, 265
Sociobiological theories, 294n2
Split-parent identification, 156

Status, 3, 6, 24, 201, 202–203, 212–220; in adult friendships, 250–251; in boys' play, 248; in peer interactions, 256. *See also* Power
Stereotypes, 1, 7, 8, 129–130, 151, 168, 175, 227–228, 231–233, 236–238; self-reports influenced by, 33–34. *See also* Display rules
Suppression, 63, 73–74, 205, 265, 273, 278
Sympathetic nervous system, 60
Sympathy, 88–91, 138

Television. *See* Media
Temperament, 5; gender differences in, 128, 130–131; parental responses to, 128–129, 140–142, 165, 175–176, 185–186
Testosterone: and aggression, 102, 105, 107–112, 126; and brain organization, 102, 112–113; and mother-infant interaction, 102; and puberty, 109; and sexual behaviors, 107; and status, 111
Themes for Emotional Development-Revised (TED-R), 9
Transactional relationships, 5, 129, 130, 140, 145–146

Unconscious, role in emotional expressiveness, 19

Verbalization, 28–29; gender differences in, 35–36, 56, 79, 131, 132; and health, 268–270; and left hemisphere, 120; and physiological arousal, 67–68; and social sharing, 28
Vocal expressiveness, 45–48; gender differences in, 46–48; and right hemisphere, 120

Warmth, 22, 79, 139, 205, 216–217, 221, 222, 223, 224, 251. *See also* Affection; Happiness
Withdrawal, 54–55
Worry, 92, 169